Contents

KU-125-359

SOUTHERN HISTORY

A Review of the History of
Southern England

edited by J.R. Lowerson

Volume 5/1983

Edited by
J. R. Lowerson

Reviews editor
W. N. Yates

ALAN SUTTON

© Alan Sutton Publishing Limited, 1983

All rights reserved. No part of this publication may be reproduced, stored in a retrieval system, or transmitted, in any form or by any means, electronic, mechanical, photocopying, recording or otherwise without the permission of the publishers.

First published in Great Britain 1983
Alan Sutton Publishing Limited
17a Brunswick Road
Gloucester
GL1 1HG

KING ALFRED'S COLLEGE
WINCHESTER.

942.2
SOU   51251

British Library Cataloguing in Publication Data

Southern History
   Vol. 5
   Great Britain—History—Periodicals
   942.2'005   DA20

   ISBN 0–86299–059–9
   ISBN 0–86299–060–2 Pbk
   ISSN 0142-4688

Typesetting and origination
by Alan Sutton Publishing Limited
Printed in Great Britain
by Redwood Burn Limited, Trowbridge

Notes on Contributors

J. Kent is Professor of Theology at Bristol University. A Cambridge graduate, his publications include *Holding the Fort: studies in Victorian Revivalism* (1978) and *The End of the Line?, the development of Christian theology in the last two centuries* (1982).

Dom F. Hockey O.S.B. is a monk of Quarr Abbey, Isle of Wight. His publications include *Quarr Abbey and its lands* (1970), *The account book of Beaulieu Abbey* for the *Camden Series* (1976), and he has edited a number of cartularies.

Dr G. J. Mayhew, a York graduate, works in East Sussex Record Office and teaches part-time for the Centre for Continuing Education, University of Sussex. He is currently working on Tudor Rye.

Dr R. Whiting, a Devonian, did postgraduate research at Exeter after graduating in history from Cambridge. He is now senior lecturer in history at the College of Ripon and York St John and is completing a book on the Reformation in the south-west.

G. Woodward studied at Sheffield, Cambridge and Bristol. The author of a number of papers, he is deputy head of the history department at Millfield School.

Rev. A. F. Munden is on the staff of Jesmond Parish Church, Newcastle-upon-Tyne, with responsibility for student members of the congregation. He is currently working on nineteenth-century Evangelicalism.

W. N. Yates is Reviews Editor of *Southern History,* Kent County Archivist and the author of many papers on church history, including a recent Historical Association pamhlet on the Oxford Movement.

Dr Bruce Coleman is a lecturer in history and dean of the Arts Faculty, University of Exeter. His work on the 1851 religious census includes the Historical Association pamphlet, *The Church of England in the mid-nineteenth century, a social geography* (1980).

Rev. W. M. Jacob read law at Hull and theology at Oxford. He was vice-principal of Salisbury and Wells Theological College until 1980, when he became secretary to the Committee for Theological Education of the Advisory Council for the Church's Ministry. He is completing an Exeter Ph.D. on the clergy and society in Norfolk, 1707–1806.

Canon J. Thurmer has been Chancellor of Exeter Cathedral since 1973 and is a part-time lecturer in the department of history and archaeology, University of Exeter.

T. A. Macdonald studied with the Open University and then did postgraduate work at Bristol. He is currently writing a Southampton Ph.D. on the economic and social history of Poole since 1815. He teaches English and general studies at the College of Nautical Studies, Warsash, Southampton.

P. S. Morrish read history at King's College, London and became a librarian. He is now sub-librarian, University of Leeds, with charge of manuscripts and special collections. He edits *Library History* and has published papers in the *Journal of Ecclesiastical History* and a number of other journals.

Editor's Preface

This volume, dedicated entirely to the theme 'Church and Society', came out of a realisation that publication of the 1983 *Southern History* would coincide with the 150th anniversary of the beginnings of the Oxford Movement. On 14 July 1833 John Keble preached the Assize sermon in Oxford, published shortly afterwards as *On National Apostasy;* his text, from the book of Samuel, ended with 'I will teach you the good and right way'. The immediate occasions of his theme were the Irish Church Bill, the apparent designs on the Church of England of the post-Reform Act government, and the need to protest against the fudging of political and religious distinctions which denied the apostolic Catholicism of Anglicanism. The *Tracts* which followed and the liturgical revivals which flooded in the wake of Keble's modest theological protest changed the face of the Church of England for ever, altering many a local landscape as determined clergy and architectural renewal swept across it, and provided a sharp edge to some political debates that lasted well into the twentieth century. Indeed, the recent rejection of the Covenant with nonconformist churches by the Anglican synod shows that the issues Keble raised are far from dead.

The paradoxes of religious liveliness in a world rapidly secularising have fascinated historians. We felt that, given the importance of the Oxford Movement in our region, part of this isue should be dedicated to papers concerned with it. There followed a flow of essays on religious themes which shaped the whole of the volume and made it convenient and stimulating to collect them together to demonstrate some of the themes and controversies currently occupying historians of the churches. There are many obvious gaps — Roman Catholicism since the Reformation and modern popular religion amongst them. We hope that this issue may stimulate work on those themes and on some of the others suggested by our contributors. Such papers will certainly be welcomed to leaven future issues crowded with more secular concerns.

The publication of this extended issue has been made possible by a generous grant from the Twenty-Seven Foundation, for which we are particularly grateful.

Editorial Changes
This will be the last issue I shall edit solely. Volume 6 (1984) will be edited jointly with Dr J.G. Rule, who will take over as sole General Editor for subsequent volumes. From the time this volume appears, correspondence about contributions, offers of papers etc., should be addressed to: Dr J.G. Rule, Editor, *Southern History*, Dept. of History, The University, Southampton SO9 5NH.

When this volume appears, there will also be a change of Reviews Editor. Mr. W.N. Yates has resigned, and will be succeeded by Professor Ivan Roots, Department of History, University of Exter, to whom all correspondence should be addressed.

J. R. Lowerson

Problems in Church History:
twenty years on

J. KENT

If one goes back twenty years one finds that a significant change had already taken place in the attitude of many church historians to their subject. Traditionally, in Britain, the specialist 'church historian' studied the institutions, beliefs and political fortunes of christian bodies of all kinds: he wrote from the Church outward, so to speak, and one of the most important roots of his discipline had been incessant argument about what happened to 'the Church' in England in the sixteenth century — an argument by no means closed at the present time. He usually had an overriding belief in the providential direction of history: when one of the founders of the modern discipline, Mandell Creighton, gave his inaugural lecture as professor of Church History in Cambridge in 1885 he said that the church historian saw in the history of Christianity the traces of God's working in the world, and burned to show how the Church had knit European society together in the past and must be its bond in the future.[1] Even now standard textbooks like J.R.H. Moorman's *A History of the Church of England* (1953) reflect Creighton's point of view. Indeed, the church historian may sometimes still appear in a theologically partisan role: Edward Norman, for example, in his *Church and Society in England 1770–1970* (1976), bowed to contemporary fashion in his title (which reflected the influence of sociology on church history), but the book was essentially about the Church of England, and its later chapters paid less attention to 'history' than to the author's passionate opposition to the prevalence of 'radical theology' and 'christian socialism' in the governing circles of Anglicanism.

Nevertheless, by the 1960s the signs of a change had become apparent. There was a perceptible shift away from the history of the 'Church' as a (perhaps) divine society, a special case, to the study of the history of religion itself, and especially the western religious tradition, inside or outside Britain. There were many reasons for this. As the British Empire dissolved, for example, the study of the impact of Christianity on Africa, China and India passed into the hands of historians with little theological or sentimental attachment to what the missionary societies had done. They saw the history of christian missions, not as part of a divine plan, but as an alien episode in the history of religiously self-providing societies. Paul Cohen's *China and Christianity* (Harvard, 1963), Thomas Metcalfe's *The Aftermath of Revolt in India 1857–70* (Princeton, 1964), J.F.A. Ajayi's *Christian Missions in Nigeria 1841–1891* (1965), and Robert Rotberg's *Christian Missionaries and the Creation of Northern Rhodesia* (Princeton, 1965), all came out in the 1960s: in them, the historian's interest was moving, not from the Church outwards, but from the non-christian society towards the christian community and its institutions. In the long run the dramatic alteration in the position of Christianity outside Britain was bound to affect the way in which British church historians regarded the history of religion in Britain itself. Moreover, in Britain after 1945 younger church historians were conscious that christian institutions seemed to be in decline, and this decline gradually affected their perspective of British religious history at least as far back as the Reformation, though it is one of the points of this essay that 'church history' has not yet been sufficiently transformed. Other powerful influences came from Marxism (through Christopher Hill and Edward Thompson, for example), from anthropology (through Keith Thomas), and from the sociology of religion (through Bryan Wilson).

These new influences and interests produced valuable new work. This included, for example: (a) a fresh reading of English Roman Catholic history since the Reformation, and a more sophisticated study of J.H. Newman (John Bossy, Stephen Dessain); (b) research into sixteenth-century puritanism and popular religion (Keith Thomas, Alan Macfarlane, Christopher Hill, Michael Walzer); (c) new approaches to the history of Methodism (Edward Thompson, Bernard Semmel, John Kent, Reginald Ward); (d) a wave of research into Victorian church history, including Victorian sects and working-class religion (Owen Chadwick, Brian Harrison, James Obelkevich, Kenneth Thomas among many). Side by side with this one must set comparative failures, such as the lack of a reinterpretation of English Protestantism equivalent to John Bossy's new understanding of Catholicism in England; the reluctance to study eighteenth-century English religion; the feeling that Victorian 'church history' still sits too complacently in a frame largely invented by Victorians themselves; a gap in the area of women's history, so that one can find little written about English church history to set beside Ann Douglas's fascinating book, *The Feminization of American Culture,* which, despite its title, is about what happened to American religion between the 1780s and the 1880s; and finally, the fact that nothing significant has been done on the Ecumenical Movement since the publication of Bryan Wilson's rather brutal attack on the problem in *Religion in Secular Society* in 1966. We must look at these points in more detail.

(a) John Bossy's *The English Catholic Community 1570–1850* (1975), and J.H.C. Aveling's *The Handle and the Axe* (1976), which covered much the same period, completed the revival of modern English Catholic historical studies which might be said to have begun with the publication in 1961 of the first volume of the still unfinished edition of *The Letters and Diaries of J.H. Newman,*[1] edited by Stephen Dessain of the Birmingham Oratory. Bossy's work is important because he argued in detail that the history of the post-Reformation Catholic community in England was not a process of continuous decline which reached bottom in the eighteenth century, thence to be rescued by a miraculous 'second spring' for which Newman and the Oxford converts were responsible, but a patient growth from small beginnings in which the eighteenth century was marked by modest progress and careful preparation for the future; this means that he also rejected the other widely-held view that the Catholicism of modern England is the result of Irish emigration into an alien land which had little or no indigenous Catholic tradition. He also situates the history of the Englsih Catholic community within the general history of nonconforming bodies in England: he divides English Dissent into a Protestant and a non-Protestant segment, placing in the first the earlier Presbyterians, the Congregationalists, Baptists and Methodists, and in the second Catholics, Quakers and Unitarians. Of course, both Bossy and J.H.C. Aveling are reacting to the need of present-day English Catholicism to adjust its past in terms of its changed position in the religious sub-culture of British society, but what matters more is that one is persuaded to look again at the traditional myths of British religious history. A similar reexamination of myth has affected the study of Newman: in *Newman and the Common Tradition* (1970), John Coulson offered a vision of a moderately liberal Newman integrated into an Anglican tradition which could be described in terms of Coleridge and F.D. Maurice. In English ecumenical politics, of course, Newman (like Sir Thomas More) has long been a major Catholic counter, and there is a well-organised campaign for his canonization. This sometimes leads to extravagant claims on his behalf in ecclesiastical circles, as when Dermot Fenton wrote that 'it was left to Newman to demonstrate that development in doctrine, far from being a mark of infidelity, was in reality a sign of the Church . . . Newman accomplished an understanding of the question which entitles him to be ranked among the great theologians of all time. His *Essay on Development* alone makes it not ridiculous to speak of him in the company of Augustine and Aquinas: it is perhaps the greatest work of theological genius since the *Summa Theologica* . . it gave the definitive reply to the argument that the Catholic Church was historically responsible for a false development of christian doctrine'.[3] Of course, Newman's *Development* offered an able defence of the historical growth of the official system of Roman Catholic doctrine, but it was no more; he did not anticipate the direction in which modern criticism of the dogmatic principle would go.

(b) When one comes to the sixteenth and seventeenth centuries as such one finds that 'church history' and 'political history' overlap so much that this must be my ground for the omission of many useful books. Nevertheless, the new interests did stand out for a time, especially in Keith Thomas's monumental *Religion and the Decline of Magic: Studies in popular beliefs in sixteenth and seventeenth-century England*, (1971), as well as in Alan Macfarlane's *Witchcraft in Tudor and Stuart England: a regional and comparative study* (1970); *The Family of Ralph Josselin* (1970); and *The Diary of Ralph Josselin 1616–83* (1976). Keith Thomas (like Macfarlane) applied the insights of recent social anthropology to the history of religion in England at its most critical point; in doing so he violated, from the point of view of traditional 'church history', a slowly forming consensus that the English Reformation was an institutional matter, to be looked at institutionally; that English Protestantism was to be defined in Anglican terms as a series of relatively minor theological and ecclesiastical modifications to the English medieval Church, and that 'separatists', 'radicals' and 'puritans' were outsiders. (Indeed, 'puritans' became increasingly difficult to define at all, perhaps because neither Anglican nor Roman Catholic historians had any real use for them, historically speaking.)

Keith Thomas, however, having devised a clear account of how the medieval English Church combined religion and magic, saw the main thrust of Protestantism as expressing a widespread rejection of the traditional set of religious practices: "the decline of the old Catholic beliefs was not the result of persecution; it reflected a change in the popular conception of religion . . . Protestantism presented itself as a deliberate attempt to take the magical elements out of religion, to eliminate the idea that the rituals of the Church had about them a mechanical efficiency, and to abandon the effort to endow physical objects with supernatural qualities by special formulae of consecration and exorcism'.[4] Paradoxically, this gradual semi-secularization of the English Churches meant that magic had a temporary increase of popularity; nevertheless, the hold of both magic and Christianity on English society had drastically weakened by the eighteenth century.[5] One might add that the attempts of various nineteenth-century movements to return to more primitive versions of Christianity did not restore Christianity to the cultural centre, and that this helps to justify the use of the 'history of religions' approach. Keith Thomas's interpretation seems to me more subtle than that of Christopher Hill, for example, in *Society and Puritanism in Pre-Revolutionary England* (1964), where the alleged 'puritan' creed is translated as the ideology of a new class emerging from the wreckage of feudalism, and the late seventeenth-century crisis of 'modernity is left as an inexplicable shift from religious individualism to market economy rationalism; or for that matter Michael Walzer's *The Revolution of the Saints* (Harvard, 1965), in which the 'puritans' are better-class but more totally alienated from both the social and ecclesiastical society: Thomas was allowing 'religion' its own history, instead of always reducing it to non-religious factors. In fact, Frank Manuel's *Religion of Isaac Newton* (1974) probably tells one more about seventeenth-century religion than either Hill or Walzer, because Manuel enables one to see how Newton's mind was littered with Biblical prophetic furniture not only antique, but useless, like the long galleries at Knowle. One has a vivid glimpse of a religious world of prophecy which might still have been intelligible to Newman in the nineteenth century, but is no longer part of our culture in the way in which it was taken seriously by Newton.

A younger generation of church historians, however, has not been unduly impressed by the 'history of religion' approach. When Rosemary O'Day and Felicity Heal edited and contributed to *Continuity and Change: Personnel and Administration of the Church in England 1500–1642* (Leicester 1976), Patrick Collinson, who had himself written on Elizabethan Puritanism, commented that 'it will be useless to seek here for signs of that millenium anticipated in the sixties by Mr Keith Thomas and other advocates of the 'new ways'; no anthropology, little 'popular religion', not as much as a cross-reference to *Annales* . . . But the editors can point to the neglect of the institutional history of the post-Reformation Church of England. The attention paid since the war to the local ecclesiastical archives on which almost everything in this book is based has not been adequately reflected in print'.[6] O'Day and Heal edited two further books of essays: *Church and Society in England: Henry the Eighth to James the First* (1977); and *Princes and Paupers in the English Church 1500–1800* (Leicester, 1981). The former collection turned to the question: 'How significant was religious ideology in England in the sixteenth century?' and argued, rather against the drift of Thomas and Macfarlane, that provincial society remained religious at all levels down to 1600; the latter volume was devoted to the economy of the Church of England, concentrating on the income of the bishops, parish clergy, chaplains and so on.[7] This institutional interest has bred a steady shift to regional and diocesan studies. For those interested in regional studies there are, for example: *The Reformation in Essex* (1965) by J.E. Oxley; *Religion and Society in Elizabethan Sussex* (1969) by R.B. Manning; *Reformation and Resistance in Tudor Lancashire* (1975) by C. Haigh; and *English Provincial Society from the Reformation to the Revolution* (1977) by P. Clark, a book about Kent between 1500 and 1640, which made much of 'radical' religion.

(c) Non-Anglican church history has been fully professionalised only since 1945. The study of Methodism profited most, though more in terms of the nineteenth than of the eighteenth century. Little, however, was done to clarify the problems of the origins of the eighteenth-century Protestant religious recovery, between John Walsh's essay, 'Origins of the Evangelical Revival' (in *Essays in Modern Church History,* ed. G. Bennett and J. Walsh, 1966), which discussed the possible internal English sources of the various movements; and W.R. Ward's essay, 'Power and Piety: The Origins of Religious Revival in the early Eighteenth Century' (in *The Bulletin of the John Rylands Library,* 1980), which sought to relate what happened in England to sources in European Protestantism. In fact, insufficient work has been done on popular religion in England in the eighteenth century to make sound judgements possible; even the relations between Anglicans and Wesleyans between 1740 and 1815 have not been properly worked out. The Oxford University Press has started to publish a 34-volume edition of *The Works of John Wesley* under the general editorship of Frank Baker, and three volumes have so far been issued, but this project will probably only prolong the tendency of historians of Methodism to concentrate on Wesley instead of on the religious movement with which he was associated. There is an excellent antidote to this obsession, V.H.H. Green's short, incisively critical biography, *John Wesley* (1964).

In recent years the principal thrust of 'church history' and 'history of religion' has been in nineteenth-century studies, and the interpretation of Methodism has been a central issue. Since 1960 fresh versions have been offered of the familiar but quite unproveable Halévy thesis[8] that one should first suppose that English society was threatened with revolution between 1740 and 1840, and then assume that one can find in the history of Methodism an important part of the explanation of the apparent non-occurrence of this revolution. In these new versions, inter-pretations of religion interlock with class-based interpretations of the development of English society between about 1780 and the High Victorian years. E.P. Thompson, for example, in *The Making of the English Working-Class*, (1963) seemed at times to argue that the psychological content of Methodist revivalism emasculated the proletariat.[9] Harold Perkin, in *The Origins of Modern English Society 1780–1880* (1969), lumped Methodism and the remainder of Nonconformity together (but did not anticipate John Bossy by adding Catholicism to the mixture) and described this total Nonconformity as the 'midwife' of the nineteenth-century class-structure. The role of sectarian religion, he said, was threefold: 'to give expression to emancipation from the dependency system before it hardened into overt antagonism; and not so much by passive teaching of patience as by active example of the benefit of non-violent organisation, to influence class-conflict in the direction of non-violence'. Perkin did not make clear just how Nonconformi-ty produced such a powerful effect specifically on the English working-class, but he certainly saw membership of movements like Wesleyanism as tending to neutralise a political stance. Bernard Semmel, on the other hand, in *The Methodist Revolution* (1974), interpreted Wesleyan theology in terms of R.R. Palmer's 'demo-cratic revolution of the eighteenth century' — see *The Age of the Democratic Revolution* (Princeton, 1959): Wesleyan doctrine con-stituted an essentially liberal, progressive ideology which confirmed and helped to advance the shift from a traditional to a modern society. For Thompson, then, the effect of the Wesleyan ideology was to corrupt the working-class, whereas for Perkin and Semmel the effect was socially healthy. A 'good' revolution was substituted for Halevy's 'bad' revolution, so to speak. In the meantime, E.J. Hobsbawm (in *Labouring Men*, 1964) doubted the connexion between Methodism and the absence of revolution, as did John

Kent, (especially in 'Salvation and Politics', Open University broadcast, 1975–82).

In all these studies Methodism was being examined from the outside, and attempts were being made to see it as religion acting in society, though not all these writers had a very clear idea of what they meant by religion. Perhaps Thompson tried harder than any of the others to convey what he thought that the world might have looked like through the eyes of a Wesleyan adept; in fact, however, Thompson could not establish that Wesleyanism functioned as the working-class religion of consolation which his Marxism permitted him; moreover, he seemed to be describing a 'chiliasm of despair' much less typical of the Wesleyans than of Anglican Evangelicals and members of the millenialist sects. These latter have been studied with half an eye on anthropology by W.H. Oliver, in *Prophets and Millenialists: the Use of Biblical Prophecy in England from the 1790s to the 1840s* (Auckland University Press, 1978), which contains work on the Southcottians, the Irvingites and the Mormons; and in *The Second Coming: Popular Millenarianism 1780–1850*, by J.F.C. Harrison (1979), which covers similar ground, and in which millenarianism is used as a conceptual tool with which to explore what Harrison calls a 'popular culture', but which looks more like the survival at a very much lower intellectual level of the interest in 'prophecy' which had been natural in the mind of Isaac Newton. These books depended less on Marxism, or on traditional 'church history', than on English work in the sociology of religion, notably that of Bryan Wilson, whose *Sects and Society* (1961) was based on valuable research into the Victorian history of Christian Science and Christadelphianism, and whose *Magic and the Millenium* (1973) was a sociological analysis of religious movements of protest. By the beginning of the nineteenth century, however, English institutionalised Christianity was already contracting into a sub-culture distinct from the mainstream culture of the society as a whole, and what Oliver and Harrison are describing was probably more important for the understanding of the Churches than some 'church historians' assume, and less important for the understanding of 'popular culture' than Thompson and Harrison supposed.[10]

A much more sustained historical discussion of nineteenth-century 'popular religion' and its relation to popular culture, at any rate in the countryside, is contained in *Religion and Rural Society: South Lindsey 1825–75*, by James Obelkevich (1976), which was an examination of Anglicanism, Methodism (Wesleyan and Primitive), and popular religion in the central districts of Lincolnshire.

Obelkevich defined popular religion as 'the non-institutional religious beliefs and practices, including unorthodox conceptions of christian doctrine and ritual, prevalent in the lower ranks of rural society. It was not a unitary phenomenon: it can best be understood as an amalgam, a loose combination of unofficial Christianity and a rather larger measure of pagan 'survivals' . . . Yet even if it was not hostile to Christianity, the Church could not avoid being hostile to what it regarded as superstition . . .'.[11] Obelkevich said that in the course of the nineteenth century a process of depersonalization affected popular religion and superstition: 'superstition subsided to the level of luck, its impersonal lowest common denominator'.[12] Obelkevich thought that this was the 'most important set of changes in popular religion since the Reformation', and he inevitably sought an explanation in social change, because he was committed to the Feuerbachian position that the secret of religious history is social history. This led him to adopt what seems to me an implausible argument that these changes depended on the replacement of an older village 'community' by a fully developed class society in village terms.[13] This sentimentality apart, *Religion and Rural Society* makes a remarkable contribution to the study of modern English religious history.

As for the 'church history' of early nineteenth-century Methodism, much new light has come from W.R. Ward's edition of the letters of the Wesleyan leader, Jabez Bunting, in *The Early Correspondence of Jabez Bunting 1820–29* (1972), and *Early Victorian Methodism: The Correspondence of Jabez Bunting 1830–58* (1976). A final section of the Bunting letters was published, edited by A.J. Hayes and David Gowland, in *Scottish Methodism in the Early Victorian Period: the Scottish Correspondence of Jabez Bunting 1800–57* (Edinburgh, 1981). On the basis of this and other research Professor Ward produced his own interpretation of the period in *Religion and Society in England 1790–1850* (1972). There is little or no trace of the 'history of religion' approach; one glimpses society as the background of the incessant internal upheavals of Methodists, Dissenters, Unitarians and Anglicans, with the north and especially Manchester — alas for *Southern History* — as the principal battleground, with Leeds, Liverpool, Rochdale and Stockport in close attendance. What emerges in the Methodist case is the image of a conflict between open, popular, lay forms of religious organisation on the one hand, and on the other 'denominational', authoritarian, clerical organisations strongly supported by locally successful businessmen. The authoritarians triumph, and this becomes a paradigm for the whole society, in which Christianity (not religion, which is not Ward's subject) contracts in consequence. Professor Ward sees the subject-matter of 'modern church history' as the decline of the Churches, and he holds that 'church history' ought to be able to provide an understanding of that recent history from its own resources. When he reviewed the second volume of Owen Chadwick's *Victorian Church* (1970), he complained that ecclesiastical history seemed incapable of providing such a framework of explanation and added: 'If general historical scholarship can do no better, then both religion and history may succumb to the myth-making skills of the sociologists'.[14] As for the sociologists, he might have had in mind such confident pronouncements as this by Thomas Luckmann: 'the degree of involvement in the work processes of modern industrial society correlates negatively with the degree of involvement in church-oriented religion'.[15] With such theories, who needed history? Ward himself, however, was coming close to a reassertion of the traditional view that 'church history' constitutes a special case because its subject-matter in the last analysis is a supernaturally-supported institution.

(d) Nevertheless, historians influenced by sociology and social anthropology have had a field-day with Victorian religious history, if only because the sense of the imminent institutional collapse of Christianity (which they share with writers like Professor Ward) has made theory seem at least as important as the grind of establishing a detailed narrative. The situation does not altogether differ from that in contemporary Marxism, where historians of the Althusserian school assert that theory must precede any kind of praxis, while rebels like Edward Thompson reply that 'the relation between historical knowledge and its object cannot be understood in any terms which suppose that one is a function (inference from, disclosure, abstraction, illustration etc) of the other. Interrogation and response are mutually determining, and the relation can be understood only as a dialogue'.[16] When one looks at the apparent conflict in the Church of England in the nineteenth century, for example, it seems amazing that the basic narratives — accounts of the Evangelical and Anglo-Catholic groups, for instance — have not even been written; and much the same is true of the non-Anglican Protestants.[17] Even in the case of a less restricted approach, as when Professor Chadwick covered the whole period in *The Victorian Church,* one finds that when he tackled the second half of the century he was unable to disentangle events from the web of Anglican myth in which they had already become enmeshed; one need only compare his weak section on 'secularization' (in the second volume of *The Victorian Church*) with his far more penetrating treatment of the same problem in *The Secularization of the European Mind in the Nineteenth Century* (1975) to accept that we shall have to set up a new dialogue between theory and event before a plausible fresh narrative becomes available. One cannot simply 'go back to narrative': the myth-making of the sociologically-minded historian has its uses. In the meantime, 'church history' has not yet fully absorbed the material with which it has to deal.

As this volume of *Southern History* is devoted to English ecclesiastical history and particularly to the Anglo-Catholic movement whose centenary and a half falls in 1983, it is appropriate to take as an example of the orthodox tradition one of the few books published recently on an aspect of Anglo-Catholic history: *Ritualism and Politics in Victorian Britain,* by James Bentley (1978).[18] This is the first detailed account of the unsuccessful campaign by the late Victorian bishops, led by Archbishop Tait, to stop the spread of Anglo-Catholicism by fixing new legal limits to the freedom of the parish clergy to introduce ritual innovations into their parish services. Tait hoped to discipline the Anglo-Catholic 'ritualists' by means of the Public Worship Regulation Act, and Bentley described both the passage of the Act (1874) and how it was reduced by non-compliance to a dead letter by 1906, when a Royal Commission on Ecclesiastical Discipline was set up as a screen for the official retreat. Bentley made good use of the recently available papers of Lord Cairns, Disraeli's evangelical Lord Chancellor, and of material from the provincial press, but his analysis was firmly controlled by Anglo-Catholic tradition — religious groups are quite as skilful myth-makers as sociologists. He concluded that 'by refusing to be put down the ritualists not only preserved the Anglican clergyman's ancient freedom; they also advanced the cause of toleration in Victorian Britain'.[19] This was to interpret the 'ritualists' as they interpreted themselves. The three-way struggle between very moderate institutionalists like Tait, Anglo-Catholic extremists like Pusey, and Evangelical Anglican extremists like J.C. Ryle, was not about individual liberty and toleration, but about the credibility of 'Anglicanism' as either idea or institution; about the role of the laity (quite as much as of the priesthood) in the Established Church; and about the credibility of Christianity in a modernising society. That Tait failed to make Anglo-Catholicism 'Anglican' cannot be disputed; that his defeat was all part of Anglo-Catholicism's regeneration of the Victorian Church of England — the traditional view — is what the critical historian has to test. My own view of both Anglo-Catholicism and Anglican Evangelicalism as 'undeclared sects' is set out in *Holding the Fort* (1978).[20]

Although we have not yet succeeded in rewriting the accepted myth of Victorian 'church history' in terms of a history of nineteenth-century English religion, it is not difficult to make a list of books which are already helping to transform our understanding of our recent religious past. This list would have to include: *Bureaucracy and Church Reform: The organizational response of the Church of England to Social Change 1800–1965* (1970) by K.A. Thompson; *Drink and the Victorians: The Temperance Question in England* (1971), by Brian Harrison; *Religion and Social Class: the Disruption Years in Aberdeen* (1974), by A.A. Maclaren; *Class and Religion in the Late Victorian City* (1974), by Hugh McLeod; *Pitmen, Preachers and Politics: the effects of Methodism in a Durham mining community* (1974) by Robert Moore; *Religion and Society in Industrial England: Church, Chapel and Social Change 1740–1914* (1976), by A.D. Gilbert; *Religion and Voluntary Organisations in Crisis* (1976) by Stephen Yeo; *Churches and Churchgoers: Patterns of Church growth in the British Isles since 1700* by R. Currie, A. Gilbert and L. Horsley; and Susan Budd's *Varieties of Unbelief: Atheists and Agnostics in English Society* (1977).[21]

Obviously, my space is limited, and only one of these books is much concerned with Anglo-Catholicism. This is Kenneth Thompson's *Bureaucracy and Church Reform,* which was based on the premise that since 1800 outside changes in society had compelled the Church of England to face the theoretical need both to 'rationalize' its structure and to create the centralising bureaucracy which such a programme entailed. In practice, no 'Anglican' consensus could be formed in the Victorian period to achieve such ends. As Thompson said: 'nothing deterred Newman from leading a movement to fight the rationalistic pragmatism of the new middle class, under the banner of the Church as the embodiment of transcendental values and supernatural qualities'.[22] If one attempts to interpret Anglo-Catholicism along these lines, one may regard it, together with 'Anglicanism's' other undeclared sect, Anglican Evangelicalism, as being at least as much a ground of decay as of regeneration. 'What was needed in the long run was a theory which could reconcile expediency in adapting norms (the concern of the reformers) with legitimacy in terms of religious principles (the emphasis of the Oxford Movement',[23] but neither of the 'church parties' was able either to produce such a theory itself, or to accept, within the Victorian period, a theory proffered from outside. This was analysis in the spirit of Weber rather than Durkheim, and the emphasis is not congenial to church historians for whom the Church (however visible) still retains a supernatural origin, but, as Professor Ward suggested, myth, or analytical structure there must be, and if the historians hesitate to criticise the myths of the institutions whose stories they narrate, then the social scientists will do the criticising for them.

Notes

[1] M. Creighton, *Historical Lectures and Addresses* (1903), p. 22. As to providence, no one was more aware than Creighton, who studied the sixteenth century, that the history of the Church was full of 'corruption', but he saw these imperfections theologically, as part of a divine order.

[2] The first published volume was actually number eleven in the whole series, and began the publication of the letters of Newman's Catholic period; it was entitled *Littlemore to Rome*. The Catholic letters were completed with the publication of volume thirty-one. Publication of the Anglican letters started with volume one, *Ealing, Trinity, Oriel*, ed. Ian Ker and Thomas Gornall, in 1978.

[3] D. Fenton, Interpretations of Catholic History', in *The Journal of Ecclesiastical History*, April 1982, pp. 264–5. The *Journal* was started in 1950 to fill an obvious professional gap; for many years it was edited by Professor C.W. Dugmore. The Ecclesiastical History Society was formed some years later and has now published nearly twenty volumes of *Studies in Church History*, containing papers given at the Society's annual Conference. The *Journal* and the *Studies* are evidence of the liveliness of 'church history' in the past twenty years.

[4] K. Thomas, op. cit., p. 87.

[5] See also Bernard Capp, *Astrology and the Popular Press: English Almanacs* (1979): Capp thought that after the Reformation, astrologers supplied a need unsatisfied by Anglicanism, 'the harnessing of supernatural powers to help men avert dangers' etc. The golden age of the almanac was 1640 to 1700. Equally interesting, but much less influenced by Thomas, is *Popular Religion in Restoration England*, by J.C. Sommerville (Florida, 1977), which was based on best-selling devotional works published between 1660 and 1711. In both cases the social science technique has its limits, but the approach suggests results, as when Sommerville concludes that the allegedly 'puritan' line on sex usually appears in 'anglican' best-sellers.

[6] Rosemary O'Day has also recently published *The English Clergy: the Emergence and Consolidation of a Profession 1558–1642* (Leicester, 1979); and Felicity Heal has published *Of Prelates and Princes: a study of the economic and social position of the Tudor episcopate*, (1980).

[7] Halévy originally advanced his views in an essay, 'La Naissance de Methodisme', published in the *Revue de Paris* in 1906, and translated and published by Bernard Semmel as *The Birth of Methodism* (Chicago, 1971). Halévy's essay was partly given over to the troubles in the woollen industry in Wiltshire and Gloucestershire in the earlier eighteenth century. Most of the argument seems to me very implausible.

[9]   Thompson relied on G.R. Taylor, *The Angel-Makers (1958)* for this.

[10]   For *Southern History* readers, the Southcottians are interesting because of their West country connexions, and so are the Brethren, who do not come into the books mentioned above. The best introduction to their history is in *The Roots of Fundamentalism, British and American Millenarianism 1800–1930* (Chicago, 1970), by E.R. Sandeen, while H. Rowdon (*The Origins of the Brethren,* 1967) discussed the work of Robert Chapan at Barnstaple, Robert Gribble in Devon and Somerset, and George Brealey in the Black Down Hills, all in the first half of the nineteenth century. As for Methodist West Country sect-life, see also *The Shearers and the Shorn,* by E.W. Martin (1965), which is a sociological and historical study of the Okehampton area in the same period. Bristol University is now helping to publish material on the Bible Christians in Somerset.

[11]   Obelkevich, *Op.cit.,* pp. 261–62.

[12]   Obelkevich, *Op.cit.,* p. 311.

[13]   This prompted the comment: 'And when the farmers became a class, with their own class values, they rejected traditional moral values, shattering the traditional moral consensus', (p. 312), for example.

[14]   ·Ward, *Journal of Ecclesiastical History,* April 1971, p. 160.

[15]   T. Luckmann, *The Invisible Religion* (ET 1967), p. 30. Marxist sociologists commonly hold that church-oriented groups in Western society are peripheral to the structure of modern society.

[16]   E.P. Thompson, *The Poverty of Theory* (1979), p. 232.

[17]   Michael Watts's *The Dissenters* (1978) ends at the French Revolution.

[18]   Two recent articles deserve notice: 'Unenglish and Unmanly: Anglo-Catholicism and Homosexuality, by D. Hilliard, *Victorian Studies,* Winter 1982; and 'The Last Victorian Anti-Ritualist Campaign, 1895–1906', G.I.T. Machin, *Victorian Studies,* Spring, 1982.

[19]   Bentley, *Op.cit.,* p. 128.

[20]   Kent, *Holding the Fort,* pp. 236–94, 'Anglo-Catholic Revivalism'. The extent to which Anglo-Catholicism still dominates the image of the recent Anglican past may be seen in another recent book, which set out to harness 'church history' and sociology, and failed partly for that reason. This was: *A Social History of the Diocese of Newcastle,* edited by W.S.F. Pickering (1981), intended as a centenary volume for a diocese started in the 1880s. Some contributions still reflected how much Anglo-Catholicism resented opposition to its claims. What was even clearer, however, was that this diocese, set up at the peak of the Victorian movement to reform the Establishment, never took off — the story is one of gradual decay, speeding up from the mid-twentieth century. This narrative of decline has to be written into the myth before a fresh understanding of 'the Victorian Church' can form.

[21]   Obelkevich would be in this list, but I have already mentioned his work. McLeod's book is about London, Stephen Yeo's about Reading; Marxism influences Maclaren and Yeo, but not the others; Susan Budd's *Sociologists and Religion* (1973) is also valuable.

[22]   Thompson, *Op.cit.,* p. 45.

[23]   Thompson, *Op.cit.,* p. 49.

Immunity, Exemption and the Sussex Monasteries

F. HOCKEY

It is too easy to forget that whereas the kingdom of Wessex possessed a group of famous anglo-saxon monasteries, Winchester, Malmesbury, Glastonbury, and also venerable nunneries, Winchester again, Wherwell, Romsey and Shaftesbury, all with great estates, the kingdom of Sussex had to wait until after the Norman Conquest for its two great monasteries. Battle and Lewes are both early Norman foundations, owing nothing to the older anglo-saxon traditions. The Normans had no esteem for the English abbeys and sought to put them under Norman abbots, for no doubt they saw in them centres of resistance to normanization. The anglo-saxon monasteries had been all closely linked to the English kings, while the episcopate was largely drawn from their monks.

Both Lewes and Battle contributed new elements to monastic life in England which were to be of great significance, particularly concerning the constitutional framework of the life — the election of abbots, independence from external interference, whether from bishops or secular government, that is to say 'exemption'.[1] This can be studied both in the intentions of the founders and in the regulations of the Rule of St Benedict which was to order the life of the foundations of both Battle and Lewes. St Benedict did not legislate for an order, but wished every monastery to be autonomous, to be a separate unit; the monks were to promise stability in the house of their choice, to live under the rule of an abbot they themselves had chosen and under his guidance to live out the counsels of the Gospels. But for mutual protection or support, monasteries have tended to group themselves into families or congregations, usually for reasons based on some historical situation. Even so, what is perhaps the chief characteristic of the Benedictine family is the lack of any clear-cut organisation or interpretation of how the Rule is to be lived out at any period. St Benedict does not give any role to the local bishop in the organisation of the monastery, except to remove an unsatisfactory abbot or to punish a rebellious priest (c.64); but, in his day, the priest in the monastic family was the exception.

According to the law of the early medieval Church, every Christian was a subject of a bishop, whose authority belonged to a particular territory only, his diocese; every Christian was at the same time a subject of the sovereign pontiff, to whom he could appeal over the local bishop. But the person who enters the monastic state becomes thereby a subject of his religious superior, his abbot. One cannot conceive of a monastery in which the abbot has not the final decision, just as one cannot conceive of a diocese in which the bishop has not the final word in the admission to holy orders. Hence there arose certain exceptions to the territorial jurisdiction of bishops; monastic life demands a certain independence, and if there are priests in the monastery, they cannot be completely under the jurisdiction of the local bishop. To be truly subject to their abbot, they must be exempt from the authority of the ordinary. This is not just a medieval problem, for it was discussed at the Council of Chalcedon in 451, hence monastic superiors came to have powers more or less equivalent to those of bishops. The first clear example of exemption from episcopal jurisdiction was that granted by pope Honorius I to the Irish foundation of Bobbio in 628. Such a privilege was particularly useful to a religious family with houses in more than one diocese, to congregations of monasteries. The great monastery of Cluny was exempt from its origins and by reason of its structure was able to hand on its exemption to all its foundations — a practice which the papacy did not seek to curb, since it worked in favour of monastic and ecclesiastical reform generally. Hence monks came to rely upon kings and popes to secure exemption from being subject to the local bishop: he was not to interfere in elections of abbots, though he could and did claim the right of conferring the abbatial blessing. The monasteries had to turn to their bishop for the ordinations of their subjects, though they could in practice avoid this by having recourse to some other bishop. Similarly when monasteries came to own churches, they had to present to the local bishop the clerks they intended to place in the benefices. Certain monasteries succeeded in extending their privileges to a limited area, usually two miles, around the monastery, the *sacrum bannum,* the *banleuca;* this was the case for Battle. The Sussex abbey of Robertsbridge[2] is not to be considered here, for the family of Cîteaux was a federation under a superior-general with an annual general-chapter; all its monasteries were exempt, as laid down by the *Carta caritatis* (1119).

The question of the right to make a visitation,[3] the equivalent of a 'general inspection', is a corollary of exemption. From ancient times it has been a duty and a right of bishops to enquire into the temporal and spiritual affairs of the different religious corporations within their dioceses. The bishop would hear complaints and ask questions with a view to drawing up injunctions for the future and maintaining good ecclesiastical discipline. Whether or not a diocesan did have the right to make the visitation of a monastery was part of the privilege of exemption, hence the cause of endless disputes, especially since the large number of cases heard by papal judges - delegate within a century of pope Gregory VII had built up a very clear body of papal decisions concerning exemption. Even if visitation is not mentioned in a case, it was obviously involved. If the monastery could prove its exemption, it was outside the jurisdiction of the ordinary, as today Westminster Abbey is exempt from the diocese of London.

After the battle of Hastings the Conqueror determined to build a monastery on the high ridge where Harold fell. He would in this way commemorate the event, secure prayers for the slain and make amends for his own sins. He did not take into consideration the difficult site he was imposing, the poverty of its soil or the inadequacy of the water-supply.[4] Though it was to the Norman abbeys of Caen and Bec that he normally turned for men to present to the English monasteries, since the nomination of abbots was a royal privilege,[5] William went outside Normandy and requested a colony of monks for his new foundation from Marmoutiers, near Tours. This famous abbey was dedicated to St Martin, for the soldier-saint had lived there centuries before; Battle abbey, also dedicated to St Martin, was destined to take its place by the side of the old pre-Conquest abbeys in England.

To us it seems only natural that a founding monastery should have some responsibility, or at least take some interest in its foundation, but when Battle was vacant for five years the claim of Marmoutiers to intervene was rejected. The Conqueror had clearly wanted his abbey to be under his own protection and control, just as he had endowed it with lands and privileges, but he had not set out these privileges and rights in any documentary form; the monks knew everything from word of mouth. The *Chronicle of Battle*[6] needs, therefore, all the care in its interpretation that its latest editor has brought to the task. When the time came for the canon lawyers to insist on written evidence of jurisdictional privileges, the grants from the founder had to be written up in charter form — hence the forged charters[7] which are extant and the chronicle which puts these charters in their historical setting. The monks themselves certainly considered themselves free from interference by royal officials and agents in their lands, probably also from most forms of ecclesiastical supervision. In England the bishops and local lords had always exerted a considerable influence in the anglo-saxon monasteries, but the new spirit of ecclesiastical reform associated with the name of Gregory VII was everywhere working to exclude lay interference in the affairs of the Church.

Now Battle had built for the use of the inhabitants of its *banlieu* a church dedicated to St Mary.[8] It was the bishop of Chichester's claim to exactions from this church which seems to have precipitated the famous crisis of 1157. How helpful it would be to have at hand precise information concerning the situation before that date, independent of the charters and the *Chronicle*. After failing to become archbishop of York, Hilary was bishop of Chichester from 1147 to 1169 and, having worked at the papal curia as an advocate and acted many times as papal judge-delegate, he was an accomplished canonist, fully aware of the niceties of exemption and privilege. He knew quite well that Battle had no papal privileges and no papal documents. It did not resemble the ancient English abbeys in being held by knight service, nor was its revenue shared between abbot and community.[9] But it received continual royal visits; when William Rufus was prevented from leaving the country by bad weather, he ordered the monks to arrange the consecration of their abbey church in the presence of the king in 1094.[10] Again, when abbot Gausbert died in 1095, it was the same king who after some delay nominated as abbot a monk of Bec, Henry, at the time prior of Canterbury. Battle was, then, very much an *Eigenkloster,* closely protected by the kings until the reign of John and the foundation of Beaulieu. Hilary began by claiming jurisdiction over the abbey and making demands on abbot Walter de Luci (1139–71), forgetting that the abbot's brother was the justiciar of England. At a first hearing of the case in the Tower of London before the king, the bishops of Winchester and Ely with the abbot of Westminster, Hilary seems to have left the court and it was thus in his absence that the king declared the abbey of Battle not to be subject to the bishop of Chichester. This did not, however, settle matters, since the abbot was ecclesiastically suspended for being contumacious; after not appearing a year later, the abbot found himself excommunicated. Finally, the case was heard at Colchester before the king, when Hilary disputed the validity of the Conqueror's charters in favour of Battle. Thereupon in anger the king rebuked the bishop for attempting to dispute and diminish the prerogatives of the Crown. Hilary submitted and renounced his rights of jurisdiction over Battle.[11] At this point it is useful to recall that, at the consecration of the abbey church, Ralph, bishop of Chichester (1091–1123), had been present and that he had persuaded abbot Henry (1096–1102) to receive his abbatial blessing at Chichester.[12] But it would be presumptuous to go over here all the important work on this case: the study of the personality of Hilary as an 'opportunist' by Dom Knowles,[13] the examination of the privileges and consequences of exemption by Lemarignier,[14] the problem of the loyalty of Hilary to the Crown and to the papacy examined by Mayr-Harting[15] and more recently, Professor Searle's penetrating examination of the forged charters and the *Chronicle*. Nonetheless, Battle was in the diocese of Chichester; it was essential to build up some *modus vivendi* with the diocese, while being outside its jurisdiction. To this we now turn, for if Battle was exempt, it was still not canonically exempt: exempted by the king, contrary to canon law.

By royal nominations Battle was in fact ably served by a line of superiors from outside the community; their quality was never in question. Odo (1175–1200), who had been prior of Canterbury, though invited for his abbatial blessing by the bishop of Chichester, was instead blessed at the archbishop's manor of Malling.[16] After 1215 royal nomination of abbots ceased and future abbots were elected by the community of Battle. The king had been treating the abbey as a royal peculiar, a royal demesne chapel, though the abbey but little resembles a royal free chapel. Battle still had not secured papal exemption, nor had it attained the status of an ancient royal chapel. However, even if the ordinary had been excluded from Battle by a confirmation[17] of its exemption by pope Gregory IX in 1234, the archbishop of Canterbury was not excluded from exercising his metropolitan rights. A composition, quite unusual, was reached a year later by a papal commission, carefully picking its way between king and bishop, smoothing over the disputed territory.[18] In future the bishop of Chichester had to be satisfied that the election had been canonically conducted, then he could give the abbatial blessing, but the ceremony must take place in some other church than Battle, where the prior would install the new abbot. The bishop could come to the abbey, but only every three years and with only twenty-five horses, remembering all the time that he had no jurisdiction within the *banleuca*. As regards visitation, the bishop would nominate one monk, the community selecting another, these two would then report their findings to the bishop. The archbishop of Canterbury, however, could make this visitation and in 1283 John Pecham did so.[19] By chance we have his injunctions. In this rich abbey, he complained that the monks were not being supplied with the necessaries; he felt that the abbot was not in full control of the monastery. It was a situation unique in England and other archiepiscopal registers show that the archbishops did make the visitation of Battle with reasonable regularity. The general history of the abbey shows a monastery of good observance and regularity; it maintained its original spirit and lived amicably with the little township which had grown up around it.[20]

Lewes was the foundation of William de Warenne and his wife Gundreda, lords of the rape and town of Lewes.[21] He had already a distinguished career before the Conquest and when William returned to Normandy in 1067, he was one of the vice-gerents during the absence; again in 1075 he acted as chief justiciar with Richard de Clare in the absence of the king. He had been granted land in Sussex, also in Conisborough in the West Riding and by 1086 possessed land in twelve English counties. It was therefore as one of the leading Norman barons that he set out on pilgrimage to Rome with his wife. The foundation charter, though interpolated, tells how they were prevented by war from proceeding to Rome, but instead made their pilgrimage to St Peter and Paul at Cluny. There is no adequate reason for rejecting the story that they were so hospitably received and edified with the spectacle of Cluny that they decided to found a monastery on their own land with monks from this famous abbey. We might have said earlier that William the Conqueror had already appealed to Cluny, to abbot St Hugh, for monks to found Battle abbey, offering to pay an annual pension of 100 pounds in silver for each monk. The abbot did not accept the proposal; for one thing he did not wish to have any monasteries beyond the seas; also he objected to the financial suggestion.[22] When William de Warenne made his request for a foundation, St Hugh again demurred and for the same reasons.

The Burgundian abbey of Cluny was then at the height of its repute for the standard of its observance, upheld by a series of distinguished abbots. The abbey had enjoyed canonical exemption since 931 and temporal immunity since its formation. It was subject only to the Holy See. Cluny had not sought for power, but it progressively became an order, securing freedom from lay and canonical jurisdiction for all the monasteries depending upon it. During the anarchy of Europe in the tenth century this great abbey had been able to bring a certain stability and reform to the Church. Freedom from external interference by secular lords or bishops was the chief factor in its growth and influence. It was the great abbot, St Hugh (1049–1109), who consolidated the order of Cluny, in which, as compared with the Rule of St Benedict, the principle of authority was exaggerated and the autonomy of the individual priories was diminished. Each dependent house in the family was a priory and not an abbey, for which the abbot of Cluny nominated the superior. The individual monk made his profession to the abbot of Cluny rather than to his prior, in something like a feudal link. It will be clear that in the nomination of superiors, too much depended on the qualities of the abbot at the centre, making his decision with insufficient knowledge of local circumstances. The abbot of Cluny acted personally without any general chapter to guide him in the government of the numerous priories of the family loosely linked together.

It required a personal visit to Cluny for earl William de Warenne to be granted three monks for his foundation at Lewes. It was not a very encouraging beginning, but Cluny was accustomed to making foundations insufficiently manned, whereas the founder was prepared to support twelve monks with their prior. Lewes was fortunate to have as its first superior Lanzo, whose long rule of thirty years secured for the priory a sound foundation. But when we consider the principles of the Cluniacs on freedom from the influence of lay lords, we may well be surprised at the terms and conditions earl William was in a position to lay down. St Hugh promised not to interfere unnecessarily in the internal affairs of Lewes and to appoint Lanzo as prior for life (he was the first prior to be granted this privilege). The abbot promised he would always set over Lewes one of his most outstanding monks, after the prior of Cluny and the prior of La Charité: the prior of Lewes was to be subject to the abbot of Cluny only in matters of observance and discipline. Lewes was to be considered one of the chief priories of the order, and these arrangements were sealed by the grant from Lewes to Cluny of 50 *solidi* every year. It has been observed that, in endowing Lewes with land in Falmer (which had simply been taken from the nuns of Wilton at the Conquest), William de Warenne did not impoverish himself by his generosity.[23]

Earl William was killed in 1088 and buried in the chapter-house at Lewes (to be re-discovered and re-interred elsewhere in 1845). Almost all the members of the family seem to have been buried there.[24] It is good here to keep in mind that the English kings, beginning with the Conqueror, held Cluny in high regard. The English Cluniac abbots or bishops were among the foremost Cluniacs of their day on either side of the Channel. Even though Lewes remained the focus and pattern of Cluniac observance,

Cluniac influence was exerted rather through those English bishops who had been monks of Cluny.

After a century of seemingly good relations between the monks of Lewes and the de Warenne family, a long dispute[25] arose when Hamelin de Warenne (d. 1202) claimed the right to have a hand in the patronage of the priory. He was only a de Warenne by right of his marriage to Isabella de Warenne, and had earlier been rebuked for witholding tithes due to Lewes. Hamelin disapproved of Alexander, the prior nominated by the abbot of Cluny; he argued that the prior should be elected by the monks and that as patron he had the right to approve of their choice; then he sequestrated the goods and put the priory under a kind of siege, ordering the prior to leave. The patron similarly occupied the dependent priory of Lewes at Castle Acre in Norfolk. At first a section of the Lewes community sided with Hamelin, no doubt feeling that the founding family should have some interest in the priory to which it had long been associated. The pope set up a commission of enquiry under the archbishop of Canterbury and the bishops of Ely and Chichester, as papal judges-delegate with a few laymen, ordering the earl to restore the goods seized.[26] Thereupon earl Hamelin excluded the prior. The arrival of the abbot of Cluny, Hugh V (1199–1207), who had been abbot of Reading, did not change the situation. While the case was still pending, Hamelin prevented the abbots of Battle and Robertsbridge from installing the new prior, Alexander, when, suddenly, perhaps because the whole community had come over to the side of the new prior and the bishop of Chichester was preparing to excommunicate, the dispute ended in an unexpected calm. There followed the composition of 1201; the importance of the case had been shown by the choice of the judges-delegate. It was agreed that in future Cluny would propose two candidates for the choice of the earl. The delegates from the priory and from the earl would go to Cluny for the abbot to present the successful candidate to the earl's representative. This rather clumsy arrangement safeguarded the principle that it was the abbot of Cluny who was nominating and, as before, presenting two of his best men. It left a prominent place for the local patron, passing quietly over the question of election by the community. It was a solution that was contrary to canon law and Gregory IX in 1229 restored to Cluny the choice of the prior of Lewes. Only in 1298 was the prior at last an Englishman, John of Newcastle (1298–1301). A national sentiment can be seen developing at Lewes, as in so many alien houses at this period. The monks pleaded with the abbot of Cluny, that since the earl of Warenne was of such high rank, any action against him would be resented by the king and the nobility. There was a good deal of truth in their argument.[27]

Archbishop John Pecham, whom we have seen at Battle, had been brought up at Patcham, near Lewes, where he may well have received some of his education and derived his devotion to the official worship of the Church. However, he became a Franciscan, an able canonist, being both ardent for monastic reform and the care of souls in parochial life. In 1284 he made a purely ceremonial visit to Lewes, where he sang the Mass and preached to the assembly. Then, as a private guest without his attendants, he sat with the monks in their refectory.[28] After his visit, the archbishop felt obliged to make known to the abbot of Cluny that he was disturbed about certain things of which he could not approve. His letter of 1 June, 1285, is carefully worded, for he knew he had no jurisdiction whatever, yet wanted to lodge his complaint.[29] The archbishop was distressed at the *desolatio* of Lewes, calling attention to three points. First, the superiors appointed should be men of quality, who could maintain the observance and the standard of hospitality. Then, since Lewes was wealthy, its wealth should be expended in proper directions, with less *ambitio*. Lastly, he appealed for a more realistic attitude towards the de Warenne family as patrons; there was an obligation of gratitude to the family and also a risk of offending the English nobility and the hierarchy. Even if the abbot of Cluny was impressed by the letter from the archbishop of Canterbury, as we have noted above, no Englishman was appointed to Lewes until 1298, by which time England and France were at war. All the alien monastic houses were now afflicted by disabilities and restrictions, while questions of immunity and exemption lost almost all their relevance. By the Statute of Carlisle 1307, Cluny could no longer receive its annual pension, while the very privileges of the Cluniac order only served to underline that its houses were in opposition to the English king. In 1374 Lewes purchased its denization, thus breaking its financial and administrative link with Cluny. In 1376 the English parliament asked that foreign abbeys should appoint English superiors to their dependent priories. A plan was elaborated and then approved by Boniface IX in 1410 for a vicar-general, an Englishman, to deal with elections and professions, but the abbot of Cluny, Raymond de Cadouène, through old age or the pride of the ancient abbey, refused. Only in 1480 did Edward IV secure the independence of Lewes by a bull of Sixtus IV. Cluny had lost its chance and time was running out; Lewes surrendered in 1537.[30]

This enquiry into the efforts two very different monasteries to maintain their rights and privileges reflects somewhat the wider problem of lay patronage and the investiture struggle. The Church had granted to the founders of churches certain rights and privileges in gratitude for the endowment conferred on the particular churches; it was only natural that founders of monasteries also would expect some parallel privileges. It is true that patronage carried with it certain obligations, but there was a tendency for patrons and founders to be possessive and the strife which ensued usually had to be settled by some form of compromise. But too often privileges and principles overlapped; on both sides there was an insistence on safeguarding privileges once received, with insufficient openness to new situations. The immunity of monasteries from secular liabilities and from ordinary diocesan jurisdiction carried with it the risk of a clash of interests, which the canonical definitions reached in the XII century did much to help smooth out.

Notes

[1]   D. Knowles, 'The growth of Exemption', *Downside Review*, L (1932), pp. 201–231, 396–436; *Dictionnaire du Droit Canon*, v, c.637–665.

[2]   For Robertsbridge, *V.C.H.*, *Sussex*, ii, p. 71.

[3]   C.R. Cheney, *Episcopal Visitations in England in the thirteenth century* (Manchester, 1931).

[4]   D.C. Douglas, *William the Conqueror: The Norman Impact on England* (London, 1964); J. Le Patourel, *The Norman Empire* (Oxford, 1977); Eleanor Searle, *Lordship and Community: Battle Abbey and its Banlieu, 1066–1538* (Toronto, 1974); Rose Graham, *English Ecclesiastical Studies* (London, 1929), ch. viii.

[5]   D. Knowles, *Monastic Order in England* (Cambridge, 2nd ed., 1963), pp. 113–115.

[6]   *The Chronicle of Battle Abbey*, ed. E. Searle (Oxford, 1980).

[7]   E. Searle, 'Battle Abbey and exemption: the forged charters', *English Historical Review*, LXXXIII (1968), pp. 449–480.

[8]   J.H. Denton, *English Royal Free Chapels of the twelfth century*, (Manchester, 1970), p. 83.

[9]   M. Howell, 'Abbatial Vacancies and Divided Mensa in Medieval England', *Journal of Ecclesiastical History*, XXXIII (1982), p. 180, 183, 185.

[10]   *Anglo-Saxon Chronicle*, ed. D. Whitelock and others (London, 1961), p. 171.

[11]   A. Saltman, *Theobald, archbishop of Canterbury* (London, 1956), pp. 243, 156–158.

[12]   H.G. Richardson and G.O. Sayle, *Governance of Medieval England* (Edinburgh, 1963), pp. 287, 290.

[13]   D. Knowles, *The Episcopal Colleagues of Archbishop Thomas Becket*, (Cambridge, 1951), p. 27.

[14]   J.F. Lemarignier, *Etude sur les privilèges d'exemption et de juridiction*

ecclésiastique des abbayes normandes, (Paris, 1937).

[15] H. Mayr-Harting, 'Hilary, bishop of Chichester and Henry II', *E.H.R.*, LXXVIII (1963), pp. 209–224.

[16] *Chronicle*, pp. 305–306.

[17] *Registres de Grégoire IX*, ed. L. Auvray, nos. 1738, 1772, 1776.

[18] Denton, *op.cit.*, p. 87.

[19] Decima Douie, *Archbishop Pecham* (Oxford, 1952), p. 156.

[20] *V.C.H., Sussex*, ii, pp. 53–54.

[21] *Early Yorkshire Charters*, ed. C.T. Clay, *Yorkshire Arch. Record Series*, VIII (1949), pp. 59–62.

[22] Migne, *P.L.*, CLIX, c. 922; N. Hunt, *Cluny under St Hugh, 1049–1109* (London, 1967).

[23] B. Golding, 'The coming of the Cluniacs', *Proceedings of the Battle Conference, 1980* (Woodbridge), pp. 65–77.

[24] v. *D.N.B.*

[25] L. Guilloreau, 'Les prieurés anglais', *Millénaire de Cluny* (Macon, 1910); *Orderic Vitalis: Ecclesiastical History*, iv, ed. M. Chibnall (Oxford, 1973), p. 180–181.

[26] C.R. Cheney, *From Becket to Langton* (Manchester, 1956), p. 158.

[27] Guilloreau, *op.cit.;* Susan Wood, *English Monasteries and their Patrons in the thirteenth century* (Oxford, 1955), both using Bruel, *Recueil des Chartes de Cluny*.

[28] Douie, *op.cit.*, p. 4.

[29] *Reg. Epist. Pecham, (R.S.)*, iii, pp. 902–905.

[30] *V.C.H., Sussex*, ii, pp. 64–71; *Dict. d'Histoire et de Géogr.*, (Louvain), xiii, c. 140.

The Progress of the Reformation in East Sussex 1530–1559: the evidence from wills

G. J. MAYHEW

Since the publication of A.G. Dickens's *Lollards and Protestants in the Diocese of York* in 1959, the value of wills' formulae as an indicator of the changing religious outlook during the middle decades of the 16th century has been well recognised by historians. Dickens, who rightly stressed that the results of such analysis should not be presented in any spirit of statistical pedantry confined his own survey to printed collections and to the evidence of preambles alone, dividing them into two categories (traditional and non-traditional). The former comprised the standard bequest of the soul to Almighty God, Blessed Virgin and Glorious Company of Saints, sometimes with the specific request to pray for me. The latter comprised all those wills in which the soul was left to God alone together with a smaller number in which the testator stressed a clear Protestant belief in salvation through Christ's merits or God's mercy alone.[1]

More recently David Palliser's study, *The Reformation in York* (1971) divided wills' preambles into traditional, non-traditional and Protestant, essentially using Dickens' criteria, though with the qualification that the main component of the non-traditional category, bequest of the soul to Almighty God, was really a neutral type of bequest.[2] Peter Clark's study of Kent (1977)[3] also confines itself to preambles alone and adopts much the same classifications of conservative (soul to Almighty God, Virgin Mary and/or saints in heaven), reformist (testator omits all references to intermediaries with the deity) and radical (salvation through the merits of Christ alone) together with a fourth category for those wills without preambles, a type he regards as probably without religious significance.[4] Most recently Claire Cross's paper in *Studies in Church History* (1979) which compares the evidence from wills for the progress of the Reformation in York and Hull makes use of preambles as an indication of changing religious attitudes.[5]

Both Palliser and Cross make reference to the relatively high number of bequests for obits and masses during the period prior to the 1540s, and Dickens, whilst including those wills with the preambles soul to Almighty God and holy company of heaven in his 'traditional' category notes that the increased omission of reference to the Virgin in the latter years of Henry VIII's reign is probably not without significance. However none of these writers makes any attempt at a systematic analysis of such factors. Whilst accepting Dickens' caution, it seems to the present writer that there is a need to explore the religious evidence from wills more systematically than hitherto, in particular, as Michael Zell's article on the limitation of preambles as an indicator of religious beliefs suggests,[6] by taking into account the full range of religious bequests contained in any one will rather than relying on preambles alone for the purpose of statistical analysis. It is as a partial solution to that problem that this paper is offered.

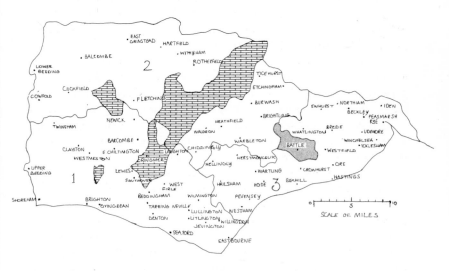

PECULIAR JURISDICTIONS

▨ BATTLE

▦ SOUTH MALLING

GEOGRAPHICAL AREAS
1 DOWNLAND
2 MARSHLAND & EASTERN COASTAL PARISHES
3 WEALD

East Sussex Protestantism — places mentioned in the text.

The study itself is based upon the evidence of some 2375 wills contained in the registers of the Lewes Archdeaconry Court, together with a further 28 wills from 7 parishes in the Peculiar of South Malling and 92 wills from the registers of the Peculiar of the

Deanery of Battle, covering the period c.1530–59, all of which (with the exception of the South Malling register)[7] are held at the East Sussex Record Office.[8] Each of these wills was card-indexed by the author according to date of composition, name of testator and parish. The exact wording of the preamble was noted, together with other evidence of religious opinions such as bequests for masses, obits, sermons, church ornaments, etc., poor bequests and requests for the disposal of part of the testator's goods 'for the health of my soul' and otherwise. Finally any references to education, learning, books, etc. was included, together with the names of any witnesses to the making of the will.

In the early stages of analysis it soon became clear that the traditional three categories were insufficient to accommodate the main variables, and a new classification system of 6 categories was evolved: Traditional, Reformist, Protestant, Neutral/Indeterminate, Mixed Traditional/Reformist and Mixed Protestant/Traditional (these last two containing only some 2% and 4% of the total respectively). The primary determining factor in the classification of individual wills was the theological bias of the preamble itself, but equal significance was accorded to specific requests for masses and other services or other overt acts of piety indicative of a particular religious outlook. In the absence of any such determining factors the language of any admonition to the executor concerning the disposal of any part of the estate was taken into account as evidence of religious bias. This proved especially important in the classification of wills with the otherwise indeterminate bequest of the soul to Almighty God.

With over 50 variant forms of preamble alone plus the possibility of their combination with a range of other variables it is inevitable that the exact dividing line between the major categories at their margins is somewhat arbitrary. The overall pattern is, however, unlikely to be seriously affected by such marginal cases since they comprise only some 1–2% of the total in any one group or year.[9]

The Traditional category is chiefly comprised of those wills with the preamble leaving the soul to Almighty God, Our Lady and the Company of Heaven, plus those with the more specific bequest for the latter to 'pray for me'. Other wills in this category may contain an element of the new style but retain all these traditional elements as for example in the relatively common Henrician bequest of the soul to Almighty God, maker and redeemer, Our Lady and all the holy company of heaven. In addition, wills with 'neutral' preambles such as those leaving the soul to Almighty God (and holy company of heaven), but containing requests for masses

(75 and 39 respectively) have been included within this category as have those other wills with these same preambles which contain other traditional bequests or the traditional bestowal of a portion of the estate 'for my soul and all christian souls'.

The Reformist category contains all those wills whose preambles dispense with both virgin and (in the majority of cases) saints (e.g. soul to Almighty God, maker and redeemer, or soul to Jesus Christ, saviour and redeemer), but where the religious language falls short of an overt declaration of Protestant doctrine. Trinitarian preambles are also included in this category, as are wills with indeterminate preambles but containing bequests of a clearly 'reformed' nature (e.g. soul to Almighty God plus disposal as executor thinks most best), or other indications of a reformist outlook (e.g. soul to Almighty God plus burial 'with the faithful').

The Protestant category has been reserved for those wills with a specific Protestant bias and is comprised mainly of wills whose preambles refer to a belief in salvation through the merits of Christ's death (and/or passion). Other overt declarations of the Protestant faith have been included in this category, such as the bequest of the soul to Almighty God my maker, to Jesus Christ my only redeemer and saviour 'by whom *my assured hope is to be saved*'; and also a small number of 'neutral' wills with specific Protestant bequests (e.g. soul to Almighty God plus a bequest for the buying of a Bible). The neutral category (18% of total) consists mainly of those wills with the simple bequest of the soul to Almighty God (including 8 with the addition of 'etc.'), or of the soul to Almighty God and the holy company of heaven, plus a number of nuncupative wills and a further eight without preambles. The Traditional/Reformist and Traditional/Protestant categories combine major elements of two types, usually by the inclusion of a bequest for masses in a will with a Reformist or Protestant preamble, though occasionally the preamble itself contains the two elements. These two categories should be seen as essentially transitional, and appear in their greatest number during times of change (e.g. during the move towards Protestantism in 1546–7 and during the increasing Catholic reaction towards the end of Mary's reign).

The wide range of variations in the wording of wills' preambles, even within each basic category suggests a lack of standardisation. Probably there were a few set formularies in circulation. The majority of parish priests (the usual authors of mid-sixteenth century wills) however, drawing their inspiration from current church usages (the impact of the two Edwardian Prayer Books is especially noticeable) composed their particular formulation on the spot at the time of writing.[10] John Reder, Vicar of Beddingham, for example, employed the phrase 'soul to Almighty God, my only creator, redeemer (and saviour)' in eleven wills which he witnessed in 1552–3, with, on nine occasions, a general admonition at the end to the executor to fulfil the testator's wishes 'as seems most best to be done, to the pleasure of Almighty God', in four cases adding 'and his own soul's health' (i.e. the executor's).[11] George Fairbancke, Rector of Tarring Nevill, employed a Trinitarian formula on the wills he witnessed in several parishes in 1549–54, bequeathing the soul 'to Almighty God, the Father, Son and Holy Ghost'.[12] When William Harward, a small farmer of Iden, made his will on 16th March, 1554, he commended his soul 'into the hands of God the Father, trusting assuredly to be saved by the merits and passion of my saviour and redeemer Jesus Christ and to be raised up again at the last day of judgement with the righteous people', 'and this I protest to be my faith' he concluded. Yet even this apparent personal declaration of faith was nothing of the kind. Almost identical words appear in nine other Iden wills in the years 1548–53.[13] However, even if wills' formulae cannot provide any firm guide to a testator's personal beliefs, they are nevertheless a good indication of the views of the clergy and the doctrine current in particular parishes at the time.

In the larger parishes, such as Battle or Rotherfield for example, or towns such as Lewes or East Grinstead, the variety of formulations in any one year suggest that testators often either chose the fomulation they preferred, or went to a priest of a sympathetic outlook. Robert Robson, curate or Battle, was quite prepared to use either Traditional or Protestant formulations. In 1557, for example, he commended the soul of George Shether to God, Our Lady and all the holy company of heaven, while in the same year committing Richard Porter's soul to God 'through the blood of Jesus Christ which I believe to be shed for the whole remission of all my sins' — both which formulae he used again the following year.[14] Occasionally one will from a particular parish stands out as quite exceptional, and is probably therefore an indication of the personal wishes of a testator, as for example, John Cotmot, the elder, of Lewes (1559), Senior Constable in 1551 and until his death a member of the Society of the Twelve, the governing body of the town, to which he left 2s yearly for four years for their Whit Sunday night feast. In language quite distinct from any other Lewes will up to that time, he commened his soul 'into the most merciful hands of Almighty God, the Father, Son and Holy Ghost, three persons and one God in trinity, most humbly beseeching him and most assuredly trusting in him that as I once being lost was by the death of Christ redeemed, so now being redeemed, that his almighty goodness will likewise see me saved'.[15]

Two East Sussex wills of this period stand out as being quite different in nature from any others in the registers. One is overtly conservative, the other, quite definitely Protestant. Both are in the nature of a (somewhat lengthy) personal declaration of faith. The earlier of the two is the will of Richard Colbrand of Wartling, a small farmer, made on 18th December, 1548. It was apparently written by Colbrand himself (no priests are among the witnesses and he adds as a postscript that 'Nicholas Yong doth owe unto me xls which I did lend him'). In it he rehearses his faith in salvation through Christ alone, specifically rejecting priestly (or any other) mediation, and quoting Biblical passages in support of this view:

> 'First and before all other things I commit myself to Almighty God and to his mercy, trusting without any doubt that by his grace and the merit of his passion of (sic) his resurrection I have and shall have remission of my sins and resurrection of body and soul according as it is written in John the xix chapter: I believe that my redeemer liveth and in the last day I shall rise out of the earth and in my flesh shall see my saviour. This is my hope, it is laid up in my bosom and touching the wealth of my soul the faith that I have taken and rehearsed is sufficient and, as I suppose, without any other man's work or works. My ground and my belief is that there is but one mediator between God and man but only Jesus Christ, and all other be but peticioners in receiving of grace, but none able to give influence of grace . . . .'.[16]

Since there is no other will of its type in the Lewes Archdeaconry registers of the period, it would seem reasonable to conclude that it represents the personal views of the testator, formed from his own reading of the Bible. However, Professor Dickens found an almost identical will, that of Edward Hoppay, yeoman, of Wakefield (1548) in the York registers.[17] And both Hoppay's will, and that of Richard Colbrand closely follow the even longer preamble in the will of William Tracy, yeoman, of Toddington, Gloucestershire (proved at Canterbury according to Foxe in 1532), for the use of which words Tracy's body was reportedly dug up and burnt for heresy.[18] Each of these three wills has separate features in common with each of the other two, whilst every one of the three has additional features unique to itself. Colbrand's, for example, gives the chapter reference of the quotation 'I know that my redeemer liveth . . .', though it should be Job, not John. It seems inescapable therefore, that all three wills were based on an even longer, more fully comprehensive version, from which each selected more or less the material available, and that here at least is indisputable evidence of the circulation of at least one Protestant formulary.

The second unusual will from the Lewes Archdeaconry registers of the period is that of George Lowes of Winchelsea, several times Mayor and onetime MP for Winchelsea during the Reformation Parliament, made on 18th September, 1553. Written at the beginning of Mary's reign, while the Edwardian services were still in full force, in it he recounts how 'auricular confession is not with all men allowed and now little used', yet he remembering the counsel of St James the Apostle, 'confess your sins one to another that you may be saved' has determined to confess and acknowledge himself both 'to God and also to all such as shall read or hear this my present testament:'

'Myself to be most miserable and wretched sinner. That I greatly and unkindly, through the weakness and frailty of my flesh, have often and many times offended my Lord God, in thought, word and work, as in breaking and transgressing his 10 Commandments, wherein hangs the whole Law and the prophets. And by the breaking of them I have committed the 7 deadly sins, and the branches of them. And also the 7 works of mercy, both bodily and ghostly, that is to wit, bodily I have not succoured, helped and relieved the poor so duly, willingly and liberally as I should, might and of power and ability was able to do. And also my five wits that God hath lent me, here to conduct and lead me, in this present world to guide me; I have misused them contrary to my bounden duty, and also all my sinful body and wretched, miswrought to the great displeasure of Almighty God.

For the which, with a contrite heart, I bewail, sorrow and lament my sins, and with that heart, I most humbly and meekly pray, require and desire of Almighty God that he would of his clemency, pity and mercy, forgive (me) being a wretched sinner, but yet his creature, my sins and trespasses, and for the attainment of the same, I most heartily desire you all of your charity to pray for me to him that it would please his majesty not to enter into judgement with me his poor creature, for in righteousness, neither I, nor no man living, is nothing worth in the sight of him. Wherefore I utterly leave and forsake his justice, and wholly trust, cleave and stick to his abundant mercy, whereupon I surely believe and hope to be saved through the passion and death of his only Son, our Lord and Saviour, Jesus Christ, and through shedding of his most precious blood. And also because I am baptised and truly believe in the Catholic and apostolic Church as the holy prophets, apostles and Evangelists have declared in the scriptures, in the Old Testament and the New, which scriptures the whole congregation of christ's whole church, in their councils and synods, hath allowed, confirmed and set forth to be the true prophet and lively word of God . . .'.

He went on to declare his belief in the three Creeds, the Common Creed, the second creed that 'is said in the Holy Communion', and the third creed 'made by the good Catholic man Athanasius, contained in the Psalm *'Quicunque vult'*. He then continued:

'And as to the last article, I believe that I must die and change my life, and as Christ saith, 'nisi granum frumenti cadens in terra mortuum fuerit, ipsium solum manet'. And I know my wretched and sinful body must rot and turn to earth and dust again, yet I believe that at the last Day of Judgement my said body shall rise again, whole and perfect, and come before the High Judge of all the world, to whom I most humbly pray. And also I most heartily and most instantly desire you all, of your charity to pray with me and now for me that I may, by the great and glorious mercy of that High Judge, be one of them that shall be called to be saved at his right hand and have the fruition and glory of him in the life everlasting. Amen'.[19]

George Lowes clearly had no great liking for the Edwardian changes. His stress on auricular confession and his desire to be prayed for indicate that quite clearly. Yet his knowledge of the Bible, the Creeds and doctrine easily rival that of any Protestant layman. His will indicates that even at the end of Edward's reign, and in such a Protestant town as Winchelsea, there were often powerful local figures who were quite unmoved by the religious changes that had taken place, and would be ready to welcome the Catholic reaction when it came.[20]

Testators such as Colbrand or Lowes were, however, only a minute percentage of the whole. Most seemed quite content with the standard formulae offered them by the local clergy, who were themselves apparently largely willing to adapt their usages to the religious changes dictated from above. This becomes clear when the changes in wills' formulae during the Reformation period are analysed. The results of this analysis of East Sussex wills is set out in Table 1 (p. 46).

A striking feature of the early years is the continuing high proportion of traditional wills to the mid-1540s, whereas in Kent, Clark found a marked shift away from traditionalism after 1538. Reformed ideas evidently came to East Sussex somewhat later, and it is interesting to note in this connection that two of the three entirely Protestant wills of Henry VIII's reign for Eastern Sussex

Table 1: Changing Religious Attitudes From Wills:
Lewes Archdeaconry 1530–59

Year	T	T/R	R	T/P	P	N	Total
1530–40	106	4	5	4	–	7	126
1541	39	2	3	1	–	3	48
1542	61	2	1	2	1	2	69
1543	73	7	–	4	1	6	91
1544	61	4	1	2	–	4	72
1545	89	6	2	–	–	12	109
1546	70	7	7	5	1	11	101
1547	51	6	11	5	4	18	95
1548	23	3	22	2	7	15	72
1549	16	3	29	1	7	22	78
1550	14	6	35	1	12	20	88
1551	10	3	35	–	10	31	89
1552	8	–	46	–	17	34	105
1553	9	3	66	3	16	31	128
1554	35	6	37	1	11	26	116
1555	29	5	25	–	10	18	87
1556	54	2	34	4	12	21	127
1557	121	12	69	3	11	42	258
1558	143	17	72	10	22	52	316
1559	56	8	113	3	42	68	290

See Appendix 1 for details of classification.

came from Rye and Winchelsea, both parishes close to the Kent border.[21] In 1546 there is a marked swing away from traditionalism, becoming more pronounced the following year — a pattern familiar elsewhere. Edward VI's reign (1547–53) marked a concerted government attempt to change religious attitudes. The success of that policy is seen in the fall of traditional formulae to barely 8% of the annual totals in 1552 and 1553, and the increase in overtly Protestant formulae to almost double that of the traditional in the same period — a rather higher proportion than in Kent.[22] The eradication of 'mixed' formulae in 1551–2 is a further sign of that success.

In 1554 the beginnings of the impact of Marian policies can be seen in the increase of traditional formulae to some 30%. This level was, however, barely half that of the last year of her father's reign (1546). Despite rigorous pressure for a return to Catholic practices, in no year during her reign did traditional wills form more than 50% of the total, whilst Protestant wills continued at a level of some 10% until 1557, when they fell by half, recovering somewhat the following year. In 1559, the first full year of Elizabeth's reign, traditional wills fell to just 19%, only slightly higher than Protestant ones. Evidently the impact of the Marian reaction in East Sussex was relatively shortlived.

These bare annual totals obscure a number of interesting local variations in the overall pattern. As Table 2 indicates, although in Henry VIII's reign all three major geographical divisions of East Sussex are remarkably similar in religious outlook, from then on, the three regions diverge quite dramatically. The downland parishes remain the most conservative both in Edward's reign and under Mary. The wealden parishes show a more marked swing away from traditionalism in the earlier period and a noticeably lower traditionalist proportion in Mary's reign. Finally the eastern coastal and marshland parishes show both a significantly higher Protestant commitment under Edward and a marked resistance to the imposition of traditionalism in Mary's reign, being the one

Table 2: Changing Religious Attitudes From Wills by Geographical Area 1530–58

Region	Percentages 1530–46						1547–53						1554–58						Total Wills
	T	T/R	R	T/P	P	N	T	T/R	R	T/P	P	N	T	T/R	R	T/P	P	N	
Downland	83	4	3	2	–	8	26	3	35	2	11	23	54	5	15	2	6	18	777
Wealden	83	7	3	3	1	4	16	7	38	2	8	29	41	5	31	1	8	14	627
Marsh/coast	81	5	3	2	1	7	20	3	36	1	16	24	31	4	33	3	9	20	836

Table 3: Changing Religious Attitudes From Wills East Sussex Towns 1530–58

Numbers of wills

	1530–46						1547–53						1554–58						Wills
Bexhill	9	1	–	–	–	–	1	–	3	–	4	8	–	4	4	–	3	3	40
Brighton	4	–	–	–	–	4	–	1	3	–	–	6	3	1	3	–	10	2	37
Eastbourne	25	–	1	–	–	–	4	–	2	–	–	1	3	1	2	–	–	3	42
E.Grinstead	9	2	–	–	–	–	–	1	11	–	–	3	9	1	7	–	3	3	49
Hastings	12	4	4	–	1	3	3	3	17	–	5	8	9	–	26	–	2	7	104
Lewes	27	–	2	1	–	1	7	–	12	1	2	2	19	1	9	1	1	6	92
Pevensey/Westham	4	–	–	–	–	–	6	–	6	–	–	1	4	–	–	6	3	4	34
Rye	23	3	2	3	1	4	1	–	15	2	7	1	4	1	11	–	3	4	85
Seaford	2	–	–	–	–	–	2	–	–	–	–	2	1	–	–	–	–	2	9
Shoreham	2	–	–	–	–	2	1	–	1	–	–	2	1	–	1	–	–	2	12
Winchelsea	7	1	–	–	1	1	–	–	3	1	4	1	6	–	4	1	1	3	34

region in the country where reformist and protestant wills outnumber traditional ones in those years.

The explanation for these marked regional variations would appear to lie in the differing geographical and social compositions of the three divisions. The relative ease of the transition from reformist to conservative in the downland region in Mary's reign is made more comprehensive when it is remembered that the region centres on Lewes, both the ecclesiastical and administrative headquarters of the eastern half of the county, where it might be expected that enforcement would be greatest. Secondly, most downland parishes were comparatively small in area, usually comprising single nucleated villages, centred on church and manor house, where social control was relatively easy. At East Chiltington, for example, (a detached chapelry of Westmeston parish), the local Lord of the manor, Nicholas Chaloner, who incidentally left an overtly Protestant will, clearly regarded that church somewhat in the light of a proprietorial chapel, specifying in his will (1554):

> 'Item. I will that all those ornaments that I have already bought for the furniture of the divine service within the chapel of Chiltington shall be had, used and occupied in the said chapel whensoever and as often as the said divine service shall be there in the said chapel celebrated. Otherwise I will it to be to the only use of me and mine heirs of the manor of Chiltington Ferrings, remaining in safe custody and keeping forever'.[23]

In such circumstances, clearly the views of the local lord would be a major factor in determining the religious life of the parish. Finally, the downland was also the area of greatest influence of the Gage family, whose major seat was Firle Place, and who, it is clear from Foxe, played the leading role in rooting out persistent heresy and enforcing traditionalism in Sussex during Mary's reign.[24] Again it is unlikely to be entirely coincidental that the parish of West Firle continued to produce a majority of traditionalist wills, even in Edward VI's reign.[325] The one exception amongst the downland parishes east of Lewes was Laughton, providing one solitary protestant will in 1551, and two reformist ones in the same period. But this was the home of Sir Nicholas Pelham, head of the Pelham family, strongly Protestant from the late 1530s, whose eldest son, John, was to be found amongst the Marian exiles in Geneva in 1557.[26]

Further east, the coastal and marshland parishes were at a much greater distance from ecclesiastical and judicial authority, in a region dominated by such early Protestant centres as Rye,

Winchelsea and Hastings; though a number of parishes such as Battle, from 1538, seat of Sir Anthony Browne, Viscount Montague, and his family, or Brede and Udimore, home of the Oxenbridge family of Brede Place, both families being staunchly traditionalist in outlook,[27] returned majorities of traditional wills throughout the period. The influence of Rye on surrounding parishes was especially noticeable, Iden (10), Peasmarsh (4), Icklesham (3), Beckley (3) and Ewhurst (2), all providing a substantial proportion of Protestant formulae in the period.[28] The contrast between eastern and western parishes shows up particularly clearly when the preponderance of the major types of wills' formulae is arranged by parishes in each region, as in Table 4.

Table 4: Religious Preferences of Testators Arranged by Parishes 1547–1558[29]

Region	1547–53			1554–58		
	Traditional	Mixed	Reformist/ Protestant	Traditional	Mixed	Reformist Protestant
No. of parishes ( )						
Downland (69)	21	10	22	48	5	12
Wealden (37)	7	6	12	13	11	10
Marsh/coast (35)	6	5	17	10	8	12

What is perhaps most significant about the results of this analysis is the much larger number of 'mixed' parishes in the Wealden zone in the Marian period. Here the parishes were far greater in area, generally consisting of many separate small communities and farmsteads, often some miles from the parish church in a region where climate and geological conditions often made communications difficult except on horseback. This was the area, stretching across the Kent/Sussex border, where Lollardy had proved impossible to stamp out in the previous century.[30] Now once again in this region the new Protestant beliefs retained their hold on a proportion of the population, despite the persecutions of the Marian period when the Wealden parishes provided 15 of the 25 Sussex martyrs whose place of origin is known.[31] In East Grinstead parish, for example, from which according to Foxe five martyrs came, the influence of Edwardian preachers like Thomas at Hothe, vicar there in the early 1550s who styled himself 'mynister' left a legacy of Protestant sentiment which continued throughout the next reign.[32] Under Mary, East Grinstead produced twenty-four wills almost evenly divided between traditional and reformist/

protestant. Not so Rotherfield, which produced at least one martyr, Alexander Hosmer, and a further six accusations of heresy in Mary's reign. Here the twenty-three Marian wills were overwhelmingly reformist/protestant, following a pattern which had begun in 1546 with the wills of William Hosmer, cousin to the martyr and Robert Farmer, whose son Alexander took over the martyr's lands following his execution.[33]

Turning now to the towns, what is perhaps at once most striking is the strength of Protestantism, especially amongst the Cinque Port towns of Rye, Winchelsea and Hastings; and the relative conservatism of smaller towns further west such as Eastbourne, Seaford and Shoreham. Lewes, regarded by the Bishop of Chichester as one of the two centres of Protestantism (together with Rye) in the diocese in 1538, also produced few overtly protestant wills throughout the period and an especially high proportion of traditionalist ones with specific requests for masses in Mary's reign. It did however produce the earliest bequest for sermons in the Archdeaconry registers (1539) by Peter Flusher, a substantial local merchant and property-owner both of whose overseers were to serve as High Constables of the town. As well as leaving 20s for five masses and to the poor on his burial day, he also left a further 40s for eight sermons to be preached 'by some discrete and well learned man whom my executor and supervisor shall name and appoint . . . whereof one to be at the day of my burying and another to be at the day of the month's mind and the rest to be preached within the precinct of the said Town of Lewes as soon after my burial as may (be) conveniently, to the setting forth of God's holy word and to the furtherance of the christian people hearing the same, the preacher to have for every sermon vs'.[34] In 1564 Bishop Barlow, in his return of the religious state of the diocese to the Privy Council reported Lewes, together with Rye, Hastings and Brighton as 'governed with such officers as be faithful favourers of God's word and earnestly given to maintain godly orders'.[35] It may well be, therefore, that Protestantism was at its strongest amongst the urban, mercantile and governing classes, both in Lewes and probably elsewhere.[36]

From the evidence of surviving wills, Rye was both the earliest centre of Protestantism in the county and the most consistent, followed closely by its neighbours Hastings and Winchelsea. Both Rye and Winchelsea had a tradition of Protestant sentiment going back at least to the early 1530s, and strong Protestant elements amongst their town corporations. At Hastings, where unfortunately the corporation records only begin in 1598, the presence of John

Melvyn, self-styled 'preacher' and 'mynyster' as a witness to two wills both written in November 1552 is evidence of Protestant influence in the town. One of these wills, for example, that of John Regles, after opening with a confession 'of perfect, stedfast and most constant faith' in Jesus Christ "son of the Living God, mine only saviour" went on to bequeath his soul 'redeemed with the most precious blood of the Immaculate Lamb Jesus Christ into the hands of God my heavenly and eternal father, praying him for his Son's sake mercifully to receive my spirit into his hands, and to cleanse away for his blood shed my most filthy sins'.[37] This will, as with a number of others, bears the name of Robert Fawkener Town Clerk (or 'common clerke') at the end of the witnesses, suggesting the latter's authorship, as with the will of John Francys, fisherman (1553) which is somewhat similar in sentiment, concluding with a request for burial in St. Clement's churchyard 'among the faithful bodies there in the sure hope of the everlasting Resurrection of God's elect'.[38]

Contrary to the overall trend, in a number of towns Mary's reign marked a substantial shift towards protestant preambles — most notably at Brighton, but also at Pevensey and East Grinstead. In Brighton this change occurs in 1556 with the coming of Laurence Plumpton, curate, who witnessed ten wills drawn up between September 1556 and September 1558.[39] On his death (?) he was replaced by John Cartwright, deposed Rector of Ore, and previously of Hastings St. Clements (1556–8) who habitually used a rather unusual reformist preamble during Mary's reign, leaving the soul 'to Almighty God, my Maker, Redeemer and Comforter', often with the admonition to the executor to dispose of the estate 'both to the quietness of my friends and the glory of God, to whom be given high honour, power and praise, now and ever. Amen'. In the first will that he witnessed in Brighton after the death of Mary he added to his usual preamble the words 'by whose mercy and tender love and through the merits of the Passion of Jesus Christ my Saviour, I believe and my very hope is that he will receive it in his eternal glory and bliss everlasting', a formulation he continued to use in subsequent wills.[40]

Pevensey produced both traditional and protestant wills in Mary's reign, together with five with 'mixed' preambles leaving the soul both to Almighty God, Virgin and Saints *and* 'trusting to be saved by the merits and passion of our Saviour, Jesus Christ', the wording frequently employed by Henry Miller, Vicar of Westham.[41] Of the three entirely Protestant wills, two were made by Jurats, the earlier, that of John Comber (1555) instructed his

Table 5: The Changing Nature of Religious Bequests From Wills:
Lewes Archdeaconry 1530–1559

Year	Totals	Masses	Obits	Poor Obits	Lights	Orna-ments	Bestowals	Disposals	Sermons	Poor Bequests	Com-munions	Others
1530–40	126	63	23	–	9	1	12	9	1	37	–	–
1541	48	27	9	1	1	1	6	6	1	19	–	–
1542	70	40	11	–	2	4	6	6	1	31	–	1
1543	91	50	7	–	5	3	1	–	1	35	–	–
1544	72	41	12	–	1	1	11	3	2	28	–	–
1545	109	62	14	1	7	2	14	9	–	52	–	–
1546	101	48	11	1	2	3*	16	4	1	38**	–	–
1547	94	33	5	5	3	3	13	5	–	37	–	–
1548	72	7	1	2	–	–	1	5	3	49	–	–
1549	78	–	–	1	–	–	2	4	–	49	1	–
1550	87	–	–	–	–	–	3	3	1	52	3	–
1551	90	–	–	–	–	–	3	1	1	45	1	–
1552	105	–	–	2	–	–	1	3	1	68	–	–
1553	129	–	–	1	–	–	2	–	1	79	–	–
1554	116	9	1	2	1	1	2	4	–	67	–	–
1555	87	12	1	–	–	1	3	2	–	43	–	–
1556	128	27	3*	2	–	1	3	4	–	61	–	–
1557	256	60	1	4	1	3	11	13	–	132	–	–
1558	317	78	5*	4	1	10	15	3	–	182	–	–
1559	290	34	–	5	2	2	11	6	–	140	–	1

Notes:

*   includes 1 unspecified.
** includes one bequest of £10 towards building an almshouse at Rye. If the corporation is unwilling to proceed with the project then the money is to be used to buy a principal suit of copes or solemn vestment for the parish church. W/A1/107 (Jone Ashe, widow).

Bestowals indicates wills containing instructions as to money to be bestowed at burial (and month/year) but no indication as to how the sum is to be used.

Disposals indicates wills containing no other instructions or religious/poor bequests save the general instruction to the executor to dispose (some part of) testator's goods for the health of his soul.

Poor Bequests indicates specific mention of poor in will, i.e. refreshing of poor at burial, poor disbursements, poor box, etc. Wills providing for refreshments, etc. at burial (month/year) not specifying for poor then present are not included.

Others indicates bequests to the church of a non-traditional nature, e.g. for obtaining Bibles.

wife to send his son to Eton for the two years following his decease and thereafter to keep him at one of the Inns of Chancery or an Inn of Court until he reached the age of twenty-one. The third Protestant will was that of William Comber, presumably a close relative of John's.[42] Evidently higher education as a means of social advancement might appeal to some of the wealthier local townsmen of the period. More usually however the educational wishes of the testators were limited to ensuring that their sons (and heirs) would learn to read and write, presumably for the purpose of carrying on the family business.[43]

Apart from the changing language of preambles, a range of different types of religious bequest indicate changing religious attitudes, including such provisions as for masses and obits, lights and ornaments, etc. The changing pattern of such bequests is set out in Table 5.

An obvious indicator of religious outlook is provision for masses. Throughout the early 1540s slightly under 60% of wills specifically requested masses. In 1546 this figure fell by some 10%. Following Edward VI's Injunctions of 31 July 1547 that money hitherto expended on obits, lights, etc. should instead be diverted to relief of the poor and church repairs, bequests for masses fell dramatically in the latter half of 1547 and 1548. The 1549 Prayer Book did, however, authorise Holy Communion services for the dead and there are five such requests in the Archdeaconry registers. Three are from parish priests and stress the intercession of the Virgin and Saints and are therefore probably an indication of conservatism accommodated under the new forms, all five wills providing sums specifically for communicants, four stipulating that they should be 'poor bodies' presumably to ensure an appropriate lay participation.[44] However, after 1551 such provision apparently ceased until, with the restoration of Catholicism, masses begin to appear again from 1554 onwards, though at a significantly lower level than in Henry VIII's reign, reaching a peak of only 26% in 1558 — rather less than half the level of the mid-1540s.

A similar pattern is apparent in bequests for obits, lights and ornaments, with a noticeable recovery in the second half of Mary's reign, but with levels still very much lower than those prior to the Edwardian reformation. With obits there is a noticeable shift away from masses and the substitution of annual charitable disbursements to the poor, though few were as elaborate as William Alfrey the elder of Hartfield (1556) who set aside 10s a year to the poor of Hartfield and Withyham each Good Friday for seven years, plus to the poor of Hartfield for fifteen years, seven bushels of wheat and six-hundred herrings every Good Friday and each Sunday in Lent, this to be divided into parcels of twenty loaves and five herrings to be given to twenty poor householders on each occasion, plus 1d each on Good Friday.[45]

Even this slight recovery of traditional bequests in Mary's reign masks a decline in the extent of individual provision. In the earlier period it was not unusual for the better off yeoman/husbandman or townsman to set aside substantial sums of money for such purposes, as for example George Mercer of Rye, Jurat (1541), who instructed his executor to set forth an honest priest to sing *dirige* and mass at Jesus Altar in the parish church for six months for his soul, his late wife's, their parents, children and all christian souls, or Thomas Thetcher of Willingdon who set aside, conditionally, five marks for an honest priest 'being an Englishman' to sing for his soul for six months in his parish church.[46] Eight wills made such provision in the 1530s and seven in the years 1541–5. There are no such bequests in Mary's reign.[47]

In regard to bequests for masses, this same pattern is apparent. In Lewes, for example, the majority of Henrician wills contained bequests for trentals at burial, month and year or provided for between five and ten priests on each occasion. Sometimes even the particular masses to be used were stipulated, as in Thomas Kayforth's will (1543) which requested five priests on each occasion to sing *dirige* and mass 'in honour of the five wounds of Our Lord'.[48] Yet in Mary's reign, of ten Lewes wills requesting masses, only one, the will of Gabriel Fowlle, schoolmaster, asked for ten priests, and then with the added proviso 'if they can be got'. Of the remainder, two asked for five masses, four for three masses and the remainder for one or two.[49] Clergy wills, often more specific in their religious provisions, tell a similar story. There is nothing in the Marian period for example to compare with the will of William Grenehyll, parson of Twineham (1542), who asked for ten masses at his burial, specifying that one should be a Mass of the Nativity, one a Mass of the Resurrection, another a Mass of the Ascension, another a Mass of the Holy Ghost, another a Mass of the Five Wounds, and others Masses of the Assumption, the Passion, All Saints, the Mass of the day and one a Mass of Requiem.[50] After the abrupt changes in religious policy of the 1540s and 1550s it was hardly surprising that some testators resigned themselves to unforseen alterations in the services, as the Laughton testator, who early in 1559 wrote 'I will that there be said for me at my burying such service as shall please the Queen's highness to set forthe' in anticipation of the imminent changes.[51]

Others, like Richard Russell of Lewes (1559), took a more resolute line specifying mass and *dirige* at burial 'according to the laudable custom of this realm' surely in implicit approbation of the impending Protestant reforms.[52]

Certainly the restoration of Catholicism under Mary met with approval in some quarters, as with Robert a Wyke (1555) of Westfield (a strongly traditionalist parish) who returned half the proceeds of the vestments and ornaments which he had bought from the parish and resold in the previous reign; or John Rige, husbandman of Ovingdean (1558) who left his parish church 6s 8d. 'that I have paid for an Image of St Ulfran'.[53] The sharp increase in bequests for ornaments in 1557–8 is further testimony of a revived interest in traditional forms by the end of Mary's reign. A further indication of Catholic revival after 1557 was the increase in numbers of wills requesting the bestowal of various amounts at burial (and often month/year), which presumably indicates a desire both for services (i.e. masses) and refreshments. There was also a similar, though less pronounced, increase in requests for disposals of part of the testator's goods for the health of his soul in the same period. The death of Mary however ended any possibility of a major Catholic revival, and 1559 shows a consequent slump in each of the various categories of traditional bequest.

Amongst more positive indications of the shift towards Protestantism in the period is the gradual change from bequests for masses to poor bequests, already noted in the case of obits. The growth of poor bequests from around 30% of the total in the 1530s to 40% at the end of Henry VIII's reign when, for the first time, they began to approach the level of provision for masses is an indication of an underlying trend. Under Edward VI, helped by government encouragement, specific bequests for the poor occurred in 61% of wills proved in the years 1547–53, entirely replacing traditional usages by the end of the reign. Under Mary, with the option of masses restored, poor bequests fell back only slightly, to an average level of 54% of the annual totals, rather more than double the annual provision for masses — a reversal of the position in the 1530s.

The 1547 Injunctions as well as their other provisions required the setting up of poor boxes in every parish church and the proper organisation of disbursements to the needy through the churchwardens. The practical effect of this can be seen in increasing reference to the poor box by testators after 1547 (six times), until, by 1552 it is mentioned in forty-seven wills, representing some 69% of all poor bequests and 45% of the total sample. Under

Mary its use fell back sharply to only fifteen wills in 1554 and six in 1556, representing an average of around only some 15% of annual poor bequests, though its use recovered somewhat in 1557 and 1558.[54] The use of the Poor Box facilitated another shift in the nature of poor bequests which had been taking place since the mid-1540s away from the mere provision of refreshments for the poor and other members of the congregation attending the burial services, to the setting aside of sums of money to be disbursed either in cash or in kind to poor parishioners on either that or another occasion. Symptomatic of the change was the will of John Agate senior, of Cowfold (1548) who left 5s for the relief of poor parishioners after his burial 'besides an honest drinking then to be had'.[55] Agate was clearly trying to differentiate between the traditional social occasion and poor relief, something extremely difficult to disentangle in bequests such as that of Richard Hart (Crowhurst, 1544) who requested *dirige* and three masses 'and bread and drink to refresh poor people and my neighbours to pray for my soul and all christian souls',[56] the type of bequest that formed the overwhelming proportion of charitable provisions in Henrician wills, where provision of bread, cheese, beer (and less commonly meat and/or pies) was the charitable norm.[57]

Alternative forms of poor bequest included set amounts to specified numbers of poor householders within the testator's parish, for example 8d each to five poor householders (Hellingly, 1545), or 6s 8d in 1d dole (Whatlington 1550).[58] Occasionally money was set aside for coals or firewood (Lewes St. Michael's 1553), clothing might be left to the poor (Rye 1552) or blankets, etc. left to the local almshouse (Rye 1552, Lewes, Southover 1554).[59] Another widespread form of poor relief was provision of a small sum for a set number of poor men to bear the deceased's body to church — usually something of the order of 16d between four poor men. This type of bequest occurs on 43 occasions in wills from 25 parishes scattered throughout the county (though with a preponderance in and around Rye) between 1543 and 1559, numbers increasing throughout the period from only three in Henry VIII's reign to twelve under Edward VI and eighteen under Mary, some ten wills containing this provision in 1559.[60] Finally, another type of poor bequest gaining currency during the period, especially in Edward VI's reign was the provision of money for poor maidens' marriages. This type first appears in the will of Edward Martyn of Rye in 1541 who left five marks for the purpose at 3s 4d a time on the death of his brother. It occurs in all twelve times, on seven occasions at Rye and once each at Brede,

Ewhurst, Hastings, Willingdon and Lewes.[61]

Finally, amongst the prime indicators of changing religious attitudes and the gradual coming of Protestantism are the requests for sermons which occur from 1539 onwards. The earliest of these was from Peter Flusher of Lewes. Others followed from Fletching (1541) Heathfield (1542), Waldron (1543), Herstmonceux and Peasmarsh (1544), Litlington (1546), East Grinstead, Etchingham and Northiam (1548), Rye (1550), Winchelsea (1552) and Hastings St. Clement's (1553). At Heathfield, the testator, Thomas Pellying, also left instructions for the provision of a desk for the Bible that his wife was to pay for, whilst at East Grinstead the desire for proselytisation was made clear by the further provision of 30s in meat, drink or money to the poor 'coming to the same preaching, or to such as would be there but cannot'. At Rye, the request for 'one solemn sermon to be made' was coupled with a request for the singing of the *Te Deum* in English during the burial service. Sermons, however, were unlikely to be afforded by many. In six out of thirteen cases the payment to the preacher was 3s 4d per sermon — compared to 6d for most masses. In two cases it was 5s, and three 2s or less. Hence requests for sermons were largely restricted to the more substantial members of society, apart from Flusher comprising Henry Garrard, yeoman and porter of Camber Castle (Winchelsea), Robert Symkyns, Rector of Hastings St. Clement's, who left over £120 in moveable goods and at least five fairly prosperous local farmers with inventory totals ranging from £58 to £87.[62] Good preaching, like sound learning, was evidently not bought cheaply, presumably because well-educated clergy were in short supply — especially in the early period.

Conclusion

There is much that surviving wills can tell us about changing religious attitudes in the formative years of the English Reformation. In sheer bulk alone they provide the one major source for popular attitudes in the period. The problems of classification are enormous and until common criteria of analysis and categorisation have been evolved and applied by researchers in different parts of England, the overall pattern will remain relatively unclear. But despite the difficulties of analysis, mid-sixteenth century wills provide, in many cases, the only surviving evidence from an overwhelming number of parishes and localities where other sources, such as churchwardens' accounts or contemporary correspondence are entirely lacking for the Reformation years.

In Eastern Sussex the broad indications from this analysis of Reformation period wills are clear, and do much to corroborate the evidence from other sources. This area, which produced the highest number of Protestant martyrs after London, Kent and Essex, does indeed show abundant evidence of the spread of the new ideas and of the difficulties encountered by the Marian authorities in countering them. Chief amongst the Protestant strongholds were the coastal towns and parishes to the east, followed by the more inaccessible Wealden parishes. Only the relatively compact downland parishes around Lewes remained solidly conservative. The new ideas seem first to have taken hold of the wealthier sort, in many cases the more substantial townsmen and yeomen farmers for whom the benefits of education were just beginning to be appreciated. Through preaching and especially as a result of the Edwardian services, a loyalty to the Protestant faith developed which even the Marian persecutions could do little to reverse. In the decline in masses and other traditional bequests and in the shift away from traditionalist language in wills' preambles in Mary's reign compared to the last years of her father, the extent of the change becomes clear. Although there is evidence of a conservative revival after 1556 the persistence of a hard core of Protestant beliefs throughout the 1550s indicates the degree of resistance that Marian religious policies encountered. The quite dramatic change in the 1559 figures suggests widespread, underlying support for the broad changes initiated by the English Reformation, and which the accession of Elizabeth now made secure. It would be interesting to see which other counties followed a similar pattern.

Appendix 1

Wills Preambles and Religious Bequests — Classification:
Traditional

Soul to Almighty God, Blessed Virgin Mary and all Holy Company of Heaven.
S to AG beseeching B L St Mary and HCH to pray for me.
S to AG Maker Redeemer/Redeemer and Saviour, BL St M and all HCH.
S to AG M R & S desiring all H & BCH to pray for me.
S to AG Father Son and Holy Ghost, Our BL and all BCH.
S to GA, to his only begotten son our S JC, to his B & HVM his mother and to all HCH.
S to only mercy of AG beseeching our L & HCH to pray for me that my

soul may the rather at their contemplation have the fruition of God's deity (+ masses).

S to AG the F, our L St M & all HCH.

S to hands of G trusting through the inercession of our BL the mother of Christ & the HCH to be associate with them.

S to AG plus either Masses or deriges or Obits or to be prayed for or disposal/bestowal for health/wealth of soul, or to be done for.

S to AG & HCH plus either Masses or bestowal for me or disposal etc as above for S to AG.

S to AG the FA and disposal for wealth of soul.

S to AG M & R and HCH plus Masses.

My S very God's Image unto the celestial father of heaven my Creator, unto JC my Redeemer and all celestial hierarchy and C of H plus Masses.

Reformist

S to AG M & R (S & R).

S to AG MR & Comforter.

S to AG S & R and all HCH.

S to AG S & R in whom I put my trust and confidence.

S to AG M & R by whom I trust to have salvation.

S to AG Creator Redeemer & only Justifier and Saviour.

S to AG F S & HG.

S to hands of blessed trinity.

S to AG in whom I believe my Creation and Redemption in the F S & HG.

S to AG the eternal F & to JC my only R & to the HG the Comforter of all good christian creatures.

S to AG my M and JC his only son my R & S.

S to blessed Trinity trusting to have forgiveness of my sins for my S C's sake.

S to G the FA and to his dear son JC my R.

S to AG our Lord & R JC and all HCH.

S to AG desiring him in this world for his S JC's sake pardon and forgiveness of my sins and in the world to come both for soul and body everlasting rest.

S to AG my CR & S JC and all HCH.

S to AG desiring my S of his infinite mercy to have mercy upon me.

S to Almighty JC.

S to hands S & R JC.

S to AG the searcher and trier of man's conscience.

S to AG thanks to the Living Lord.

S to AG as the most precious jewel that I have.

S to AG my M.

S and body to God.

S to AG our heavenly F.

My soul, spirit and life into the hands and mercy of our Lord God.

S to GA in whom is my only help of salvation.

S to AG plus disposal as exec thinks most best (and poor bequests).

S to AG and all HCH plus disposal by exec as she will better be seen of AG.

S to AG into fellowship of BCH plus disposal to God's honour and soul's health.

S to AG plus disposal to honour of God and wealth/health of soul.

S to AG my maker redeemed by the precious blood of the Immaculate Lamb.

S to JC my only very Mediator & Saviour.

S to great mercy of G to have the fruition of his glory with all the heavenly C.

A to AG and ministrations for me . . . as shall be agreeable to scripture.

S to AG and burial with faithful.

S to AG and godly fellowship of all saints.

Protestant

S to AG trusting to be saved by the merits of Christ's (death &) passion.

S to AG by the Merits of C's (d &) p.

S to AG through the merits of our Lord & S JC.

S to AG and his mercy trusting without any doubt or mistrust I have & shall have remission of my sins and resurrection of soul & body.

S to AG faithfully believing that it shall have eternal rest (by the merits of C's p) with Abraham, Isaac and Jacob in the K of H.

S to hands of Our heavenly F desiring him for the sake of our S JC that I may rise again among the elect and chosen that do die in the christian faith at the day of judgement.

S to hands of AG and his mercy trusting by his grace and his mercy to have forgiveness of my sins plus bestowal as exec shall answer at day of judgement.

S to mercy of AG the F and his S JC in whom & through whom I believe to have forgiveness of my sins, to rise at the Latter Day and to have life everlasting.

S to merciful hands of my heavenly F to have the fruition of his everlasting K.

S to JC my only R & S in whom is my full trust for the remission of all my sins.

S to G by the mediation of our Lord and S JC.

S to AG my M, to JC my only R & S by whom my assured hope is to be s.

S to AG M & R and only S by whom my assured trust is to be s.

S to AG M & R and only S J by whom I believe assuredly to be s.

S to AG plus bequest towards buying Bible for church.

S to hands of my only S JC who with his most precious blood hath redeemed the same plus Sermon and English Te Deum.

S to AG only R & S plus books of Peter Martyr and Cyprian.

Neutral

S to AG.

S to AG & HCH.

No preamble or other religious bequests.

Mixed Traditional/Reformist

S to AG MR (& S) plus masses, or disposal/bestowal for health/wealth of soul.

Trinitarian formulae plus masses or to be done for.

S to AG my C plus masses or disposal/bestowal for soul.

S to AG only R & S plus masses.

S to AG only R & S, our BL St M and all HCH.

S to AG M and R JC, our L St M and all HCH.

S to F of Heaven and to his dear S JC my R and all HCH to pray for me.

S to JC only S & R and all BCH plus disposal/bestowal for soul, or masses.

S to the Very Image of God, into the hands of deity my Creator plus Masses.

S to JC my R, BVM and all celestial C of H plus masses.

S to AG M & R plus bequest for lights.

Mixed Protestant/Traditional

S to AG trusting to be s by the m's of C's (d) & p plus masses.

As above plus exec to do for me in deeds of charity, refreshing the poor at her discretion.

S to AG & all HCH and to the merits of our S JC.

S to the intercession of the blessed merits of Christ's passion, the BVM mother of God and all HCH.

S to mercy of G beseeching our BL and whole C of H to pray that my said soul may be partaker of Christ's passion.

S to Ag, our L st M and all elect in heaven.

S to bosom of Abraham and corruptible body to be buried . . . plus masses.

S to AG BV M and all HCH plus sermon and bequest for Bible for church.

S to AG my R plus Masses and Sermons.

S to AG plus masses and sermons.

Appendix 2

East Sussex Parishes Classified by Main Type of Will

(a) *1547–53:*   i) *Traditional*

Downland -Arlington, Beeding, Berwick, Chailey, West Dean, West Firle, Henfield, Little Horsted, Litlington, Lullington, Portslade, Poynings, Preston, Shermanbury, Telscombe,

Wilmington, Wivelsfield, Eastbourne, Seaford, Southwick, Jevington

Weald -   Ashburnham, Frant, Heathfield, Horsted Keynes, Ifield, Withyham, Worth

Marsh/
Coast -   Battle, Brede, Ore, Sedlescombe, Udimore, Westham

ii) Evenly Divided Traditional/Protestant, Reformist

Downland -Aldrington, Alfriston, Barcombe, Shoreham, Piddinghoe, Selmeston, Streat, Westmeston, Hove, Hurstpierpoint, Henfield

Weald -   Ardingly, Etchingham, Fletching, Hartfield, Waldron, Cowfold

Marsh/   Beckley, East Guldeford, Hellingly, Herstmonceux, Ninfield,
Coast -   Westfield

iii) Reformist and Protestant

Downland -Albourne, Beddingham, Chalvington, Clayton, Ditchling, Falmer, Hamsy, Iford, Keymer, Laughton, Meeching, Newtimber, Patcham, Plumpton, Ripe, Rodmell, Southease, Tarring Nevill, Willingdon, Woodmancote, Brighton, Lewes

Weald -   Bolney, Brightling, Burwash, Cuckfield, Dallington, West Hoathly, East Grinstead, Maresfield, Rotherfield, Salehurst, Ticehurst, Warbleton

Marsh/   Bexhill, Catsfield, Fairlight, Hailsham, Hastings, Hollington,
Coast -   Hooe, Iden, Northiam, Peasmarsh, Pett, Pevensey, Rye, Wartling, Whatlington, Winchelsea

(b) *1554–59*   *i) Traditional*

Downland -Alciston, Aldrington, Alfriston, Arlington, Barcombe, Beddingham, Bishopstone, East Blatchington, Chailey, Chalvington, Clayton, East Dean, West Dean, Denton, Falmer, West Firle, Hamsey, Heighton, Henfield, Little Horsted, Hurstpierpoint, Iford, Keymer, Kingston, Friston, Litlington, Newtimber, Patcham, Piddinghoe, Portslade, Preston, Ripe, Rodmell, Rottingdean, Selmeston, Shermanbury, Southease, Southwick, Streat, Tarring Nevill, Telscombe, Twineham, Westmeston, Wilmington, Wivels-field, Eastbourne, Lewes, Seaford

Weald -   Ashburnham, Brightling, Chiddingly, Cowfold, Dallington, Etchingham, Fletching, Frant, West Hoathly, Horsted Keynes, Ifield, Slaugham, Worth

Marsh/   Brede, Crowhurst, Herstmonceux, Hooe, Iden, Ninfield,
Coast -   Sedlescombe, Udimore, Westfield, Whatlington

ii) Divided Traditional/Protestant, Reformist

Downland -Ditchling, Kingston Buci, Laughton, Shoreham, Pyecombe
Weald - Ardingly, Balcombe, Bolney, Cuckfield, Heathfield, East
Grinstead, Salehurst, Ticehurst, Warbleton, Withyham,
Lindfield
Marsh/ Battle, Beckley, Bodiam, Hellingly, Hollington, Northiam,
Coast - Wartling, Winchelsea

iii) Reformist and Protestant

Downland -Albourne, Beeding, Berwick, Brighton, Folkington,
Jevington, Meeching, Ovingdean, Plumpton, Ringmer,
Willingdon, Woodmancote
Weald - Burwash, Buxted, Hartfield, East Hoathly, Maresfield,
Mayfield, Penshurst, Rotherfield, Wadhurst, Waldron
Marsh/ Bexhill, Catsfield, Ewhurst, Guestling, Hailsham, Hastings,
Coast - Icklesham, Mountfield, Peasmarsh, Pevensey, Playden, Rye

1 The geographical division of downland, weald and marsh/coast closely follows
that of C.E. Brent: *Employment, Land Tenure and Population in Eastern Sussex
1540–1640* (University of Sussex D.Phil thesis 1973), esp. pp. 356–64.
2 Types i) Traditional, and iii) Reformist and Protestant have been reserved for
those parishes where at least 50% of wills are of that type or where a substantial
majority (i.e. 2:1 or more) are of type i) rather than type iii). Parishes more evenly
divided between traditional and reformist/protestant wills have been placed in type
ii).
3 Not every parish had wills written in each period.

Notes

[1] A.G. Dickens, *Lollards and Protestants in the Diocese of York 1509–1558*,
(London, 1959), p. 172.
[2] D.M. Palliser, *The Reformation in York 1534–1553*, (York, 1971), pp. 28, 32.
[3] P. Clark, *English Provincial Society from the Reformation to the Revolution:
Religion, Politics and Society in Kent, 1500—1640*, (Hassocks, 1977).
[4] *Ibid.*, pp. 58–9, 76.
[5] C. Cross, 'Parochial Structure and the Dissemination of Protestantism in
Sixteenth Century England: A tale of two cities', in *The Church in Town and
Countryside: Studies in Church History, XVI*, ed. D. Baker (1979), pp. 269–78. I
would like to thank Dr. Cross for her helpful comments on an earlier draft of the
present article. M.L. Zell, 'The Use of Religious Preambles as a Measure of
Religious Belief in the Sixteenth Century', in the *Bulletin of the Institute of
Historical Research*, 50 (1977), pp. 246–9.
[6] Dickens, *Lollards and Protestants*, p. 172.
[7] W(est) S(ussex) R(ecord) O(ffice) STA 1/2.
[8] E(ast) S(ussex) R(ecord) O(ffice) W/A 1–7, W/BAT 1, W/C 4.
[9] See Appendix I.
[10] For a fuller discussion of the influence of printed formularies on the wording
of wills' preambles, see M.C. Cross's forthcoming article in *Northern History*: 'The

development of protestantism in Leeds and Hull 1520–1640: the evidence from wills', and her forthcoming article in D. Loades (ed.), *The end of strife: death, reconciliation and expressions of Christian spirituality*, C.I.H.E.C. Durham Colloquium Papers 1981, 'Wills as evidence of popular piety in the Reformation period: Leeds and Hull 1520–1640'.

[11]   W/A 3, ff. 59v (John Hyve), 61r (John Thatcher), 61v (Thomas Als), 64v (Rayffe Gur), 81r (Richard Collyn), 81v (Richard Lover), 82r (John Baker), 82v (Elisabeth Buckhold, widow), 96r (Phyllyppe Brekeden), 96v (Richard Baker), 114r (Agnes Barber, widow).

[12]   Hailsham: W/A 3, ff. 2v (Thomas Reder), 131v (Richard Twysden), 170, 173 (Norman Dalton); Tarring Neville: W/A 3, f. 63r (Jone Waterman, widow); Warbleton: W/A 3, f. 56 (Robert Smyth).

[13]   W/A 3, ff. 5v (William Harward), 10v (Nicholas Dyryke), 11v (Symon Russell, Thomas Havenell als Onell), 26v (Henry Swane), 36r (John Walter), 54v (Thomas Croche), 92r (Alexander Maynarde), 227r (Olyver Vane); W/A5, f.474 (William Aderfold).

[14]   W/BAT 1, ff. 84 (Shether), 81 (Porter), 1557; 81 (Robert Banyster), 84 (Alce Egylden, widow), 1558.

[15]   W/A 5, f. 144. He was Senior Constable 1551–2, *The Town Book of Lewes 1542–1701*, ed. L.F. Salzman (Sussex Record Society, 1945), p. 6.

[16]   W/A 1 f. 198r.

[17]   A.G. Dickens, *Lollards and Protestants*, pp. 216–17; this will has recently been transcribed as part of a collection of documents, *The Reformation in the North to 1558*, ed. W.J. Sheils (York, 1976), produced by the Borthwick Institute of Historical Research.

[18]   John Foxe, *The Acts and Monuments of the Church*, ed. J. Cumming, II (1875), p. 351.

[19]   W/A 3, f. 126r.

[20]   Lowes had been associated with several prominent Kent conservatives, clergy and gentry, since at least the early 1540s, Cf. e.g. L(etters and) P(apers), Henry VIII, XVIII (2), no. 546 (iv); Clark, *English Provincial Society*, pp. 60–74.

[21]   Clark, *English Provincial Society*, p. 58; W/A 1, ff. 75r (Roger Okeman, hookmaker, Rye, 1542), 132r (Tristram Cosker, Winchelsea, 1546); W/A 3, f. 99r (John Breet, Balcombe, 1543).

[22]   Clark, *English Provincial Society*, p. 76.

[23]   Chalenor was also generous in his poor bequests, leaving 4d. to every poor householder in Chiltington and 'to iiii poor persons of the said chapelry . . . one mass of meat with bread and drink for dinner every Sunday after service, by the space of one whole year next after my decease'. Evidently as lord of the manor he felt it incumbent upon himself to make adequate provision for his poorer tenants. W/A 3, f. 184v.

[24]   Foxe, *Acts and Monuments*, III, pp. 333, 337, 872, 874–5, 888–96. Sir Edward Gage served as High Sherrif of Sussex and Surrey 1555–6. Sir John Gage served as Lord Chamberlain of the Household from Mary's accession until his death in April 1556.

[25]   Three of six. Two further were neutral. Of the traditional wills, in one Edward Gage Esq. appeared as a witness, in another as overseer: W/A 3, f. 25v (Robert Ballerd, 1550), 87r (William Grynt, 1552). Grynt's will also included a number of personal bequests to members of the Gage family.

[26]   Three Laughton wills were proved 1547–53. Protestant: W/A 3, f. 241r (John Saverye); Reformist: W/A 3, ff. 30r (Thomas Pupp, 1549), 91v (Thomas Walshe, vicar, 1553 — a second copy is registered W/A 4, f. 327v). For the religious outlook

of the Pelham family, see A. Pelham and D. McLean, *Some Early Pelhams*, (Hove, 1931), pp. 141, 193–4. Sir William (d.1538), in his will, proved P.C.C., left £6 13s. 4d. for twenty sermons to be preached at Laughton and surrounding parishes. John Pelham and William Morley (of Glynde) arrived together at Geneva, from Padua University and were received into Knox's congregation there on 26 November 1557. C.H. Garrett, *The Marian Exiles: A Study in the Origins of Elizabethan Puritanism* (1938), pp. 231, 247–8.

[27] A.G. Dickens, *The English Reformation*, (Fontana, 1967), pp. 279–80; E. Austen, *Brede, the Story of a Sussex Parish* (Rye, 1946), pp. 34–5.

[28] Peasmarsh:W/A 2, f. 23v (Ralph Dison, vicar, 1548), W/A 3, ff. 137v (Robert Squyre, 1554), 216v (Agnes Squyre, widow, 1556), 220r (Robert Rowbottom, 1556); Icklesham:W/A 3, f. 259r (Robert Nasche, 1557), W/A 4, ff. 8v (Dennys a Mylls, 1557), 174v (John Wolbrege, husbandman, 1558); Beckley: W/A 1, f. 142v (Agnes Sampson, widow, 1547), W/A 4, ff. 245v (Denys Ive, husbandman, 1558), 419v (Thomas Harroll, 1558); Ewhurst: W/A 4, ff. 42v (John Acars, 1557), 68r (William Chesman, husbandman, 1558). For Iden, see above, n. 12.

[29] For a list of parishes under each heading and details of method of classification used, see Appendix 2.

[30] Foxe, *Acts and Monuments*, I, p. 923; II, pp. 724–7; *The Victoria History of the County of Sussex*, ed. W. Page, Vol. 2 (1907), p. 15.

[31] Foxe, *Acts and Monuments*, III, pp. 333, 346, 735, 907; L.F. Salzman, 'Sussex Excommunicates', *Sussex Archaeological Collections*, 82 (1942), p. 140; W.H. Hills, 'A Sentence of Excommunication', *Sussex Notes and Queries*, I (1926), pp. 51–3.

[32] The indictment against Anne Tree, burnt at East Grinstead 18 July 1556, specifically refers to the influence of Thomas at Hothe's teaching: Hills, *S.N.Q.* I, p. 51. Thomas at Hothe, 'mynyster' of East Grinstead c. 1549–54 can presumably be identified with Thomas Hoth, precentor of Hastings New Priory convicted of heresy in 1533 for his advanced Protestant opinions, apparently learnt at Cambridge: C.E. Welch, 'Three Sussex Heresy Trials', *S.A.C.* 95 (1957), pp. 60–63. At Hothe witnessed four East Grinstead wills: W/A 2, f. 13r (Thomas Grantam, Forest Row, 1549), W/A 3, ff. 9r (William a Woode, 1550), 8r (Katherine Dyllyng, widow, 1551), 110v (Robert Nycholl, 1552), but not, apparently, that of Edward Goodwyn, snr, 1543 (W/A 2, f. 7r), with its request for preaching 'the word of God' and 'redying and other service . . . . as shall be then allowed and set forth by the king, our sovereign lord'.

[33] W/A 1, ff. 119r (Hosmer), 149v (Farmer). Both wills were composed June 1546. See also C. Pullein, *Rotherfield: The Story of Some Wealden Manors*, (Tunbridge Wells, 1928), pp. 264–75 and Hills, *S.N.Q. I*, p. 51.

[34] L.P. XIII (2), no. 278; W/C 4, f. 106.

[35]*Collected Original Letters from the Bishops to the Privy Council 1564*, ed. M. Bateson (Camden Miscellany IV, 1895), pp. 8–11.

[36] Such was certainly the case in Rye. See my article, 'Religion, Faction and Politics in Reformation Rye: 1530–59', in *S.A.C.* 120 (1982).

[37] W/A 3, ff. 53r (Regles), 70v (Thomas Nokes, beer-brewer).

[38] W/A 3, ff. 72r, 276r (Francys), 71r (William Benett, 1551).

[39] 1556: W/A 3, ff. 238r (John Smyth), 240r (Robert Herseu, fisherman), W/A 4, f. 49v (Thomas Stoneham, fisherman); 1557: W/A 3, ff. 235v (Christopher Hune, fisherman), 238v (William Baker), W/A 4, ff. 75r (John Allen, fisherman), 164v (John Fartom), 309r (Robert Scott); 1558: W/A 4, ff. 139v (James Lambert, fisherman), 145v (John Cowper, the younger, yeoman).

[40] e.g. the will of Pharowe Townsend, fisherman, Hastings (1556), W/A 3, 219v, 276r; and of Symonde Tranckmore, Brighton (1558), W/A 4, f. 322r.

[41]   1556: W/A 3, f. 230r (Thomas Pylcher, husbandman); 1557: W/A 4, f. 28v. (Denys Hart, widow), W/A 5, f. 126 (William Eryge); 1558: W/A 4, f. 52v (William Hart), W/A 5, f.105 (Thomas Drynker).

[42]   W/A 3, ff. 161v (John Comber, jurat), 212v (Thomas a Vale, jurat, 1557), 172v (William Comber, 1555).

[43]   Eleven wills (excluding Comber's) contained such provisions, three from the 1540's, eight from the 1550's. All appear to have been made by yeomen or husbandmen: 1554, Bartholomew Collen, Burwash, W/A 3, f. 108r and Thomas Pykenall, Streat, W/A 1, f. 38v; 1545, Edward Wheatley, Pevensey, W/A 1, f. 195v; 1553, John Benjamyn, Chalvington, W/A 3, f. 205r; 1556, Edward Feld, Battle, W/BAT 1, f. 73, John Trayton, Ditchling, W/A 3, f. 207r, John a Brooke, West Dean, W/A 3, f. 198r; 1557, John Scras alias Shether, W/A 4, f. 11v; 1558, Richard Wyllard, Etchingham, W/A 4, f. 146v; 1559, Awdryan Holland, Eastbourne, W/A 4, f. 375r, Richard Markewyck, Wadhurst, W.S.R.O. STA 1/2, f. 56r. There was no obvious correlation between such bequests and any particular type of religious outlook.

[44]   1549: W/A 1, f. 189v (William Marley, vicar, Lullington); 1550: W/A 2, ff. 30r (Henry Marshall, vicar, Wilmington), 19r (Stephen Goodsall the elder, Burwash), 18v (John Denet senior, Burwash); 1551 W/A 3, f. 66r (Edmund Pelham, clerk, Hellingly).

[45]   W/A 3, f. 243v.

[46]   W/A 1, f. 27r (Mercer), W/A 3, f. 243v (Allfrey).

[47]   W/C 4, ff. 1 (John Fenell, Eastbourne 1530), 2 (William Berde, Beeding, 1530), 6 (John Fychas, Brighton, early 1530s), 8 (William Hesman, Barcombe, early 1530s), 9 (Roger Gate, yeoman, Cowfold, early 1530s), 21 (John Chauntler, Barcombe, 1535), 30 (Thomas Kyng, Cuckfield, 1536), 31 (John Shepard, Denton, 1526); W/C 4, f. 75 and W/A 1, f. 160r (John Roger, labourer, Brightling, 1542), W/A 1, ff. 9r (Thomas Standen, yeoman, Ticehurst, 1542), 51v (William Hunt, senior, yeoman, Ticehurst 1544), 55v (Thomas Thetcher, Willingdon, 1544), 66v (Margery Oxenbridge, widow, gentlewoman, Ewhurst, 1545), 77v (George Mercer, Rye, jurat, 1541), 199r (James Fletcher, Iden, 1545).

[48]   W/A 1, f. 12v (Thomas Kayforth, Lewes All Saints); and cf. W/A 1, f. 201v (Robert Branfeld, Lewes All Saints, 1543). Examples elsewhere include: W/A 4, f. 376v (Thomas Balcombe, Balcombe, 1539).

[49]   Fowle also left 1d. each to his pupils to pray for him, plus 1s. each to five (named) pupils 'for their diligence about me'. He left his 'newe graylle imprinted' to Ringmer church and his 'wrytten masse booke' to Southover church: W/A 3, f. 170r. Agnes a Stable, widow (1556) and Alice Duplake (1554) W/A 3, ff. 265v and 128, requested five masses at burial and month; Johane Phylypp, Thomas Parys, Richard Pawley (1557) and Edward Wyckam (1558), W/A 3, ff. 229r, 265v W/A 4, ff. 7r, 90, requested three; John Gurnett and Alice Copland, widow, W/A 4, 136r, 138, requested two; and William Gyfforde (1556), W/A 3, f. 240v. one. A further twenty-seven wills of Lewes testators 1554–8 made no reference to masses.

[50]   W/A 1, f. 12v.

[51]   W/A 5, f. 355 (John Rickefeld, als Saverye).

[52]   W/A 4, f. 293r.

[53]   W/A 3, f. 164r (a Wyke), W/A 4, f. 110r (Rige).

[54]   The annual totals were 1547 6; 1548 25; 1549 22; 1550 34; 1551 25; 1552 47; 1553 52; 1554 15; 1555 10; 1556 6; 1557 31; 1558 27; 1559 36.

[55]   W/A 1, f. 181v.

[56]   W/A 1, f. 59v.

[57]   e.g. the will of Richard Jorden, yeoman, of Warbleton (1542) which provided

for masses and a 'drynkyng' for 'the povertie of the parish' at burial and year, and on the month day specified in addition the killing of a wether, to be baked into pies, together with bread and drink for the poor. W/A 1, f. 26v.

[58] W/A 1, f. 97v (Thomas Pelham, Hellingly, 1545) and W/A 3, f. 11v (Aleyne Edgyngworthe als Gybon, Whatlington, 1550).

[59] W/A 3, f. 96 (Johane Walker, widow, Lewes St. Michael's 1553), W/A 3, f. 26r (James Mercer, Rye, 1552), W/A 3, f. 41r (Alice Dier, widow, Rye, 1552), W/A 3, f. 122r (John Aylen, Southover, 1554).

[60] The annual totals were 1543 1; 1545 2; 1547 1; 1548 2; 1549 1; 1550 5; 1551 1; 1552 1; 1553 1; 1554 1; 1555 2; 1556 1; 1557 7; 1558 7; 1559 10. Parishes where such bequests occurred were: Ticehurst (4); Beckley, Icklesham, Rye (3); Brede, Burwash Crowhurst, Ewhurst, Fletching, Lewes (2); Bexhill, Chiddingly, Clayton, Heathfield, Hooe, Jevington, Hastings, Lullington, Ore, East Grinstead, Twineham, Newick, Udimore, Westfield, Winchelsea (1).

[61] Rye: W/C 4, f. 70 and W/A 1a, f. 13 (Martyn, 1541), W/A 2, f. 9v (Alexander Wulphyn, jurat, 1549), W/A 2, f. 16r (Henry Sowggs, 1550), W/A 3, f. 8v (Robert Gaymer, 1550), W/A 3, f. 27r (John Joysse, als Fillylad, fisherman, 1551), W/A 3, f. 41r (Alice Dier, widow, 1552), W/A 4, f. 35v (William Alye); Ewhurst: W/A 1, 163v Thomas Thomset, yeoman, 1546); Willingdon: W/A 1, f. 103v (Richard Wright, 1546); Brede: W/A 1, f. 151r (John Mychell, 1548); Hastings: W/A 3, f. 71r (William Benett, 1551); Lewes St Michael's: W/A 3, f. 96 (Johanne Walker, widow, 1553).

[62] W/C 4, f.106 (Flusher), W/A 1, ff. 16r (Joachyn Godfray, Fletching), 200v (Thomas Pellying, Heathfield), 171v (John Bodyll, senior, Waldron), 42r (John Henarye, Herstmonceux), 136r (William Gate, Peasmarsh), 95v (William Chamber, Litlington), 181r (Thomas White, Northiam), 177r (Morgane Brode, Etchingham), W/A 2, f. 7r (Edward Goodwyn, senior, East Grinstead), W/A 3, ff. 100r (Johane Blacke, widow, Rye), 93v (Henry Garrard, Winchelsea), 72r (Robert Symkyns als Hayton, rector, Hastings St Clement's).

'For the Health of my Soul': Prayers for the Dead in the Tudor South-West

R. WHITING

How was the 'average man' affected by the Reformation? After more than four centuries, the answers given to this apparently simple question are in fact diverse and often conflicting. Some historians have emphasized the element of change. Professor Dickens, for example, has claimed to discern a fundamental re-orientation of religious attitudes, even in supposedly conservative areas like Yorkshire and Nottinghamshire.[1] Other writers, however, particularly in recent years, have maintained that the implementation of reform was frequently restricted and delayed. In Lancashire, for example, Dr Haigh has argued that religious change was seriously obstructed by a combination of official weakness and local resistance.[2] The precise popular impact of the Reformation remains, in short, highly problematic.

In a previous examination of the Henrician campaign against images, the present author adduced evidence to suggest that the local enforcement of religious change may have been markedly more effective than recent historians have usually allowed.[3] The following study represents an extension of the investigation into a second and even more crucial area of reform: the assault upon prayers for the dead. Was the traditional popular devotion to such practices effectively eradicated during the Reformation decades? Or was it able, in reality, to survive substantially intact? Seeking answers to these questions, the present examination focuses upon the English South-West, a region which possesses a valuable range of sources — including wills, and an unusually rich collection of churchwardens' accounts — for the study of religious development at the popular level. Chronologically, however, this investigation is wider than its predecessor, extending from the decades immediately preceding the Reformation, through the upheavals under Henry VIII, Edward VI and Mary, and on to the establishment of official Protestantism under Elizabeth I.

I

'*Orate pro animabus Katharine Burlas, Nicholai Burlas, et Johannis Vyvyan, qui istam fenestram fecerunt fieri*'. Thus pleads an early-Tudor window — which also portrays the donors themselves — in the parish church of St Neot. A similar inscription, in English, is still to be seen on the exterior of the church at Cullompton. It reminds us that John Lane and his wife founded one of the chapels in 1526, and asks us to say a *Pater Noster* and *Ave* for them, their children, and their friends; it also expresses the hope that God will have mercy on their souls and finally bring them to glory. Even more explicit were the texts formerly to be seen in the chapel founded by another prosperous merchant, John Greenway, at Tiverton in 1517. 'O that the Lord may / Grant unto John Greenway / Good fortune and grace / And in Heaven a place'. 'Of your charity, pray for the souls of John and Joan Greenway, his wife . . . and for their fathers and mothers, and for their friends and their lovers. On them Jesu have mercy. Amen. Of your charity, say *Pater Noster* and *Ave*'.[5]

The prayers thus requested supposedly speeded souls through the purifying torments of Purgatory and into the eternal blessedness of Heaven. Pre-Reformation worshippers at Exeter Cathedral were indeed bidden to pray 'for all the souls [that] bideth the mercy of God in the bitter pains of Purgatory: that God, of his mercy, the sooner deliver them through your devoted prayers'.[6] It was therefore inevitable that intercessions should lie close to the very heart of the popular religion. They began within hours of the death itself. Until the 1530s, parsons of Down St Mary would visit the corpse of each newly-deceased parishioner in his own house, 'where they were wont to say *dirige* and other prayers, with the neighbours of the dead man, for the souls of all such corpses'.[7] Further prayers attended the burial: '*hic roget sacerdos orare pro anima defuncti*', instructs a late-medieval service-book discovered at Coldridge.[8] But these were merely the initial stages of a highly-organized intercessory process which might continue for months, years or even generations after the body had been laid to rest. Wills, churchwardens' accounts and chantry certificates leave no doubt that on the very eve of the Reformation, an overwhelming multiplicity of 'masses', '*diriges*', 'trentals', 'obits', 'mind-days', 'anniversaries' and similar rites were still being celebrated throughout the region on behalf of the dead. 'There is no day', the heretic Thomas Benet reportedly complained to the clergy at Exeter in 1531, 'but ye say divers masses for souls in feigned Purgatory'.[9]

Nor were these merely the endowment of earlier generations. Wealthier members of the laity continued to invest substantial sums in such intercessions for themselves, their families and their friends. In 30 wills made by Cornish or Devonian laypeople, from below the level of the gentry, between 1520 and 1529, prayers or masses were endowed in no less than 21 (70%).[10] Some prayers were to be said by fellow-laymen. John Trotte, founding an almshouse at Cullompton in 1523, required its inmates to pray for his and certain other souls, while Joan Tackle, at Honiton in 1528, left 4d to each householder in the town to pray for her. John Greenway, arranging his burial in his superb new chapel at Tiverton in 1529, sought to ensure grateful prayers for his soul by ordering a dole of £20 and a dinner for the poor; and more money and food were to be distributed at his 'month's mind'.[11] Most intercessions, however, were entrusted to the acknowledged specialists. Friars were specified in 5 of the 21 wills. Nicholas Ennis of Luxulyan left 10s each to the friaries at Bodmin and Truro in 1522, in return for trentals for his soul, while at Exeter in 1523 John Bridgeman gave 53s 4d to the Franciscans for a perpetual obit. William Sellick of Tiverton bequeathed 10s in 1524 to 'all the houses of friars within Devonshire', for trentals on behalf of his soul, and in 1529 Gilbert Rugge of Widecombe left 2s to the Exeter Franciscans. In the same year John Greenway of Tiverton left 40s to the Dominicans of Exeter, 'to the intent that the friars there being shall devoutly say and sing four trentals for my soul and all Christian souls, immediately after my decease'; and he ordered similar trentals from the Franciscans at Exeter, and from the Franciscans and Dominicans at Plymouth.[12]

Even more frequently hired for such intercessory purposes were the secular priests. It was such a priest that John Hugh of Branscombe, for example, required to 'pray for my soul' in 1521. Another priest was hired by Nicholas Ennis of Luxulyan in 1522 'to pray for the soul of an old woman which lost her purse with 2s 8d therein; that I found when I was young, and did never recompense her'. In 1526 Thomas Hamlyn of Totnes arranged annual intercessions in his parish church: the vicar, Lady priest and parish clerk were to say 'placebo and dirige with lauds', perform a requiem mass, and pray for his and certain other souls. In 1529 John Greenway endowed a priest to pray and sing for his soul for seven years in his new chapel at Tiverton, while another merchant, John Lane, endowed a priest for the new chapel of Our Lady at Cullompton. Lane also donated a total of £33 6s 8d to no less than 100 neighbouring churches — on condition that they enter him on their bede-rolls, 'to pray for me in their pulpits'.[13]

Even laymen incapable of financing individual intercession found prayers and masses available on a communal basis. A relatively modest offering procured the addition of a name to the parochial bede-roll. Such receipts appear frequently in the accounts of pre-Reformation churchwardens, together with payments to priests for reciting rolls from the pulpit. Even more attractive was the membership of a religious gild. This privilege was sometimes restricted to a specific trade: thus the fraternity of the Holy Trinity at Helston in 1517 was for local cobblers. Most groups, however, seem to have drawn support and finance from a variety of occupations within the parish. The gild of St Katherine at Chagford — which may have operated from a house still standing near the church — received income from parishioners' gifts, as well as from the local sale of its sheep and wool. The gild of the High Cross at Stratton (whose accounts commence in 1512) was financed by fees, gifts and a yearly Ale, while the gilds at North Petherwin drew revenue from the sale of bread and ale.[14] Although such groups differed in composition and in organization, their primary function seems everywhere to have been similar. This was the hastening of departed members through the 'bitter pains of Purgatory'.

Many, like the High Cross at Stratton, began by arranging their members' burial, often with knell, cross and tapers. Most also maintained their own bede-roll. At Stratton, most years between 1512 and 1530 saw local people buying places on the High Cross roll, which the vicar would recite regularly. Thus in 1527 Alison Pudner paid 6s 8d 'for her husband's grave, and to set him apon the bede-roll', while Robert Hecket gave a piece of pottery worth 10s 'for to set three names apon the bede-roll'. Such rolls actually survive among the early-sixteenth century accounts for North Petherwin. Folio 38*v*, for instance, begins with an exhortation to pray for the deceased brothers and sisters of St Michael's gild, and then lists their names. Usually, moreover, the fraternity hired a priest to celebrate at a particular altar in the parish church. Masses for departed brothers and sisters of the Holy Trinity were performed in Helston church, each surviving member reciting a Lady Psalter on their behalf. St Katherine at Chagford hired priests and organized obits, including an anniversary for its departed on the morrow of St Katherine; and Stratton's High Cross maintained its own chantry-priest, as well as paying the vicar to perform perpetual obits. Even in smaller communities, like North Petherwin, gilds arranged *dirige* and mass for their dead. On occasion the rites organized by such groups were impressively elaborate. At Lostwithiel in the reign of Henry VIII, St George's gild held an annual parade along the main street. One member, riding on horse-back and attended by mounted followers, was dressed as St George himself, with armour, crown, sceptre and sword. At the church he was received by the priest, and escorted inside to hear a *dirige* in the gild's chapel; then the whole company retired to a local house, for their customary feast.[15]

The continuing popularity of such groups is attested by their very number on the eve of the Reformation. Several of the j20 or so 'stores' at Ashburton, for example, were certainly associated with altars, and chapels were dedicated to Our Lady, St John, Sts Katherine and Margaret, St Thomas and St Nicholas. Chagford boasted not only St Katherine but also the Blessed Virgin, St Antony, St George, St Nicholas, St Lawrence, St Eligius, the Name of Jesus, and Young Men. There were about 9 groups at Stratton, and about 10 at Camborne: several of the latter were dedicated to local saints like Ia, Winwaloe and Meriasek, and at least four arranged *diriges*. Numerous such groups operated even in relatively small communities like Morebath, South Tawton, Winkleigh, Anthony and North Petherwin. At both Antony and North Petherwin they totalled about 11, those in the latter parish being named after St Nicholas, St Patern, St George, St Michael, St Luke, St Thomas, St John, St Christopher, Allhallows, Our Lady and the Trinity.[16] The persistence of popular support for such gilds is confirmed, moreover, by the 30 surviving wills from 1520–9. Bequests to them appear in 17 (57%). Some testators left money, like the 3s 4d donated by John Hart at Bovey Tracey in 1520; other contributions were in kind, like the sheep given by Christopher Stephen of Highbray in 1524. At Totnes in 1526 Thomas Hamlyn bequeathed money to five groups in the parish church; and to one, dedicated to Our Lady of Pity, he left also the income from certain land, requiring its priest to pray for him and his family. In the same year a merchant of South Molton, Thomas Leigh, not only ordered an annual *dirige* and mass from a local gild of the High Cross, but also gave 12d each to seven groups in the parish church, as well as money, cloth and timber 'to the building of the chantry-house belonging to the gild of the Trinity'.[17]

The available evidence can thus leave little doubt that, on the very eve of the religious upheavals, the traditional apparatus of intercession continued to play a vital role in the lives of individuals and of communities throughout the South-West. It was a central and flourishing feature of popular piety that was soon to encounter hostility from the reforming regimes.

II

The next problem is to evaluate the impact of the Henrician Reformation upon such intercessions. Did the policies decreed by Henry VIII, Cromwell and Cranmer in 1529–47 actually initiate significant changes in the pattern of popular practice? Or did official decrees, in reality, pass over the heads of the average man? The evidence required for the formulation of answers to these crucial questions is to be sought in the four major indices of religious change that survive from the Henrician years. These are wills, legal records, chantry certificates, and the accounts of church- and gild-wardens.

Wills, at first sight, might appear to indicate that popular enthusiasm for intercessions sustained little substantial damage from the Henrician Reformation. In 1536, for example, Joan Bidwell of Shobrooke arranged her registration on a local bede-roll, 'to be continually prayed for, for ever'; she also ordered a trental and required a priest 'to sing and pray for my soul, my friends' souls, and for all the souls departed, abiding the mercy of God; and that to be done in Shobrooke church'. In 1540 Robert Hone arranged an elaborate burial at Ottery St Mary, complete with psalter, knell and black-clothed mourners, and a gift of 1d to the spectators to pray for his soul. He also ordered obits and a place on their bede-rolls ('there to be prayed for, amongst the brothers') from fraternities at South Molton and Cullompton, and other masses including a trental, 'with masses, fasting, and prayers, after the old customable usage'. He even forgave his debtors on the condition that they pray for him, and left his god-children 12d each 'to say a *Pater Noster, Ave,* and Creed, praying for my soul'. Gilbert Kirk of Exeter similarly left 4d to each householder in the parish of St Mary Arches in 1546, 'to pray to Our Lord God to have mercy on my soul and all Christian souls'.[18]

A closer examination of the wills, however, suggests that in significant respects the traditional patterns were already beginning to change. The most obvious disruption occurred in 1536–9, when the suppression of religious houses brought to a sudden end the intercessions endowed within them by laymen. As late as 1534–5 Robert Hooker of Exeter had arranged for the local Dominicans and Franciscans to say a trental for his and certain other souls, and John Flood of Topsham had commissioned a trental, for 10s, from the Exeter Franciscans.[19] But such endowments declined as the government's hostility to religious orders became increasingly explicit. They appear in only 1 of the 22 wills from 1536–9 — when

John Forde of Ashburton ordered trentals from friaries at Exeter and Plymouth in April 1538[20] — and disappear totally from west-country wills thereafter. Even more significant is the evidence relating to religious gilds. Bequests to these still appear in 11 of the 19 wills from 1530–5 (58%). John Brown of Uffculme, for instance, left a silver chalice, a mass-book, a bell, cruets and vestments to a local fraternity of Our Lady in 1535.[21] Such bequests, however, are found in only 10 of the 22 wills from 1536–9 (45%); and for 1540–6 the figure falls to 19 of 69 (28%). These statistics would suggest that investment in intercessory gilds may have been in decline from as early as the 1530s.

Most notable of all, however, is the apparent change in the overall volume of intercessory endowment. Prayers and masses had been arranged in 21 of the 30 wills from 1520–9 (70%). Of the 41 wills from 1530–9, by contrast, they were endowed in only 21 (51%); and of the 69 wills from 1540–6, in no more than 23 (33%). Despite their relatively small number, the surviving wills would therefore seem to indicate a marked decline in intercessory investment from the onset of the Henrician Reformation. Such a modification of the established patterns of piety is rendered the more significant by the inherent probability that most testators, being of above-average age, were slower to abandon traditional religion than were the young and the middle-aged. In sources relating to a wider range of age-groups, the signs of incipient change are even more strikingly apparent.

One such source is the legal record. In the Consistory Court, and in central courts like Chancery and Star Chamber, several cases of a type rare in 1500–29 indicate that devotion to the traditional apparatus of intercession was beginning to wane. As early as 1530, at Cullompton, several local men (headed by the More family) reportedly occupied the chapel erected only four years previously by John Lane. Lane had intended a chantry-priest to celebrate there; the intruders outraged his widow by using it for their burials instead. Similar disruption occurred at Exeter, where property had formerly been bequeathed to the parish churches of St Kerrian and St Martin for the maintenance of intercessory prayers and masses. In 1533–8 Richard Drewe prevented their continuance by appropriating the income for his own use. At about the same time, Edward Thorn of Sheepwash was detaining certain deeds, so as to hinder the collection of a rent which maintained intercessions in the parish church at Silverton. A comparable situation arose at Shillingford, where land had once been granted to the dean and chapter of Exeter on condition that they kept an obit in the cathedral and prayed for their benefactor's soul. In 1537–8 the land was appropriated by John Blackaller, one of Exeter's leading citizens. He refused to allow the clergy their rent, to the inevitable detriment of the customary obit.[22]

In 1538–44 there was similar disruption at Holsworthy, Marwood and South Petherwin. Land had been given to maintain a priest who served the gild and altar of St Katherine at Holsworthy; but the donor's heir now detained its deeds, preventing its use for the original pious ends. Richard Frear similarly claimed land at Clayhanger which, according to a local priest, belonged to St Katherine's chantry at Marwood. Again, land used by a gild of Jesus at South Petherwin to hire a priest — who sang 'Jesus masses' in the parish church — was now claimed by John Blackmore. By 1544–7 such attitudes were no longer uncommon. At Halberton, for example, Christopher Sampford and John Warren reportedly dismissed a stipendiary priest from his post, 'commanding him to depart, saying to him that he should serve there no longer'. At Davidstow, the local constable John Jelley persuaded the parishioners to sell certain oxen, the hiring-out of which had maintained a priest 'to the laud and praise of Almighty God'. He then kept the proceeds for himself. At Aveton Giffard, in about 1547, a local man claimed land which (according to other parishioners) belonged in fact to a neighbouring chantry.[33]

Internal dissensions as well as external assaults are revealed by the legal records. At Zeal Monachorum, money belonging to the stores of St John and St Katherine was dishonestly retained in 1534. In the same year, the responsibilities of gild-wardenship were refused by a parishioner at Crediton. At Cullompton in 1538–44 the members of the gild of St John not only quarreled with their stipendiary priest, but also argued bitterly amongst themselves, the Mores claiming pre-eminence on account of their benefactions. At Yealmpton in 1544, Nicholas Thorning refused to return rings and money worth over £16 that had been entrusted to his care by the store of Our Lady. They had originally been collected for 'divers good and godly purposes and intents' within the parish church.[24] Evidence of this nature serves to strengthen the impression that between 1530 and 1547, enthusiasm for intercessory institutions experienced a significant decline.

Further light upon developing attitudes is provided by the chantry-certificates of the Henrician and Edwardian commissioners. These reveal that, on the eve of their suppression, many chantries were already in serious decay. At Creed, for example, land once donated for the maintenance of a priest to celebrate 'Jesus masses' had been 'conveyed from the churchwardens of long time'; a house belonging to a chantry at Helston was in ruins; and an obit at St Winnow had been discontinued. A hospital at Kingsteignton had a chapel in which the five poor inmates were supposed to hear divine service; but it now lacked ornaments, jewels, plate, goods and chattels, 'for that it hath not been maintained according to the will of the founder'. Property given to maintain a chantry-priest in the parish church at South Petherwin had been in dispute, and 'a great part of the issues of the said lands' was thus 'expended in the suit of the same'.[25]

Most of the disruption seems to have occurred in the last years of Henry's reign. An endowment at Truro had maintained a priest to pray for the founder and his family; but it ended in the early 1540s, the mills which provided its income being allowed to decay. In about 1543 a chantry at Bampton, founded by Humphrey Calwoodley in about 1521, was dissolved by Michael Mallett; he discharged the incumbent and assumed the property for himself. John Trotte's almshouse at Cullompton, the inhabitants of which had prayed for the founder's soul since its establishment in about 1523, was dissolved by his own sons in about 1544 — an act symbolizing the attitude frequently adopted by this generation towards the piety of its fathers. It was similarly in about 1544 that land originally given to maintain obits at Looe was employed by the townsmen to finance the repair of their bridge. The commissioners also reported that a chantry on the 'isle of Laman' now lacked all equipment and property, 'for that the service in the chapel hath of late discontinued'.[26] The certificates thus confirm that devotion to intercessions was often in decline several years before the advent of a Protestant regime.

The final source of evidence is the account of the church- or gild-warden. This, too, provides indications of change. At the parish church of St John's Bow in Exeter, for example, annual payments for 'obits of St Gregory' were recorded in the accounts until 1535–6 — but then ceased altogether. Payments to a priest in the parish church at Ashburton, for the celebration of mass at an altar dedicated to Our Lady, similarly ended after 1536–7; and several gilds made their last appearance in the Ashburton accounts in 1537–9. The gild of St Antony at Chagford, which organized masses on St Antony's Day, disappeared from the accounts after 1536–7, at which date a gild of St Nicholas in the same town seems also to have ended. The accounts of a group at St Thomas-by-Launceston, dedicated to the Blessed Virgin and maintaining its own bede-roll, similarly ceased in 1537. Two 'stores' at

Broadhempston, named after St Christopher and Our Lady, apparently ended after 1539. In the same year, no less than four groups — dedicated to St Antony, St Sidwell, St Sunday and Our Lady — seem to have disappeared from the parish church at Morebath.[27]

A gild of St Eligius at Chagford seems to have ended in about 1540; and several of the groups recorded in the Camborne accounts up to 1540 — notably 'Yea', 'Gwynwala', 'Nyales', 'Bastyen', and 'Jane and Margaret' — are conspicuously absent thereafter. 'Our Lady Holmadons' at Stratton apparently suspended operations after 1541–2 — when, in fact, John Mock was paid 'for drawing down of Our Lady chapel'. Another group dedicated to Mary, at Woodbury, appears to have dissolved in 1542–3, when its goods were transferred to the central wardens. At North Petherwin, the last account for St George's gild is dated 1543; and no accounts from the 1540s exist for several gilds known to have operated here in previous years. Similarly suggestive absences occur in the accounts for Ashburton and South Tawton.[28] Allowance being made for the incompleteness of some account-sequences, it is again difficult to avoid the conclusion that intercessory institutions were frequently disappearing several years before the arrival of official Protestantism in 1547. The accounts confirm also that even the surviving groups did not necessarily continue to flourish. They record (for example) that gild-wardenship was refused at Morebath in 1536, and that many of the gilds at Antony in the last years of Henry VIII were owed money by local men: these proved so slow to repay that the 'Six Men' of the parish began to threaten legal action. The accounts show also that bede-rolls were still recited, and new names occasionally added; but the particularly full records of Stratton's High Cross group reveal a decline in enrolments from 1540. There was but one name added in 1541, 1542, 1544 and 1546 and one in 1540, 1543 or 1545.[29]

The combined testimony of wills, legal records, chantry-certificates and wardens' accounts can thus leave little doubt about changing attitudes to the traditional apparatus of intercession. Between 1530 and 1547 the decline in popular enthusiasm appears to have been both widespread and rapid. The study of prayers for the dead — like the study of image-veneration — renders it difficult to maintain the thesis that the Henrician Reformation passed 'over the head' of the average man. On the contrary, it appears probable that fundamental changes in his religious activity were initiated in these tumultuous years.

If a decline in enthusiasm for intercessions can be asserted with relative confidence, the factors behind this trend are less immediately apparent. In most cases, nevertheless, it appears to have been non-ideological in origin, and to have represented an essentially pragmatic response to the unambiguously hostile activities of the government and of the local gentry.

The intentions of the government became increasingly clear from 1529, when the acceptance of stipends for singing masses for the dead was restricted by statute.[30] The suppression of religious houses in 1536–9, moreover, not only ended lay-endowed intercessions within them, but also publicized governmental doubts about the efficacy of any prayer or mass for the dead. 'The founding of monasteries argued Purgatory to be', observed Latimer; 'so the putting of them down argueth it not to be'.[31] Even more disturbing were the statute of 1545, which threatened to transfer the property of chantry foundations to the Exchequer, and the associated activities of the chantry commissioners — 'the king's visitors for the church lands', whom the churchwardens of Woodbury (for example) had to meet in 1545–6.[32] The expectations of an imminent dissolution that were inevitably aroused by such developments can only have served to undermine popular confidence in intercessory institutions, discouraging new investment and stimulating the diversion of existing endowments to essentially secular ends.

At the same time, the population of the South-West saw chantries come under inceasing attack from members of the gentry. Motivated more often by material interest than by Protestant conviction, this development can be traced to the earliest years of the Reformation. In 1529–32 the deeds of a Trinity gild at Exeter were detained by Charles Coplestone, and an annuity maintaining a chantry-priest at Tretherf was appropriated by the founder's son. A stipendiary chaplaincy at Thornbury was dissolved by a gentleman named Specott in about 1531; property at St Winnow, granted by William Casely to maintain an obit, was reclaimed by his heirs in about 1537; and at Colyford, in the early 1540s, Robert Stowford refused to pay the chantry-priest more than half his stipend. Another gentleman, meanwhile, claimed land at Lansallos that had maintained the performance of obits, while chantries at Halberton and Colebrooke were dissolved by members of the gentry in about 1545.[33] The example thus set by his social superiors must have eroded even further the confidence of the average man in the traditional organs of intercession.

III

Intercessory institutions had thus already lost much of their vitality when, after the accession of Edward VI, they were subjected to an official assault unprecedented in rigour and in scope. By the Act of 1547, all properties, rents and annuities providing stipends for chantry-priests were transferred to the Crown, along with the funds of parish gilds and fraternities assigned to 'superstitious' purposes. The ultimate aim of this campaign was the total demolition of the intercessory structure.[34] To what extent, in reality, was it effectively implemented?

In the parishes of the South-West, the characteristic response seems usually to have been a dutiful — if unenthusiastic — conformity to official decrees. Wardens' accounts indicate that in most parish churches, the recitation of bede-rolls was obediently abrogated in 1548. At Stratton, for example, names ceased to be added to the roll, and payments to the vicar for reading it now came to an end.[35] Extant accounts record also an almost invariable cessation of masses for the dead at about the same time.[36] Even more remarkable was the alacrity with which parishes obeyed the official instructions for the dissolution of religious gilds. By 1550, these once-vital institutions appear to have been virtually eliminated from every parochial community for which accounts remain.

At Stratton, for instance, the stockwardens' account for 1547 (made on 1 January 1548) indicates the existence of gilds known as Allhallows, Our Lady and St George, Our Lady, St Andrew, St Thomas, St Armil, Christ, the Trinity, and the High Cross. The next account, made at the feast of St Andrew in 1548, records only four. By 1549, only the High Cross survived; and it, too, seems to have been suppressed thereafter. The last account of All Saints' gild at Launceston was compiled on All Saints' Day in 1548. The 'Brewers of the Processional Ale', who had organized rites at North Petherwin as well as selling bread and ale, similarly ended in 1548. Morebath lost its 'Young Men' and 'Young Women' at about the same time. Annual *diriges* for a fraternity at Woodbury ceased in 1548; and in 1550 the parish sold three ewes which had belonged to St Margaret's store. By 1549, the former complexes of 10 or 11 groups at Camborne and at Antony had dwindled to one and three respectively; and even these were soon to end.[37] The few groups that survived this deluge of destruction were invariably shorn of their 'superstitious' functions. At North Petherwin, for example, St Christopher's store had organized a regular *dirige,* mass and bede-roll. The store continued to exist throughout the reign of

Edward VI, but from 1548 these activities disappeared entirely from its accounts; its traditional identity had been effectively effaced.[38]

The suppression of intercessory institutions was followed by the dispersal of their property. A single day — 25 February 1549 — saw the sale by the government of land belonging to a chantry at Beaford, of a house at Broadhempston that had maintained an anniversary, and of property at Exeter which had supported the singing of an antiphon in St Petrock's parish church, as well as the disposal of land at Ashburton which had belonged to the fraternity of St Lawrence.[39] Sometimes the former premises of a chantry were converted to non-religious use. St Nicholas' chapel at Looe, for example, became the hall of a secular gild.[40] Some, moreover, were subjected to physical attack. In 1549, following the dissolution of St George's gild at Lostwithiel and the cessation of its annual procession, *dirige* and feast, the gild's chapel in the parish church was deliberately 'defaced' by the townsmen. They acted on the orders of their mayor, Richard Hutchings.[41]

The general passivity of popular responses to this unprecedented assault upon the intercessory system is indicated also by surviving wills. Only 6 of the 30 testators in 1547 (20%) still thought it judicious to invest in prayer for the dead; the prevalent uncertainty is evident in the request of Peter Amis of Lanlivery for a trental, 'if it may be'. Such investment, moreover, appears in no more than 3 of the 17 wills from 1548 (11%), and in only 1 of the 20 from 1549 (5%). The sole exception in the latter year was John Southwood of Hemyock, who on 10 March left 12d to a priest in return for his prayers.[42] Bequests to gilds, furthermore, are found in no more than 6 of the 77 wills from 1547–9 (8%). The import of these statistics is clear. As the Protestant proclivities of the Edwardian regime became increasingly explicit, testators grew correspondingly reluctant to risk investment in the traditional apparatus of intercession. A rising number, significantly, were beginning to divert their bequests towards the poor of this world instead.

For more than two years, until the summer of 1549, any attempts at resistance to this devastation of traditional religion seem to have been remarkably restricted in scale. They were limited to localities like Ashburton, where some of the inhabitants attempted with violence to prevent the confiscation of lands and market-tolls formerly owned by the gild of St Lawrence.[43] Most parishes, by contrast, seem to have submitted to the commissioners without overt dissent. Woodbury was again typical, dutifully sending its representatives to Exeter in 1547–8 'for the church lands',[44] while at Morebath the Three Men and the wardens rode to meet the commissioners at Tiverton 'to make an answer for chantry ground'. Nor should it be too readily assumed that even the Western Rebellion of June-August 1549 necessarily indicates a determination by the majority of west-countrymen to restore the intercessions by force. It is true that the rebel articles declare that 'we will have every preacher in his sermon, and every priest at his mass, pray specially by name for the souls in Purgatory, as our forefathers did'. They demand also the confiscation of 'the half part of the abbey lands and chantry lands in every man's possession, howsoever he came by them', in order to finance the restoration of two establishments in each county 'for devout persons, which shall pray for the king and the commonwealth'.[45] Since, however, the articles were almost certainly formulated by the traditionalist priests who led the revolt, the extent to which they accurately represent the attitudes of the rebel rank-and-file must remain open to doubt. Cranmer told the rebel laymen that they had been deceived by their priestly leaders, 'which devised those articles for you, to make you ask you wist not what';[46] and it is certain that several of the insurgents' motives — notably their desire for plunder, their fear of taxation, and their bitter antagonism towards members of the gentry — were essentially secular rather than religious in nature. It is equally important to note the apparent failure of the rebellion to engage more than a relatively small minority of the regional population — an estimated 7,000 out of perhaps 100,000 inhabitants of the South-West. The resigned conformity of Morebath seems to have been markedly more typical than the desperate resistance of Sampford Courtenay. At the same time, moreover, there were significant individuals and groups, both within Exeter and beyond, who proved actively loyal to the Edwardian regime.[47]

The revolt's bloody defeat by Lord Russell, and the ensuing campaign of fines, confiscations and executions, would appear in fact to have extinguished the last sparks of organized resistance to the assault upon intercessions. Certainly the official orders for the dismantling of altars, at which prayers and masses for the dead had been offered, were implemented with conspicuous compliance in most parishes for which accounts survive. The parishioners of Woodbury, for example, pulled down their altars in 1550, paying James Croft 'for carrying out of the rubble of the altars', and selling 'stones of the altars', as well as 'three broad stones that lay apon the altars'. The wardens at Stratton paid for 'drawing down of the altars' in 1551, and sold 'stones of the altars' for 4s 4d, while at Dartmouth in 1552 old altar-stones were to be found lying out in the church-yard.[48] At the same time, vast quantities of vestments and altar-plate, much of which had been used in intercessory rites, were disappearing from the parish churches, either by sale, by theft, or by official confiscation.[49] That the prevailing popular attitude to this new wave of destruction was again characterized by resignation and compliance is confirmed by the apparently total lack of resistance recorded in the surviving sources. It is also revealing that, in the 32 wills made between January 1550 and July 1553, there was not a single attempt to arrange intercessions in any form. Nor was there even one recorded bequest to a religious gild. Gifts to the poor, by contrast, were included in no less than 15 of the 32 wills.

IV

Was devotion to prayers for the dead eliminated permanently by the Edwardian regime? Or could it revive and flourish in the more favourable climate of Mary's reign? How effective, at local level, was the alleged 'restoration' of Catholicism in 1553–8?

There is no doubt that many subsidiary altars at which intercessions had once been performed — like St Margaret's at Woodbury — were re-erected by parishes within months of the queen's accession in July 1553. Others, however, were restored only after considerable hesitation — until 1554–5 at Chagford and Braunton, for instance, and until 1555–6 at Morebath — while in some parishes they may never have been restored at all.[50] It is also suggestive that, of the 22 parishes for which accounts survive, there is certain record of the revival of intercessory activity in only 13. Again, moreover, the revival was not necessarily spontaneous. It was deferred until 1555–6 at Exeter St Petrock and at Woodbury, until 1557 at Chagford, and until as late as 1558–9 at Exeter St John's Bow. In 9 parishes there is no evidence of intercessions at all. Equally notable is the absence from all the accounts, with the sole exception of those for Dartington, of payments to priests for the recitation of bede-rolls — a virtually ubiquitous feature of pre-Edwardian accounts. It would therefore appear that most communities never succeeded in reviving these prayers for the dead.[51]

Even more revealing is the light thrown by accounts upon the restoration of religious gilds. Of the 22 recorded parishes, not one seems ever to have approached the total of 9, 10 or 11 groups maintained by several pre-Edwardian communities. Only 7 appear to have revived as many as 2, 3 or 4. Seven restored a single group, while the remaining 8 seem to have restored none at all. Nor did the Marian gilds necessarily resume their pre-Edwardian functions. St Brannoc's at Braunton might buy 'vittle against St Brannoc's obit for the brother and sisters', hire a priest 'to come to say mass when our Ale was', and pay a man 'for going about the town the brotherhood day' to proclaim it;[52] but many of the revived gilds were little more than fund-raising agencies for the parish church. St Christopher's at North Petherwin, for example, failed to revive the *diriges*, masses and bede-roll readings that it had organized regularly until 1548. Nor do the accounts of the High Cross store at Stratton — formerly the organizer of a popular bede-roll — record a single new registration upon it in the reign of Mary.[53] When every allowance has been made for incompleteness, the unavoidable impression given by Marian accounts is that the restoration of intercessory institutions and activities was never, in reality, more than a very tentative and limited phenomenon.

This impression, moreover, receives substantial confirmation from contemporary wills. Prayers or masses for the dead had been endowed in 70% of the wills from 1520–9, in 51% of those from 1530–9, and in 33% of those from 1540–6. Of the 60 wills from 1553–9 — i.e. from Mary's accession to the Elizabethan injunctions — such bequests appeared in no more than 11 (18%). John Tuckfield, alderman of Exeter, might still in 1554 leave money to his apprentice, servants and maids, 'to pray for me', and Richard Friend of Ermington might still in 1557 endow a priest 'to sing for my soul and all my friends';[54] but even amongst testators, with their generally conservative tendencies, such confidence in the ancient modes of intercession was no longer common. Even more striking is the failure of all but one of the 60 testators to include bequests to religious gilds. The sole exception was Robert Easton of Chudleigh, who as late as April 1559 left 6s 8d to the local store of Our Lady.[55] This dramatic reduction of support for such institutions, which contrasts so markedly with their popularity on the eve of the Reformation, provides further substance for the conclusion that the Henrician and Edwardian upheavals had dealt the traditional piety a crushing blow — a blow from which it was never, even in the favourable circumstances of Mary's reign, to recover.

It was, therefore, a religious practice in unmistakeable decline that came under renewed and determined attack from the Elizabethan regime. The royal commissioners reached Exeter in

September 1559 and, according to the contemporary Exonian John Hooker, 'did deface all the altars and monuments of idolatry, and forbade any more masses or popish services to be used'.[56] Once more the most frequent local response to official instruction seems to have been a dutiful conformity. The destruction of altars is recorded even in the accounts of villages that were relatively small and remote. Thus the parishioners of Coldridge sent representatives to meet the visitors at Barnstable, and then paid for 'ridding of the altars of the church'. Similarly at Woodbury, after the wardens' appearance before the visitors at Exeter, men were paid for pulling down St Margaret's altar, and for carrying away the stones.[57] Soon, moreover, the parish churches were to be stripped again of their vestments and plate.[58] In every parish for which relevant accounts survive, furthermore, prayers and masses for the dead appear totally to have ceased in 1559. By the 1560s, therefore, the ancient practices of intercession seem to have been wellnigh eradicated from the pattern of parochial religion.

Belief in Purgatory, inevitably, did not vanish overnight. Some testators, like William Spiring of Bradninch in 1560, would still arrange the disposal of their property 'for the wealth of my soul and all Christian souls'.[59] Such belief, nevertheless, could no longer be expressed in ritual performance. Of 90 testators from 1560–9, only one dared even to request the performance of intercession. This was William Turner of Cullompton, who in January 1561 still hoped for an annual dole to the poor on his burial-day, 'to pray for me and my father and mother and my two wives, Thomasine and Joan, and all Christian souls'.[60] At the same time, moreover, religious gilds were experiencing a further reduction both in number and in importance. Many of the groups revived under Mary were ended in 1559–60. In several parishes, including St Petrock's, St John's Bow, and St Mary Steps at Exeter as well as Ashburton, Crediton, Dartington, Kilmington and Woodbury, not one such gild appears to have survived into the 1560s.[61] Other communities rarely retained more than one or two, and even these had invariably been divested of their original intercessory functions. St Katherine at Chagford seems merely now to have raised money for the church by selling ale. The two groups dedicated to Sts John and George and St Brannoc at Braunton, though still dispensing food and drink to the poor on 'brotherhood day', no longer arranged their traditional intercessions. St Christopher at North Petherwin similarly survived into the 1560s, but its customary *diriges*, masses and bede-roll recitations had long since been abandoned.[62] It is scarcely surprising that such emasculated institutions were no longer able to attract the enthusiastic support of former years. Their wardenship now was often refused, as at Chagford and Chudleigh.⁶³ More significantly, they failed to receive a single bequest in any of the 90 westcountry wills from this decade.

The conclusion to be drawn from the different types of surviving evidence is therefore relatively clear. Whatever the case in other regions, the impact of the Reformation upon intercessions in the South-West can in no way be dismissed as either 'restricted' or 'delayed'. On the contrary: the effects of official pressure upon this crucial component of the popular religion appears to have been increasingly noticeable at parish-level from as early as the 1530s, and ultimately to have proved devastating. Both the magnitude and the speed of these developments are suggested by Graphs 1 and 2, which depict the pattern of testatorial investment in intercessions and in gilds between the eve of the Reformation and the first decade of Elizabeth's reign. What is indicated by these statistics, as well as by evidence of a less quantifiable nature, is a fundamental reorientation of religious activity — a virtual eradication, within one life-span, of practices which had for generations lain close to the very heart of the popular piety.

V

Long-established patterns of religion were thus erased, by what were they replaced? Was the ancient enthusiasm for intercession transmuted into a corresponding acceptance of the 'Protestant' view of salvation? To what extent was the decline of the old ideology accompanied by a rise of the new?

There is no doubt that, even at relatively low levels of west country society, authentically Protestant attitudes to salvation were occasionally emerging in the Reformation decades. They received their clearest expression in the tracts written in 1547–9 by Philip Nichols, a young Devonian layman of comparatively humble social origins. Nichols rejected the entire concept of Purgatory as unscriptural. 'Christ speaketh not any one word of Purgatory — no, nor any place of all the scriptures, from the first word of *Genesis* to the last of St John's *Revelation*'. Equally characteristic of Protestant emphases was Nichols' confidence that believers are assured of an immediate passage to Heaven after death by the atoning work of Christ. Since the wicked proceed immediately to Hell, there is no need for a 'third place'. (One might equally claim a fourth place for the Devil, he argues; if God refuses souls entry into Heaven until they are cleansed of wickedness, may not Satan debar souls from Hell until they are purged of virtue?) Since Purgatory does not exist, prayers and masses for the dead are no more than fraudulent inventions of the priesthood, devised in order to increase its wealth and to maintain its ascendancy over 'simple consciences here, in this world'. 'As for matins-mumblers and mass-mongers, with *diriges* and trentals, with such superstitious prayers: the scripture speaketh not of them'.[64]

That Protestant views of the after-life were occasionally to be found at a relatively low social level in the mid-Tudor South-West is thus beyond dispute. The extent of their acceptance by the regional population at large, however, is markedly more problematic. One source of evidence is provided by the records of the Consistory Court at Exeter. Its act-books and deposition-books, which run intermittently from Henry VII to Elizabeth I, offer strikingly little indication of popular Protestantism in the diocese before 1570.[65] A similar impression is given by the Exeter episcopal registers for this period. John Atwill of Walkhampton might in 1506 dismiss bede-rolls as more effective in enriching clerics than in saving souls, and Otto Corbin at Exeter in 1515 might declare, 'I care not for my soul, so I may have an honest living in this world; and when ye see my soul hang on the hedge, cast ye stones thereto';[66] but the marked rarity of such cases again suggests that neither 'Lollard' nor 'Protestant' attitudes to salvation ever attracted widespread support in the region before 1570. The same conclusion is to be drawn from the records of other contemporary courts, some of which (notably Chancery and Star Chamber) dealt tangentially with religious affairs. The only court-cases from this period to reveal unambiguously Protestant conceptions of the after-life are in fact the two recorded by John Foxe. The first concerns Thomas Benet, a private schoolmaster who was burned at the stake at Exeter in 1532; he reportedly accused the clergy of selling masses for souls in 'feigned Purgatory', and declared salvation to be dependent upon Christ's atonement rather than upon human achievement. The second case is that of Agnes Priest, an uneducated woman from near Launceston; she also was burned as a heretic at Exeter, in 1558. Agnes regarded trentals, *diriges,* soul-masses and purchased prayers as 'foolish inventions'; for, 'God's Son hath, by his Passion, purged all'. These are the sole instances of such belief to be recorded by the *Acts and Monuments* for the entire diocese in the Reformation decades.[67]

Further clues are provided by wills. Authentically Protestant formulae, expressing confidence in the soul's immediate passage to

Heaven by virtue of Christ's atoning work, are conspicuously absent from all 30 west-country wills with recorded formulae from 1520–9. Of the 30 with formulae from 1530–9, moreover, only 2 contain possible indications of such belief. The Cornishman William Nanfan avowed in 1536 that God would grant, 'after this present and miserable life, eternal life to all faithful souls in the joy everlasting', while John Forde of Ashburton in 1538 commended his soul 'to Almighty God and to his infinite mercy, trusting that by the merits of his Passion [I am] to have the fruition of his Godhead in Heaven'. Yet the Protestantism of even these two testators is doubtful: Forde in fact arranged prayers and masses for his soul in no less than twenty local churches.[68] Solifidian assertions, moreover, appear only once in the 21 wills with formulae from 1540–6, and only twice in the 16 from 1547–9. Two of these three testators — Nicholas Wise in 1540, and Richard Colwill under Edward VI — may not have been resident in the region, since Wise (despite his west-country associations) requested burial at Shoreditch, and Colwill owned land both in Devon and outside. The only certain resident to express Protestant convictions in his will before 1550 is therefore John Bougin of Totnes. In 1548 he bequeathed his soul to God and his body to Christian burial, 'abolishing all feig[ned] ceremonies contrary to Holy Scripture, which is God's word and commandment'. Instead he arranged psalms, 'in the honour of God and with thanksgiving that it hath so pleased him to call me to his mercy and grace'.[69]

Only after the defeat of the Western Rebellion in 1549 — and after the replacement of the conservative John Veysey by the vigorously Protestant Miles Coverdale as bishop of Exeter in 1551 — did the pattern begin to change. Of 18 testators between January 1550 and July 1553, confidence in the sufficiency of Christ's atonement was expressed by 6; namely John Harris, John Bond of Crediton, John Anthony of Dartmouth, William Amadas of Plymouth, and Philip Mayhew and John Hurst of Exeter. Thus Anthony, a merchant, bequeathed his soul to God in 1552, 'believing that by the merits of Christ's Passion [I am] to have remission of all my sins, and to be one of the same number that are elected to be with him in everlasting glory'; and Amadas, in June 1553, commended himself to Christ, 'in whom and by whom is all my whole trust of clean remission and forgiveness of my sins'.[70] Amadas himself was undoubtedly committed to Protestantism.[71] In the five other cases, however, it is less clear that solifidian assertion reflects a personal conviction rather than a dutiful conformity to official norms. A high degree of conformism is certainly suggested by the rapidity with which such formulae ceased to appear after Edward's death: only 2 are found in 32 wills made between Mary's accession and Elizabeth's injunctions. Although Harry Reynold in 1554 required burial 'according unto God's holy word', and John Lane of Broadhembury in October 1558 declared himself 'perfect in mind and, trusting in Jesu, safe in soul', a clearly Protestant attitude to death seems to have been expressed only by two citizens of Exeter, namely John Drake (in 1554) and Griffith Meredith (in 1557). Drake, a merchant, proclaimed his 'faithful trust and hope in the infinite goodness of Almighty God, my Maker and Redeemer', and his expectation of eternal life 'after my departing out of this wretched and transitory life'. Meredith committed himself to God, 'trusting to be saved by the shedding of Christ's blood, and in all the merits of his Passion'.[72]

Even after the return of Protestant government under Elizabeth I, such statements of faith remained strikingly rare. Of 30 west-country wills with recorded formulae from 1560–9, they appear in no more than 4. William Lake, a merchant of Plymouth, described himself in 1560 as a 'most miserable sinner', and asked God 'that the merits of thy son Jesus Christ may be a full redemption and satisfaction for the trespasses that I have done or committed since I came into this wretched world, so that my most wretched soul may be saved amongst thy saints'. Joan Lake of Plymouth — possibly his wife — proclaimed in 1562 a similar confidence in salvation 'by no other means' than the Passion of Christ. In the same year a yeoman from Combe Pyne, John Helier, declared that he expected to receive, through Christ's work, 'the fruition of his Godhead in Heaven'. In 1566, finally, Robert Ebsworthy of Bridestow bequeathed 'my soul to God, and my body to the earth, and my sin to the Devil, desiring God for Christ's sake to forgive them'.[73] Such declarations would seem still to have been uncommon at the popular levels of west-country society. Most of the extant wills from this decade are suggestively silent about the fate of the testator after death.

What conclusions are to be drawn from the available evidence? Protestant views of the after-life were undoubtedly beginning to attract support from at least some members, both male and female, of the lay population below the level of the gentry. Though found in some rural communities, this support appears to have been strongest in the larger towns, particularly Exeter and Plymouth; here the literacy required for Bible-reading was relatively high, Protestant preaching was comparatively frequent, and trade-links with Protestant London were often strong. By 1570, nevertheless, it was still limited to a relatively small proportion of the regional population. The traditional apparatus of intercession had been progressively dismantled, and was now beyond repair; but in the minds and hearts of most west-countrymen it had yet to be replaced by an enthusiastic commitment to the new and alien doctrine of justification by faith alone. In reality, it seems more often to have been replaced by uncertainty, confusion, and indifference to the officially-sanctioned forms of religion. In their campaign to suppress the ancient piety, the agents of Reformation had achieved substantial success; but the substitution of an alternative spirituality was proving to be a separate and a markedly more difficult problem.

For his generous advice in the preparation of this article, I am again indebted to Dr Nicholas Orme of the University of Exeter.

Abbreviations

BL   British Library
CRO   Cornwall County Record Office, Truro
CWA   Churchwardens' accounts
DC   Dean and Chapter Library, Exeter Cathedral
DRO   Devon County Record Office, Exeter
ERO   East Devon Record Office, Exeter
PRO   Public Record Office

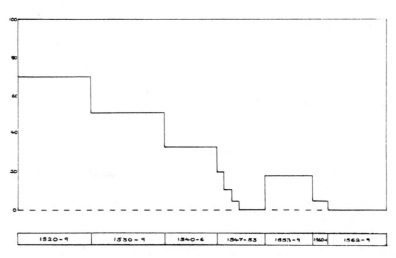

Graph 1: The percentage of wills with endowments of intercession, 1520–69

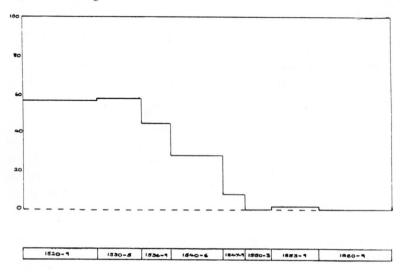

Graph 2: The percentage of wills with bequests to religious gilds, 1520–69

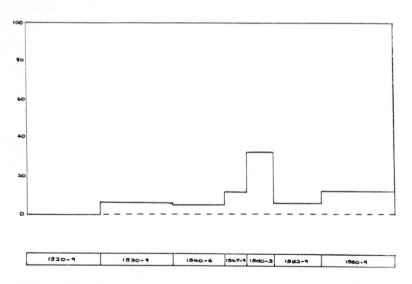

Graph 3: The percentage of wills with 'Protestant' formulae, 1520–69

Notes

[1] A.G. Dickens, *Lollards and Protestants in the Diocese of York, 1509–1558* (1959).

[2] C. Haigh, *Reformation and Resistance in Tudor Lancashire* (1975).

[3] R. Whiting, 'Abominable Idols: images and image-breaking under Henry VIII', *Journal of Ecclesiastical History*, January 1982.

[4] G. McN. Rushforth, 'The windows of the church of St Neot, Cornwall', *Exeter Diocesan Architectural and Archaeological Society Transactions* (1927).

[5] J. Prince, *Worthies of Devon*, (1701), 324, 325.

[6] DC 2864 (bede-roll, late-fifteenth century).

[7] PRO, Chancery, Early Proceedings (C 1), 900/34,35 (1533–8).

[8] DRO, 745C (service-book, late-medieval), p. 3.

[9] J. Foxe, *Acts and Monuments*, (1583), Ii, 1039.

[10] This and all subsequent references to wills (unless otherwise indicated) relate to the author's analysis of (a) 177 wills from 1520–69, as preserved in PRO, Prerogative Court of Canterbury, Wills (PROB 11), and (b) 221 testamentary abstracts from 1520–69, as preserved in DRO, Moger Abstracts of Devon Wills (47 typescript volumes); Devon and Cornwall Record Society Library, Exeter, Oswyn Murray Abstracts of Wills (39 typescript volumes), and C. Worthy, *Devonshire Wills: a collection of annotated testamentary abstracts* (1896). The 221 abstracts are summaries of the originals; the 177 wills are complete copies. The testators came from a wide range of parishes, both urban and rural.

[11] PRO, Prerogative Court of Canterbury, Wills (PROB 11), 21, fo. 18*v*; 23, fo. 71; 24, fo. 10.

[12] PRO, Prerogative Court of Canterbury, Wills (PROB 11), 20, fo. 229*v*; 21, fos. 128, 202*v*; 22, fos. 8, 302; 24, fo. 10.

[13] PRO, Prerogative Court of Canterbury, Wills (PROB 11), 20, fos. 229, 229*v*; 23, fo. 29; 24, fo. 10; DRO, Moger Abstracts of Devon Wills, 19, Thomas Hamlyn, 1526.

[14] C. Henderson, *Essays in Cornish History*, (1935), 75–9; DRO, Chagford CWA, 1500–30, *passim*; BL Additional MS 32243, Stratton High Cross wardens' accounts, 1512–30, *passim*; CRO, North Petherwin CWA, fos. 14, 22*v*, 32*v*, 38*v*, etc.

[15] BL Additional MS 32243, Stratton High Cross wardens' accounts, 1512–30, *passim*; CRO, North Petherwin CWA, fo. 38*v*, etc; Henderson, *Essays*, 75–9; DRO, Chagford CWA, 1500–30, *passim*; R. Carew, *Survey of Cornwall* (1811 ed.), 322–323; PRO, Exchequer, Court of Augmentations, Proceedings (E 315), 122/15–28.

[16] A. Hanham, ed., *Churchwardens' Accounts of Ashburton, 1479–1580* (1970), xii-xv; DRO, Chagford CWA, 1500–30, *passim*; BL Additional MS 32243, Stratton High Cross wardens' accounts, 1512–30, *passim;* BL Additional MS 32244, Stratton Stockwardens' accounts, 1532 *et seq.;* CRO, Camborne CWA, 1535 *et seq.;* J.E. Binney (ed.), *The Accounts of the Wardens of the Parish of Morebath, 1520–73,* (1904) *passim*; Devon and Cornwall Record Society Library, Exeter, transcript, South Tawton CWA, 1524 *et seq.;* ERO, Winkleigh CWA, 1519 *et seq.;* transcript in the possession of Mr F.L. Harris, Antony CWA, 1538 *et seq.;* CRO, North Petherwin CWA, *passim*.

[17] PRO, Prerogative Court of Canterbury, Wills (PROB 11), 19, fo. 208; 22, fo. 191*v*; 23, fo. 54; DRO, Moger Abstracts of Devon Wills, 19, Thomas Hamlyn, 1526.

[18] PRO, Prerogative Court of Canterbury, Wills (PROB 11), 27, fo. 69*v*; 29, fo.

201; 31, fo. 44.

[19]   PRO, Prerogative Court of Canterbury, Wills (PROB 11), 25, fo. 280v; 26, fo. 76.

[20]   PRO, Prerogative Court of Canterbury, Wills (PROB 11), 26, fo. 79v.

[21]   PRO, Prerogative Court of Canterbury, Wills (PROB 11), 25, fo. 227v.

[22]   PRO, Star Chamber Proceedings, Henry VIII (STAC 2), 25/80,142; PRO, Chancery, Early Proceedings (C 1), 781/26 (1533–8); 786/54 (1533–8); 930/1 (1533–8).

[23]PRO, Star Chamber Proceedings, Edward VI (STAC 3), 2/20; 7/45; PRO, Chancery, Early Proceedings (C 1), 959/35–7 (1538–44); 976/32,33 (1538–44); 986/44 (1538–44); 1042/7–9 (1538–44); 1200/10,11 (1547–51).

[24]   DRO, Consistory Court Book 778, *sub* 12 January 1533/4, 17 March 1533/4; PRO, Chancery, Early Proceedings (C 1), 1029/46–50 (1538–44); 1162/52 (1544–7); 1185/31 (1547).

[25]   L.S. Snell, ed., *The Chantry Certificates for Cornwall* (1953) pp. 21, 27, 42, 53; L.S. Snell, ed., *The Chantry Certificates for Devon and the City of Exeter* (1961), xxii, 41.

[26]   Snell, *Cornwall*, 34, 48, 50; Snell, *Devon*, xxi, xxii, 23, 24. For Trotte, see also above, 5.

[27]   ERO, Exeter St John's Bow CWA, *passim;* Hanham, *Churchwardens' Accounts, passim;* DRO, Chagford CWA, *passim;* CRO, St Thomas-by-Launceston CWA, *passim;* DRO, transcript, Broadhempston CWA, *passim;* Binney, *Accounts, passim.*

[28]   DRO, Chagford CWA, *passim;* CRO, Cambrone CWA, *passim;* BL Additional MS 32244, Stratton Stockwardens' accounts, 1541, 1542, *et seq.;* ERO, Woodbury CWA, 1543 *et seq.;* CRO, North Petherwin CWA, *passim;* Hanham, *Churchwardens' Accounts, passim;* Devon and Cornwall Record Society Library, Exeter, transcript, South Tawton CWA, *passim.*

[29]   Binney, *Accounts,* 73; transcript in the possession of Mr F.L. Harris, Anthony CWA, 69–86 (c.1543–5); BL Additional MS 32243, Stratton High Cross wardens' accounts, 1540–6.

[30]   G.H. Cook, *The English Mediaeval Parish Church,* (1954), 261.

[31]   G.W.O. Woodward, *The Dissolution of the Monasteries* (1966) 171, 172.

[32]   ERO, Woodbury CWA, 1546.

[33]   PRO, Chancery, Early Proceedings (C 1), 601/1 (1529–32); 631/4 (1529–32); 1228/63 (1547–51); Snell, *Cornwall,* 28, 53, 54; Snell, *Devon,* xxi, xxii, 25.

[34]   Cook, *Parish Church,* 262.

[35]   BL Additional MS 32243, Stratton High Cross wardens' accounts, 1547, 1548, *et seq..* The abnormal number of registrations in 1547 (20) may represent a panic-reaction to the advent of Protestant government; they were certainly the last at Stratton.

[36]   E.g. ERO, Exeter St Petrock CWA; ERO, Exeter St John's Bow CWA; DRO, Exeter Holy Trinity CWA; Hanham, *Churchwardens' Accounts, passim;* CRO, St Thomas-by-Launceston CWA; BL Additional MS 32244, Stratton Stockwardens' accounts; ERO, Woodbury CWA.

[37]   BL Additional MS 32244, Stratton Stockwardens' accounts, 1547, 1548, 1549; BL Additional MS 32243, Stratton High Cross wardens' accounts, 1549; CRO, St Thomas-by-Launceston CWA, 1548; CRO, North Petherwin CWA, fos. 28, 28v; Binney, *Accounts, passim;* ERO, Woodbury CWA, 1548, 1549, 1550; CRO, Camborne CWA, *passim;* transcript in the possession of Mr F.L. Harris, Antony CWA, *passim.*

[38]   CRO, North Petherwin CWA, fos. 3, 30–2. The erasure of the word

'bede-roll' from the 1548 account indicates its suppression in that year.

[39]   *Calendar of the Patent Rolls, Edward VI* (1924–9), II, 259.

[40]   C. Henderson, *Cornish Church Guide* (1925) 126.

[41]   PRO, Exchequer, Court of Augmentations, Proceedings (E 315), 122/15–28; above, 9.

[42]   PRO, Prerogative Court of Canterbury, Wills (PROB 11), 32, fo. 15*v;* DRO, Moger Abstracts of Devon Wills, 39, John Southwood, 1549.

[43]   PRO, Star Chamber Proceedings, Edward VI (STAC 3), 2/14.

[44]   ERO, Woodbury CWA, 1548, Binney, *Accounts*, 159.

[45]   BL, Royal MS 18 B XI, 'An Answer to the Articles'.

[46]   J. Strype (ed.), *Memorials of Archbishop Cranmer* (1848), II 502, 503.

[47]   R. Whiting, 'The Reformation in the South-West of England', unpublished Ph.D. thesis, Exeter University, 1977, 197–201; A. Fletcher, *Tudor Rebellions* (1973) 48–63.

[48]   DRO, Episcopal Registers, Veysey (RE XV), fos. 119*v*, 120; ERO, Woodbury CWA, 1550; BL Additional MS 32243, Stratton High Cross wardens' accounts, 1551; ERO, Dartmouth CWA 1552 (and page following).

[49]   Whiting, 'Reformation', 202–4.

[50]   ERO, Woodbury CWA, 1554; DRO, Chagford CWA, 1555; DRO, Braunton CWA, 1555; Binney, *Accounts*, 189.

[51]   Intercessions recorded: ERO, Exeter St Petrock CWA; ERO, Exeter St John's Bow CWA; DRO, Exeter Holy Trinity CWA; J.R. Chanter and T. Wainwright (eds.), *Reprint of the Barnstaple Records*, (1900) I, 212, 213; DRO, Chagford CWA; DRO, Crediton CWA; CRO, St Thomas-by-Launceston CWA; transcript in the possession of Mr F.L. Harris, Antony CWA; DRO, Braunton CWA; ERO, Dartington CWA; Binney *Accounts*, 175–202, *passim;* CRO, North Petherwin CWA; ERO, Woodbury CWA. Intercessions not recorded: ERO, Exeter St Mary Steps CWA; Hanham, *Churchwardens' Accounts,* 128–141, *passim;* CRO, Camborne CWA; ERO, Dartmouth CWA; BL Additional MS 32243, Stratton High Cross wardens' accounts; DRO, Coldridge CWA; R. Cornish, ed., *The Churchwardens' Accounts of Kilmington, 1555–1608* (1901), *passim;* J. Phear (ed.), 'Molland Accounts', *Transactions of the Devonshire Association* (1903), *passim;* Devon and Cornwall Record Society Library, Exeter, transcript, South Tawton CWA.

[52]   DRO, Braunton CWA, 1555–9. Cf. DRO, Chagford CWA; CRO, St Thomas-by Launceston CWA; transcript in the possession of Mr F.L. Harris, Antony CWA; CRO, North Petherwin CWA; ERO, Woodbury CWA.

[53]   CRO, North Petherwin CWA, fos. 3*v*, 4; BL Additional MS 32243, Stratton High Cross wardens' accounts, 1553–9.

[54]   PRO, Prerogative Court of Canterbury, Wills (PROB 11), 39, fo. 203; DRO, Consistory Court Book 855A, fos. 311*v*, 312.

[55]   DRO, Moger Abstracts of Devon Wills, 13, Robert Easton, 1559.

[56]   ERO, Book 51 (John Hooker, Commonplace Book), fo. 352.

[57]   DRO, Coldridge CWA, 1560; ERO, Woodbury CWA, 1559.

[58]   Whiting, 'Reformation', 212, 213, 224, 225.

[59]   PRO, Prerogative Court of Canterbury, Wills (PROB 11), 50, fo. 152*v*.

[60]   PRO, Prerogative Court of Canterbury, Wills (PROB 11), 44, fo. 159*v*.

[61]   ERO, Exeter St Petrock CWA; ERO, Exeter St John's Bow CWA; ERO, Exeter St Mary Steps CWA; Hanham, *Churchwardens' Accounts*, 141–166, *passim;* DRO, Crediton CWA; ERO, Dartington CWA; Cornish, *Kilmington, passim;* ERO, Woodbury CWA.

[62]   DRO, Chagford CWA, 1560–70; DRO, Braunton CWA, 1560–70; CRO, North Petherwin CWA, fos. 4, 4*v*.

[63] DRO, Chagford CWA, 1560–70; ERO, Chudleigh CWA, 1561.

[64] BL, Royal MS 18 B XI, 'An Answer to the Articles', fos. 25–26; BL Reading Room 4404 B 61, P. Nichols, *A Godly New Story* (1548) 47.

[65] DRO, Consistory Court Books 41, 775, 776, 777, 778, 779, 854 (I,II), 854A (I,II), 855, 855A, 855B, 856.

[66] DRO, Episcopal Registers, Oldham (RE XIII), fos. 144v, 145, 179v–181.

[67] Foxe, *Acts and Monuments*, II, 1039, 2050–2052.

[68] PRO, Prerogative Court of Canterbury, Wills (PROB 11), 26, fo. 79v; 27, fo. 4v.

[69] PRO, Prerogative Court of Canterbury, Wills (PROB 11), 28, fo. 149; F. 44 Alen; Devon and Cornwall Record Society Library, Exeter, Oswyn Murray Abstracts of Wills, 3, John Bougin, 1548. For the Protestant minority under Edward VI, Whiting, 'Reformation', p. 182.

[70] PRO, Prerogative Court of Canterbury, Wills (PROB 11), 33, fo. 155; 34, fos. 154v, 225; 35, fo. 169; 36, fo. 20v; 44, fo. 274.

[71] For his sponsorship of Protestant preaching, Whiting, 'Reformation', p. 74.

[72] PRO, Prerogative Court of Canterbury, Wills (PROB 11), 37, fos. 144, 178; 41, fo. 243; 42A.

[73] PRO, Prerogative Court of Canterbury, Wills (PROB 11), 45, fo. 60v; 46, fos. 128v, 258v; 48, fo. 459v.

The Dispersal of Chantry Lands in Somerset

G. WOODWARD

Although the condition of the English chantries at the dissolution has been the subject of a recent study[1] and the chantry certificates of at least twenty-six counties have been printed, historians have shown little interest in examining the consequences of the dissolution. In 1970 Christopher Kitching studied the administration and disposal of chantry property in the diocese and county of York during the reign of Edward VI and in 1980 the present writer examined the dissolution of the Somerset chantries for the period 1548 to 1603.[2] Apart from these two pieces of research, there has been no detailed study of the disposal of chantry land.[3] The purpose of this essay is to examine the disposal of chantry land and property in Somerset between 1548 and 1603 and, where possible, to identify the new owners and secondary purchasers.[4]

A chantry was an endowment — usually in real estate but occasionally in cash or goods — for a priest to sing a mass for the repose of the founders and of specified persons at an altar of a church or chapel. At the dissolution in 1547, Somerset possessed 108 chantries, twenty-one free chapels, thirty-two chapels, four hospitals, one chantry school, nineteen guilds and fraternities, one college and 258 obits and lights.[5] These were founded in cathedrals, churches, chapels, churchyards, schools, castles and manor houses, endowed by individual benefactors and collective corporations and appear to have been evenly distributed throughout the county with 51 per cent of all parishes possessing at least one foundation at the dissolution.[6] When the Crown carried out a survey of its new possessions at Easter 1548, it discovered that the property in Somerset was worth £733 13s 11½d per annum.[7] If all outgoing rents and rents which were incorrectly included in the survey are deducted from this figure, the Crown had at its disposal chantry property valued at £628 1s 8½d per annum. In the course of the next fifty-five years, 6 per cent was granted away in gifts and exchanges and a further 75 per cent was alienated in sales, four-fifths of which occurred in Edward VI's reign when the Crown was faced first with a war and then an economic crisis. At

Michaelmas 1603 the Crown held less than 20 per cent of its original chantry property valued at £117 14s 9d.[8]

Before considering the identity of the new owners of chantry lands and property, an examination albeit brief of the source material is essential. The principal source for a study of the dissolution of the chantries is the Patent Rolls, a collection of documents at the Public Record Office which contains the names of grantees, dates of enrolment, amounts paid, rents, reprises, tenants and conditions of each grant.[9] As far as Somerset is concerned, seventy-six patents have survived containing the names of 116 different grantees. Over 80 per cent of these men lived or worked in London as officials of the royal household, court and privy council, like William Manne, Sir William Paulet and George Cotton; employees at the Court of Augmentations such as John Dodington, John Grene and Richard Duke; lawyers like Edward Stanhope and Robert Wood; merchants like Andrew Salter and Robert Thomas; MP.s such as William Morgan and John Aylworth, or were wealthy gentlemen like William Breton, Thomas Cecill, Henry Codenham and William Wynlove. Each of these men was well placed to negotiate chantry sales with the Crown.

Two-thirds of all Somerset grants were made to groups of two or three men who probably combined together to raise the large sums of money — usually in excess of £1000 — for properties which in most cases were located the length and breadth of the country. Thomas Reve and George Cotton, for example, received a grant worth £1877 in March 1553 containing lands in twenty-five counties; the chantry property in Somerset — Backwell land and a chapel at Dundry — amounted to less than 0.1 per cent of the total grant.[10] Similarly, in July 1563 John Gifford and Robert Hitchcock acquired lands in sixteen counties for £2295 but their chantry possessions at Ilminster accounted for just £21 (or 0.3 per cent) of the grant.[11]

For many years historians believed that the names contained in the patent rolls were the real purchasers of the grants who had acquired composite grants of widely dispersed land as speculators.[12] In the 1950s, however, Professor H.J. Habakkuk and Miss Joyce Youings demonstrated that the patentees were often London agents acting on behalf of clients in the country.[13] Shortly after the letters patent were granted, the grant was broken down into its constituent parts and each parcel of land was conveyed to its prospective owner. More recent studies have confirmed the danger of placing too much dependence upon the patent rolls as a method of identifying the real owners.[14] Significantly, of sixty-six new owners of Somerset lands who can be identified with a degree of certainty, only twenty performed the role of patentees.

A second source of material is the collection among the records of the Court of Augmentations known as the Particulars for Grants.[15] These documents contain the value of individual chantry properties, the rate or purchase price determined by the commissioners for sales and the name of the person for whom the rating was made (for convenience sake he may be termed the 'ratee'). The ratee's role in the transaction was to negotiate the purchase price and, as such, he usually had a personal interest in securing the best possible terms. As far as Somerset is concerned, at least thirty-six out of ninety-five ratees appear to have been prospective owners. However, over 40 per cent of the Somerset ratees lived or worked in London and, like many of the patentees, were well placed to conduct sales on behalf of clients. John Bellowe, Laurence Hyde, Giles Keylway, Jerome Halley, Thomas Reve and Richard Roberts, for example, appear to have acted as agents or attorneys in the transactions and were not the actual purchasers of chantry property in Somerset. In a recent study of the disposal of Somerset monastic land, Miss Katherine Wyndham stated that 'It does not appear possible, as a general rule, to consider the ratee the more likely purchaser than the patentee',[16] an opinion which may equally apply to the disposal of chantry property in the county.

The true identity of the new owners is further obscured by the fact that most chantry land was small in size and value and therefore hard to trace and because a royal licence was not required to alienate crown lands held in socage.[17] However, a statute of 1536 did require the enrolment of land sales either in 'one of the King's Courts of Record at Westminster, or else within the county where the lands lie', and these documents often reveal the names of the purchasers.[18] Occasionally, references occur in the records of the Courts of Chancery, King's Bench, Star Chamber and Augmentations, and even less frequently among wills and *inquisitions post mortem*.[19] In some cases estate papers have survived containing rentals, surveys, deeds of lease, sale and conveyance and, in two cases, the original letters patent.[20]

While all the above sources have been examined, it has only been possible to identify sixty-six new owners whose properties comprised some 56 per cent of all Somerset chantry grants. Although the names of all the remaining patentees and ratees are known, no firm conclusion can be reached as to the identity of the purchasers.

One would expect, perhaps, the largest and most valuable parcels of chantry land to have been bought by wealthy local landowners, but in fact only three members of the aristocracy are known to have purchased Somerset property and each held his main estates outside the county. Francis Hastings, first earl of Huntingdon, for example, held estates and manors in fourteen counties centred on Leicestershire. Described perhaps not unfairly as 'an opportunist on the alert to promote his own interest',[21] in 1550 he paid £146 8s for Aller chantry lands which formed part of his Somerset manorial estates. He appears to have personally conducted the grant through its transaction : in the course of 1548 he asked William Cecil, secretary to the duke of Somerset, to reserve the lands for him; on 6 December 1548 he appeared before the commissioners for sale, over a year later on 24 December 1549 he paid the Treasurer £996 for this and other lands and on 2 January 1550 he and Thomas Hasilwood, a Leicester landowner, were in receipt of the letters patent.[22] A Staffordshire peer, Sir George Audley of Helley Castle, paid nearly £300 for twenty-three parcels of land in Taunton in August 1548 and May 1549. Each of his two grants was initially acquired by centrally placed agents : John Browne and William Twysden, and William Breton and Humphrey Luce.[23] Although Audley held lands in the county, these properties may have been conveyed to Sir John Tuchet, Lord Audley, who was granted Stowey manor by the Crown in 1553.[24] Sir William Paulet, marquis of Winchester and Lord Treasurer to Edward VI, Mary and Elizabeth, held estates mainly in Hampshire and Wiltshire. In 1561 he bought a house and garden in Nunney and two cottages and 3¼ acres in Trudoxhill, valued at £7 10s 4d per annum, which formerly had provided endowments to Nunney Chantry.[25]

Six new chantry landowners held the rank of 'knight', three of whom resided in Somerset. By far the most important was Sir Hugh Paulet whose estates lay in the south of the county around Hinton St. George. Assessed in the lay subsidy of 1551 at £200 in lands, he served Somerset as a J.P., M.P. and on two occasions as its sheriff.[26] On 6 March 1549 he paid nearly £198 for 200 acres in Curry Mallet and Crewkerne, which had formerly been endowed to the chantries in Langport, Crewkerne and Curry Mallet. Each of these properties was conveyed to Paulet by Laurence Hyde fourteen days after the Crown granted the letters patent.[27] Sir Thomas Dyer lived at Sharpham, was M.P. for Bridgwater in 1544, 1553 and 1559, sheriff of Somerset in 1559 and, like Paulet, had served as a chantry commissioner for Somerset and Dorset in

1548.[28] In 1554 he paid nearly £80 for Woolavington and Weston chantry lands, acquiring his patent on 11 June from the grantees, William Morgan of Monmouth, M.P., and Jerome Halley of London. They had held the patent for less than twenty four hours.[29] The third Somerset knight to acquire chantry land was Sir John Horsey who bought 30 acres of arable and 8 acres of meadow formerly endowed to Charlton Mackrell Chantry. Although these lands were sold to Thomas Bell of Gloucester and Richard Duke of London in 1548, neither appears to have received them as Horsey claimed they formed part of his manor of Cary Fitzpaine.[30]

Three knights lived outside the county. Sir John Thynne, a Wiltshire and Somerset J.P. and sheriff of Somerset and Dorset in 1548–9, bought extensive lands in Somerset and Wiltshire where at Longleat he established his family estates.[31] In August 1548 he bought properties belonging to four chantries at Frome, Cannington, Croscombe and East Horrington, valued at £36 9s 6½d per annum, together with woods worth £4 14s 4d, for which he paid nearly £730.[32] The lands at Croscombe, East Horrington and Frome were rated for him by two servants, Thomas Byflete and Thomas Chaffyn on 7 June, whereas Idstoke Free Chapel in Cannington was rated by Thynne himself on 27 June 1548.[33] When he took possession of East Horrington Free Chapel, he discovered that the county surveyor, William Moryce, had over-assessed its rental value by 6s 8d for which Thynne claimed a £7 rebate from the Crown. Although he has been described as a covetous man 'obsessed with money', on this occasion he was fully justified and the Court of Augmentations duly awarded him the money.[34] Another Wiltshire landowner and J.P. was Sir William Sharington from Lacock who bought Knowle Free Chapel, Bedminster in 1550, valued at £3 6s 8d per annum. In 1548 he served on the chantry commission for Bristol where until 1551 he was Master of the Mint.[35] Perhaps these connections explain his interest in this chantry property. The chapel and its site were purchased for him by a business associate Richard Roberts of London, who received its rating on 8 December 1549 and its letters patent on 9 January 1550 before conveying it to Sharington on the following day.[36] Sir Roger Blewet came from Holcombe Rogus in Devon and served Somerset and Devon as a J.P. in Edward VI's reign. In 1549 he bought two cottages and 24 acres at Newton Placy for £35 1s 4d and one year later nine burgages and 5 acres at North Petherton for £83 13s 8d.[37]

Most new owners of Somerset chantry property were gentry and esquires living in the county. Some were lords of the manor like

William Hodges, John Horner and John Payne. In 1549 Hodges of Middle Chinnock bought the chantry house in Charlton Adam. The auditor noted at the time of the sale that Hodges 'claims this house saying that he has bought the same house by general words of the King's majesty'.[38] The most likely explanation of this wording is that Hodges claimed that the house which adjourned the rectory formed part of the manor of Charlton Adam which he had bought from the King in 1546.[39] Nevertheless, he was obliged to pay £4 for the house which, according to the particulars, was an increase of £1 on its valuation.[40] The Horner family from Cloford had bought land and acquired leases to monastic property in the 1540's. In November 1548 John Horner paid over £357 for lands in Ashwick, Kilmersdon, Shepton Mallet, Stoke St. Michael, Holcombe, Yeovil, Elleston, Barwick and Stoford which had provided the endowments to the Trinity and St. John the Baptist Fraternity in Shepton Mallet. In addition, he bought 90 acres of woodland in Kilmersdon for £9.[41] Horner's grant was the most valuable Somerset chantry property alienated by Edward VI. John Payne from Hutton in the north-west of Somerset was lord of Christon manor who purchased chantry land at Christon, Cheddar, Loxton and Sandford for £125. He most probably took possession of these lands in July 1548 when the patent was granted by the Crown to Robert Norton of Suffolk, although a licence to re-grant the lands to Payne was not recorded until 13 May 1551.[42]

Several local gentry acquired chantry property which was located near to or adjoining their own lands. In December 1549 George Payne paid over £172 for lands at Alston Sutton, Axbridge, Badgworth, Blagdon, Cheddar and Winscombe, not far from his home at Hutton.[43] Elizabeth Fitzjames was a wealthy Temple Combe widow who held at the dissolution the lease to South Cheriton Free Chapel, worth £1 6s 8d per annum. The property appears to have been rated on her behalf by James Fitzjames of Redlinch in May 1548, granted to Laurence Hyde on 6 March 1549 and then coveyed to Elizabeth.[44] Robert Hyatt was a prosperous Street landowner who bought extensive crown lands in central Somerset in 1554, including over 60 acres of chantry land at Curry Rivel valued at £3 6s 8d a year.[45] Chantry lands in North Curry, valued at £8 11s 5½d per annum, were bought in two grants in 1548 and 1549 by a Lillesdon gentleman, William Lyte, for £121 11s.[46] In 1555–6, however, a court action arose concerning his right to possess Nythe chantry lands. John Newton and Gregory Rowsewell, representing the inhabitants of North Curry, claimed that the lands should have been exempt from dissolution since no chantry priest had ministered there since 1543. Lyte denied these accusations stating that a priest had served there 'from time to time' and that any money left over from the annual rent of £4 15s, once the priest had deducted his salary, went towards the repair of bridges and 'any manner of harness or other common charges'.[47] The court appears to have dismissed the complaint as Lyte continued to hold the disputed chantry property until his death in 1559.[48] Two other families who extended their estates by acquiring chantry lands were the Phelipps' of Montacute and the Wroths of Newton Placy. In 1553 Thomas Phelipps, esquire, bought a chapel, church house and 30 acres of land at Shepton Beauchamp, Foddington and East Pennard at a cost of £55. Although the properties were intially granted to two London agents William Breton and William Webb on 24 February 1553, within two days they had been conveyed to Thomas Duport, a local landowner, who subsequently transferred them to Phelipps on 14 May 1553.[49] The Wroth family had held the office of keeper of Newton Placy park and farmer of the chantry tithes since the dissolution. In 1590 Richard Wroth appears to have asked William Wroth, an Essex gentleman, to acquire the unsold chantry lands worth £3 17s per annum on his behalf. On 1 February 1592 they were duly conveyed to William by the patentees John Wells and Hercules Witham, renowned London land agents.[50]

Several new owners were emerging as important figures in local politics. Nicholas Halleswell, a J.P. from Goathurst, served as M.P. for Bridgwater in both Mary's and Elizabeth's reign. Assessed in the 1549 subsidy at £80 in goods, he bought two tenements and 40 acres of chantry land at Chedzoy, Cossington, Huntspill and Taunton, worth £3 1s 8d per annum.[51] John Norres, M.P. for Taunton in 1554, bought his local chantry chapel at West Monkton for £2 13s 4d in 1549.[52] A Bridgwater landowner, William Halley, who became a J.P. in Elizabeth's reign, acquired chantry property in the town valued at £2 10s in 1553[53] and Humphrey Colles, J.P. for Devon and Somerset and sheriff of Dorset and Somerset in 1557, purchased a chantry house in Ilminster, a tenement and chapel in Taunton and a chapel in Milverton for £26 12s in 1549.[54] Humphrey Walrond came from Sea near Ilminster and worked as an attorney to the sheriffs of the south-west counties in the Court of Chancery. On 16 May 1549 he and Henry Greenfield of Ilminster paid £126 to Giles Keylway of Dorset and William Leonard of Taunton for three leases to several Ilminster chantry lands. Keylway and Leonard, who received the royal grant on 2 April, most probably acted as agents on behalf of Walrond and Greenfield; on 18 May the Ilminster men donated the lands for the establishment of a new grammar school in the town.[55] Between 1552 and 1563 Walrond acquired five more grants comprising nearly 200 acres of former chantry land centred on Ilminster at a cost of over £326. Each of his grants was obtained by deeds of conveyance; none was rated or patented in his name. On three occasions in 1552, 1553 and 1563, the rating and patenting was done for him by Thomas Reve, an employee at the Court of Augmentations; the remaining grants were acquired for him in 1554 by Jerome Halley, clerk of the petty bag of Chancery, and in 1557 by Henry Simson, a local landowner.[56] Walrond was still in possession of these properties at his death in 1580.[57] The St. Barbe family, who had their estates at Ashington, served at the court in the royal household. William St. Barbe, a groom of the chamber, acquired Yeovilton Free Chapel in 1550 for £45 16s 8d.[58] In the same year his eldest son Edward, who served in Edward VI's household, bought a chantry house, garden and stable in Trent for £8.[59] John Reynon, the deputy auditor for Somerset, and his brother Peter held land at Chewton Mendip and West Coker; in 1554 they bought three messuages, three cottages, six orchards, 91 acres, a chapel and a croft in East Coker. The Crown first granted the property to Edward Nevill, lord of East Coker manor, on 17 December 1554 in part exchange for lands in Kent; three days later, he conveyed the Somerset property to the Reynons for £80.[60]

A number of gentry, who were living outside the county at the time of their purchase, already held Somerset property. John Cleves, for example, was a Dorset gentleman who combined with a Kingston yeoman, John Dyrdo, in 1564 to buy six properties in Yeovil worth £4 6s per annum.[61] In 1591 Thomas Freke of Dorset and Richard Swayne of Kingston, each of whom held lands on the Somerset-Dorset border, bought a burgage in Yeovil valued at 10s a year.[62] Richard Duke and John Aylworth worked at the Court of Augmentations and were principally Devon men. Duke, who was clerk to the court, had acquired several crown lands in Somerset in Henry VIII's reign and served Devon, Dorset and Somerset as a J.P. in 1547. In August 1548 he bought Einston Farm in Henstridge, which had provided part of the endowments of St. Katherine's Chantry, Ilminster, for £96.[63] Aylworth, the Crown's receiver for the south-west region, acquired lands in Devon and Somerset in the 1540's and 1550's before settling in Wells, where he was M.P. from 1557 to 1572. Although in 1548 he received with William Lacy of Shepton Mallet a grant comprising seven Somerset chantries, he is only known to have retained the lands and possessions of Mountroy College, Wells, worth £15 0s 4d a year, most of which he still held at his death in 1574.[64] It seems probable that the remaining lands in Combe Florey, Bawdrip, Portbury, Sherston and Yeovil were either acquired by Lacy or, as in the case of Norton Hawkfield, re-granted to local tenants.[65] John Bowyer, a bailiff of the honour of Petworth, Sussex, also bought Somerset chantry land and subsequently settled in the county. He first acquired property in 1553 when he bought monastic land in Bridgwater and Stoke sub Hamdon and chantry land in Chewton Mendip. By the time he received Cannington manor in 1557, his family was well established in Somerset.[66]

Many purchasers were small landowners who bought local parcels of chantry property. John Easton, for example, acquired a house, garden and 4 acres of land in Limington in 1549 for £8 16s. He most probably took possession of his property in advance of the date of enrolment as the conveyance was not recorded in the Court of Chancery by the patentees, Gibbes and Were, until 14 July 1552.[67] John Maundry, a yeoman from Beercrocombe, bought 5 acres in 1549 for £14 13s 4d from the grantee, Laurence Hyde, who had received his patent some nine months before.[68] William Coke, the Crown's farmer of Catcott chantry tithes, acquired in 1551 a house, garden and 24 acres, including the site of Catcott chapel, for £16.[69] Although one can only speculate upon his motives in acquiring the chapel, several villagers had little doubt that his intentions were far from good. Their suspicions were confirmed when he told them that they could no longer use the chapel and prevented them from entering by appearing at the door with a 'hand-gun charged upon his shoulder and his servant with a forest bill'. Then, in April 1552, he proceeded to dismantle the chapel, stone by stone, until nothing remained.[70] Although Coke subsequently defended his action on the grounds that the chapel was a free chapel and legally belonged to him, the Court of Star Chamber upheld the plea from the incumbent and parishioners that the chapel was really a chapel of ease and should not have been dissolved in the first place. Coke was therefore ordered to restore the chapel in 'as good estate as it was when he pulled it down'.[71] Despite further protests, litigation, and a spell of thirteen months in prison, Coke reluctantly rebuilt the chapel and, rather surprisingly, recovered his office as the Crown's collector of chantry tithes in Catcott.[72]

Some new owners were tenants of chantry land who took the opportunity to purchase their property. John Michell, the former chantry priest of Our Mary in the Churchyard at Crewkerne, acquired his house, garden and orchard from the patentees, John Whitehorne and John Bayly of Chard, for an undisclosed amount.[73] John Collyns paid over £20 for 26 acres of land, 2 acres of pasture and 6½ acres of meadow in East Coker on 26 July 1549; he received his grant from chantry land agents, Hugh and Thomas Pomeroy, five days after the letters patent were first granted by the Crown.[74] Robert and Elizabeth Wyther held a house in Taunton worth 10s a year which they bought for £5 in 1549. They received it on 7 May from a Taunton merchant, William Leonard, who had himself acquired it on 6 May from the patentees, Nicholas and Roger Prideaux.[75] In 1549 Robert Freke, a Crewkerne man, employed two Kent agents, Were and Gibbes, to acquire on his behalf the chapel in the churchyard at Yeovil, for which he paid £4.[76] At Long Load, a local landowner Robert Dyer bought the chapel, cottage and 2 acres for a 'certain sum of money' on 25 May 1549. Although the villagers were apparently not prepared to defray any of Dyer's costs, he placed the chapel and its property 'in trust to the use of the said inhabitants'.[77] At nearby South Petherton, John Kingman paid £3 4s for his 4 acres of land in 1549, which he and three other tenants held at the dissolution.[78]

Wealthy Somerset merchants figure prominently among the purchasers of town property. John Whitehorne and John Bayly from Chard bought all the town's chantry property valued at £20 12s 4d for £406 3s 4d in August 1548.[79] Each of the forty-five parcels of property was purchased on behalf of local inhabitants many of whom were chantry tenants at the dissolution. Although only one deed of conveyance has survived, the inhabitants appear to have received their property by buying it directly from the grantees.[80] For example, on 31 August 1548, twelve days after the granting of the letters patent, William Moryn paid Whitehorne and Bayly £13 6s 8d for a burgage and an unnamed property, worth 10s and 6s 8d per annum respectively.[81] Much of the chantry property in Yeovil was bought by a local merchant, Giles Hayne from Kingston-next-Yeovil, who paid over £271 in 1564 for seventeen parcels of land.[82] William Gifford, a well-to-do Wellington mercer, paid over £34 in 1549 for most of the chantry properties situated in and around the town.[83] Three merchants — William Leonard, William Chaplyn and William Horsey — bought properties in Taunton in 1549. Leonard received two grants on 1 May and 26 May for eighteen burgages, tenements and shops overlooking the market, valued at £7 6s 8d per annum.[84] Chaplyn, who rated several particulars for Leonard, acquired a burgage and a plot of land worth 13s 8d a year, while Horsey bought three burgages in

North Street valued at £3 13s 4d a year.[85] According to a Taunton rental *circa* 1555, Leonard, Chaplyn and Horsey appear to have sub-let most of their property to the pre-dissolution tenants.[86] John Smythe, on the other hand, was a Bristol merchant who bought lands which were formerly part of his manor of Long Ashton. On 18 April 1549 he paid nearly £290 for Chocke's Chantry and Meryatte's Chapel in Long Ashton, and a further £6 for chantry lands in Gloucestershire.[87]

Institutions as well as individuals acquired chantry lands. In May 1550, 30 acres of land at Simondsbury in south Dorset worth £2 per annum, which had provided part of the revenue for St. Katherine's Chantry, Ilminster, over 800 acres in Dorset worth £14 15s per annum and a house in Martock worth 4d per annum which together had comprised the entire endowments of Martock Chantry, were granted as a gift by the Crown to help found Sherborne School.[88] In Mary's reign, the Crown made two further gifts of Somerset chantry land: in May 1554 twenty-four properties in Bridgwater worth £10 2s 8d a year were given to the mayor and burgesses, and in November 1556 Blackford Free Chapel in Wedmore, which carried an annual rent of £6, was granted to the master of the Savoy Hospital in London.[89]

While most chantry property appears to have remained in the hands of local inhabitants and landowners, at least thirteen primary purchasers seem to have had no previous connection with the county. Three new owners lived in Devon and Wiltshire and acquired lands which, although formerly endowed to Somerset chantries, lay outside the county. William Hurst was a very wealthy merchant and landowner from Exeter who in 1563 bought property in Salcombe, worth 14s a year, which had provided part of the endowments of St. Katherine's Chantry, Ilminster.[90] The Wiltshire property comprised a messuage in East Knoyle valued at £5 4s 11d per annum, which had formed part of the endowments of Compton Pauncefoot Chantry. On 20 August 1548 William Hunston and his wife, Melior, from East Knoyle, purchased the property for a little over £135.[91] At least ten purchasers came from London. Little is known about John Hyndemonds who acquired a meadow, five tenements, two burgages, three shambles, two windows and seven shops in Taunton, and a burgage in Frome. The grant, which was valued at £13 14s per annum, was conveyed to him on 17 December 1549 by the patentee, Edward Bury of Essex, who had received the letters patent the previous day.[92] Bridget Skipwith, a gentlewoman of the Queen's Chamber, bought land in Harberton, Devon, in 1560 for £50, which was formerly endowed to St. Katherine's Chantry, Ilminster.[93] Queen Elizabeth was not averse to rewarding her servants with grants of chantry land: in January 1576, John Dudley and John Ayscough acquired lands at Curry Rivel, Langford Budville, Milborne Port and Yeovil, as well as chapels at Ilchester, Upton and Knowle.[94] In March 1577 John Fortescue, a groom of the chamber, and John Walker received a gift of chantry land at Wellington worth £2 0s 4d per annum.[95] In July 1577 Henry Campion, a London mercer, and his son William acquired 24 acres of land in Bridgwater worth £1 10s per annum from Sir James Croft, the comptroller of the household, who had first received them from the Crown for his 'many services'.[96] Finally, on 27 June 1600 Michael and Edward Stanhope, grooms of the Queen's Chamber, paid £639 13s 4d for Whitehall Free Chapel, the most valuable Somerset property to be alienated by the Tudors.[97]

The main recipients, then, appear to have been the local gentry, merchants and small landowners. Some were former tenants; others acquired property for the first time or extended their estates. Very few new owners were major landowners in Somerset or neighbouring counties. It seems likely that the predominantly small parcels of land held little attraction to anyone living outside Somerset who did not already hold property in the county.

Records have survived for at least twenty-one Somerset chantry properties which were re-sold in the post-dissolution period. All but one of the secondary purchasers were existing chantry tenants or held land locally. John Drewe, for example, a yeoman-tenant of Charlton Mackrell chantry property, acquired the freehold from Sir John Horsey in 1553.[98] At Norton Hawkfield, Arthur and Margaret Payton of Chew Magna bought a chapel, 4 acres of arable, 1 acre of pasture and all tithes valued collectively at £1 6s 8d per annum, from John Aylworth and William Lacy. Shortly after the death of her husband, Margaret sold the property to her cousin John Molde in 1555.[99] Another tenant who bought the freehold to his own property was William Hodges of Middle Chinnock. In November 1550 he paid William St. Barbe £64 for 55 acres of land, appurtenances and tithes in Speckington, which had formerly provided the endowments of Yeovilton Free Chapel.[100] St. Barbe had held the lands for less than a year and seems to have made a profit of nearly £20 on the sale.

Sir Hugh Paulet was a Somerset landowner who disposed of his three grants of chantry property within fourteen months of receiving them. On 9 May 1550 he sold 81 acres in Curry Mallet, worth £1 6s 8d per annum, to a local husbandman John Hawker.[101]

Three days later, Paulet sold his chantry lands in Crewkerne to James Downham, a Chillington yeoman, for £126, thus realising a profit of £11 3s 4d.[102] Finally, on 28 May he disposed of 55 acres in Curry Mallet to Richard Palpytte, a local husbandman, for £80.[103] Paulet's profit on this sale was £28 18s 10d. In 1554 Dundry Chapel was bought by the feoffees (one of whom was a certain Mr Peyton) from two Wraxall landowners, Cocks and Tynte,[104] and local landowners also acquired chantry property at Nunney, Newton Placy and Ilchester. In 1573 William Paulet's son alienated his lands in Nunney to Swythune Thorp,[105] and at Newton Placy Roger Blewet's possessions passed first to his son, John, in 1566 and then to a fellow Devonian, Arthur Basset, in 1575.[106] At Ilchester, some of the endowments of Whitehall Free Chapel were alienated by Michael and Edward Stanhope of London although they appear to have kept most of the original grant. In February 1603 William Raymond of Ilchester bought a messuage, garden and close, which he held for two years,[107] and in January 1605 Edward Phelips of Montacute paid £73 6s 8d for 11 acres of meadow and the site of the free chapel.[108]

Former chantry lands which lay outside the county and which were first purchased by non-Somerset inhabitants, passed to natives of Devon and Wiltshire. Chantry land in Harberton, Devon, for example, which was first acquired by Bridget Skipwith of London in 1560, was sold in 1564 to an Exeter merchant, William Hurst, for £95.[109] Whether or not Bridget bought this land primarily as an investment, she realised a profit of £45 in four years. At East Knoyle, William and Melior Hunston sold their tenement worth £5 4s 11d per annum to fellow Wiltshire residents Robert Somerfield, John Apprice and Nicholas Morgan in 1570.[110]

In those cases where records of secondary sales have survived, most properties changed hands within a few years of the first sale and, where purchase prices were recorded, profits of varying amounts appear to have been made by the primary purchaser. The re-sale of chantry property at North Curry, East Coker and Wells, however, suggests that it would be unwise to draw any firm conclusions on the basis of a small number of extant documents. At North Curry, for example, property was sold to pay off debts and not to make a profit. In 1548 and 1549 William Lyte bought two grants of chantry land from the Crown worth £8 11s 5½d per annum. When he died in 1559, he left substantial debts which his executors, Thomas Lyte and John Forster, decided should be met by selling some of his chantry land. In January 1560 they sold a tenement in Lyng to an Ilminster draper, Hugh Isacks, for £6 13s

4d, and four months later disposed of the remaining chantry land in North Curry to a London clothworker, Robert Howse, for £110.[111] The executors, then, received over £116 from these two sales which represented a profit of only 6 per cent on the original purchase price. Since the 1550's was a decade of rampant inflation, it would not be unreasonable to suggest that little if any real profit was made in the course of these transactions. At East Coker, financial difficulties accounted for at least two of the three conveyances of chantry land which occurred between February 1555 and April 1588. On 21 November 1560 Edward Baeshe, lord of West Coker manor and servant of the Queen, purchased 91 acres from John and Peter Reynon but within a year he had run into debt and was forced to sell the entire property to Francis Whitton, a local landowner from Pendomer.[112] He held the property, together with 20 acres of chantry land in West Coker, for twenty-six years until in April 1588 he, too, was in financial straits and sold 18 acres of his East Coker land to a tenant, John Giles, for £160.[113] Profits may have been made in the course of these transactions but the motive behind the sales appears to have been solvency rather than speculation.

The secondary and subsequent sales of Mountroy College, Wells, well illustrate the length and continuity of ownership of some chantry properties. In the course of sixty years the site of the college changed hands on only three occasions and each time the new owner was a local man. The college and its property, valued at £15 0s 4d per annum, were first granted to John Aylworth in August 1548 for £268 9s.[114] Aylworth subsequently settled in Wells and retained his chantry possessions for at least twenty-one years. In 1569 he alienated the mansion, orchard, garden and stables, valued at £1 6s 8d per annum, to John Bridgwater, a canon of Wells Cathedral for £55, thus realising a profit of £23. Five years later, Bridgwater sold this property to a local landowner, David Jones, for £71. On Jones' death in 1581 his son, Anthony, sold it to Arthur Collinge of Lympsham for £112 and he retained it until 1607.[115] Only Anthony Jones appears to have made a substantial profit: his sales price represented an increase of 57 per cent on the value of his property over a period of seven years.

Most secondary purchasers, then, lived in Somerset or adjacent counties and were predominantly lesser gentry, merchants, husbandmen and yeomen. Although only two secondary owners, William Hodges and William Hurst, also bought chantry lands at first hand, the practice of tenants buying their freehold at secondhand may have been more widespread than the three documented cases suggest. It is, however, impossible to determine the reasons behind most sales and equally difficult to ascertain in an age of inflation what profit, if any, was made in the process. The surviving documents reveal that fourteen properties changed hands at least once within a few years of the primary sale, while others are known to have remained in the possession of primary owners until their death and then inherited by their families.[116]

In conclusion, it appears that nearly all new owners were local men. Some were chantry tenants at the dissolution with sufficient resources to acquire their own plot of land and occasionally their neighbours' as well. A few purchasers were merchants eager to invest their trading assets in landed property, but most owners came from landowning families in the county who had valuable contacts at the court or in local government. Only a handful of primary owners lived outside Somerset, and within a few years these had either sold their property to local residents or had settled permanently in the county. Since the procedure for purchasing crown lands was at times lengthy, expensive and complex, especially for those men who had a limited knowledge of the machinery of the Exchequer or who exercised little influence within the court or who lived a long way from London, most purchasers relied upon a friend, business associate or London agent to act for them as their ratee and patentee and received the letters patent by conveyance after the completion of the sale. Although small profits appear to have been made on most re-sales of chantry property, purchasers seem to have bought lands with the intention of retaining them. However, the evidence is insufficient to draw any firm conclusions as to either the motive behind such purchases or the extent to which profits were made.

Notes

[1]   A. Kreider, *English Chantries: the Road to Dissolution* (Harvard, 1979).

[2]   C.J. Kitching, 'Studies in the Redistribution of Collegiate and Chantry Property in the Diocese and County of York at the Dissolution' (unpub. Ph.D. thesis, Durham Univ. 1970); G.H. Woodward, 'The Dissolution of the Chantries in the County of Somerset' (unpub. M.Litt. thesis, Bristol Univ. 1980).

[3]   The disposal of non-chantry crown land in Somerset was examined by Miss Katherine Wyndham in 'The Redistribution of Crown Land in Somerset by Gift, Sale and Lease, 1536–72' (unpub. Ph.D. thesis, London Univ. 1976) and 'The Royal Estate in Mid-sixteenth Century Somerset', *Bulletin of the Institute of Historical Research*, L11 (1979), pp. 129 ff.

[4]   Chantry property, which was concealed from the Crown at the dissolution but subsequently discovered and alienated, has not been considered in this essay.

[5] These figures are more accurate than those compiled by William Camden in 1607 or by William Archbold in 1892. Camden believed there were two hospitals, one college and ninety-six chantries and free chapels: B(ritish) L(ibrary), Cotton MS. Cleopatra E IV, ff.458v–459r. Archbold offered a round figure of 250 chantries and chapels and does not appear to have differentiated between chantries, lights and obits, regarding them all as a single chantry; his figures should at best be regarded as an approximation: W.A. Archbold, *The Somerset Religious Houses* (Cambridge, 1892), p. 20.

[6] Kreider, *English Chantries*, p. 16.

[7] The returns are located in the P(ublic) R(ecord) O(ffice) Exchequer, A(ugmentation) O(ffice), E.301/42 and P.R.O. Land Revenue Office, L.R.2/246. Annual cash rents provided an additional revenue of £244 11s 5d.

[8] P.R.O. Special Collections, Ministers' Accounts, S.C.6 James 874.

[9] P.R.O. Chancery, C.66. They have been calendared for the years 1547–1575 and hereafter are cited as C(alendar of) P(atent) R(olls).

[10] *C.P.R., 1553*, p. 153.

[11] *C.P.R., 1560–63*, p. 560.

[12] R.H. Tawney, for example, argued in 1941 that crown lands were purchased in part by 'syndicates of speculators, who bought land in large blocks, subdivided and resold it': R.H. Tawney, 'The Rise of the Gentry', *Economic History Review*, XI (1941), p. 29. In 1950 Professor Bindoff reiterated this view when he stated that 'the groups of London businessmen who acquired estates scattered all over the country were speculators who intended to resell them at a profit in smaller parcels': S.T. Bindoff, *Tudor England* (1950), p. 116. A serious weakness in W.K. Jordan's study on the identity of chantry grantees is his total reliance on the patents: *Edward VI: the Threshold of Power* (1970), *passim*. For an appraisal of this historiographical debate, see C.J. Kitching, 'The Disposal of Monastic and Chantry Lands', *Church and Society in England: Henry VIII to James I*, ed. F. Heal and R.O'Day (1977), pp. 119 ff.

[13] H.J. Habakkuk, 'The Market for Monastic Property', *Ec.H.R.* 2nd series, X (1958), pp. 379–80; J.A. Youings, 'The Terms of the Disposal of the Devon Monastic Lands, 1536–58', *English Historical Review*, LXIX (1954).

[14] See, for example, G.W.O. Woodward, 'A Speculation in Monastic Lands', *E.H.R.*, LXXIX (1964), p. 783; Kitching, thesis, p. 119; R.B. Outhwaite, 'Who Bought Crown Lands? The Pattern of Purchases, 1589–1603', *B.I.H.R.* XLIV (1971), p. 21.

[15] Located in the P.R.O. E.318.

[16] Wyndham, thesis, p. 116.

[17] The Patent Rolls record only one licence to alienate Somerset chantry property — Whitehorne and Bayly's grant to William and Melior Hunston: *C.P.R., 1548–9*, p. 287. Furthermore, the records of the Alienation Office up to 1571 are missing although an index of their contents, compiled in the seventeenth century, remains: P.R.O. IND.9967–9976.

[18] 27 Henry VIII c.16. The main central government enrolments of Somerset chantry lands are located in P.R.O. Chancery, Close Rolls, C.54 and Records of the Court of Common Pleas, Plea Rolls, C.P.40. The S(omerset) R(ecord) O(ffice) contains ten deeds of chantry lands which were enrolled in the county courts between 1548 and 1603: S.R.O. Enrolments of Deeds, CQ 1/4,6,14,17.

[19] P.R.O. Chancery, Early Chancery Proceedings, C.1; Chancery Proceedings C.2, C.3; *Inquisitions Post Mortem* C.142; Records of the Court of King's Bench, K.B.27; Records of the Court of Star Chamber, Sta(r) Cha(mber) 2,3,4; A.O., Proceedings of the Court of Augmentations, E.321; The King's Remembrancer,

Decrees and Orders of the Court of Augmentations, E.123.

[20]   Most of these documents are located in the S.R.O.

[21]   Claire Cross, *The Puritan Earl* (1966), p. 9.

[22]   Hatfield House, Cecil Papers, Vol.144 (a microfilm is kept in the B.L. Cecil MS. M.485/36, Vol.144); P.R.O. E.318/1722; Treasurer's Receipts, E.315/343; C.66/825. Hasilwood subsequently alienated the lands to Huntingdon: P.R.O. IND. 9976,f.677 (calendar only).

[23]   *C.P.R., 1547–8*, pp. 409–10; *1548–9*, pp. 305–8; 318/1438;/2018.

[24]   P.R.O. E.318/1394; J. Collinson, *The History and Antiquities of Somerset*, Vol.3 (Bath, 1791), p. 553.

[25]   *C.P.R., 1560–63*, p. 49. Paulet was lord of Nunney manor.

[26]   He was a J.P. in the reigns of Henry VIII, Edward VI, Mary and Elizabeth, sheriff in 1542 and 1547 and an M.P. in 1572. In 1572, three years before his death, he was assessed at £266 in lands: P.R.O. E.179/171/284.

[27]   *C.P.R., 1548–9*, pp. 287–291; P.R.O. E.318/1694; C.54/459/48.

[28]   Assessed at £100 in lands in 1551, his properties lay mainly on the Wiltshire border around Wylye and Wincanton: P.R.O. E.179/170/249; *C.P.R. 1547–8*, p. 136.

[29]   It was rated for sale on 23 May 1554 by Thomas Holmes of London: *C.P.R., 1553–4*, p. 153; P.R.O. E.318/2199; C.54/501/12.

[30]   *C.P.R., 1548–9*, p. 40; P.R.O. E.318/1419; S.R.O. Cary Fitzpaine Papers DD/M1/Box 5.

[31]   In Somerset alone, he received in the 1540's eight grants of crown land worth £207 p.a. at Lullington, Marston, Frome, Capland, Rodden, Winterstoke, Langley, Monksham, Cheddar and Walton: Wyndham, thesis, p. 243.

[32]   *C.P.R., 1548–9*, p. 51; Marquess of Bath MS. (Longleat) 4775, mm.1–3; S.R.O. Thynne Papers DD/SE 17 Box 2.

[33]   P.R.O. E.315/68 ff.131–2, 245, 352–3; E.318/2008.

[34]   *Letters of Lord Paget*, ed. Sybil M. Jack and Barrett L. Beer (Camden Miscellany, XXV, 1974), p. 67; P.R.O. E.321/33/49; E.315/258 f.115. The warrant for repayment was dated 4 June 1549.

[35]   Hist.Mss.Comm., *Various Collections*, 1, pp. 64–70.

[36]   *C.P.R., 1549–51*, pp. 5–7; P.R.O. E.315/67 f.108; C.P.40/1143/11.

[37]   *C.P.R., 1549–51*, pp. 131, 374; P.R.O. E.315/67 f.323; E.318/1904.

[38]   P.R.O. E.318/1769.

[39]   *Letters and Papers, Henry VIII*, XXI (2), p. 346.

[40]   P.R.O. E.318/1769.

[41]   *C.P.R., 1547–8*, pp. 366–7; P.R.O. E.315/68 f.295; E.318/1705. The letters patent are held by Lord Oxford of Mells: Horner MS.124.

[42]   P.R.O. E. 318/1823; *C.P.R., 1547–8*, p. 319; *1552–3*, p. 60. It was not an uncommon practice for the new owner, if he was the tenant or if he held land locally, to take possession of his property well in advance of his receiving the letters patent (cf. Easton, p. 12).

[43]   The properties carried an annual rent of £9 3s 8d: *C.P.R., 1549–51*, pp. 135–6; P.R.O. E. 315/67 f.42; E.318/1850;/1851.

[44]   In the 1547 subsidy she was assessed at £70 in goods: P.R.O. E.179/170/226; L.R.2/246 f.34v; E.318/1694; ·*C.P.R., 1548–9*, pp. 287–291.

[45]   Assessed at £20 in lands in 1547: P.R.O. E.179/170/226; *C.P.R., 1553–4*, p. 338.

[46]   The grants were made to Richard Randall of London and to Nicholas and Roger Prideaux of London: *C.P.R., 1548–9*, pp. 44, 362–6; P.R.O. E.318/1890;/ 1896. Lyte was the King's escheator in Somerset and Dorset in 1550 and was

assessed in 1551 at £20 in lands: P.R.O. E.179/170/249; H.C. Maxwell Lyte, *The Lytes of Lytescary* (Taunton, 1895), p. 95.

[47] P.R.O. C.1/1371 ff.78–80. It was presumably the loss of this income which caused the villagers to initiate the law suit.

[48] P.R.O. C.142/119/165.

[49] P.R.O. E.318/2057; C.54/486/16;/17; *C.P.R.*, *1553*, p. 161.

[50] P.R.O. C.66/1370; C.54/1424; E.123/4 f.16;/9 f.192; L.R.2/70 f.173.

[51] P.R.O. E.179/170/238; E.318/1851.

[52] P.R.O. E.318/1731.

[53] P.R.O. E.318/1466.

[54] P.R.O. E.318/1694;/1997; E.315/67 f.116. In the 1540's he bought substantial monastic lands in Somerset: P.R.O. E. 318/304;/349;/458;/1060;/1998. His lands were valued at £100 in 1549: P.R.O. E.179/170/238.

[55] *C.P.R.*, *1548–9*, p. 200; P.R.O. C.54/460/4;/5. Ilminster Grammar School's charter was dated 3 June 1549.

[56] *C.P.R.*, *1550–53*, p. 251; *1553*, p. 153; *1560–63*, p. 500; P.R.O. E.318/1899j/1900;/2152;/2199;/2484; C.54/484/2;537/21.

[57] P.R.O. C.142/193/41; *Somerset Wills*, 1, ed. Rev. F. Brown (1887), pp. 60–61.

[58] S.R.O. DD/BD/88 m.117.

[59] P.R.O. E.318/1619.

[60] *C.P.R.*, *1554–5*, pp. 149–150; P.R.O. C.P.25 (2)/77/657 no. 28.

[61] *C.P.R.*, *1563–6*, pp. 12–15; P.R.O. E.318/2485; L.R.2/67 f.228; C.54/667/40.

[62] P.R.O. C.66/1345; L.R.2/70 f.242.

[63] On 10 Sept. 1548 the property was granted to him by Thomas Bell, the co-patentee: *C.P.R.*, *1548–9*, p. 40; P.R.O. C.54/469/4; E.318/1419.

[64] *C.P.R.*, *1547–8*, pp. 406–8; P.R.O. C.142/193/46; E.315/68 ff.57–8; E.318/1401; S.R.O. DD/TD Box 41/3 m.1.

[65] See below, p. 16.

[66] P.R.O. E.318/1452; L.R.2/65 f.139; C.142/257/57.

[67] P.R.O. E.318/1718; C.54/482/30.

[68] P.R.O. E.318/1694; C.54/463/21.

[69] William Moryce, the surveyor of crown land in Somerset, was granted the property on 8 July 1550 and conveyed it to Coke on 12 Feb. 1551: *C.P.R.*, *1549–51*, pp. 273–6; P.R.O. C.54/474/47; E.318/1800.

[70] P.R.O. Sta.Cha.Proc. Stac 2, Henry VIII, 8/190; Stac 4, Philip and Mary, 6/2 mm.1–3.

[71] P.R.O. E.315/105/225; B.L. Harleian MS.6967/60.

[72] P.R.O. Sta.Cha.Proc.Stac 4, Philip and Mary, 6/34 mm.1–2; E.310/23/127 m.21.

[73] P.R.O. C.3/14/48.

[74] *C.P.R.*, *1549–51*, p. 106; P.R.O. E.315/67 f.332; C.54/469/40.

[75] P.R.O. C.P.40/1143/5v;/1144A/12. The letters patent were dated 1 May 1549: *C.P.R.*, *1548–9*, pp. 362–6.

[76] P.R.O. E.318/2066; E.36/258 f.102. The chapel appears to have been converted into a schoolhouse by 1573: J. Goodchild, *The Parish Church: Yeovil* (Yeovil, 1925), p. 11.

[77] In an undated bill of complaint — probably late sixteenth century — Dyer's grandson was cited before the court to answer charges from the inhabitants of Long Load that he had taken the profits, cut down trees and destroyed the chapel hay: Winchester College MS. 13153.

[78] P.R.O. E.318/2065. Kingman was bailiff of the manor of South Petherton.

[79]   P.R.O. E.318/2075; *C.P.R.*, *1547–8*, p. 285.

[80]   One inhabitant, a certain John Budge, claimed the purchase price was too high and refused to pay it: P.R.O. C.1/1198 ff.61–2.

[81]   S.R.O. DD/SN/ Bundle A,m.1.

[82]   *C.P.R.*, *1563–6*, pp. 12–15. In 1569 he and John Hacker acquired a lease of unsold chantry property in Yeovil worth £6 17s p.a. for sixty years: *C.P.R.*, *1566–9*, p. 403; P.R.O. E.310/23/127 m.28.

[83]   *C.P.R.*, *1548–9*, 'p. 297; P.R.O. E.318/1637. The ratee, Robert Freke, was a Somerset man who worked in London. He wrote on the dorse of the particulars: 'I have released my interest of the parcel and within written to William Gyfford'.

[84]   The first patent was granted to Leonard and Keylway on 2 Apr. 1549 and formally conveyed to Leonard by Keylway on 1 May: *C.P.R.*, *1548–9*, p. 200; P.R.O. C.P.40/1144A/6. The second grant, dated 1 May 1549, was conveyed to him by Nicholas and Roger Prideaux: *C.P.R.*, *1548–9*, pp. 362–6; P.R.O. C.P.40/1144A/12.

[85]   P.R.O. E.318/1730;/1731; C.P.40/1144A/12.

[86]   S.R.O. T/PH/hps.

[87]   *C.P.R.*, *1548–9*, pp. 403–4; P.R.O. E.318/1948;/1949; Bristol Record Office, Smythe Papers, AC/C2/1–6.

[88]   *C.P.R.*, *1549–51*, p. 193; P.R.O. E.319/1/13; S.P.10/19/27; A.B. Gourlay, *A History of Sherborne School* (Sherborne, 1931), p. 11.

[89]   *C.P.R.*, *1553–4*, p. 192; *1555–7*, p. 545; P.R.O. E.318/2128. Blackford Free Chapel and its lands were surrendered to the Crown in May 1557 although there is no further record of them in the Ministers' Accounts.

[90]   He was assessed at £100 in lands in 1557–8: P.R.O. E.179/100/353; E.318/2382.

[91]   The patent was acquired by Whitehorne and Bayly on 18 Aug. 1548 and re-granted to Hunston two days later. Since the lands were held in chief and not in socage, a licence to alienate had to be procured: *C.P.R.*, *1547–8*, pp. 278, 287; P.R.O. E.318/2075.

[92]   *C.P.R.*, *1549–51*, pp. 120–1; P.R.O. C.54/463/42.

[93]   *C.P.R.*, *1558–60*, p. 318; P.R.O. C.54/664/11; E.318/2285.

[94]   P.R.O. C.66/1148; E.318/2312.

[95]   P.R.O. C.66/1155; E.318/2344.

[96]   P.R.O. C.66/1163.

[97]   It carried an annual rent of £15 19s 10d: P.R.O. C.66/1535; L.R.2/72 f.258.

[98]   The lands remained in Drewe's family until 1664: P.R.O. C.142/159/51; *C.P.R.*, *1553–4*, p. 191; S.R.O. DD/M1 Box 5, quitclaim (dated 28 Oct. 1553), general livery (17 Apr. 1583) and final concord (1664).

[99]   The conveyance from Payton to Molde was enrolled on 14 Aug. 1556: S.R.O. CQ 1/4/85.

[100]   Hodges retained the lands until January 1603 when he sold them to William Hodge, a Dorset cleric, for £260: S.R.O. DD/BD/88 mm.117–18.

[101]   The lands, which had formerly provided endowments to Heron's Chantry, Langport, were sold 'for a certain sum of money': P.R.O. C.54/459/48; S.R.O. CQ 1/4/63.

[102]   P.R.O. C.54/459/48; S.R.O. CQ 1/4/65.

[103]   In 1549 Palpytte was assessed in goods at £14: P.R.O. E.179/170/237; C.54/459/48; S.R.O. CQ 1/4/64.

[104]   Collinson, *History and Antiquities*, Vol.2, p. 105. Collinson's evidence was a 'deed in the church chest of Dundry' which is no longer extant.

[105]   Four years later on 16 Feb. 1573, Thorp granted a quitclaim to Thomas

Parker and Thomas Wyseman: S.R.O. DD/BR/1s 4.

[106]   P.R.O. IND.9973 f.68; C.142/144/164. Basset was M.P. for Devon in 1572.

[107]   S.R.O. CQ 1/17/258. On 7 Apr. 1605 he sold his freehold to the tenant, John Sawter, for £23.

[108]   S.R.O. DD/PH 52/8. Phelips was M.P. for Somerset in 1601.

[109]   P.R.O. C.54/664/11. The property, which carried an annual rent of £2, formerly provided part of the endowments at St Katherine's Chantry, Ilminster.

[110]   *C.P.R., 1569–72*, p. 115.

[111]   The Lyte family, however, retained their chantry lands at Nythe which in 1559 were leased to Joan Wadham: *Somerset Wills*, 1, p. 58; S.R.O. CQ 1/6/99;/104.

[112]   The sale was conducted on 9 Oct. 1561: P.R.O. C.54/596/25.

[113]   S.R.O. DD/WHh/717.

[114]   *C.P.R., 1547–8*, pp. 406–8; P.R.O. E. 318/1401.

[115]   Collinge sold part of the property to Humphrey Willis in 1607 and the remainder to William Evans in 1610. Both were citizens of Wells: S.R.O. DD/TD Box 41/3 mm.1–5.

[116]   For example, the chantry lands at Aller (Hastings), Newton Placy (Blewet), Shepton Mallet (Horner), North Curry (Lyte), Idstoke, Frome, Croscombe and East Horrington (Thynne) and Long Ashton (Smythe).

Radicalism versus Evangelicalism in Victorian Cheltenham

A. F. MUNDEN

In his recent work on radicalism in Gloucestershire, with particular reference to Cheltenham during the period 1832–47, Dr. O.R. Ashten maintains that it was the opposition of the incumbent of Cheltenham parish church, the Rev Francis Close, to the disparate elements — working class Chartists, Owenite Socialists and middle-class radicals — which caused them to unite as an unholy coalition against the establishment, whether it be employers, magistrates or clergy.[1]

Yet while much new material has come to light in the research, many of the underlying assumptions and evaluation of the situation in Victorian Cheltenham need to be challenged. Much of the problem is the failure to understand the nature of Evangelicalism in the Church of England, and the character of the leader of that party in Cheltenham. The research of the Rev Geoffrey Berwick has misled subsequent historians, and his distorted impression of Francis Close (1797–1882), perpetual curate of Cheltenham parish church between 1826 and 1856, reveal more about Berwick's Anglo-Catholic prejudice and misjudgment than about Evangelicalism.[2] From a different perspective, Ashten creates an impression which is a misreading of Close and his theological position. But Berwick and Ashten are not the first to misunderstand the nature of Evangelicalism in the Church of England, and the complex personality of Francis Close.

Ashten's impression is that Close was 'a Tory Evangelical cleric'[3] who, through his despotic rule impressed his 'inquisitorial control of Cheltenham life'.[4] All aspects of the social and religious life of the town were confined by 'the straight-jacket of Evangelicalism'.[5] Close attempted to obtain class control and indoctrination of the population through the erection of churches, the provision of schools, bible classes for working men, and the formation of charitable bodies. He publically opposed Chartism — notably in the two sermons preached to the Chartists assembled in the parish church in August 1839[6] — and in 1842 was instrumental in causing the arrest and prosecution for blasphemy of the freethinker, George Jacob Holyoake.

But this impression of Cheltenham is far too narrow, and should be set against a wider context, of the Evangelical character of the town which extended over a period of one hundred years from the end of the Napoleonic wars to the first world war. An Evangelical ministry was exercised at the parish church by a succession of incumbents, notably Charles Jervis,[7] Francis Close,[8] and Edward Walker. Of these three, the most outstanding was Francis Close, who had been converted to faith in Christ in 1813, and having come under the influence of Evangelicals at Hull and Cambridge, expressed in his own ministry the principles of Charles Simeon.

Simeon was one of the second generation of Evangelicals in the Church of England in the eighteenth century, and represented a moderate Calvinistic theology. During the course of his fifty-four year ministry as vicar of Holy Trinity church, Cambridge between 1782 and 1836, he established a movement with its own distinctive theology, loyal to the principles of the established church, and committed to reaching men and women at home and overseas for Christ. To solve 'the problem of continuity'[9] of a succession of Evangelical ministers, in important centres, Simeon acquired the right of presentation to twenty one livings, in spas like Cheltenham and Bath, and in urban centres like Derby and Bradford (later both of these became cathedrals). Simeon's philosophy was simple:

'There is this difference between myself and others: they purchase *income* — I purchase *spheres*, wherein the prosperity of the established church, and the kingdom of our blessed Lord, may be advanced; and not for a season only, but if it please God, in perpetuity also'.[10]

The patronage of Cheltenham was purchased in 1816 for £3000, and Close was appointed by Simeon in 1826. During Close's residence in Cheltenham, the population increased from 13,396 in 1821 to over 35,051 in 1851. The steady transformation of the town during this period from spa to educational centre, has to be seen in the light of the rise of Close to a position of unrivalled leadership, and the adoption by a large proportion of the resident population of the town to Evangelical faith and principles.

Close's concern was to reach *all* social classes for Christ, and churches and schools were erected and schemes of social relief implemented with that aim in mind. The direct outcome of lives committed to God and transformed by Christ had a profound effect on the whole of society. The research of Dr K. Heasman[11] has shown the impact of Evangelicalism on social work, and Dr I.

Bradley,[12] the impact upon the upper classes, where for example, there was a

> 'marked decline in race-going, in attendance at theatres and other entertainments, and the closing down of several gaming clubs and pleasure gardens through lack of custom'.[13]

This transformation was obvious in Cheltenham over the issue of Sunday observance. Sabbatarianism was stressed because it provided both a preparation and a foretaste of the afterlife. Close, together with most of the other Anglican and Nonconformist ministers of Cheltenham held such strongly-held Sabbatarian principles that it was said that Cheltenham as 'assumed a more sober, discreet, quiet and religious appearance than any other town in England, or . . . the United Kingdom'.[14] The *whole* community — rich and poor — should *enjoy* the Sabbath. The Cheltenham Society for the Prevention of the Desecration of the Sabbath (f1839); enabled shopworkers to have at least one day off work each week. Close encouraged his congregation to walk to church rather than hire carriages, and he expressed his concern for postmen and milkmen who were expected to work. Opposition to Sunday trains was to preserve both the peace of the town and to prevent it from becoming 'a mere tea garden . . . by the idlers and Sabbath breakers of Birmingham, Droitwich, Bromsgrove and Worcester'.[15]

Close was supported in his views by most of the Anglican clergy in the town, as well as by a large proportion of the residents. Some of the leading individuals, like Close and John Browne, the minister of Holy Trinity church, and retired army officers, were dubbed by their opponents as 'the Lieutenant General Close Brigade', whose rule was regarded as being nothing less than 'the slavery of the blackcoats'.[16] A warmer assessment was made in an illuminated address presented to Close on leaving the town in 1856.

> 'We would express our admiration of the astonishing energy of your character, and the attractive geniality of your temperament, and we believe that many who at a distance may have viewed your opinions with suspicion and distrust, would, if brought into personal communication with yourself, have entertained very different sentiments towards you'.[17]

Ashten over estimates the number of those who opposed Close and the significance of the opposition in relation to Close's other concerns. Apart from the opposition of the activities of the dissolute Colonel William Berkeley and his circle, the combined Unitarian and radical freethinking opposition was a small, insignificant minority of the resident population of the town.

In Close's own estimation, of the five hundred male Chartists who attended the parish church in August 1839, over one hundred were not from Cheltenham. This is a similar number to that of the three hundred and forty-eight individuals who in 1837 signed a petition in favour of secular education. What is clear from Ashten is that the Cheltenham Chartists were supported by those from other local centres of Chartism in Cirencester, Stroud and Gloucester. While there were no more than some five hundred Chartists in Cheltenham, Close could rely upon support from a minimum of the 1200 strong congregation of the parish church (which included a number of shopkeepers and working class) to the 13,000 who in 1837 signed a petition in favour of having a daily reading of scripture in schools. This last figure represented almost half of the resident population in 1841. Even over the vexed question of the payment of the church rate (which was hardly a 'radical' issue, but which would have gained radical support), the highest recorded number of those who opposed the rate was 1050 in 1845. Support for Close's position can be seen in 1864 (eight years after he had left the town), when Holyoake was again opposed by Cheltenham residents over giving a lecture.

Ashten traces the progress of radicalism in Cheltenham; it was absent before 1831, socialism had disappeared by 1845, and Chartism by the mid-1850s. The last Chartist meeting was held in Cheltenham in August 1856, only a few months before Close left to become dean of Carlisle. The radical cause was actively supported by the *Cheltenham Free Press* (f1834); by the congregation of about one hundred at the Unitarian Chapel; and by those who attended the Mechanics' Institute. However, Ashten overstates both the influence of the radical cause in the town, and Close's opposition to it. A far greater threat to Evangelicalism was Romanism, and from 1835 Close and Brown were active in their condemnation of that movement within the Church of England, and as expressed in the Church of Rome.

Ashten is wrong over Close's attitude to dissent and to education. To maintain that both Simeon and Close did not oppose dissent on theological grounds, but from fear that it was not tied to the *status quo* and wanted reform, is unsupported. Close opposed radical dissent (and Unitarianism) because it was unscriptural, and the independency of nonconformity, but was prepared to actively co-operate with dissenters in matters of common concern —

Sabbath observance, the British and Foreign Bible Society, the YMCA and opposition to Romanism. Close encouraged co-operation:

> 'Let us cordially fraternise with the religious dissenters — separating them from the political democrats of the day — let all bible-loving, bible-believing, bible-reading Christians unite together against Rome . . . we must shake hands on the common ground of God's truth against the world'.[18]

Close believed that an exclusively secular education was wrong, and the aim was 'scriptural education on the principles of the established church'.[19]

Church and state should co-operate in educational matters, since 'education conducted on Christian principles, is one of the greatest blessings that a people can receive, or a government impart'.[20] Part of the purpose of education was to prepare individuals for this world and the next. Well-qualified Evangelical teachers were needed for the schools, and a bible-based education would protect the middle and working classes from the twin evils of secularism and Romanism. Therefore, against Ashten, Close was *not* in favour of Sunday schools, because he deplored their poor standards, and he was *against* the National Society because it propagated Romanism. Close believed that if Christians did not educate the poor, then they would be led astray by 'knaves, traitors and Chartists'.[21] Education was not just to consist of bible teaching, as Ashten maintains, but scientific teaching was also to be given. Ashten is quite prepared to criticise the provision of Evangelical schools, and to welcome radical ones; but it radicals could provide schools, then why not Christians?

Close's views did change over alcohol; but again a wider context is essential in order to understand his position. Ashten correctly observes that Close, like most other Anglican ministers, did not support the tee-total movement because of its association with Chartism. In 1848 Close maintained that he could not be induced to become a total abstainer; but on moving to Carlisle he adopted total abstinence. This radical change of heart may well have been caused through the disability of gout from which he suffered, but he maintained that it was through his better aquaintance with the working classes. Close threw himself into the new cause. Of his eight publications between 1860 and 1862, four were devoted to total abstinence. He also became president of the Church of England Total Abstinence Society (f1862).

During Close's thirty year ministry at Cheltenham parish church, the town was transformed from a fashionable, yet declining watering place, in to an important educational centre and setting for exhibitions and conferences. How Cheltenham would have developed without Francis Close as its leading citizen is mere speculation. But what is perfectly clear is that 'his history and the history of the town are one'.[22] Any analysis of Close's leadership and philosophy which regards him as a power-hungry despotic cleric concerned with maintaining the *status quo* fails to understand the nature of the man, and of his strongly held Evangelical convictions.

Notes

[1]   O.R. Ashten, *Radicalism and Chartism in Gloucestershire 1832–1847*, unpublished Ph D thesis, University of Birmingham 1980.

[2]   G.T. Berwick, *Close of Cheltenham parish pope. A study in the Evangelical background to the Oxford Movement*, unpublished typescript in Cheltenham public library, 1938.
G.T. Berwick, Close of Cheltenham, parish pope, *Theology*, Vol 39, (September and October 1939), pp. 193–201, 276–285.

[3]   Ashten, op. cit., xi.

[4]   Ibid., 256.

[5]   Ibid., 375.

[6]   F. Close, *The Chartists' visit to the parish church. A sermon addressed to the Chartists of Cheltenham, Sunday 18 August 1839, on the occassion of their attending the parish church in a body* (1839); *The Female Chartists' visit to the parish church. A sermon addressed to the female Chartists of Cheltenham, Sunday 25 August 1839, on the occasion of their attending the parish church in a body* (1839).

[7]   A.F. Munden, 'Evangelical in the shaddows: Charles Jervis of Cheltenham', *Churchman*, Vol 96, No 2 (1982), pp. 142–150.

[8]   M. Hennell, *Sons of the Prophets, Evangelical leaders of the Victorian church*, (1979), pp. 104–121.

[9]   C. Smyth, *Simeon and church order, a study of the origins of the Evangelical revival in Cambridge in the eighteenth century* (Cambridge 1940), p. 310.

[10]   W. Carus, *Memoirs of the life of the Rev Charles Simeon MA* (1847), p. 780.

[11]   K. Heasman, *Evangelicals in Action, an appraisal of their social work in the Victorian era* (1962).

[12]   I. Bradley, *The call to seriousness, the Evangelical impact on the Victorians* (1976).

[13]   Ibid., p. 106.

[14]   *Cheltenham Journal*, 19 February 1844, p. 2.

[15]   *Cheltenham Journal*, 14 September 1840, p. 2.

[16]   *Cheltenham Free Press*, 25 December 1847, p. 408.

[17]   *Address from his parishioners and friends to the Very Reverend Francis Close, Dean of Carlisle, Presented 3 December 1856.*

[18]   F. Close, *'Missions: Protestant and Popish'* (Liverpool 1851), p. 31.

[19]   F. Close, *A sermon preached in the parish church of St Mary, Cheltenham, on Thursday, 5 November 1840* (1840), p. 16.

[20]   *National Education and Church Extension. An authentic report of the speeches*

delivered at a public meeting of members and friends of the established church . . . 9
February 1839 pp. 78–79.

[21] F. Close, *Co-operation with the Committee of Council on Education vindicated
and recommended* (1848), p. 51.

[22] *Cheltenham Free Press,* 23 December 1882, p. 2.

'Bells and Smells': London, Brighton and South Coast Religion Reconsidered

W. N. YATES

When Charles Ryder first went up to Oxford in 1922 he was warned by his cousin Jasper to 'beware of the Anglo-Catholics — they're all sodomites with unpleasant accents'.[1] Apart from the ancient universities their principal strongholds were thought to be London and the fashionable watering places along the south coast, especially Brighton. The period between roughly 1890 and 1930 marked the high point of extreme Anglo-Catholicism, a subject largely neglected by ecclesiastical historians on the grounds of its supposed irrelevance to contemporary events, and left to the sentimental pens belonging to the admirers of the more disting-uished or eccentric Anglo-Catholic clergy. Most of the literature is pure hagiography, yet anybody who has bothered to read any local newspapers, or even some national ones, during this period will be well aware that extreme Anglo-Catholicism was a subject that produced violent public reaction, both for and against, even to the extent of being a major issue in some parliamentary constituencies at election time. It was public indignation against extreme Anglo-Catholicism, and the demonstrations of Kensitites, which resulted in the setting up of the Royal Commission on Ecclesiastic-al Discipline, and led indirectly to the abortive attempts to revise the Anglican Prayer Book in the 1920s. The purpose of this paper is to look at the manifestation and geographical distribution of extreme Anglo-Catholicism in the southern counties of England in the first decade of the present century, using the vast resources of primary evidence available, and to show that, far from confining itself to London, Brighton and the south coast, extreme Anglo-Catholicism was widely distributed throughout the region, though sometimes particularly concentrated in a small area for various historical or political reasons.[2]

* * *

The best starting point for this study, in terms of contemporary evidence, is the *Ritualist Clergy List*, containing the names of those clergymen with alleged 'Romanist' leanings, first published by the Church Association in 1903, and subsequently re-issued on several later occasions with additions and deletions. The Church Association had been founded in 1865, specifically to counteract the spread of ritualism within the Church of England, and had been responsible for initiating most of the attempted prosecutions of ritualist clergy under the Public Worship Regulation Act of 1874.[3] Since 1890, however, it had found itself rather outmanoeuvred by the direct action tactics of the Protestant Truth Society, founded by John Kensit. The publication of the *Ritualist Clergy List* was an attempt by the Church Association to re-assert its leadership of the anti-ritualist movement. The *List* gave the names of those bishops who wore mitres, those clergymen who were members of the main Anglo-Catholic Societies (English Church Union, Confraternity of the Blessed Sacrament, Society of the Holy Cross, Guild of All Souls, Associates of the Society of St. John the Evangelist), those clergymen who practised what were known as the 'six points' of ritual observance (eastward position, wafer bread, mixed chalice, lighted candles, vestments and incense), and those clergymen who had seceded to Rome with details of their Anglican preferment. The *List* is arranged alphabetically by clergymen, rather than by parishes, so is less easy to use than the contemporary *Tourists' Church Guide*, published by the English Church Union, 'which showed with asterisks and paragraph marks and sections and daggers what churches throughout the United Kingdom possessed the six points'.[4] But it does give more information, such as the membership of certain Anglo-Catholic societies, which is otherwise not easily obtainable.

The *List* also gives a useful summary of ritual statistics for each Anglican diocese. By comparing these with the number of benefices in a contemporary *Clergy List* or *Crockford's Clerical Directory*, one can express ritual observance in percentage terms (Table 1). This reveals that in about two out of five churches in the provinces of Canterbury and York, the celebrant took the eastward position at the Eucharist; that in about one out of four churches candles were lighted and water mixed with wine in the chalice; and that in about one out of ten churches the eucharistic vestments were in use. Although all practices were innovations introduced by extreme 'high churchmen' in the 1830s and 1840s, the first three had become fairly widely accepted by more moderate churchmen. Only the use of vestments was still restricted to the extreme 'high churchmen': 'the wearing of vestments always meant Catholic

teaching about the Mass and the Confessional'.[5] To a large extent
the diocesan figures confirm the general belief that the Oxford
Movement had more parochial impact in the south than the north
of England. Only in half the northern dioceses were the figures for
ritual observance above or near the national average, and in the
Isle of Man ritual observance was restricted to the use of the
eastward position in one church: St. Matthew's, Douglas. In the
southern dioceses, however, only one diocese, Bath and Wells, had
figures well below the national average, and two dioceses, London
and Truro, were strongholds of Anglo-Catholic influence and
practice. In the Midlands two out of seven dioceses had figures
below the national average, but in Wales all four dioceses were in
that category.

The low incidence of ritual observance in the diocese of Bath
and Wells may have had something to do with the Evangelical
episcopate of A.C. Hervey between 1869 and 1894, though no
diocesan could ever impose his churchmanship completely on a
diocese, since the patronage of benefices was not solely in his
hands, but shared with many others. Of the other dioceses in
southern England three — Chichester,[6] Oxford[7] and Salisbury[8] —
had had a succession of 'high church' bishops, and the diocese of
Truro had had three 'high church' bishops since its creation in
1877: E.W. Benson (1877–83), G.H. Wilkinson (1883–91) and
John Gott (1891–1906).[9] John Gott is perhaps one of the most
significant of the forgotten 'high churchmen' of the late nineteenth
century, a distinguished vicar of Leeds and dean of Worcester, and
the author of the frequently reprinted pastoral textbook, *The
Parish Priest of the Town*. In other dioceses there was a more even
balance between 'high church', moderate and Evangelical episcopal
appointments, though at Exeter the 'high church' Henry Phillpotts
(1831–69) left a tradition which none of his less 'high church'
successors were entirely able to eradicate.

For the rest of this paper our attention will be confined to those
parts of southern England south of the river Thames, excluding
London and its Kentish and Surrey suburbs, and to those churches
within the very definite Anglo-Catholic category, that is those
churches in which the eucharistic vestments were worn in 1903,
and in some of which incense was also used. There were 342 of the
former and 56 of the latter, and they were widely spread
throughout the area, though rather thin on the ground in Surrey.
A summary list is given of these churches in the appendix to this
paper. Table 2 endeavours to categorise them according to the
type of community in which they were situated, and Table 3

1876

1900

1911

Ritual Elaboration — St. Bartholomew's, Brighton — the high altar.

analyses the comparative strength of Anglo-Catholicism in the major towns. The results are interesting in both cases. As one might expect, churches with both incense and vestments were mostly to be found in the major urban centres and in the resort towns. What is perhaps more surprising is the considerable strength of less extreme, though still committed, Anglo-Catholicism in the countryside, especially in Devon and Cornwall. In the major towns one notes the comparative weakness of Anglo-Catholicism in the dockyard conurbations, except for Plymouth, and the contrast between the extreme Anglo-Catholicism of Brighton and the more moderate Anglo-Catholicism of Torquay. The towns with the highest proportion of ritualist churches were Swindon and Taunton, where vestments were worn in half the Anglican churches, followed by Plymouth, Reading, Torquay, Dover, Folkestone and St. Helier, in all of which vestments were worn in between a quarter and half of all Anglican churches. It should be noted that vestments were worn in only a fifth of the churches in Brighton and Hove, though in all but one of these incense was also used. No large town in southern England had a higher proportion of Anglican churches using incense. The towns with the fewest ritualist churches were Maidstone, Aldershot, Reigate and Canterbury, in all of which not a single Anglican church used vestments. In proportionate terms ritualist churches were equally thin on the ground in Portsmouth, Bournemouth and Winchester. Even though Bristol had seen the formation of one of the earliest ritualist pressure groups, the Bristol Church Union in 1848,[10] there were relatively few ritualist churches in the city at the end of the century.

Three small towns, which will be looked at in more detail later in this paper, were strong centres of ritualist teaching and practice. These were, with their 1901 population figures in brackets, Bovey Tracey (2693), where vestments were worn in both Anglican churches and incense used in one; Frome (11,057), where vestments and incense were used in three out of four Anglican churches; and the Clewer suburb of Windsor (14,130), where, as at Bovey Tracey, vestments were worn in both Anglican churches and incense used in one.

* * *

It is obviously impossible in one short paper to consider in any detail all the known ritualist parishes in southern England, and one has to be selective. In doing this the aim has been to illustrate significant features of or trends within Anglican ritualism in the late nineteenth and early twentieth centuries. One fact which does become clear from what is known about ritualism in various parts of England and Wales is that similar themes are repeated over and over again, and the danger of quoting too many examples is that one quickly becomes repetitive. There will, therefore, be many ritualist parishes in southern England which escape mention in the main text of this paper, though careful perusal of the appendix will provide the local historian with some indications of the strength of Anglican ritualism in particular parts of the region, and the names of individual parishes that might repay further study.

Pioneer Ritualist Parishes

The five areas of southern England with the longest tradition of Anglican ritualism were, in chronological order, Clewer (1844), Plymouth (1848), Bovey Tracey (1849), Brighton (1850) and Frome (1852). One other early centre of ritualistic activity, Chislehurst (1846), being now in Greater London, falls outside the scope of this paper.[11] Important distinctions can be made between these ritualist centres. Whereas the pioneer ritualist incumbents at Clewer, Thomas Thelluson Carter (1844–80), and Frome, William James Early Bennett (1852–86), were established incumbents who were not even advanced 'high churchmen' in the first few years after their ordination, the pioneer ritualists at Plymouth, Bovey Tracey and Brighton were men of the second generation of the Oxford Movement and typical examples of its more fervent disciples. The difference in outlook between the two generations is indicated in the cautious approach of the older men towards ritual innovation as compared with the more enthusiastic excesses of their juniors.

T.T. Carter had been born in 1808, his father holding the Buckinghamshire living of Burnham and acting also as Vice-Provost of Eton College. After ordination to the diaconate in 1832 he served for a year under the 'broad church' H.H. Milman, later dean of St. Paul's, as curate of St. Mary's, Reading. Between 1833 and 1838 he acted as curate to his father at Burnham, and was then appointed to two Eton College livings in succession: Piddle-hinton, Dorset (1838–44) and Clewer, Berkshire (1844–80). He seems to have made little mark at the former, and was compelled for health reasons to be non-resident between 1842 and 1844, during which time he lived again at Burnham. Clewer was a mixed parish, partly rural and partly Windsor suburb. For someone who was later identified as one of the high priests of ritualism, Carter's progress at Clewer was very slow. It was not until 1852 that he began the restoration of the parish church, and the nave was still 'full of high pews in 1858'.[12] One of Carter's curates recorded that in 1865 'a surpliced choir was gradually supplanting the old choir of male and female voices who sat behind the pulpit. Black stoles only were worn, and, at least in the morning, the black gown was used; this was done in consideration for some of the parishioners. At first white stoles were used, but it was some time before red and green were introduced'.[13] Carter, however, was a convinced Tractarian before he came to Clewer, having been strongly influenced by the *Tracts for the Times* and the other writings pouring out from Oxford in the 1830s and 1840s. His main effort at Clewer was, however, directed towards teaching and social action rather than an obsession with the externals of public worship. He was much caught up in penitentiary work, the rehabilitation of prostitutes, and founded his own House of Mercy at Clewer in 1849, and a sisterhood to run it in 1852. Over the next thirty years almshouses, a convalescent home, boarding and industrial schools were established at Clewer. There were associated foundations at Bovey Tracey: another House of Mercy (1863) and a mission to the poor (1879). Elsewhere in southern England, two convalescent homes and a home for incurables were established at Torquay (1866–92), and another convalescent home and a mission to the poor at Folkestone in 1875, all run by sisters from Clewer.

It was largely as a result of pressure from his curates that Carter was persuaded to adopt a more extravagant ritual at Clewer, though he always denied this: 'I was thought by some an extreme Ritualist, and by others that I was led on against my own mind by my curates. But neither was true. My inclination has been for a good measure of Ritual. I have believed a higher Ritual to be our rightful inheritance . . . From the first I kept the eastward position, and, I think, the mixed chalice. In minor ways, as in processions, and choral celebrations, and the Altar cross, and flowers, I went beyond what the upper ten of the congregation at all liked, as they showed me more or less uncomfortably. But the first movement that made a commotion was lighting the candles at the early celebration. Things went on until matters became more critical, and, I suppose, the teaching disapproved. But not until the dissentients had left the church did I light the candles at the late celebration, or use vestments. After a while the attack came, and the crisis'.[14] There seems every reason to believe that the Church Association engineered Carter's prosecution under the Public

Worship Regulation Act largely because of his national standing as a confessor and retreat conductor, and as the founder and first Superior-General of the Confraternity of the Blessed Sacrament. Certainly by the mid-1870s ceremonial was very much more advanced in many other parishes than it was at Clewer, and even there the more extravagant ritual was reserved for the daughter church of St. Stephen, which became a separate parish in 1873, with Carter's former curate, G.D. Nicholas, as the first vicar. Carter's prosecution was vetoed by his bishop, J.F. Mackarness, who had made him an honorary canon of Oxford in 1870, though he made it clear to Carter that he should abandon some of the disputed innovations. Carter therefore felt that he was morally obliged to resign his living to protect the bishop from Protestant abuse, although his stand was much criticised by the more aggressive Anglo-Catholics who regarded it as unnecessarily conscientious. After his resignation Carter continued to reside at Clewer directing his penitentiary work until his death in 1901. His successor as rector maintained the liturgical and theological tradition he had established.

Developments at Frome were much the same though W.J.E. Bennett was unaffected by the ritual prosecutions or attempted prosecutions under the Public Worship Regulation Act. Bennett had been born in 1804 and served short curacies at several fashionable London churches before his appointment as minister of the Portman Chapel in 1836. He was chosen by Bishop Blomfield to become first incumbent of the new church of St. Paul's, Knightsbridge, consecrated in 1843. It was whilst at the Portman Chapel that he gradually became a Tractarian, having previously been a strong Calvinist. It was his ritual innovations at St. Paul's, Knightsbridge, and the daughter church of St. Barnabas, Pimlico, opened in 1850, which caused serious riots, a dispute with the bishop, and Bennett's resignation early in 1851. Shortly afterwards the vicarage of Frome, in the patronage of the Marquess of Bath, then a minor, fell vacant and was offered to Bennett by the marquess's mother, who was a personal friend of Keble, Pusey and other Tractarian leaders. The appointment produced a furore in Parliament, and at the local level 56 parishioners of Frome, including five clergymen, petitioned Lady Bath against the appointment. A counter-petition in favour of Bennett, however, attracted the support of 1039 parishioners, and within a few months of his institution the congregation had increased by a third to some 2000.[15]

When Bennett went to Frome in 1852 he found the parish

church 'unrestored' with box pews and three-decker pulpit. The pews in the chancel were cleared immediately and he abolished both pew rents and church rates. During 1855–6 the pulpit, nave pews and galleries were also removed, and this was followed between 1862 and 1865 by a full-scale restoration of the whole fabric. Bennett remained at Frome until his death in 1886. He introduced various parochial charities, such as a dispensary, provident clubs and soup kitchens. A home was provided for factory girls and a creche for the children of working mothers. The parish was divided into districts with the vicar and curates responsible for regular visiting, a parish magazine was begun in 1854 and parochial missions in 1868. There were local wards or branches of the Confraternity of the Blessed Sacrament, Guild of All Souls, English Church Union and Society for Promoting the Unity of Christendom.[16] Frome under Bennett was very much a model Tractarian parish.

Liturgically Bennett was a conservative. He introduced a daily communion service at 7 a.m., with once or twice a month a celebration on Sundays at 10 a.m. for the 'old and delicate', on Thursdays at 9 a.m., and occasionally on weekdays a celebration at 5.15 a.m. for 'working people' with coffee afterwards at the vicarage. He retained choral Mattins on Sundays at 11 a.m. instead of introducing a Sung Eucharist, which was instead at 8 a.m., and there was choral Evensong daily with incense on festivals. Vestments were not worn until the mid-1860s when a majority of the regular communicants requested their introduction and presented them to the vicar.[17] As patron of the daughter churches to the parish church in Frome, Bennett appointed his own curates to these livings as they became vacant, so that of the four Anglican churches in the town, three were strongly ritualist by the 1870s, whilst at the parish church successive marquesses of Bath could be relied on as patrons to continue the tradition which their family had begun there in 1852.

Compared with Carter and Bennett the younger generation represented by Prynne at Plymouth, Courtenay at Bovey Tracey and Wagner at Brighton, were much more radical. George Rundle Prynne was born in 1818 and served as curate at All Saints', Clifton, and very briefly (1846–8) as vicar of Par in Cornwall, before his appointment in 1848 by Bishop Phillpotts of Exeter to the incumbency of St. Peter's, Plymouth, where he remained until his death in 1903. Prynne's 'high church' views were well known before the appointment though Phillpotts always claimed, never very convincingly, that he had been totally unaware of them.

Plymouth was an Evangelical stronghold in the 1840s, and indeed for the rest of the century. St. Peter's was a new parish, using as its church a chapel built in 1830 by the Revd. John Hawker, who had seceded from the established church over Catholic Emancipation, and purchased for Anglican use after his death. Those who knew Bishop Phillpotts suspected that the appointment of a known Tractarian in such a delicate ecclesiastical situation was a deliberate anti-Evangelical move. The establishment of the new parish was supported by the foundation of a sisterhood under Priscilla Lydia Sellon to assist the clergy in ministering to both the spiritual and social needs of a deprived community. Phillpotts agreed to act as visitor to the sisterhood and consecrated the church, from which Prynne had removed the galleries and three-decker pulpit, in 1850. The attacks on Prynne began almost immediately, co-ordinated by the Evangelical clergy. There were public meetings to protest about the use of the surplice in the pulpit, intoning the service, bowing at the name of Jesus, and other minor innovations. There were attacks on the sisterhood and allegations made against Prynne relating to the improper questioning of penitents. Phillpotts held a series of inquiries and publicly exonerated both Prynne and the sisterhood, and was stoned at a confirmation service in protest. He gave £50 annually to augment the benefice income until his death in 1869. With Phillpotts' support, despite the fact that the bishop disapproved of extreme ritualism, Prynne developed St. Peter's as the first of what later became a significant group of ritualist churches in Plymouth. The church was always in the forefront of the ritualist movement, and was, in 1882, the first in England to begin perpetual reservation of the Blessed Sacrament.[18] Prynne was also able to enlarge the original converted chapel with a new nave designed by his architect son.

About halfway between Plymouth and Exeter lay Bovey Tracey of which Charles Leslie Courtenay was vicar from 1849 until 1894. Courtenay, born in 1816, was the son of the tenth earl of Devon. The Courtenays were like the Thynnes (marquesses of Bath) a distinguished, aristocratic, 'high church' family. Courtenay's only other preferment was, despite his known 'high churchmanship', a canonry of Windsor. As this was an appointment in the personal gift of the sovereign, it must be assumed that Courtenay's theological views were of less importance to Queen Victoria, who strongly disapproved of 'high churchmen', than his aristocratic connections. At Bovey Tracey Courtenay Tractarianised the parish church, beginning with a full scale restoration, completed with the addition of an outer north aisle in 1858. The daughter church of

St. John was built in 1852, the architect being R.C. Carpenter, one of those most favoured by Tractarian incumbents and thoroughly 'ecclesiological' in his approach. Here Courtenay introduced an even more advanced ritual than that at the parish church and ensured its continuation by assigning the patronage to Keble College, Oxford, in 1885. The warden and fellows of Keble consistently apointed ritualists to their livings, and several others were assigned to them by the founders of ritualist parishes who did not trust other possible patrons, such as the diocesan bishop or the incumbent of the mother parish, to present candidates of the right churchmanship. Other Anglo-Catholic patrons were the Guild of All Souls and the Society for the Maintenance of the Faith, but there were an even larger number of Evangelical patronage trusts. The extreme nature of the ritualist teaching and practice at St. John's, Bovey Tracey, is made abundantly clear in the verbatim report of an episcopal enquiry held at the church in 1905, recently discovered among the archives of the diocese of Exeter.[19] In the directions given to the incumbent and churchwardens the bishop ordered the former 'to submit at all times for my approval and authority all services and all prayers for which there is no express direction or authority in the Book of Common Prayer, . . . to abstain from all omissions and all interpolations and all variations in the service of the Holy Communion as it is laid down in the Book of Common Prayer, especially . . . the second fraction or intinction or commixture, and the elevation of the host accompanied by the ringing of bells, . . . to abstain from the ceremonial use of incense or portable lights, . . . to abstain from giving notice of or observing by special services any feast or other days not directed by the Prayer Book calendar to be observed, . . . [and] to abstain from placing flowers, lights or ornaments before any image or picture in the church'. He ordered the churchwardens to obtain a confirmatory faculty within six months, or else to remove, two tabernacles, two statues of Our Lady and 'the image of Our Lord displaying the Sacred Heart . . . and . . . to abstain in like manner with the vicar from placing flowers, lights or ornaments before any image or picture in the church or from authorising any other person to do the like'.

A similar state of affairs existed in the notorious group of Anglo-Catholic churches in Brighton, the majority of which owed their existence to the munificence of Arthur Douglas Wagner. Anglo-Catholicism in Brighton was less widespread than its critics frequently alleged. It was confined to about a fifth of the churches in the town virtually all of which were established as Anglo-

Catholic churches. The sole exception was St. James', a propriet-
ary chapel usually served by Evangelical ministers, which had a
flamboyant ritualist minister in the person of John Purchas
between 1863 and 1872. Much of Brighton's notoriety seems to
have been the result of Wagner's own dominant personality, which
attracted the attention of extreme Protestants, and led to John
Kensit contesting the 1900 general election there on an anti-
ritualist platform. Yet Wagner's ability to achieve what he did was
largely fortuitous. His family was immensely wealthy. His father,
Henry Michell Wagner, was vicar of Brighton from 1824 until his
death in 1870, a conservative 'high churchman' who was prepared
to make provision for his more ritualist son, born in 1825. It was
the elder Wagner who built the new church of St. Paul, opened in
1848, at a cost of £14,000, and arranged for his son to become
perpetual curate in 1850. Had it not been for the influence of his
father the younger Wagner might have had some difficulty in
securing ordination or, at any rate, his own benefice. He appears
not to have been offered any other and he died as vicar of St.
Paul's in 1902.

From the first St. Paul's, an ecclesiologically correct design by
R.C. Carpenter, was among the most extreme of the ritualist
churches in England. Although Wagner was concerned primarily
that his main mission should be to the working class of his district,
St. Paul's became the most fashionable church outside London and
'high church' visitors to Brighton, as well as the simply curious,
formed a high proportion of the Sunday congregations. Although
Wagner was an extremist he was also a politician, abandoning the
use of both incense and vestments on various occasions as a result
of episcopal requests to do so. In some matters, however, he could
be totally resolute, as in the case of Constance Kent where, despite
public abuse and even physical assault, he refused to repeat in
court what had been revealed to him under the seal of sacramental
confession.

If Wagner had merely restricted his ministry to the building up
of St. Paul's as the main Anglo-Catholic church in Brighton it is
doubtful whether the number of such churches in the town would
have inceased significantly. The ritualist experiment at St. James'
was short-lived and, on the whole, disastrous. St. Michael's, where
a strong ritualist tradition was established, was opened in 1862
and, though neither financed nor planned by Wagner, was
subscribed to by those who admired his work at St. Paul's and
were anxious to provide a benefice for one of his curates. All the
other pre-1900 ritualist churches in Brighton owed their existence

directly to Wagner himself. He personally financed the two very modest churches of St. Mary Magdalen (1862) and the Annunciation (1864), and the much more lavish, indeed positively opulent, St. Bartholomew's, opened in 1874, which cost £18,000 and could seat 2000 people. The church of St. Martin, opened in 1875 cost £12,000, but on this occasion the cost was shared between various members of the Wagner family as the building was erected as a memorial to the late H.M. Wagner. One other church, outside Brighton, built by A.D. Wagner, was at Buxted (1885–6). Altogether the younger Wagner is rumoured to have spent some £70,000 on financing churches, schools, and even houses for his poorer parishioners.[20]

Although all these churches were Anglo-Catholic there were significant differences between them. St. Martin's was fairly moderate: a weekly sung Eucharist was not begun until 1888 nor the eucharistic vestments worn until 1896.[21] At the other extreme was St. Bartholomew's where vestments and a daily eucharist had been introduced in the temporary mission church as early as 1870. Four confessionals were installed in 1879, Stations of the Cross in 1881, reservation of the sacrament in 1896.[22] It was the more extreme of the Brighton churches that produced most of the secessions to Rome: two curates and the organist at St. Bartholomew's in 1878, and another three curates in the two succeeding decades; one curate at St. Paul's in 1876 and one at the Annunciation in 1881. The most serious crisis, however, occurred in 1910 when the vicars of both St. Bartholomew's and the Annunciation resigned to become Roman Catholics, along with several members of their congregations, when the bishop of Chichester prohibited both benediction and exposition of the Blessed Sacrament. There is no doubt that successive bishops of Chichester found Brighton Anglo-Catholics an embarrassment, particularly when they promoted Protestant demonstrations, petitions and riots, even though all the bishops were themselves moderate 'high churchmen'. None, however, took any substantial action before 1910, and the services prohibited then had been specifically condemned by the Royal Commission on Ecclesiastical Discipline. Bishop Gilbert (1842–70) was probably so tired of his fruitless struggles with J.M. Neale at East Grinstead as to have no stomach for similar wrangles with A.D. Wagner. Bishop Durnford (1870–95) was even prepared to visit the offending churches; at the consecration of St. Bartholomew's in 1887 he defended outward beauty in worship but asked that the altar candles should not actually be lit whilst he was in the building.[23]

Wagner's influence and position in Brighton was unusual. The continued success and growth of Anglo-Catholicism in the town after 1900 had much to do with the way in which church extension had been organised in the town by him and his father. Successive vicars of Brighton, all at least moderate 'high churchmen' themselves, enjoyed considerable patronage, including that of St. Martin's and St. Michael's; the patronage of the churches established for or by A.D. Wagner himself was placed in the hands of a trust whose members included the bishop of Chichester, the vicar of Brighton, and the vicars of all the churches in the trust. The ecclesiastical dominance of a large town by one family had few comparisons elsewhere in England, except perhaps in Leeds where the 'Hookism' of many churches was a direct result of the patronage of the vicar of Leeds, and shared some features in common with the 'Wagnerism' of Brighton.[24]

Later Ritualist Parishes

The variety in types of parishes influenced by the Oxford Movement, encompassed in the pioneer ritualist ministries discussed above, was continued in the many other ritualist parishes of the late nineteenth and early twentieth centuries. The popularity of the 'ritualist slum priest' phrase bandied about so freely by even otherwise responsible historians has generally led to two serious misconceptions: firstly that most ritualist activity was confined to socially deprived communities, and secondly that ritualist priests were the only Anglican clergymen with a social conscience. In fact, certainly in the south of England and to a lesser extent elsewhere, the number of Anglo-Catholic clergy in the 'slum priest' category was a small minority. The majority of ritualist parishes were either in the more middle-class urban communities or in the rural areas. Five typical examples illustrate the variety of parishes involved: the urban parishes of St. Michael, Southampton, and St. Agatha, Portsmouth; the suburban parish of St. Peter, Parkstone; the rural parishes of Portleven and Tedburn St. Mary.

St. Michael's, Southampton, was one of only a few medieval churches in the larger towns of southern England to become a centre of ritualist activity, and indeed was an unlikely candidate for such innovations. During the 'papal aggression' crisis of 1850–1 the parish vestry had petitioned both the sovereign and the bishop of Winchester against 'the Romanising teaching and practices of a great number of clergymen of the Church of England', which it considered were 'calculated to undermine the great principles of

Protestantism and to set up in the land a species of priestly domination repugnant to our constitutional liberty'.[25] Yet in 1870 the same parishioners were forced to come to terms with the fact that their new vicar, Francis Maund Gregory, born in 1841 and formerly curate at the Anglo-Catholic St. Paul's, Knightsbridge (where Bennett of Frome had once been incumbent), was just such a 'Romaniser'. He inherited a church which had only been re-arranged as a preaching house as lately as 1828, but during 1872–3 the galleries, box pews and three-decker pulpit were swept away (an exceptionally late date for an important town church) and replaced by the customary Tractarian fittings. But Gregory's architectural and liturgical changes were not popular and his ministry, which lasted until his death in 1899, was in many ways a disaster. A once fashionable eclectic congregation was dispersed and replaced by a much smaller one; the number of regular communicants never rose above a hundred.[26] Despite this Gregory was succeeded by another Anglo-Catholic and St. Michael's settled down to be a typical, not very successful, Edwardian ritualist parish, rather more typical in fact than the better publicised parishes of popular memory.

One of these was St. Agatha's, Portsmouth, established in 1882 by Winchester College as its contribution towards the spiritual needs of a large and deprived urban community, and finding in its second missioner, Robert Dolling (1885–96) the ideal 'ritualist slum priest'. It is difficult to know how successful Dolling was in spiritual terms; there can be little questioning of his achievements in the social field. His own account of his work in Portsmouth and that given by his contemporary biographer[27] suggest that his spiritual success was considerable, but the surviving records of his successor, G.H. Tremenheere, suggest that congregations after 1900 were very modest.[28] Under both Dolling and Tremenheere the Winchester College Mission was conducted on aggressive Anglo-Catholic lines. Soon after the former's arrival in Portsmouth there was a daily communion service at St. Agatha's and four celebrations on Sundays, including one for children, and various extra-liturgical services such as Vespers of the Dead and of the Blessed Sacrament. Enormous emphasis was placed on the need for regular confession to a priest as the best way of leading a profoundly spiritual life. In his dealings with three bishops of Winchester Dolling refused to compromise on even the most unimportant aspects of ritual practice and he used the conflict with Davidson over the consecration of the permanent church as a convenient matter of principle on which to resign.

Many of the most successful Anglo-Catholic parishes in the long term were to be found, not in the centres of the major urban communities, but in their suburbs, and a good example is St. Peter's, Parkstone, which lay between Bournemouth and Poole and benefitted from the expansion of both towns in the period after 1850. Bournemouth itself had been a centre of much Tractarian, though largely non-ritualist, activity since 1845 when A.M. Bennett had become vicar of the parish church. Parkstone had only become an independent parish in 1833 but was to become the major ritualist centre in the area with the appointment of E.E. Dugmore to the vicarage in 1872. Dugmore, who was vicar for 38 years and who became a canon of Salisbury in 1890, was responsible for rebuilding the parish church and for building four daughter churches, two of which later became independent parish churches. These, however, were to be no ordinary buildings. St. Peter's, rebuilt in stages between 1876 and 1901, was one of the major works of the major 'high church' architect, J.L. Pearson. St. Osmund's is one of the few, and one of the most effective, neo-Byzantine churches in England. Dugmore, like many other Anglo-Catholics, believed that beautiful services required beautiful buildings in which they could be carried out; he achieved this aim spectacularly not once but twice.[29]

Ritualist activity in the rural areas has been generally underestimated by historians of Victorian Anglicanism. In the south of England it was in rural or small town parishes that the impact of the Oxford Movement was first felt. Even before 1840 there were Tractarians like Hawker at Morwenstow, Keble at Hursley and Manning at West Lavington, and later on one thinks of Butler at Wantage, Denison at East Brent and Neale at East Grinstead. In south-east Hampshire there was a significant group of rural Tractarian or ritualist parishes on the northern outskirts of Portsmouth: Farlington, Purbrook, Widley and Wymering.[30] Among the incumbents of these parishes were George Nugée and Alfred Poole, two former curates of St. Barnabas, Pimlico, where ritual riots had taken place in 1850. Another significant group of ritualist parishes was established in the Chard district of Somerset, the initiative being taken in the 1870s at Barrington and Shepton Beauchamp.[31] Rural ritualism could be detected by the end of the century in both populous as well as remote and scattered rural communities, of which Porthleven in Cornwall and Tedburn St. Mary in Devon can serve as appropriate contrasting illustrations. Porthleven was a large coastal village in the parish of Sithney, where a separate ecclesiastical district had been created in 1842.

Porthleven, like most of the larger villages in Cornwall, was a stronghold of Methodism and the appointment of the advanced ritualist, Thomas Lockyer Williams, to the vicarage in 1851 provoked considerable conflict. Despite this he remained at Porthleven until 1889 and was able to establish a successful Anglo-Catholic tradition in the parish which was maintained by his successors. The success of a strong ritualist tradition, including the use of both vestments and incense, in a village like Porthleven was of considerable significance for the later ecclesiastical development of Cornwall, which reacted against the strength of Methodism by becoming almost universally 'high church' by the end of the nineteenth century. Indeed by the early years of the twentieth century Cornwall numbered among its clergy two who were so extreme as to have little in common with their Anglican brethren, and whose churches were clearly meant to resemble their Roman Catholic counterparts in Brittany: Sandys Wason of Cury and Gunwalloe and Bernard Walke of St. Hilary. In 1910 the bishop of Truro inhibited Wason from religious duties outside his own parish and refused to visit his churches. His response was to introduce the Roman Catholic service of Benediction and in 1919 a group of irate local farmers 'arrived at the vicarage' and 'bundled the vicar and his belongings unceremoniously on a cart and carried them over to St. Hilary', as a result of which he resigned.[33] Walke was appointed to St. Hilary in 1912 and mixed extreme ritualism with extreme socialism. All efforts by the bishop and disaffected parishioners to tone down the ritual at St. Hilary failed and eventually in 1932 'a party of Kensit supporters came in cars and a coach from Plymouth and elsewhere outside the county. By a deception they got into the church, brushed aside the vicar . . . and with crowbars and hammers broke down statues, pictures, the reredos of the high altar . . . In the church strewn with stone dust, fragments of plaster and wood, and with the altar linen bedraggled and torn, Kensit read prayers and the Ten Commandments. They had . . . allowed Walke to remove the Sacrament, which he did through a path lined with kneeling parishioners holding candles'.[34] Four years later Walke resigned. Some years earlier, C.W.E. Tothill, rector of Tedburn St. Mary, a scattered rural parish in Devon, had suffered similar attacks on his rather milder ritualism. Tothill became curate of the parish in 1862 and succeeded to the rectory in 1865. By the end of the century it was one of four rural parishes in Devon in which both incense and vestments were used. In 1886 a petition, signed by one of the churchwardens and 62 parishioners, was sent to the bishop of Exeter asking him to allow the prosecution of Tothill under the Public Worship Regulation Act. The bishop, the Evangelical E.H. Bickersteth, however, indicated that he would veto the prosecution on the grounds that he had received a counter-petition supporting Tothill signed by 90 parishioners. The churchwarden alleged that most of these were schoolchildren and that the counter-petition had been organised by the schoolmaster who supported Tothill; he claimed that most parishioners had ceased to attend the parish church, but instead attended either neighbouring parishes or the Methodist chapel which had recently been opened in the parish, no doubt to take advantage of the conflict. Tothill himself, however, considered that it was the churchwarden, a newcomer to the parish, and a handful of dissenters who had stirred up the people against him. He admitted that his congregation had declined but believed that this was entirely the fault of the churchwarden who had deliberately persecuted him since he had moved into the parish.[35]

One group of ritualist parishes that requires specific consideration is those to be found in the larger seaside resorts. The general assumption has been that inland watering places, such as Cheltenham and Tunbridge Wells, were centres of Evangelicalism and that the seaside resorts were strongholds of ritualism. Whilst there is some general truth in this view it requires some modification. Bath, for instance, though certainly an Evangelical stronghold, had three well-established ritualist parishes by the last quarter of the nineteenth century, and at Tunbridge Wells, despite Evangelical protestations, the new church of St. Barnabas was established in 1881, under the patronage of Keble College, Oxford, specifically to offer a Tractarian alternative to the Evangelical monopoly of Anglican worship in the town.[36] The level of ritualist activity in seaside resorts varied considerably. As we have seen it was extreme, though limited to a smallish number of churches, in Brighton; it was more widespread, though also more moderate, in Penzance and Torquay. The least ritualistic seaside resorts seem to have been the Kentish ones of Herne Bay and Margate, the latter as strongly Evangelical as Tunbridge Wells. But at another Kentish resort, Folkestone, there was nearly as much conflict over ritualism, with Matthew Woodward at the parish church, Husband at St. Michael's and Ridsdale at St. Peter's, as there was in Brighton. Ritualist churches in many seaside resorts were frequently built as a result of donations or legacies from wealthy visitors, and occasionally even after mass lobbying for their erection. Christ Church, St. Leonards-on-Sea, was built in 1859–60 at the sole cost of Lady St. John, mother of the first rector, Charles Lyndhurst

Vaughan (1828–95). Vaughan was vicar of St. Neots in Hunting-donshire from 1854, and his mother had arranged for the new church to be looked after by the clergy of the neighbouring 'high church' parish of St. Mary Magdalen, until he resigned St. Neots to reside at St. Leonards-on-Sea in 1863. There were daily services from 1863, a weekly early communion service from 1864, and choral celebrations of Holy Communion from 1865. By 1868 lighted candles and vestments were in use, and a daily communion service began in 1870. Between 1872 and 1875 the first church was replaced by a much larger building designed by Sir Arthur Blomfield. The new church was consecrated by Bishop Durnford of Chichester in 1884. The use of incense began in 1886 though it was only used on the major festivals until the congregation became accustomed to it. Although Christ Church clearly drew a large proportion of its congregation from amongst the wealthy residents and visitors, it was envisaged that, like the ritualist churches in Brighton and other seaside resorts, it should function as a centre of social concern for the less well-to-do inhabitants: a creche for working mothers was begun in 1872 and in 1891 the clergy of the church spearheaded a mission supported by all the Anglican churches in Hastings and St. Leonards.[37] The eventual establish-ment of the ritualist parish of St. Andrew's, Worthing, in what was, like Margate, an Evangelical stronghold, is particularly interesting for the light it throws on the development of English seaside resorts. In 1878 the Anglican Community of St. Mary the Virgin established a convalescent home in Worthing, and a small group of lay people who had recourse to their chapel formed the nucleus of a campaign to establish a 'high church' parish in the town. A site was purchased and a building committee formed in 1885 though, as at Tunbridge Wells, the local Evangelical clergy endeavoured to frustrate these efforts by offering to enlarge the accommodation of existing churches. The new church was, howev-er, built, with the support of the bishop who secured the assignment of a small ecclesiastical district from three existing parishes, which meant that an independent parish could be created. It was, however, realised that the congregation would always be eclectic and that many would be visitors. Indeed it would seem that the likely benefit for the tourist trade was one of the most powerful arguments in favour of the new church, if one newspaper report was to be believed: 'We warmly congratulate the people of Worthing . . . No watering place has a chance of doing well that has not at least one decent church . . . a health resort which does not provide for the Ritualist cuts itself off from a large section of the community'.[38] St. Andrew's, Worthing, was consecrated in 1888, and once again the patronage was vested in Keble College, Oxford. Vestments and incense were in use from the beginning. A crisis over the insistence that private confession was an obligatory preliminary to confirmation, and the subsequent episcopal enquiry, resulted in the secession of the vicar and one of the curates to Rome in 1905. The tradition was, however, continued by the next and all subsequent incumbents.

Patronage and Societies

Two aspects of parochial ritualism which have in the past received insufficient attention from ecclesiastical historians have been the role of patrons in promoting ritualism and the strength given to the ritualist clergy by the various national societies founded to protect 'high churchmen' or to popularise their teaching. Tables 4 and 5 summarise the situation in both respects in the parishes of southern England, firstly for a group of parishes throughout the region and secondly for a group of parishes in its most 'high church' county, Cornwall, which was practically coterminous with the diocese of Truro.

Looking first at the patrons it is very clear how much the spread of the Oxford Movement in the parishes owed to non-episcopal patronage. We have noted how on several occasions patronage was vested in Keble College, Oxford, which, as a Tractarian foundation, could be relied on to appoint 'high churchmen', indeed almost always extreme ritualists, to its parishes. But Keble College, Oxford, were not the only collegiate patrons of ritualist parishes, similar appointments being made by Eton College at Clewer and Winchester College at Portsmouth. The role of private patrons, very frequently members of the aristocracy, in presenting 'high churchmen' to livings was also significant. In the south of England the most important patrons in this category included the Marquesses of Bath and Salisbury, and the Earl of Shaftesbury. The role of the last-named is particularly interesting, since the seventh earl, who died in 1885, was the noted Evangelical philanthropist and politician. It was his son's widow, the eighth earl dying in 1886, acting on behalf of the ninth earl during his minority, who presented ritualist incumbents to the Dorset parishes of Hinton Martell and Horton, and who built the chapel of Woodlands as daughter church to the latter in 1892. Although the diocesan bishops presented to fewer than a quarter of the ritualist livings in the south of England, their role in promoting ritualism was certainly not negligible and the statistics do give some support to the contemporary Evangelical assertion that the bishops were doing little to curtail parochial ritualism, particularly when they themselves were known to have presented ritualists to their own livings. One parish in which a dispute over the appointment of a ritualist incumbent actually led to a change of patronage was St. Stephen's-by-Launceston, where the patrons were the ratepayers and feoffees of the parish. In 1900 a vacancy occurred in the living. The previous incumbent had been a 'high churchman' and the feoffees wanted the tradition to continue. The ratepayers were, however, of a different opinion, and the two groups presented rival candidates. After six months, with no settlement, the right of presentation lapsed to Bishop Gott, who passed over both the rival candidates, but appointed another 'high churchman', the vicar of Lostwithiel. As a result of this dispute the patronage of the living was transferred from the original patrons to the dean and chapter of Truro.[39]

There is no doubt that without the Anglican system of patronage, under which no individual or institution had a monopoly of presentation to benefices in any diocese, the parochial success of the Oxford Movement could have been very severely hampered. The fact that it was not hampered had much to do with the significant network of private patrons, supported by a small number of collegiate institutions, supplemented later on by a number of ritualist patronage trusts, who made it their business to see that ritualist clergy were presented to benefices and thereby allowed to impose their liturgical and theological views on a frequently suspicious laity.

The role of the ritualist societies was complementary to that of the ritualist patrons. They provided a network of support for ritualist clergy under attack from their laity. They provided a mechanism whereby ritualist opinions could be promoted in the national and diocesan and even parochial organisations of the established church. Finally, they provided a forum where like-minded people, clerical and lay, could get together to discuss their beliefs and problems. The largest of the ritualist societies was the English Church Union which had branches in many of even the more moderate 'high church' parishes in England and Wales. Of the two societies which promoted special 'high church' concerns, the Confraternity of the Blessed Sacrament, founded by T.T. Carter of Clewer, enjoyed very considerable support in ritualist parishes; the appeal of the Guild of All Souls, which encouraged prayers for the departed, was slightly more limited. The national organisation with the most restricted membership, confined to priests and ordinands, was the Society of the Holy Cross, but its influence was considerable. It was this society which was particularly active in the promotion of retreats and auricular confession. It operated as a secret society, which greatly assisted its influence among the clergy, and its surviving membership records reveal that its support tended to be concentrated in particular localities. Many of its members were beneficed in the south of England, and although they included well-known ritualists like Bennett, Carter, Courtenay and Prynne, and their curates, there were a fair number of country clergymen whose parishes were not among the more well-known centres of ritualism: Purbrook and Wymering (Hampshire); Flimwell (Sussex); Pennard, Elworthy, Great Elm, Farmborough, Bicknoller, East Brent and Hambridge (Somerset); Landreth and St. Erth (Cornwall); Faringdon, Benson and South Morton (Berkshire); Kenn and Tallaton (Devon); Northfleet and Stone (Kent).[40] The influence and strength of these ritualist societies was considerable, and a very important factor in assisting the spread of 'high church' opinions and practices among both clergy and laity.

Conclusion

The principal aim of this paper has been to demonstrate that, contrary to popular opinion, the strength of Anglican ritualism in the late nineteenth and early twentieth centuries was not confined to the metropolis and a few specially selected resort towns. It was, apart from a fairly heavy concentration of Anglo-Catholic parishes in London, reasonably evenly distributed throughout the country. In the south of England the ritualist domination of the coastal resort towns has been grossly exaggerated, even in the case of Brighton, which owed its unique position in the development of Anglican ritualism to the influence, patronage and wealth of one clerical family, the Wagners. By contrast relatively little attention has been paid to the significant role of ritualism in the ecclesiastical history of towns such as Reading, Swindon and Taunton. It is to be hoped that the general conclusions drawn in this paper will lead in the future to some detailed studies of ritualism in these and other places, and to some consideration of why some towns attracted ritualist clergy, whilst others, such as Aldershot, Canterbury, Maidstone and Reigate, clearly did not.

As well as considering the general question of the ritualist geography of southern England this paper has also tried to show the common ground that existed between ritualist parishes in very different types of communities: the contrasting caution or rashness in the introduction of liturgical and other changes; the response of the laity; the success or otherwise of the experiment in terms of the size of the congregation; the reliance on wealthy benefactors to provide buildings and endowments; the role of both aristocratic and ecclesiastical patrons, and of the national ritualist societies. It is important neither to underrate nor to overrate the success of the Oxford Movement's parochial impact. In terms of the number of parishes that were fully ritualist by *c.*1900 that success was severely limited. Overall, vestments were worn in about 12% of the Anglican churches in the south of England, whilst incense was used in less than 2%. Yet when one considers the enormous public hostility to ritual innovations, together with the legislative attempt to control ritualism through the Public Worship Regulation Act and two royal commissions into the subject, then the fact that extreme ritualism had established even such a limited foothold in the Church of England was indeed remarkable. And it has to be remembered that many other Tractarian practices, still violently condemned by Evangelicals, such as lighted candles, the mixed chalice and the eastward position at the eucharist, had become the norm in dioceses such as Canterbury and Truro by 1900, and accepted in more than a quarter of all the parishes in every diocese of southern England, with the sole exception of Bath and Wells.

The plain fact was, and the Evangelicals recognised this, that the ritualists had outmanoeuvred both their critics and the Anglican establishment. Many Evangelicals blamed the bishops for this, but in reality the real cause of the ritualist victory was the same Anglican system which had allowed the Evangelicals themselves to survive in the face of much hostility in the late eighteenth and early nineteenth centuries. There was no adequate mechanism in the Church of England for securing uniformity of doctrine and liturgical practice. Parishes were effectively independent, bishops did not have a monopoly of patronage (some of which was exercised by highly eccentric landowners), incumbents once appointed had security of tenure and it was notoriously difficult to secure their deprivation on anything except grounds of gross immorality or neglect of duty. When attempts were made through the courts to define the historic practice and teaching of the church they frequently produced either conflicting legal opinions or, as in the case of the Gorham Judgement, a wholly unsatisfactory attempt at compromise. Efforts to regulate ritualism through the Public Worship Regulation Act were frustrated, partly through the ability of bishops to veto what they considered were unwise prosecutions, and partly through the stubbornness of the ritualist clergy, who realised that, if they stood firm and were imprisoned for contempt, they would quickly be seen as martyrs to a cause. One of the most remarkable changes in public opinion was that which took place between the mid-1870s, when everybody was demanding the suppression of ritualism, and the mid-1880s, by which time the popular view was enormously hostile to the imprisonment of clergymen who believed that what they were doing had divine authority.

But a further factor in the growth of ritualism was a growing appreciation of ritual by Anglican worshippers. There had been from the 1830s a forceful lay lobby, mostly aristocratic, in support of Tractarian principles. As the decades passed this lobby grew considerably and gained a very strong adherence from the female middle class element in Anglican congregations. There were of course still cases of parishes, even in the late nineteenth and early twentieth centuries, and indeed later than that, where ritualist incumbents imposed unwanted ceremonial on hostile congregations and either divided their parishes or emptied their churches. But equally there were many parishes where the pace of ritual change was determined by the congregation, where 'high church' clergy were deliberately encouraged to introduce a more elaborate ritual by popular demand.

The various attempts to control ritualism put forward by the bishops — not all, of course, since some were either secret or open supporters of the ritualists — and by Parliament were doomed to failure. Frequently battles were still being fought after the issue had been effectively conceded, and it has been argued that if greater flexibility had been shown some of the more extreme manifestations of ritualism could have been suppressed. It is doubtful if this would have been the case. What is remarkable about Anglican ritualism is the speed at which it developed once it had begun. The critics never really came to terms with this and clearly misjudged the key support for ritualists in certain areas, or the determination of the ritualist clergy to fight for what they believed in.

Ritualism in southern England in 1900 was, therefore, well entrenched and widely distributed throughout the region. There was nowhere, with the possible exception of Surrey, where ritualism had made little headway, as it had in parts of Wales and East Anglia. In social terms it had as much effect on the prevailing ecclesiastical climate as the challenges provided by the growth of dissent and the break-up of the Anglican domination of religious life over the previous century. Its detailed manifestations and its progress in different parts of the region would certainly repay further attention, and one hopes that the historians of local communities will be looking out for the way in which the teachings of the Oxford Movement affected the Church of England in their community in the years after 1840.

Table 1: Ritual Observance in the Provinces of Canterbury and York, 1903

Churches adopting	Eastward Position (%)	Lighted Candles (%)	Mixed Chalice (%)	Eucharistic Vestments (%)
Diocesan average	39	26	24	10
Southern dioceses				
Truro	84	62	56	24
London	70	52	45	24
Canterbury	72	47	38	12
Oxford	53	39	32	14
Winchester	55	36	31	9
St. Albans	47	34	31	11
Chichester	48	31	31	10
Gloucester	43	31	28	11
Salisbury	42	30	32	9
Exeter	40	33	28	12
Rochester	40	30	27	14
Bristol	38	29	24	14
Bath & Wells	27	21	19	10
Midland dioceses				
Lichfield	52	31	34	14
Worcester	44	27	28	11
Lincoln	40	29	27	13
Peterborough	44	27	26	9
Ely	38	30	26	12
Hereford	30	20	15	5
Norwich	20	16	15	8
Northern dioceses				
Newcastle	48	32	31	14
Wakefield	46	27	36	12
Southwell	37	27	27	15
Durham	43	22	30	9
Chester	40	25	24	7
York	35	25	21	12
Ripon	28	20	17	5
Manchester	30	11	18	4

Table 1: Ritual Observance in the Provinces of Canterbury and York, 1903

Churches adopting	Eastward (%) Position	Lighted (%) Candles	Mixed (%) Chalice	Eucharistic (%) Vestments
Northern dioceses				
Liverpool	29	11	16	5
Carlisle	15	3	3	1
Sodor & Man	4	–	–	–
Welsh dioceses				
Llandaff	32	23	21	12
St. Asaph	18	9	8	3
St. Davids	11	8	7	3
Bangor	19	5	3	1

Table 2: Anglo-Catholic Churches in different types of Communities in Southern England, 1903

Churches with:	Vestments	Incense
Principal urban centres	31	12
Resort towns	47	16
Large market towns	11	4
Small market towns	48	5
Rural parishes	205	19
Total	342	56

Table 3: Anglo-Catholic Churches in the larger towns of Southern England, 1903

Town:	Population	Anglican Churches	Churches with Vestments	Churches with Incense
Bristol	328,945	73	10	4
Portsmouth/Gosport	217,017	30	3	2
Plymouth/Devonport	178,073	28	7	4
Brighton/Hove	160,013	35	7	6
Medway Towns*	110,177	15	2	1
Southampton	104,824	18	3	1
Reading	72,217	14	6	–
Bournemouth/Poole	66,466	30	3	2
Hastings/St. Leonards	65,528	21	3	1
Thanet Towns*	57,317	13	2	–
Bath	49,839	21	3	2
Exeter	47,185	28	3	2
Swindon	45,006	6	3	1

Town:	Population	Anglican Churches	Churches with Vestments	Churches with Incense
Eastbourne	43,344	9	2	–
Torquay/Paignton	42,010	17	6	–
Dover	41,794	8	2	–
Maidstone	33,516	10	–	–
Tunbridge Wells	33,373	8	1	–
Aldershot	30,974	4	–	–
Folkestone	30,650	8	2	1
Gravesend	27,196	5	1	–
St. Helier	26,418	8	3	1
Reigate/Redhill	25,993	5	–	–
Canterbury	24,899	15	–	–
Taunton	21,087	6	3	–
Winchester	20,929	15	1	1
Worthing	20,015	6	1	1

*Medway Towns: Chatham, Gillingham and Rochester

*Thanet Towns: Broadstairs, Margate and Ramsgate

Table IV: Patronage of Anglo-Catholic Churches in Southern England, 1903

Churches in:	Group A[1]	Group B[1]
Private patronage	14	21
Bishop's patronage[2]	12	11
Incumbent's patronage	10	6
Trustees' patronage	8	–
Collegiate patronage	6	–
Crown patronage[2]	3	5
Capitular patronage	2	3
Other patronage[3]	1	3
Total no. of parishes	56	49

Notes:

(1) Churches in Group A includes all churches with incense and vestments in southern England; those in Group B include all churches with vestments in the county of Cornwall and diocese of Truro.

(2) In two churches in Group A and four in Group B, the diocesan bishop and the Crown presented alternately.

(3) The Lord Chancellor was patron of one church each in Groups A and B; the Duke of Cornwall and the ratepayers and feoffees of the parish were the patrons of one parish each in Group B.

Table 5: Membership of Ritualist Societies among Clergy of
Anglo-Catholic Churches in Southern England, 1903

Members in:	Group A	Group B
English Church Union	50	28
Confraternity of Blessed Sacrament	46	17
Guild of All Souls	22	1
Society of Holy Cross	15	1
Associates of Society of St. John Evangelist	3	–
Total no. of parishes	56	49

Note:
Groups are the same as in Table 4 above. Numbers are counted as one
per parish even if more than one clergyman belongs to the same society in
the same parish.

Appendix: Summary List of Ritualist Churches in Southern England in 1903

Berkshire:
Vestments were worn in 23 churches including six in Reading; the
parish churches of Abingdon, Hungerford and Newbury; St.
Andrew's and St. Stephen's, Clewer, Windsor; All Saints, Boyne
Hill, Maidenhead, where there had been a celebrated confessional
scandal in the late 1850s; St. Leonard's, Wallingford; and All
Souls, South Ascot. Incense was used in only one church, St.
Stephen's, Clewer.

Channel Islands:
Vestments were worn in three churches in St. Helier, Jersey: St.
Luke's, St. Mark's and St. Simon's, in the last named of which,
established as a ritualist church in 1865 and designed by the
distinguished Tractarian architect, G.F. Bodley, incense was also
used. Vestments were not worn in any churches in Guernsey
though at both the ancient parish church and the new church of St.
Stephen's in St. Peter Port candles were lighted, the chalice mixed
and the eastward position taken at the eucharist.

Cornwall:
Vestments were worn in 49 churches including Truro Cathedral;
three churches in Newlyn and Penzance; and the parish churches
of Bodmin, Camborne, Hayle, Launceston, Padstow, Redruth, St.
Columb Major, St. Ives, St. Just-in-Penwith, Saltash and Torpoint.
Incense was used at Breage, Germoe, Lezant and Porthleven.
E.M. Phillipps-Treby, rector of Forrabury, became a Roman
Catholic in 1895.

Devon:

Vestments were worn in 58 churches including seven in Plymouth and Devonport, six in Torquay and Paignton, three in Exeter and two in Bovey Tracey; in the parish churches of Bideford, Dartmouth, Kingsbridge, Okehampton, Plympton St. Mary, Plympton St. Maurice, Salcombe and Shaldon; and, among the 27 village churches, at Lew Trenchard, where the distinguished antiquarian, folklorist and hymn-writer Sabine Baring-Gould, author of *Onward Christian Soldiers*, had been rector since 1881. Incense was used at four churches in Plymouth (All Saints, St. James', St. Peter's and St. John's, Sutton-on-Plym); two in Exeter (All Hallows and St. Mary Steps); St. John's, Bovey Tracey; and in the village churches of Bridgerule, Chardstock, Mary Tavy and Tedburn St. Mary.

Dorset:

Vestments were worn in 16 churches, all but two of which were in rural parishes, the exceptions being St. Peter's, Parkstone, and St. James', Shaftesbury. Incense was used at St. Peter's, Parkstone, and in the village churches of Alderholt, Hinton Martel, Horton and Woodlands.* J.B.M. Camm, rector of Monkton Wyld, became a Roman Catholic in 1891.

*The *Ritualist Clergy List* implies that both vestments and incense were used at both Horton and its dependent chapelry of Woodlands, but it is possible that they were only in use at Woodlands and not at Horton.

Hampshire:

Vestments were worn in 30 churches including three in Portsmouth and Gosport; three in Southampton; two in Bournemouth; in Romsey Abbey; and in the parish churches in Basingstoke and Farnborough. The village churches in which vestments were used included those at Hursley and Wymering, where the eminent Tractarians John Keble and George Nugee, respectively, had been beneficed. Incense was used at St. Clement's, Bournemouth; St. Agatha's and St. Michael's, Portsmouth; St. Michael's, Southampton; and Holy Trinity, Winchester. Vestments and incense were also in use at Alton Abbey, but this was not a parish church. W.B. Drewe, vicar of Longstock, became a Roman Catholic in 1885.

Isle of Wight:

Vestments were worn in Holy Trinity, Cowes; St. Michael, Swanmore, Ryde, in which incense was also used; St. Alban, Ventnor; and in the village churches at Arreton, Chale, Godshill, Gurnard, Haven Street and Whitwell.

Kent:

Excluding the area now in Greater London, vestments were worn in 33 churches including two each in the Medway Towns, Thanet, Dover, Folkestone and Whitstable, and one each in Gravesend and Tunbridge Wells. Incense was used in St. Saviour's, Folkestone; St. Mary's, Strood; and in the village church of Egerton. It was alleged in the *Ritualistic Clergy List* that S.R. Hole, 'late Dean of Rochester', wore vestments, took the eastward position, and used both lighted candles and the mixed chalice at the eucharist. C.J. Ridsdale, vicar of St. Peter's, Folkestone, since 1869, who had been prosecuted under the Public Worship Regulation Act of 1874 and had sought a dispensation from Archbishop Tait to be absolved from his obligation, according to his interpretation of the Ornaments Rubric, to wear the eucharistic vestments, appears not to have resumed the use of vestments in 1903.

Somerset (inc. Bristol):

Vestments were worn in 55 churches including ten in Bristol; three each in Bath, Frome and Taunton; two each in Clevedon and Yeovil; St. John's, Bridgwater; All Saints, Weston-super-Mare; and the parish churches of Bruton and Radstock. Although vestments were worn in 24 village churches, these did not include East Brent, where Archdeacon Denison had been beneficed between 1845 and 1896. Incense was used in four churches in Bristol (All Saints, Clifton; Holy Nativity, Knowle; St. Raphael's and St. Simon's; St. Raphael's was actually closed between 1878 and 1893 because of 'ritualistic difficulties'); three churches in Frome (St. John's, St. Mary's and Christ Church); two churches in Bath (St. John's and St. Mary's, Bathwick); All Saints, Clevedon; and the village churches of Chaffcombe, Cloford and Hambridge. W.M. Hunnybun, vicar of Bicknoller, became a Roman Catholic in 1872, as did F.B. Lord, rector of Farmborough, and Lord F.G. Osborne, rector of Great Elm, in 1877.

Surrey:

Excluding the area now in Greater London, vestments were worn in only nine churches, all rural with the exception of St. Nicholas, Guildford. There were no churches in the county in which incense was used.

Sussex:

Vestments were worn in 34 churches including seven in Brighton and Hove, three in Hastings and St. Leonards and two in Eastbourne; St. Mary's, East Grinstead; St. Michael's, Lewes; St. Mary's, Littlehampton; St. Andrew's, Worthing; and, among the 17 village churches, Buxted, founded by A.D. Wagner, and West

Lavington, where Cardinal Manning had been rector and archdeacon before he became a Roman Catholic. Incense was used in six churches in Brighton (All Souls, The Annunciation, St. Bartholomew's, St. Martin's, St. Mary Magdalene's and St. Michael's); Christ Church, St. Leonards-on-Sea; St. Andrew's, Worthing; and the village church at Hadlow Down. J.H. Spelling, rector of Westbourne, became a Roman Catholic in 1888.

Wiltshire:

Vestments were worn in 23 churches including three churches in Swindon; St. Mary's, Marlborough; St. Martin's, Salisbury; and All Saints, Westbury. Incense was used in St. Paul's, Swindon, and in the village church at Baverstock.

Notes

[1]   E. Waugh, *Brideshead Revisited* (1945), bk. 1, cap. 1.

[2]   On later Anglo-Catholicism generally the best introductions, though superficial, are A. Hughes, *The Rivers of the Flood* (1961), and P.F. Anson, *Fashions in Church Furnishings* (1965), especially pp. 206–17, 303–27.

[3]   See P.T. Marsh, *The Victorian Church in Decline* (1969), pp. 158–92, and J.F. Bentley, *Ritualism and Politics* (Oxford 1978), the latter reviewed by the present writer in *Southern History*, i, pp. 252–3.

[4]   C. Mackenzie, *Sinister Street* (1913), bk. 2, cap. 6.

[5]   A. Hughes, *op. cit.,* p. 34.

[6]   Bishops: A.T. Gilbert (1842–70), R. Durnford (1870–95), E.R. Wilberforce (1895–1908).

[7]   Bishops: S. Wilberforce (1845–69), J.F. Mackarness (1870–89), W. Stubbs (1889–1901), F. Paget (1901–11).

[8]   Bishops: E. Denison (1837–54), W.K. Hamilton (1854–69), G. Moberly (1869–85), J. Wordsworth (1885–1911).

[9]   See H.M. Brown, *A Century for Cornwall* (Truro 1976), especially pp. 22–64.

[10]   See M.A. Crowther, *Church Embattled* (Newton Abbot 1970), pp. 186–95.

[11]   A study of Chislehurst and its ritualist rector, Francis Henry Murray (1846–1902), by the present writer will appear in *Archaeologia Cantiana*, xcviii, during 1983.

[12]   *Life and Letters of Thomas Thelluson Carter,* ed. W.H. Hutchings, (1903), pp. 34, 39.

[13]   *Ibid.,* p. 41.

[14]   *Ibid.,* p. 173.

[15]   F. Bennett, *The Story of W.J.E. Bennett* (1909), pp. 159–68.

[16]   *Ibid.,* pp. 206–9.

[17]   *Ibid.,* pp. 200–1.

[18]   For a recent assessment of Prynne see G.C.B. Davies, *Henry Phillpotts* (1954), pp. 287–306; the contemporary biography by A.C. Kelway was published in 1905.

[19]   Now in the Devon Record Office; I am extremely grateful fo Mr. Dickinson of that office for bringing this document to my attention.

[20]   The best reassessment of Wagner and Brighton Anglo-Catholicism is E.P.

Hennock, 'The Anglo-Catholics and Church Extension in Victorian Brighton', *Studies in Sussex Church History*, ed. M.J. Kitch, (University of Sussex 1981), pp. 173–88. H.H. Maughan, *Wagner of Brighton* (Loughlinstown 1949), is brief and slight.

[21] M.J. Leppard and K.H. Hackman, *St. Martin's History and Guide* (Brighton 1975), p. 19.

[22] *St. Bartholomew's, Brighton: A Short Story of the Last Fifty Years* (Brighton 1924), pp. 8, 20–1, 33.

[23] *Ibid.*, p. 22.

[24] See W.N. Yates, 'Leeds and the Oxford Movement', *Thoresby Society Publications* lv (1975), especially pp. 19–24.

[25] D.C. Cotton, *History of St. Michael's Church*, (Southampton 1970), p. 22.

[26] Service registers and other very full records of the parish in Southampton City Record Office; see W.N. Yates, 'Urban Church Attendance and the Use of Statistical Evidence, 1850–1900', *Studies in Church History*, xvi (1979), p. 397.

[27] R.R. Dolling, *Ten Years in A Portsmouth Slum* (1896), and C.E. Osborne, *Life of Father Dolling* (1903).

[28] Service registers and some other records in Portsmouth City Records Office; for a re-assessment of Dolling's ministry at St. Agatha's, see the present writer's forthcoming study of 'The Anglican Revival in Victorian Portsmouth' in the *Portsmouth Papers* series.

[29] Dugmore's building achievements are chronicled in *Records of the Church of St. Peter* (Parkstone 1926).

[30] See W.N. Yates, *Ritual Conflict at Farlington and Wymering*, Portsmouth Paper no. 28 (Portsmouth 1978).

[31] R. Dunning, 'Nineteenth Century Parochial Sources', *Studies in Church History*, xi (1975), pp. 302–6.

[32] H.M. Brown, *The Catholic Revival in Cornish Anglicanism*, (St. Winnow 1980), pp. 40–1, 63–4.

[33] H.M. Brown, *A Century for Cornwall* (Truro 1976), p. 80.

[34] *Ibid.*, p. 99.

[35] *Royal Commission on Ecclesiastical Discipline:* minutes of evidence nos. 3116–74.

[36] Correspondence in Kent Archives Office, P371L/28/10.

[37] See H.V. Nicoll, *The Story of Christ Church* (St. Leonards-on-Sea 1909).

[38] *Church Times*, 23 May 1888, quoted in D.R. Elleray, *St. Andrew's Church* (Worthing 1977), p. 9.

[39] M. Fisher, 'The St. Stephen's Patronage Dispute of 1900', *Old Cornwall*, ix (1980), pp. 137–42.

[40] Details from the 1855–81 roll of members of the Society of the Holy Cross in the temporary custody of the Kent Archives Office.

Southern England in the Census of Religious Worship, 1851

B. I. COLEMAN

It is more than a quarter of a century since historians began to make serious use of the evidence provided by the unique official Census of Religious Worship in 1851.[1] Since then calendars of the MS returns for several areas have been published and a number of monographs have utilized the returns for particular localities.[2] It is surprising, however, given its obvious importance, how much of the statistical material readily available in the Census volume remains less than fully exploited. The purpose of the present article is to provide a statistical analysis in some (though far from full) detail of the patterns of worship which the Census revealed in the ten counties grouped in registration districts II (South-Eastern Counties) and V (South-Western Counties). These counties, in their Census order, were extra-metropolitcan Surrey, extra-metropolitan Kent, Sussex, Hampshire and Berkshire in Division II and Wiltshire, Dorset, Devon, Cornwall and Somerset in Division V. They are, conveniently, the ten counties which lay wholly within the area to which *Southern History* is now devoted.

The outline given here of patterns of worship in the region is heavily statistical in character and is based almost entirely upon the printed figures of the Religious Census volume. No attempt has been made for the purposes of this article to make use of the MS returns in the Public Record Office.[3] Nor does the article address itself to most of the questions of analysis and interpretation which the figures raise. One question or set of questions has, however, been borne in mind: namely, in what senses did the ten counties constitute a 'region'? What, if anything, were the area's distinctive features and how far was there a characteristic 'southern England' pattern of religious performance? How homogeneous was the area? What were its significant internal divisions? Such a discussion will certainly not end the need for more detailed studies by county and local historians, but it should provide an appropriate framework for such work. In what follows 'region' refers to the area of the ten counties, and 'division', 'county' and 'district' are all used in the technical sense as defined for the purposes of the

Census of Religious Worship. For Surrey and Kent 'county' should be understood to mean the extra-metropolitan county.

Students of the Census material know that it cannot lay claim to pinpoint accuracy, even as a record of attendances on a single Sunday. There were deficiencies in the original returns and the smaller the area of study by the historian, the less satisfactory the figures tend to be. But for large areas, including nearly all the registration districts, the printed figures convey a reasonably accurate impression of the scale of attendances on 30th March, 1851. The mode of calculation adopted in the tables below is a variant of the 'index of attendance' method. The index figure is produced by aggregating the morning, afternoon and evening attendances and presenting the total as a percentage of the population of the area in question. The figure for England and Wales at the head of Table 1, for example, shows that the total of attendances at all recorded services on 30th March amounted to 58.1% of the population. (Corrected figures which made allowance for deficient or missing returns raised the figure to 60.8%.) Similar calculations can be made for individual denominations or groups of denominations. In our tables the index of attendance (IA) is shown for the aggregate of all forms of worship, for the Church of England, for the aggregate of non-Anglican attendances, for the sum of the Old Dissenting denominations, for the sum of the various Methodist denominations and for Roman Catholics. Also shown is the percentage share (PS) of total attendances gained by the Church of England and by the other denominational categories. The first line of Table 1 shows that Anglican attendances (uncorrected), which amounted to 27.6% of the population, accounted for 47.4% of all attendances in England and Wales. Table 1 provides the figures for the region, for the two divisions and for the ten counties; Table 2 gives them for each of the 174 registration districts in the region.

Two further points need to be made. First, the figures for the divisions, counties and districts are all 'uncorrected'; an estimate for underreturn was made by the Census office only for England and Wales as a whole. The incidence of missing and deficient returns was uneven and for a number of smaller districts it may have vitiated the figures as printed. No allowance for this has been made in the tables. Second, the figures all refer to attendances, not to the numbers of people who attended. Some people attended worship more than once that Sunday — sometimes, it seems, in more than one denomination — and this explains how the IA could exceed 100 in some cases.

Before considering the detailed figures, we might note something of the character of the region as it is generally understood. It is a commonplace among historians of the period that southern England was characterised by strong Anglican practice. Here was the *milieu* of Trollope's Barsetshire. But even the opening lines of *The Warden* (1855) might give us pause. Three cathedral cities in our region — Wells, Salisbury and Exeter — and two outside it — Hereford and Gloucester — were named as possible proto-types of Barchester, and the city was located somewhere in 'the West of England', not in 'the South'. Trollope seems to have been assuming that the Anglican hegemony that characterised Barsetshire was not confined to the ten counties of our region and that some parts of the region were more suitable for his purposes than others. There were certainly a number of counties outside our area with high Anglican attendances.[5] In fact of the twelve counties with the highest Anglican attendances in England and Wales, only five were in the region.[6] Some of the highest Church attendances were to be found in a belt running from East Anglia through the South Midlands into the inner West Country and this zone lay as much outside our region as within it. The counties abutting the region — Gloucestershire, Oxfordshire, Buckinghamshire and extra-metropolitan Middlesex — did not reproduce precisely the figures for any county among our ten, but nor were they so far out of line with performances south of that boundary as to suggest that our area of study formed an easily definable and self-contained region. One should recall that the 'southern England' of Anglican dominance is more often defined as the area south of a line drawn from the Severn to the Wash than as the counties south of the Thames. It is also true — as Table 1 makes manifest — that some parts of England south of the Thames sustained distinctly stronger Anglican practice than others. Whether he recognised it or not, Trollope placed Barsetshire in the inner West Country where many of the region's highest attendance figures were recorded in 1851.

It would be wrong anyway to characterise the region's religious culture only in terms of Anglican attendances. The latter were only one criterion of religious performance. Another was the level of religious practice in aggregate (i.e. across all denominations); another was the level of non-Anglican attendance; and another the relative shares of attendances enjoyed by the Church of England and by other denominations. Does one, for example, judge the Church's position by its index of attendance or by its share of attendances? The two criteria provide rather different regional patterns, as a comparison between Maps 2 and 4 will indicate. Our ten counties came out of the second test rather more Anglican than in the former. They included eight of the twelve highest Anglican PS figures among the counties of England and Wales. Once the criteria of religious performance are multiplied in these various ways, the picture which emerges becomes a complex one which lends itself less easily to neat generalizations about regional characteristics.

Something of this complexity emerges even from the figures for the counties in Table 1. The level of religious practice *in toto* was clearly not uniform across the region. In the three most eastern counties attendances, though close to the national average, were well below the regional average; as one moved westwards the level rose to well above the national average; it peaked in Wiltshire, but then declined again through the south-western peninsula, though even Cornwall recorded figures above those at the eastern end of the region. The average for Division V was significantly higher than that for Division II, but the county figures make it clear that there were more than two recognizable zones of religious performance in the region. One might note that the region itself was not characterized by unusually high attendances. Only Wiltshire and Dorset were among the counties with the twelve highest figures in the country.

A comparable unevenness emerges from the figures for non-Anglican attendances. The index ranged from Surrey's 12.2 to Cornwall's 48.7 and the PS from 22.5 to 71.8 for the same two counties. If Cornwall was something of a special case, even the rest of the region divided into several distinguishable zones with the peak of Nonconformist support showing in Wiltshire. A rather different and less clear-cut pattern emerges from the county figures for the non-Anglican share of attendances. The PS is rather stabler than the index simply because some of the highest Nonconformist attendances occurred in areas where Anglicanism was also strong and some of the weakest where the Church was relatively poorly supported. Wiltshire, for example, appears to be a strongly Nonconformist county, at least by regional standards, if one considers only the non-Anglican IA, but it is much less remarkable if one takes the PS into account. It was a county where religious practice in aggregate was notably strong and where there was room enough for both the Church of England and various kinds of Nonconformity to flourish. Only Cornwall was remarkable for both the IA and the PS, and it is already apparent that, whatever regional homogeneity the rest of southern England might display, Cornwall has to be counted out.

The county figures disguise a good deal of variation among the component registration districts. Table 2 sets out the figures for the region's 174 districts. In 55 districts, nearly one-third of the total, aggregate attendances fell below the national average, and most of those districts were in the three eastern counties. Only 26 and 29 districts, however, fell below the national figures for the Anglican IA and PS respectively. Cornwall provided about two-fifths of these totals and only three other counties — Hampshire, Wiltshire and Devon — made any significant contribution. It was in these respects that the region, Cornwall excepted, came closest to something like homogeneity. But the picture changes when one turns to the non-Anglican figures. Now 109 districts fall below the national IA with around two-fifths of the total above that figure. A considerably larger number — 145 — were below the national PS. Cornwall contributed heavily to the number of districts with above-average Nonconformity, but Surrey was the only one of the ten counties that failed to do so at all. Quite clearly, it was the unevenness of the strength of Nonconformity in absolute terms (rather than in relation to Anglicanism) that made the greatest contribution to the heterogeneity within the region.

The tables distinguish two main elements within the non-Anglican attendances: the sum of the old Dissenting denominations and the sum of the various kinds of Methodism. The IA for Old Dissent fell below the national average in 98 of the districts and the Methodist IA failed to reach its national score in 118. Thus, though both categories of Nonconformity were weaker in the region than in the country as a whole, Old Dissent performed rather the better. In fact it attracted higher attendances than Methodism in 99 of the districts. Here, though, a pattern stands out within the region. Though the two elements achieved parity in Kent, Old Dissent was the stronger in a clear majority of the districts in every county westwards until Dorset, Somerset and Devon. In Cornwall Methodism was the stronger in all fourteen districts. The third element distinguished within non-Anglican practice in the tables is Roman Catholicism. It was not notably strong anywhere in the region. What support it possessed was largely in coastal areas, particularly in the larger ports where there was Irish immigrant labour.

Even before detailed consideration of the district figures for each county, the conclusion stands out that the region, less Cornwall, displayed a considerable degree of differentiation and diversity within a framework of Anglican predominance. If the ten counties formed what might be called a region, it was neither self-contained nor homogeneous. The two registration divisions are not an adequate framework for analysis, for in each case there were unmistakable east/west contrasts and no two counties were identical in their patterns of religious practice. One could distinguish a number of sub-regional zones within our area but they would differ in number and size according to the criterion of religious character one adopted. As Table 2 shows, there was significant differentiation even within individual counties and one must go to the district figures to gain a fuller picture of the region's patterns of religious performance. The sections that follow examine the figures of religious worship in each of the ten counties. They should be read in conjunction with Tables 1 and 2.

South-Eastern Counties

Surrey (extra-metropolitan)
The aggregate of observance in the county was rather below the national average and considerably below the figures for the region and for Division II. In fact Surrey returned the lowest attendances among the ten counties. It was also notable for the extent and uniformity of Anglican predominance. The Church of England index of 42.0 was above the national, regional and divisional figures and the PS was spectacularly high at 77.5, the highest county figure in the region and, indeed, in England and Wales. This Anglican strength was, however, more relative than absolute. It co-existed with a rather low level of observance in general and the Anglican IA was bettered by three counties in the region, though none in the south-eastern division. Wiltshire, for example, returned an Anglican PS of 52.2, far below Surrey's, but an IA rather higher at 44.7. Though enjoying nothing like the easy dominance it did in Surrey, the established church attracted a larger proportion of the population to worship.

What Nonconformity there was in Surrey was predominantly in the older Dissenting denominations. The Independents were easily the largest Nonconformist denomination, followed by the Baptists and then by the Wesleyan Methodists. Only in Middlesex among the counties of England and Wales was Methodism weaker than in Surrey where it attracted fewer than half the attendances of Old Dissent.

The index of aggregate attendance was fairly stable among the registration districts, though rather higher at the western end of the county than in some of the eastern districts. The Anglican IA was more variable, with Farnborough conspicuously high and

Dorking and Reigate notably low, but the PS was remarkably stable. Even where Anglican attendances were low, there was little sign of an aggressive Nonconformity to exploit the weakness. Even the highest non-Anglican IA was below the divisional average and in four districts (of only thirteen such in the region) non-Anglican attendances were less than one-tenth of the population. In no district did the Nonconformist denominations command as much as one-third of all attendances and in five districts the figure fell below one-fifth.

The denominational breakdown reveals the almost uniform weakness of Methodism within the county. In none of its forms had it made a major impact upon any district by 1851. In every district except one at the western end of the county Old Dissent achieved higher attendances than Methodism, but in only three districts did its attendances exceed one-tenth of the population. The Methodist denominations reached that figure nowhere and the Reigate district was one of only three in the region without a single Methodist congregation. Roman Catholicism was of significant strength only in Croydon and Richmond, both of them bordering the London registration division.

Surrey thus revealed little internal differentiation. In fact it was the most homogeneous of the ten counties. It was, however, not entirely of a piece with its division or its region. In two respects, indeed, it produced figures at the end of the regional spectrum. Neither Kent nor Berkshire matched the Surrey pattern of religious performance closely; the nearest thing to it elsewhere in the region was in the western half of Sussex.

Kent (extra-metropolitan)

The county's attendance figures were much closer than Surrey's to the divisional ones. The aggregate index was rather above Surrey's and close to both the national and divisional figures. Kent's Anglican IA, however, fell below Surrey's. In fact, though still well above the national figure, it was lower than in any other county in the region except Cornwall. The non-Anglican PS was again close to the divisional average and this reflected a much stronger performance by the Nonconformist denominations than in Surrey. Old Dissent, within which Independents and Baptists were evenly balanced, was rather stronger and Methodism considerably stronger than in Surrey. Here too Kent was close to the divisional and regional figures. Two points have to be set, though, against Kent's claims to be typical or representative of the region. One is that Kent's figures resembled those of no other county very closely, though Sussex and Hampshire were perhaps the nearest. The other is that the figures for Kent as a whole disguised considerable unevenness within the county.

Kent displayed much more internal variation than Surrey. Most of the below-average figures for aggregate attendance occurred in the north-west of the county — in the districts stretching from the metropolitan suburbs to the Medway — and most of the high figures in the south and east, though a few districts broke this pattern. With Anglican attendances too the figures were highest in the southern and eastern districts and depressed in the more densely populated north-west. The correspondence between the two patterns was, however, far from exact. Thanet, which returned the highest figure for total attendance, recorded Anglican attendances below the average. The Anglican PS, which fell below fifty in only one district, Sheppey, showed no very marked pattern. The range of variation in Nonconformist strength was much wider than in Surrey. It was generally weak in the centre of the county but performed more strongly in the north-west, in the Weald and in the coastal districts. In only three districts, though, did the non-Anglican index exceed the national figure and the PS did so only once.

Old Dissent tended to be strong in the more urbanized districts, particularly in the north-west, and was weakest in the east-central area, while such support as Methodism enjoyed lay predominantly in the coastal districts. Unlike Surrey, Kent contained a number of districts where Methodism had made a significant impact and in two of them its index was higher than Old Dissent managed anywhere in the county. Roman Catholicism was weak and was largely confined to the coastal districts.

The figures for Kent as a whole suggest that the county was fairly representative of its division, even perhaps of the region, but its internal differentiation, less sharp than that in Sussex but in clear contrast to the degree of uniformity in its other neighbour Surrey, showed that a characteristicly Kentish pattern of performance was not particularly evident at the district level. The variability was greatest in respect of the strength of Nonconformity. Anglican attendances were a majority of the total in all but one district, but in the degree of Anglican predominance and in other respects the picture was rather patchy and Kent was a difficult county to characterise. Even the internal differentiation did not form a very clear pattern. What pattern there was, however, seems to have been influenced by the proximity of London in the north-west and by the county's long coastline.

Sussex

Aggregate attendance in the county as a whole was rather below the national and well below the regional figure but of a piece with the divisional performance — midway, in fact, between Surrey and Kent. This was the broad picture in other respects too. The Anglican index and PS were well above the national average and non-Anglican attendances were well down on national levels, but all these figures came somewhere between those for Kent and Surrey. Not too different from its northern and eastern neighbours, Sussex lacked the stronger Nonconformity which began to appear in Hampshire to the west. In the context of its division, Sussex stood out neither for strong Anglican practice (perhaps surprisingly considering that it was one of the few counties retaining a majority of Anglican places of worship in 1851) nor for strong Nonconformity. The Anglican share of attendances was, however, second only to Surrey's in the region.

Both Old Dissent and Methodism achieved figures above Surrey's and below Kent's, and the former was once again the stronger of the two groups. The Independents were the largest single denomination, followed by the Baptists and the Wesleyan Methodist Original Connexion. There were more 'isolated' or 'undefined' congregations than were found in most counties; this category accounted for 2.6% of all attendances against only 1% in Kent. There was little Roman Catholicism.

Unremarkable as the figures for Sussex as a whole were, there was a more interesting and distinct pattern among its registration districts than was found in the two counties considered above. Although the range of variation in aggregate attendance was considerable, only one district, Hailsham, reached a notably high figure. Attendances, however, were generally high in the coastal districts and significantly lower inland and also rather higher in the west of the county than in the east. All five coastal districts from Eastbourne westwards returned IAs over 60. The inland zone of weak performance covered both halves of the county, though it did not extend as far north as East Grinstead on the border with Kent and Surrey. Anglican attendances also showed a wide range of variation and again the figures were higher in the west and along the coast than in the east and inland, though Brighton, with the largest and densest population, returned Anglican attendances below the county average. There was a concentration of weak Anglican performance in the predominantly Wealden districts of Ticehurst, Uckfield and Battle. The Anglican share of attendances was similarly patterned: less than half the total in Hailsham and

Ticehurst and generally low in the east, especially inland, but higher along the coast and very high in the west of the county. In seven of the county's twenty districts the Anglican PS was over 80, a figure exceeded in only nine other districts in the region, all of them in Division II. As for non-Anglican attendances, they were heavily concentrated in the eastern half of the county, Eastbourne excepted, and in the western districts they were as low as almost anywhere in southern England.

The denominational distribution revealed similar contrasts. Methodism had a significant presence in some of the districts bordering Kent where Anglican performance was weak, but it came a bad second to Old Dissent, particularly the Independents, in the central and western districts. Methodism was at its weakest at the county's western end. Here several districts were without an Original Connexion congregation and one, Thakeham, without Methodism of any description — one of only three such districts in the region. The Old Dissenting denominations were more evenly spread over the county than Methodism, though they were strongest in the central districts, notably Lewes and Hailsham. Brighton accounted for most of the county's Roman Catholic attendances and none at all were recorded in the eastern districts.

At first sight Sussex seems to fit into a characteristic 'south-eastern' pattern of religious performance as represented, with certain differences, by its neighbours Surrey and Kent. Yet the idea of a single dominant pattern becomes hard to sustain when one examines the district figures. Sussex was a county more clearly divided into zones of religious practice than either Surrey or Kent. There was a double division: first, between the coastal districts and the inland (and largely Wealden) districts, and, second, between the eastern half of the county (which had much in common with adjacent parts of Kent) and West Sussex which was very like Surrey to the north. Few of the region's counties had such sharp internal contrasts.

Hampshire

The county's aggregate attendances, significantly higher than in the counties to the east, were also the highest in the division. Berkshire also displayed this rather stronger religious performance, though neither county recorded the levels of attendance to be found further to the west in Division V. Hampshire's Anglican attendances, though lower than Surrey's, were slightly above the divisional figure. What distinguished Hampshire from the eastern parts of the division was not its Anglican practice but a level of non-Anglican attendance very much stronger than across the county boundary in Surrey and West Sussex. Nonconformist attendances accounted for two-fifths of the total, the highest figure in the division. Both Old Dissent and Methodism were rather stronger than they were further east. Indeed Hampshire's figures for Old Dissent were the highest in its division and second only to Wiltshire's in the region. The Independents and the Wesleyan Original Connexion were the largest Nonconformist denominations.

The index of aggregate attendance never fell below fifty in any district, though Portsea only just exceeded that figure, but there were two areas of very high attendance, in the south-west of the county and in the north-west. They included three of the region's seven districts in which attendances exceeded population. Religious practice was weakest in and around the conurbations of Portsmouth and Southampton. The Anglican IA also was low in and around the large towns and was depressed in some of the west-central districts too. Though there were exceptions to the pattern, Anglican attendances tended to be low along the seaboard and higher inland, the opposite of the situation in Sussex. Nonconformist attendances were conspicuously high in the south-west corner of the county and in the Isle of Wight and lowest in the centre and north-east. Generally speaking, they were higher in the coastal districts than inland and higher in the west than in the east of the county.

Old Dissent was rather more evenly distributed than Methodism (though this was so in nearly every county in the region) but it was still stronger in the coastal districts than inland and particularly strong in the south-west. Methodist strength was much patchier and its best figures were distributed around the county rather than concentrated in contiguous districts. None of its best districts was along the border with Sussex and in Catherington there was no Methodism at all. Methodist support was heavily concentrated in the west of the county. Roman Catholicism, which was stronger in Hampshire than in any other of our counties, was concentrated mainly in the coastal districts and there was little inland.

Hampshire came closer to the regional averages than any other county we have considered so far but the county was some way from the divisional figures and was clearly a rather different case from its eastern neighbours, Sussex and Surrey. Berkshire, in fact, was the most comparable county. In both Hampshire and Berkshire we find higher aggregate attendance than in the east of the division but not markedly stronger Anglicanism, the increase stemming mostly from stronger Nonconformity with a consequent depression of the Anglican share of attendances. Hampshire displayed some marked internal contrasts — both between east and west and between the seabord and the hinterland — though they were not as sharply defined as those in Sussex. Perhaps Surrey, west Sussex and eastern Hampshire can be seen as forming a distinguishable zone or sub-region of religious practice. If so, western Hampshire was clearly the start of something different.

Berkshire

Both the aggregate index and the Anglican figures were close to Hampshire's. Indeed Berkshire was broadly similar to its southern neighbour, though Nonconformity was rather weaker than in the latter. Old Dissent was significantly weaker but Methodism rather stronger. Berkshire, in fact, sustained the strongest Methodism in Division II and it was the only county of the five where the Methodists attracted more attendances than Old Dissent. It was also the only county in the region where the Wesleyan Original Connexion was not the largest Methodist denomination; the Primitive Methodists were and they were also the largest of all the Nonconformist sects.

Aggregate attendance was higher in the west of the county than in the east, though even its peaks did not approach the levels reached in a number of Hampshire districts. The lowest figures occurred in the two easternmost districts which, in this respect, replicated the characteristics of neighbouring Surrey. The Anglican IA, though highest in Abingdon and lowest in Windsor, displayed less of an east/west contrast than the aggregate index and it was rather depressed in the centre of the county. The Anglican share of attendance was higher in the east while Nonconformity was stronger in the western districts.

Like Hampshire, Berkshire — if its summary figures are to be taken at anything like their face value[7] — showed a pattern of observance intermediate between that of the counties to the east and that found further west. One feature which stood out as one moved westwards was the growing strength of Nonconformity, particularly of Methodism. In this and in other respects Berkshire, like Hampshire, displayed some internal contrasts between east and west. Its situation between two strongly contrasting counties, Surrey and Wiltshire, helped to explain why its registration districts showed such a wide range of variation for a relatively small county. Berkshire also had its distinctive features. The denominational make-up of its Nonconformity was an unusual one, not reproduced elsewhere in the region.

South-Eastern Counties

The division was thus far from uniform. There were not only considerable differences among its 95 districts but also, in several cases, major contrasts between different parts of the same county. Only Surrey could show anything approaching homogeneity. The division could perhaps be divided into three main areas of religious performance, though without very clearly defined boundaries. The central zone consisted of Surrey, west Sussex and the eastern parts of Hampshire and Berkshire. The dominant characteristics of this area were an overwhelming Anglican supremacy and very low levels of Nonconformity, particularly of Methodism, though with some unevenness in the level of aggregate observance. Further to the east, Kent and east Sussex formed a zone much more mixed in character. Aggregate observance was only slightly higher but, within that, Anglican strength was less pronounced and support for Nonconformity, particularly for Methodism, considerably stronger though rather patchy in its incidence. At the western end of the division, beyond the central zone, Nonconformity was stronger still and approached balance with the Church of England. Here, in the western parts of Hampshire and Berkshire, aggregate observance was much stronger than in the central zone. The feature of note was not so much a falling away of Anglican attendances as the markedly increased strength of Nonconformity in both its Old Dissenting and its Methodist versions. It is not clear whether this constituted a distinct zone of religious practice. Perhaps it was more the eastern outcrop of a sub-region of combined high aggregate observance and strong Nonconformity centred on Wiltshire. This analysis stresses the east/west contrasts found within the division, but the pattern was complicated by differences between coastal and inland areas that occurred in Sussex, Hampshire and, to a lesser extent, in Kent. In at least Hampshire's case one factor was the large-scale urbanization along parts of the seaboard.

South-Western Counties

Wiltshire

By a fair margin Wiltshire recorded the highest level of performance in the region. Its index of aggregate attendance was the sixth highest among the registration counties of England and Wales. The county was distinctive in other respects. It had the second highest

Anglican index in the region, but the strength of Nonconformity meant that the Anglican PS was the lowest except for Cornwall. Wiltshire was a county of very high levels of practice within which both the Church of England and Nonconformity found room to flourish — a situation more common in East Anglia and some of the other eastern counties than in our region. Methodism was stronger in Wiltshire than in any other of our counties except Cornwall and Old Dissent achieved its best figures in the region. The Particular Baptists were the largest Nonconformist denomination — something they achieved in no other county in the region — just ahead of the Independents who were followed by the Wesleyan Original Connexion and the Primitive Methodists.

Only one district, Calne, fell below the national average for aggregate attendance. Though low by Wiltshire's own standards in the northern districts, attendances were remarkably high in the centre and south of the county. They exceeded population in three districts (out of only seven such in the region) and Warminster recorded the region's highest attendances of all. The Anglican index was less uniformly high and showed a wide range of variation, being notably low in Melksham and Calne. All the districts where Anglican attendances fell below half the total were in the county's northern half with the picture worst in the north-west. In no district was Nonconformity weak by regional standards, but its incidence was uneven. Melksham and Westbury were the region's only districts where the index for non-Anglican attendances rose above seventy — higher, that is, than anything found even in Cornwall. The Church of England could claim a majority of attendances in the southern districts, but even here strong Anglicanism might find itself accompanied by strong Nonconformity, as in Salisbury and Tisbury.

Both Old Dissent and Methodism were spread fairly evenly. There was little of the sharp contrast between different parts of the county which occurred in Sussex and Hampshire or even of the patchiness that appeared in Kent. In only two districts did the index for Old Dissent fall below ten and the Methodist index did so only once. Old Dissent, however, was strongest in the west-central districts — the old textile centre of the county — and weaker in the more simply agricultural districts along the eastern border. In these eastern districts Methodism did rather better than Old Dissent and the Primitives had a significant presence alongside the Wesleyans. Melksham and Westbury were the only districts in the region where Old Dissent took over half the attendances and where the Baptists were the largest single denomination — larger even than the Church of England. Nowhere else in the region, indeed, did any non-Methodist denomination achieve this position. Roman Catholic places of worship were recorded in only three districts, all of them in the south of the county.

Wiltshire was one of the more remarkable counties. It was scarcely typical either of the region or of its division. Indeed it was clearly untypical for both its aggregate observance and its strong Nonconformity, though its high level of Anglican practice was more characteristic of the region. Wiltshire, perhaps surprisingly given its size, was a county with relatively little internal differentiation. The absence of a coastline perhaps contributed to the absence of major contrasts.

Dorset

The county sustained a high level of religious practice, well above the national figure and second only to Wiltshire in the region. One of the few counties where Anglican places of worship remained the majority, Dorset returned the region's best figures for Anglican attendances. The Church's share of attendances, though the highest in the division, was less remarkable, falling below the levels achieved in the three most eastern counties of the region. The non-Anglican index, which came close to the national average, was the second lowest in Division V but exceeded every county figure in the south-eastern division. The non-Anglican share of attendances, however, fell far below the national figure and was the lowest in the south-western division. Thus, by the region's standards at least, Dorset provided a picture of Anglican strength more than of Dissenting weakness and so showed more than a passing resemblance to its northern neighbour, Wiltshire. The balance between the Methodist denominations and Old Dissent was about even. The only two denominations of major significance across the whole county were the Independents and the Wesleyan Original Connexion, though neither could attract as much as one-quarter of Anglican attendances.

The aggregate index was above the national figure in every registration district, a more even pattern than in most counties. Attendances were, however, rather higher in the east of the county than in the west. The Anglican index was also above the national level in every district, but the figures at the low end of the range were mainly in the coastal districts while the highest occurred in the central and northern districts. The Anglican PS was fairly stable and nowhere was the Church notably weak, though it achieved only around half the attendances in five districts.

Nonconformity was strongest in the coastal districts, particularly in the east, and weaker inland. As in Hampshire, the seabord sustained above-average Nonconformity.

The performance of individual denominations varied considerably from district to district. Methodism was stronger than Old Dissent in the north but weaker than it in the west of the county. Both kinds of Nonconformity were well-established in most, though not all, of the coastal districts. The Independents were the largest of the old denominations almost everywhere, as the Wesleyans were among the Methodists, though the Primitives had a pocket of strength in the north-eastern corner of the county. What little Roman Catholicism there was occurred mainly in the coastal districts.

Dorset, one of the region's smallest counties, was relatively homogeneous. The internal contrasts were less sharp than in most counties. The county can be seen as broadly representative of an inner-West Country pattern of religious performance found also in southern Wiltshire, much of Somerset and east Devon as well as in some of the districts across the border with Hampshire. But that hardly made Dorset typical of the region as a whole. Its level of aggregate observance was unusually strong for southern England. Though weaker in Nonconformity than most of Division V further west, it was stronger than the counties to the east. Dorset was one of those counties that looks typically southern only if one does not stop to ask what 'typically southern' really means.

Devon

The largest of the ten counties in both population and area, Devon returned figures for aggregate attendance well above the national level though rather below the divisional average. The Anglican index was rather above a divisional average reduced by the impact of Cornwall. In fact Devon's Anglican attendances fell below the levels of the three counties to the east. Nonconformity ran well below the levels in Wiltshire and Cornwall but slightly above those in Somerset and Dorset. As in the last two counties, Old Dissent and Methodism were in roughly even balance. The Independents and the Wesleyan Connexion were the major denominations, though the Bible Christians also had a significant presence. Devon was unique in recording no Primitive Methodists. In terms of the county figures, however, Devon was scarcely remarkable among the counties of its division and region. The main interest, predictably enough in a county so large and geographically diverse, lay in the internal variations of performance.

There was no firm pattern to aggregate observance, though the highest figures occurred in the east and north of the county and in Kingsbridge at its southern tip. Attendances were lowest in the central (predominantly moorland) districts and in the south-west, especially in Plymouth and its environs. The pattern of Anglican practice was rather clearer. The index was high in east Devon but much lower in the west, particularly in and around Plymouth. In the north and north-west, areas conventionally depicted as strongly Nonconformist, Anglican attendances held up quite well, as they did in Kingsbridge. It was only in the moorland and Plymouth districts that Anglican attendances fell to something like Cornwall's levels. The Anglican share of attendances, highest in the south-east of the county, dropped badly only in the Plymouth area. The non-Anglican index was highest in the north-west and in Kingsbridge; the PS peaked in the north-west and in Plymouth.

Old Dissent was stronger than Methodism in the eastern and east-central districts where there ended the belt of Dissenting strength in the old textile districts running from East Anglia through the south Midlands into the inner West Country. The Methodist denominations were much stronger in the west of the county, especially in the three north-western districts. In Holsworthy, where Bible Christians as well as Wesleyans were numerous, the sum total of Methodists had a majority of attendances, though in no district in the county did a single denomination exceed the Anglican attendances. Methodism was well established in the Plymouth area too, but the most remarkable feature was the size of the 'isolated congregations' category in the Plymouth district itself. It was credited with an index of 12.9 and a PS of 23.4, easily the highest such figures in the country and apparently a reflection of the local strength of the Brethren whose congregations declined to identify themselves as a denomination. There was little Roman Catholicism anywhere in the county except in East Stonehouse where chapels served the whole Plymouth area and which returned the highest Catholic figures in the region.

The county figures are thus rather deceptive. They make Devon look fairly representative of the south-western division, Cornwall excepted, but the district figures reveal a county containing major divisions and contrasts. Historians of the county sometimes argue that the significant line of division ran north-to-south down the middle of the county; others argue an antithesis between north and south Devon. But the county's complexities went beyond a two-fold or even a four-fold division. There were perhaps eight or nine zones of religious performance within the county and there are very few generalizations one could frame for the county as a whole. Devon illustrates how misleading county averages can be and its internal contrasts indicate how difficult it would be to fit the whole of the county (as opposed to some of its parts) into a regionalization or sub-regionalization of southern England.

Cornwall

Aggregate attendance was above the national average and similar to the regional level though below the division's. (Unlike most of Wales, Cornwall did not combine unusually high levels of aggregate observance with its rampant Nonconformity.) The Anglican figures were quite out of line with the other counties in the region and were even below the national figures. The non-Anglican index was higher even than Wiltshire's and the PS was very considerably higher. If southern England had a characteristic pattern of religious performance, Cornwall certainly did not conform to it. The balance within Nonconformity was also unusual. The county had the weakest Old Dissent in region, while Methodism was far stronger than elsewhere. The Methodist index was 2½ times that of the next highest figure, Wiltshire's, and the PS was more than three times that of Berkshire.

The district figures show that aggregate attendance was rather higher in the east of the county than in the far west, the Scillies excepted. Apart from the three far western districts only Liskeard fell markedly short of the county figure. The Anglican index was below the divisional and regional averages in every district except the Scillies but still showed some east/west differentiation. St. Austell joined the three most westerly mainland districts in returning notably low Anglican attendances, Redruth's being the lowest in the region. The Scillies excepted, all the districts with an Anglican index over 25 were along the Devon border. St. Austell's Anglican PS was the lowest in the region and, conversely, its non-Anglican PS the highest. The non-Anglican index exceeded the national and regional averages in every district and the divisional average in every district save one. No district, however, achieved the non-Anglican index over 70 which occurred in two Wiltshire districts. There was no clear east/west pattern here. In fact the highest figures were returned by the mid-Cornwall districts of Truro and St. Austell, with Launceston next in order, while Helston had the lowest non-Anglican index in the county. Something of an east/west division appears more in the share of attendances. The Nonconformist PS was generally higher in the western and central districts than in the eastern ones.

Methodism was stronger than Old Dissent in every district. In four districts, the only ones of the kind in the region, no Old Dissent was recorded at all. The Independents, the largest of the old denominations, had most of their support in the eastern and central districts, while Baptists were concentrated in the west. In nine of the fourteen districts a Methodist denomination was the largest single denomination, the Church of England included; in eight cases it was the Wesleyan Original Connexion, in Camelford the Bible Christians. In twelve of the fourteen districts the Methodist denominations aggregated over half the total attendances, an achievement found otherwise in the region only in one west Devon district. The predominance of the Wesleyan Connexion among Methodists and in Nonconformity as a whole was more marked in the west of the county than in the east, where the Bible Christians and the Wesleyan Association were significant forces. Roman Catholicism recorded its lowest figures in the region and seems to have been largely confined to the ports. As every registration district save one incorporated sections of coastline, it is impossible to tell from the printed figures whether significant differences existed between coastal and inland areas.

Cornwall was *sui generis*. Though parts of west Devon represented a halfway stage towards the Cornish situation, there was nothing in the rest of southern England like Cornwall. Even Wiltshire could not match its Nonconformist attendances — and Wiltshire was a very different picture in other respects. It sustained strong Nonconformity alongside strong Anglicanism and notably high levels of aggregate observance. Cornwall, however, had strong Nonconformity in a context of remarkably weak Anglicanism and aggregate observance well below Wiltshire's level. Even outside the regional context Cornwall was an unusual case. There were only seven registration counties, all of them Welsh and/or heavily industrialized, with lower Anglican indices; there were only three registration counties (the two Welsh ones and Monmouthshire) with a lower Anglican PS. Set against the whole county's distinctiveness, its internal differences paled almost into insignificance. Though Cornwall was one of the more homogeneous counties of the region, the pattern of denominational strength revealed by the Census among its various districts was of some interest.

Somerset
The county figures seem to place Somerset firmly in the inner-west Country pattern of performance. Aggregate attendance, below the

levels in Wiltshire and Dorset, was close to Devon's and to the divisional figure and was well above the national average. The Anglican index was well above the national level and of a piece with the rest of the division, Cornwall excepted. The Anglican PS, however, was high by divisional standards and only just below Dorset's; this followed from Nonconformist attendances below those in the rest of the division. Within Nonconformity the Wesleyan Connexion, the Independents and the Baptists (in that order) were the largest denominations, and Old Dissent and Methodism were about evenly balanced as in Devon and Dorset. Somerset, taken as a whole, was one of the more unremarkable counties in the region. Of more interest was the diversity to be found within it.

Most parts of the county showed moderately strong aggregate observance, the exceptions being the Bedminster district which included parts of Bristol and the two Mendip districts of Wells and Shepton Mallet. The strongest occurred in Frome, adjacent to the high attendance areas of Wiltshire, and in Wellington on the Devon border. Observance was more uneven in north Somerset than in the southern and western districts. The Anglican index showed much the same picture. The best figures occurred in the west and a range of lower ones in the central and northern parts of the county, again notably around Bristol and in the Mendips. In only one of these districts, however, was the Anglican share of attendances badly down on the national figure; the Church's weakness in Somerset tended to occur in districts where religious practice in general was at a low ebb.

The figures for Nonconformity provided greater contrasts. Though the Mendip districts returned Nonconformist attendances below the county average — they displayed weak Anglicanism rather than strong Dissent — attendances were high in the north-east alongside the strongly Nonconformist parts of Wiltshire. In Frome, Clutton and Keynsham Nonconformity accounted for over half the attendances. It was much weaker, however, in the west of the county and along the Bristol Channel coast. A similar unevenness showed in the balance between the denominational groups. Old Dissent was stronger than Methodism in nearly all the districts bordering Devon and Dorset and reached its peak in the old textile districts towards Wiltshire. Methodism was stronger in the north of the county, both in the Mendips and around Bristol. Roman Catholicism, found in only four districts, was strongest in Bath.

Though Somerset's internal contrasts were less sharp than those in Devon, Hampshire and Sussex, the county averages still masked a considerable unevenness of religious practice. Somerset sat rather uneasily between the strong Nonconformity of Wiltshire and the more assured Anglican hegemony of east Devon. As in other counties, concentrated urban growth — in this case Bristol and Bath — had left its mark on the map of religious performance, but the coastline, the Mendips and the old textile industry had also contributed to the pattern of diversity.

South-Western Counties

Division V was thus far from homogeneous. It presented, indeed, even sharper internal contrasts than Division II. Again the geographical pattern depended on the criterion adopted. The highest levels of aggregate attendance were recorded at the eastern end of the division, in Wiltshire and Dorset, and the level tended to fall as one moved westwards. Within this pattern, though, certain kinds of districts — notably upland, industrial and urbanized areas — tended to record significantly lower levels of practice than the rest. The patterns for Anglican attendance were rather different. In most of the division Anglican practice was strong by national standards. Only at the western end, in Cornwall and, to a lesser extent, in west Devon, was Anglican observance weak. In much of the division, indeed, Anglican attendances were higher as a proportion of population than in the greater part of the South-Eastern Counties. Though the Anglican share of attendances was rather low by regional standards in the east of the division, that was a matter of the local strength of Nonconformity rather than of Anglican weakness in absolute terms.

The contrasts within the division were sharpest for Nonconformist attendances. They ran at high levels in most of Wiltshire and in some adjacent parts of the neighbouring counties but were much lower in west Dorset, west Somerset and east Devon. Then in west Devon they began to climb again until they reached a new peak in central and west Cornwall. There, with Anglican practice weak, the Nonconformist share of attendances was quite out of proportion to anything else in the region, though in absolute terms Nonconformist attendances were no stronger than in some of Wiltshire's districts.

Overall one can see perhaps three zones or sub-regions within Division V. An eastern one, centred on Wiltshire, was characterized by high aggregate performance, strong Anglicanism and strong Nonconformity. The second, a zone of rather lower attendances in aggregate, strong Anglicanism still but significantly weaker Nonconformity, consisted of west Somerset, west Dorset and east Devon. The third zone, which displayed low levels of Churchmanship and rampant Nonconformity within the weakest aggregate observance of the three zones, included Cornwall and parts of west Devon. A more detailed exploration of the incidence of denominational strengths would modify this sub-regionalization but probably not invalidate it. The main conclusion — that there was no one pattern of religious performance common to all parts of the South-Western Counties — would remain.

The region
Most of the above analysis has stressed the diversity within the ten counties. What, then, is left to say of the region itself? Cornwall, as we have seen, could scarcely be counted as part of the region for our purposes, but one clear characteristic of the other nine counties was Anglican predominance. Even here, though, there was considerable unevenness both between counties and within counties, as Maps 4A and 4B illustrate. The absolute level of Anglican performance was also high by national standards over most of the region, though there was some patchiness in this respect too (Maps 2A and 2B). Even within a region of obvious Anglican strength, there were many different degrees of strength. It should also be stressed that Anglican performance in relation to population was not at all the same thing as Anglican performance relative to non-Anglican attendance, as a comparison between Maps 2A and 2B on the one hand and Maps 4A and 4B on the other will show. What has to be considered here is not simply the incidence of Nonconformity — and it was in the unevenness of this that the region displayed most internal variation (Maps 3A and 3B) — but also the variation in levels of aggregate attendance. Some parts of the region and of its constituent counties simply had higher levels of religious performance than others (Maps 1A and 1B).

Some sub-regionalization of our area seems to be necessary. The region can perhaps be divided into five broad zones of religious performance, though they rarely had anything like sharply defined boundaries. They ran, east to west, as follows.
(1) Kent and east Sussex: an area of mixed character with stronger Nonconformity than (2) but still with an Anglican majority of attendances nearly everywhere. Despite that, it was perhaps the most variegated of the five zones.
(2) Surrey, west Sussex, east Hampshire and east Berkshire: here

there was an overwhelming Anglican superiority and very weak Nonconformity (particularly weak Methodism) — in fact the weakest in the region. Aggregate attendance was on the low side by regional standards, though higher in the Hampshire districts than in the rest of the zone.

(3) Wiltshire with parts of west Hampshire, west Berkshire, east Dorset and east Somerset: here the highest levels of aggregate attendance in the region were produced by the combination of strong Anglican performance with the strongest Nonconformity outside zone (5) with both Old Dissent and Methodism well supported.

(4) West Dorset, west Somerset and east Devon: aggregate attendance was lower than in (3) though higher than in (1) and (2). Anglican predominance was more pronounced than in zone (3) and the index of Anglican attendance, though no higher than in (3), was rather stabler. Nonconformity was considerably weaker than in the zones on either side though still stronger than in (1) and (2).

(5) Cornwall with west Devon: the zone was characterized by chronic Anglican weakness and constituted the only sizeable area of Nonconformist predominance in the region. The Nonconformity was overwhelmingly Methodist. Aggregate attendance, rather lower than in zones (3) and (4), was similar to that in (2).

Some of these zones were more homogeneous than others but all had a degree of internal differentiation, and the fivefold division suggested above takes account only of the predominant characteristics of the areas concerned. One must admit that an east-to-west zonal division underrates the importance of the coastline. The contrasts we have noted between coastal and inland districts in several counties suggest that the region's long seaboard added to its religious diversity, though not, it seems, in any very consistent manner. A further *caveat* is that the effective zones of religious performance in southern England may not have been confined by the boundaries of Census Divisions II and V and that areas to the north of those boundaries may need to be added to three of our five zones.

Explanation has not been a major concern of this article but there are certain general conclusions that seem to emerge from the statistical evidence. If most of the region was characterised by Anglican dominance, what were the local circumstances that had tended to weaken or disturb that dominance? The Church seems to have been weaker, absolutely or relatively, in the upland areas of the region such as the Weald, the Mendips, Dartmoor and much of Cornwall, and so it is probable that the predominantly lowland character of the region was a crucial factor in Anglican fortunes. Another obvious influence was industrialization. Anglican performance suffered either relatively or absolutely in the industrial districts of the region like the Wealden parts of Kent and Sussex, the old textile areas of Wiltshire and east Somerset and the mining districts of Devon and Cornwall. A larger and faster growing industrial base would have altered the region's pattern of performance. A third factor was urbanization. The Church of England clearly faced problems in and around nearly all the major towns of the region, notably Portsmouth, Southampton, Bristol and Plymouth. The point would have been underlined if London had been included in our study. To take only one example of what this meant for the Church, Roman Catholicism, which was of minimal importance in most of the region, attracted most of its attendances in the larger urban districts, largely, one presumes, among Irish immigrants, and a larger number of fast-growing towns with strong labour demand would have drawn even more of the Irish into the region. As most of the very large towns were ports, large-scale urban growth was often connected with the seaboard factor we have noticed so frequently.

The greater part of the region — four of the five zones — was a predominantly lowland area relatively untouched in 1851 by major concentrations of industry and urbanization. Its religious character owed a great deal to that. The ten counties, nonetheless, contained within themselves enough uplands, large towns and industrial districts to produce considerable variety of religious performance — in Anglican, in Nonconformist and in aggregate attendance — such as to leave one doubtful of their claims to constitute a single and distinct region. But to recognize the degree of diversity is not to deny the region, in whole or in part, to be a worthwhile subject of study. Rather the opposite, for such a recognition might encourage a willingness to ask new questions about the character of the various counties, areas and localities — and, beyond that, a readiness to put each in a regional perspective, to examine one locality in the context of others and to seek to distinguish in each case the widely prevalent characteristics from those that were unique or unusual. One of the most fruitful kinds of regional history for students of southern England will be a comparative history that measures one of its areas or communities against another.

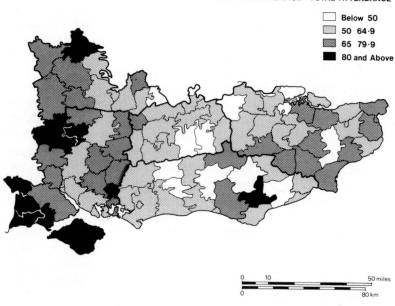

INDEX OF ATTENDANCE : TOTAL ATTENDANCE

- Below 50
- 50 64·9
- 65 79·9
- 80 and Above

0   10   50 miles
0   80 km

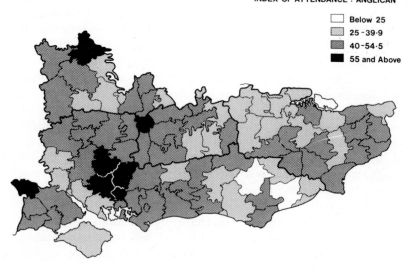

INDEX OF ATTENDANCE : ANGLICAN

- Below 25
- 25 - 39·9
- 40 - 54·5
- 55 and Above

0   10   50 miles
0   80 km

INDEX OF ATTENDANCE : NON-ANGLICAN

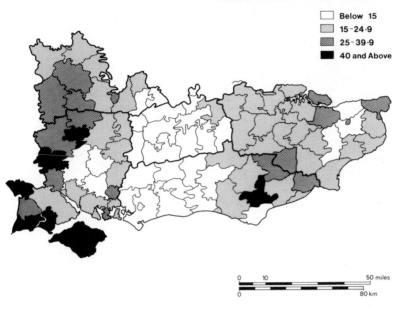

PERCENTAGE SHARE OF ATTENDANCES

ANGLICAN   NON-ANGLICAN

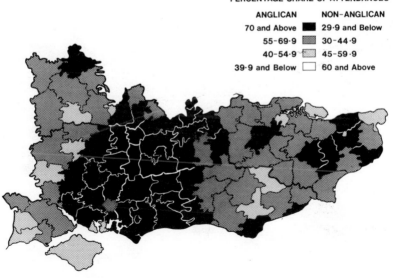

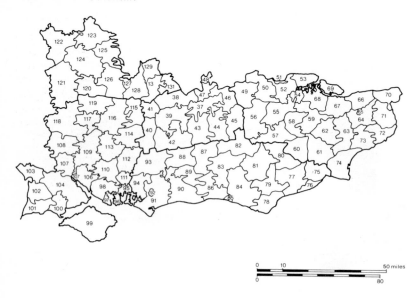

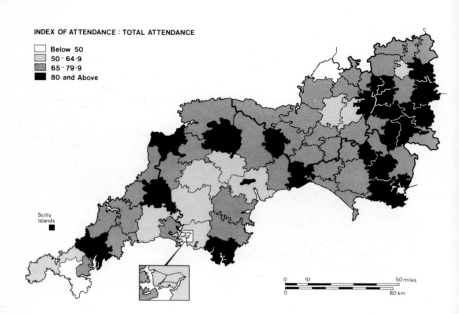

INDEX OF ATTENDANCE : TOTAL ATTENDANCE

Below 50
50 - 64·9
65 - 79·9
80 and Above

Scilly
Islands

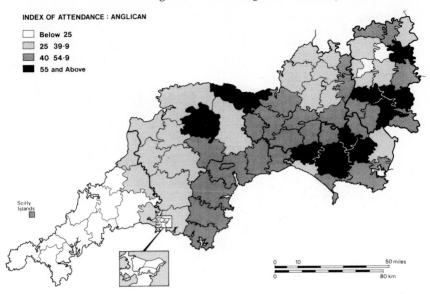

INDEX OF ATTENDANCE : ANGLICAN

- Below 25
- 25 39·9
- 40 54·9
- 55 and Above

Scilly
Islands

0   10   50 miles
0   80 km

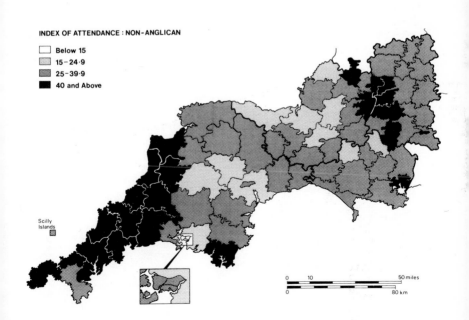

INDEX OF ATTENDANCE : NON-ANGLICAN

- Below 15
- 15 – 24·9
- 25 – 39·9
- 40 and Above

Scilly
Islands

0   10   50 miles
0   80 km

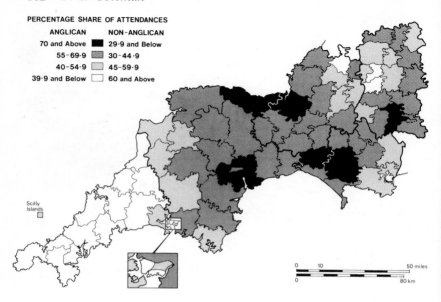

PERCENTAGE SHARE OF ATTENDANCES

ANGLICAN	NON-ANGLICAN
70 and Above	29·9 and Below
55 - 69·9	30 - 44·9
40 - 54·9	45 - 59·9
39·9 and Below	60 and Above

Scilly Islands

0   10   50 miles
0   80 km

KEY

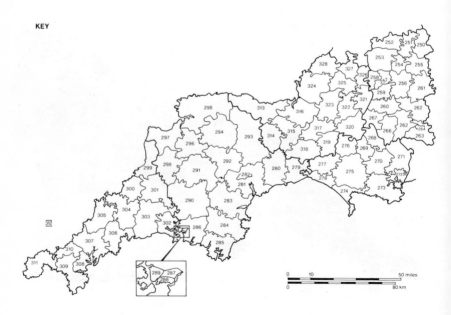

0   10   50 miles
0   80 km

Census of Religious Worship, 1851

IA (Index of Attendance) = attendances at worship as a percentage of population

PS (Percentage Share) = attendances as a percentage of all attendances

Table 1

	Population	Total	Anglican		Non-Anglican		Old Dissent		Methodism		Roman Catholics	
		IA	IA	PS	IA	PS	IA	PS	IA	PS	IA	PS
England & Wales (uncorrected)	17,928m	58.4	27.6	47.4	30.5	52.6	12.6	21.6	14.9	25.7	2.0	3.5
England & Wales (corrected)		60.8	29.5	48.6	31.3	51.4	12.8	21.1	15.2	25.0	2.1	3.5
Divisions II & V	3,431,677	67.2	38.6	57.4	28.6	42.6	12.4	18.5	14.3	21.3	0.5	0.8
Division II: South-Eastern Counties	1,628,386	61.1	39.3	64.2	21.8	35.8	11.7	19.2	8.6	14.0	0.6	1.0
Division V: South-Western Counties	1,803,291	72.8	38.0	52.2	34.8	47.8	13.0	17.9	19.5	26.8	0.5	0.6
Surrey (ex-met.)	202,521	54.2	42.0	77.5	12.2	22.5	8.1	15.0	3.8	7.1	0.8	1.4
Kent (ex-met.)	485,021	59.8	37.7	63.0	22.1	37.0	11.1	18.6	9.6	16.1	0.4	0.7
Sussex	336,844	56.5	38.4	68.0	18.1	32.0	10.3	18.2	5.7	10.1	0.4	0.7
Hampshire	405,370	67.6	40.5	59.8	27.1	40.2	15.5	22.9	10.0	14.8	1.0	1.4
Berkshire	170,065	66.0	40.1	60.8	25.9	39.2	11.2	16.9	12.8	19.4	0.8	1.2
Wiltshire	254,221	85.7	44.7	52.2	41.0	47.8	22.9	26.7	16.0	18.7	0.6	0.7
Dorset	184,207	77.6	48.2	62.2	29.4	37.8	13.8	17.8	13.7	17.7	0.7	0.9
Devon	567,098	70.5	40.1	56.9	30.4	43.1	13.4	19.0	13.2	18.7	0.3	0.5
Cornwall	355,558	67.9	19.2	28.2	48.7	71.8	4.3	6.4	43.8	64.5	0.3	0.4
Somerset	443,916	70.3	43.3	61.6	27.0	38.4	12.6	17.9	12.5	17.8	0.6	0.8

Table 2

No.	Name	Population	Total	Anglican		Non-Anglican		Old Dissent		Methodism		Roman Catholics	
			IA	IA	PS	IA	PS	IA	PS	IA	PS	IA	PS
Surrey (extra-metropolitan)													
37	Epsom	19,040	56.9	47.1	82.8	9.8	17.2	6.0	10.5	3.4	6.0	–	–
38	Chertsey	16,148	57.6	43.9	76.2	13.7	23.8	7.5	13.0	6.0	10.3	0.3	0.5
39	Guildford	25,072	57.3	43.4	75.7	13.9	24.3	10.4	18.1	2.0	3.5	0.3	0.6
40	Farnham	11,743	56.3	41.9	74.4	14.4	25.6	9.5	16.9	5.1	9.0	–	–
41	Farnborough	7,839	71.7	59.9	83.6	11.8	16.4	2.1	3.0	9.7	13.5	–	–
42	Hambledon	13,552	57.7	49.6	85.8	8.3	14.2	6.7	11.7	1.1	1.8	–	–
43	Dorking	11,353	42.8	30.1	70.5	12.7	29.5	5.9	13.9	3.0	7.1	–	–
44	Reigate	14,329	42.6	29.5	69.2	13.1	30.8	12.6	29.5	–	–	–	–
45	Godstone	8,868	56.2	46.7	83.1	9.5	16.9	6.8	12.1	3.8	6.7	–	–
46	Croydon	31,888	54.9	38.8	70.7	16.1	29.3	11.4	20.7	1.8	3.2	2.6	4.7
47	Kingston	26,783	52.0	42.7	82.1	9.3	17.9	7.1	13.7	1.8	3.5	0.4	0.8
48	Richmond	15,906	49.5	39.5	79.8	10.0	20.2	4.5	9.0	2.0	4.1	3.5	7.1
Kent (extra-metropolitan)													
49	Bromley	17,637	45.4	30.0	66.1	15.4	33.9	10.0	22.1	5.3	11.7	–	–
50	Dartford	27,330	50.2	27.8	55.4	22.4	44.6	16.5	33.0	4.3	8.6	0.6	–

No.	Name	Population	Total IA	Anglican IA	Anglican PS	Non-Anglican IA	Non-Anglican PS	Old Dissent IA	Old Dissent PS	Methodism IA	Methodism PS	Roman Catholics IA	Roman Catholics PS
51	Gravesend	16,633	48.6	26.5	54.5	22.1	45.5	13.6	27.9	7.6	15.6	0.8	–
52	North Aylesford	16,569	51.5	31.6	61.3	19.9	38.7	14.4	28.0	5.6	10.8	–	–
53	Hoo	2,845	43.0	26.6	61.9	16.4	38.1	1.4	3.2	13.7	31.8	–	–
54	Medway	42,796	47.8	25.1	52.5	22.7	47.5	8.2	17.1	12.1	25.3	1.3	–
55	Malling	19,579	52.8	39.9	75.5	12.9	24.5	7.9	15.0	5.0	9.5	–	–
56	Sevenoaks	22,095	57.3	39.4	68.8	17.9	31.2	11.4	19.8	5.6	9.8	–	–
57	Tunbridge	28,545	66.4	41.7	62.8	24.7	37.2	15.2	22.9	8.8	13.2	0.7	–
58	Maidstone	36,097	62.7	41.5	66.1	21.2	33.9	13.8	22.0	7.0	11.2	–	–
59	Hollingbourn	13,751	53.6	36.5	68.2	17.1	31.8	9.4	17.5	7.7	14.3	–	–
60	Cranbrook	13,069	70.1	40.6	57.9	29.5	42.1	16.2	23.1	8.2	11.8	–	–
61	Tenterden	11,279	72.4	48.8	67.4	23.6	32.6	9.8	13.6	14.7	20.3	–	–
62	West Ashford	13,314	69.7	49.0	70.3	20.7	29.7	9.9	14.2	10.0	14.4	0.5	–
63	East Ashford	11,960	44.3	31.4	70.8	12.9	29.2	1.5	3.4	7.5	17.0	–	–
64	Bridge	11,164	57.8	46.8	81.5	11.0	18.5	1.2	2.1	9.5	16.4	–	–
65	Canterbury	14,100	64.1	32.4	50.5	31.7	49.5	15.6	24.3	14.8	23.1	–	–
66	Blean	14,661	55.7	43.7	78.4	12.0	21.6	5.5	9.9	6.4	11.5	–	–
67	Faversham	16,684	65.5	39.2	59.9	26.3	40.1	8.1	12.3	17.4	26.5	–	–
68	Milton	12,026	71.2	48.4	68.0	22.8	32.0	8.9	12.5	15.0	21.0	–	–
69	Sheppey	13,385	53.4	22.3	41.8	31.1	58.2	11.5	21.5	14.7	27.6	2.5	–
70	Thanet	31,798	76.4	39.9	52.2	36.5	47.8	16.6	21.7	15.6	20.5	1.2	–
71	Eastrey	25,162	70.8	47.0	66.4	23.8	33.6	15.1	21.3	6.1	8.7	0.8	–
72	Dover	28,325	62.1	44.0	70.8	18.1	29.2	7.9	12.8	8.8	14.2	–	–
73	Elham	18,780	66.9	44.3	66.1	22.6	33.9	7.8	11.7	14.8	22.2	–	–
74	Romney Marsh	5,437	68.2	47.1	69.0	21.1	31.0	3.1	4.6	17.9	26.2	–	–
Sussex													
75	Rye	12,349	57.0	31.5	55.4	25.5	44.6	8.0	14.1	17.4	30.6	–	–
76	Hastings	21,215	54.6	38.3	70.1	16.3	29.9	6.0	10.9	9.2	16.8	–	–
77	Battle	14,232	40.2	22.5	56.0	17.7	44.0	6.2	15.5	11.3	28.2	–	–
78	Eastbourne	8,347	63.8	53.8	84.4	10.0	15.6	6.7	10.5	3.2	5.1	–	–
79	Hailsham	13,289	84.6	41.5	49.1	43.1	50.9	29.9	35.4	10.2	12.0	–	–
80	Ticehurst	15,507	54.9	26.4	48.1	28.5	51.9	13.6	24.8	11.9	21.6	–	–
81	Uckfield	17,631	37.2	20.5	55.1	16.7	44.9	8.1	21.8	4.9	13.2	–	–
82	East Grinstead	13,216	67.0	42.6	63.6	24.4	36.4	15.9	23.8	8.5	12.6	–	–
83	Cuckfield	15,607	48.5	33.7	69.6	14.8	30.4	13.7	28.3	1.0	2.1	–	–
84	Lewes	25,719	67.4	39.0	57.9	28.4	42.1	21.9	32.4	4.3	6.3	–	–
85	Brighton	65,569	55.8	33.5	60.0	22.3	40.0	12.5	22.4	6.8	12.2	1.4	2.5
86	Steyning	16,867	60.6	51.1	84.3	9.5	15.7	5.2	8.6	2.1	3.4	–	–
87	Horsham	14,018	56.3	44.2	78.5	12.1	21.5	10.6	18.9	0.8	1.4	0.6	1.1
88	Petworth	9,629	44.5	36.7	82.5	7.8	17.5	6.6	14.9	–	–	–	–
89	Thakeham	7,434	47.9	45.5	94.9	2.4	5.1	0.7	1.4	1.8	3.7	–	–
90	Worthing	18,746	62.2	48.9	78.7	13.3	21.3	5.7	9.2	4.9	7.9	0.2	0.2
91	Westhampnett	14,649	60.7	54.4	89.7	6.3	10.3	1.5	2.4	4.8	7.9	–	–
92	Chichester	15,037	53.7	42.6	79.3	11.1	20.7	6.0	11.1	2.5	4.6	1.4	2.6
93	Midhurst	13,599	51.7	42.2	81.6	9.5	18.4	7.8	15.1	1.4	2.6	1.0	1.8
94	Westbourne	6,944	56.9	47.1	82.7	9.8	17.3	7.7	13.5	2.2	3.8	–	–

No. Name	Popu-lation	Total	Anglican		Non-Anglican		Old Dissent		Methodism		Roman Catholics	
		IA	IA	PS	IA	PS	IA	PS	IA	PS	IA	PS
Hampshire												
95 Havant	7,212	73.0	54.5	74.6	18.5	25.4	15.3	21.0	1.3	1.8	1.4	1.9
96 Portsea Island	72,126	50.7	22.1	43.5	28.6	56.5	17.9	35.2	8.9	17.6	1.3	2.5
97 Alverstoke	16,908	52.3	34.1	65.2	18.2	34.8	11.4	21.8	4.5	8.6	1.2	2.3
98 Fareham	13,924	62.5	44.7	71.6	17.8	28.4	14.8	23.8	2.9	4.6	–	–
99 Isle of Wight	50,324	80.9	36.4	44.9	44.5	55.1	17.4	21.6	23.7	29.3	2.0	2.5
100 Lymington	12,153	93.8	52.4	55.8	41.4	44.2	33.7	35.9	6.7	7.1	0.3	0.4
101 Christchurch	8,482	92.0	43.9	47.8	48.1	52.2	43.1	46.9	4.5	4.9	0.4	0.4
102 Ringwood	5,675	82.3	45.1	54.7	37.2	45.3	29.9	36.4	7.3	8.9	–	–
103 Fordingbridge	6,834	108.5	61.0	56.2	47.5	43.8	23.6	21.8	23.9	22.0	–	–
104 New Forest	9,469	69.9	48.8	69.7	21.1	30.3	13.3	19.0	7.9	11.2	–	–
105 Southampton	34,098	63.3	35.0	55.2	28.3	44.8	16.2	25.5	6.7	10.6	2.3	3.7
106 South Stoneham	15,974	54.4	39.0	71.7	15.4	28.3	7.8	14.4	7.4	13.6	–	–
107 Romsey	10,810	65.0	36.6	56.3	28.4	43.7	19.0	29.2	9.1	14.0	–	–
108 Stockbridge	7,480	72.6	31.9	43.9	40.7	56.1	12.8	17.6	28.2	38.8	–	–
109 Winchester	25,661	52.1	40.1	76.8	12.0	23.2	4.9	9.3	4.3	8.3	2.9	5.6
110 Droxford	10,697	67.1	63.5	94.5	3.6	5.5	0.9	1.3	2.3	3.4	0.5	0.8
111 Catherington	2,493	105.4	69.0	65.2	36.3	34.5	36.3	34.5	–	–	–	–
112 Petersfield	7,814	79.5	59.3	74.6	20.2	25.4	14.4	18.1	5.4	6.7	–	–
113 Alresford	7,418	69.8	62.7	89.8	7.1	10.2	3.4	5.1	2.0	2.8	1.6	2.
114 Alton	11,910	66.5	49.6	74.6	16.9	25.4	10.9	16.4	6.0	9.0	–	–
115 Hartley Wintney	11,223	75.6	53.8	71.1	21.8	28.9	19.7	26.0	2.2	3.0	–	–
116 Basingstoke	17,466	64.0	45.2	70.7	18.8	29.3	8.7	13.6	9.8	15.4	–	–
117 Whitchurch	5,619	100.5	44.1	43.9	56.4	56.1	25.8	25.7	30.4	30.2	–	–
118 Andover	17,266	83.9	52.6	62.7	31.3	37.3	12.7	15.2	18.1	21.6	–	–
119 Kingsclere	8,909	74.0	46.4	62.7	27.6	37.3	10.1	13.7	17.5	23.7	–	–
Berkshire												
120 Newbury	20,815	69.7	29.6	42.5	30.1	57.5	13.0	18.7	22.4	32.1	2.0	2.9
121 Hungerford[1]	20,404	79.0	45.2	57.2	39.2	49.6	4.4	5.5	34.5	43.6	–	–
122 Faringdon	15,732	68.1	45.0	66.0	23.1	34.0	13.4	19.7	8.6	12.6	1.2	1.
123 Abingdon	20,946	82.3	59.9	72.8	22.4	27.2	14.7	17.9	6.1	7.5	–	–
124 Wantage	17,433	71.0	40.0	56.3	31.0	43.7	13.4	19.7	8.6	12.6	1.2	1.
125 Wallingford	14,163	61.5	38.2	62.2	23.3	37.8	13.8	22.5	7.2	11.7	0.8	1.
126 Bradfield	16,380	57.5	39.7	69.0	17.8	31.0	6.3	11.0	13.3	23.1	–	–
127 Reading	22,175	66.3	34.3	51.7	32.0	48.3	22.2	33.6	7.6	11.4	1.6	2.
128 Wokingham	13,668	57.3	41.2	71.9	16.1	28.1	11.0	19.2	5.1	8.9	–	–
129 Cookham	11,767	66.8	43.2	64.7	23.6	35.3	9.1	13.6	14.3	21.4	–	–
130 East-Hampstead	6,352	50.6	42.9	84.7	7.7	15.3	3.4	6.7	4.3	8.6	–	–
131 Windsor	19,389	37.5	25.4	67.8	12.1	32.2	8.2	21.9	3.4	9.0	0.5	1.4
Wiltshire												
250 Highworth	17,620	74.2	36.7	49.5	37.5	50.5	14.6	19.7	22.8	30.7	–	–
251 Cricklade	11,402	69.0	41.3	59.9	27.7	40.1	9.5	13.8	18.1	26.3	–	–
252 Malmesbury	14,899	72.6	40.5	55.8	31.1	44.2	22.7	31.2	6.5	8.9	–	–
253 Chippenham	21,407	74.6	37.2	49.9	37.4	50.1	24.1	32.3	12.3	16.5	–	–

No.	Name	Population	Total	Anglican		Non-Anglican		Old Dissent		Methodism		Roman Catholics	
			IA	IA	PS	IA	PS	IA	PS	IA	PS	IA	PS
254	Calne	9,173	56.3	23.1	41.0	33.2	59.0	14.9	26.5	15.4	27.3	–	–
255	Marlborough	10,263	93.4	64.4	68.9	29.0	31.1	11.4	12.2	15.7	16.8	–	–
256	Devizes	22,236	74.8	37.9	50.6	36.9	49.4	22.3	29.8	10.0	13.4	–	–
257	Melksham	18,815	99.4	23.4	23.5	76.0	76.5	52.9	53.2	19.9	20.0	–	–
258	Bradford	11,607	93.3	38.6	41.4	54.7	58.6	36.5	39.1	18.2	19.5	–	–
259	Westbury	12,530	107.9	34.3	31.8	73.6	68.2	56.9	52.7	16.0	14.8	–	–
260	Warminster	17,067	110.2	66.2	60.1	44.0	39.9	32.5	29.5	11.4	10.4	–	–
261	Pewsey	12,503	85.0	52.0	61.1	33.0	38.9	9.8	11.5	23.3	27.4	–	–
262	Amesbury	8,250	94.8	63.6	67.1	31.2	32.9	16.4	17.3	14.8	15.7	–	–
263	Alderbury	14,998	73.8	45.6	61.8	28.2	38.2	7.3	9.9	20.8	28.3	–	–
264	Salisbury	8,930	106.5	60.7	57.0	45.8	43.0	28.6	26.8	10.6	9.9	3.6	3.4
265	Wilton	10,472	96.9	68.9	71.1	28.0	28.9	18.1	18.7	10.9	11.2	–	–
266	Tisbury	10,181	97.1	53.5	55.0	43.6	45.0	19.8	20.4	12.9	13.3	1.1	1.1
267	Mere	8,433	78.0	40.0	51.2	38.0	48.8	17.5	22.4	17.4	22.3	1.5	2.0
Dorset													
268	Shaftesbury	13,029	65.8	42.5	64.5	23.3	35.5	8.4	12.7	15.0	22.8	–	–
269	Sturminster	10,382	90.3	59.4	65.7	30.9	34.3	5.8	6.4	23.1	25.5	1.3	1.4
270	Blandford	14,837	97.2	64.0	65.8	33.2	34.2	20.3	20.9	11.4	11.7	1.6	1.6
271	Wimborne	17,284	74.4	36.3	48.8	38.1	51.2	15.8	21.2	20.6	27.7	1.7	2.3
272	Poole	12,890	85.4	41.3	48.2	44.1	51.8	25.6	30.0	14.1	16.5	1.6	1.9
273	Wareham	17,417	80.6	44.2	54.9	36.4	45.1	16.6	20.5	17.3	21.4	2.4	2.9
274	Weymouth	22,037	75.0	42.7	57.0	32.3	43.0	11.8	15.7	16.1	21.4	0.3	0.5
275	Dorchester	25,002	74.3	56.4	75.8	18.0	24.2	7.3	9.8	6.7	9.0	–	–
276	Sherborne	13,081	78.9	54.0	68.5	24.9	31.5	9.9	12.5	13.3	16.8	–	–
277	Beaminster	14,270	73.1	58.1	79.5	15.1	20.5	9.3	12.7	5.8	7.9	–	–
278	Bridport	16,866	69.9	38.6	55.2	31.3	44.8	19.7	28.2	9.3	13.3	–	–
Devon													
279	Axminster	20,303	82.9	53.9	65.1	29.0	34.9	20.4	24.7	7.9	9.5	–	–
280	Honiton	23,824	76.8	50.4	65.6	26.4	34.4	17.9	23.3	8.2	10.7	–	–
281	St. Thomas	48,806	63.5	48.5	76.4	15.0	23.6	6.7	10.6	4.6	7.2	–	–
282	Exeter	32,823	8.45	54.7	64.7	29.8	35.3	12.8	15.2	10.0	11.8	0.8	0.9
283	Newton Abbot	52,306	75.9	45.5	60.0	30.4	40.0	16.4	21.6	10.0	13.2	0.7	1.0
284	Totnes	34,022	78.5	45.9	58.4	32.6	41.6	16.7	21.2	12.4	15.8	0.1	0.1
285	Kingsbridge	21,377	96.9	52.2	53.9	44.7	46.1	17.8	18.4	21.7	22.4	–	–
286	Plympton St. Mary	19,723	50.1	32.2	64.4	17.9	35.6	3.7	7.3	12.4	24.9	–	–
287	Plymouth²	52,221	55.1	24.5	44.5	30.6	55.5	9.6	17.4	7.5	13.7	–	–
288	East Stonehouse	11,979	54.5	21.7	39.8	32.8	60.2	10.1	18.5	14.4	26.5	8.3	15.3
289	Stoke Damerel	38,180	57.2	22.1	38.7	35.1	61.3	15.9	27.8	14.2	24.9	–	–
290	Tavistock	27,850	60.1	26.2	43.6	33.9	56.4	8.5	14.1	24.7	41.2	–	–
291	Okehampton	20,401	59.4	35.5	59.7	23.9	40.3	9.1	15.4	13.4	22.5	–	–
292	Crediton	21,728	64.9	42.6	65.6	22.3	34.4	12.5	19.2	6.4	9.8	–	–
293	Tiverton	39,563	66.9	39.3	57.0	27.6	43.0	19.0	27.5	10.1	14.6	0.2	0.3
294	South Molton	20,566	88.1	60.0	68.1	28.1	31.9	9.3	10.5	16.5	18.7	–	–

No.	Name	Population	Total	Anglican		Non-Anglican		Old Dissent		Methodism		Roman Catholics	
			IA	IA	PS	IA	PS	IA	PS	IA	PS	IA	PS
295	Barnstaple	38,178	71.5	39.6	55.4	31.9	44.6	16.9	23.6	12.2	17.0	–	–
296	Torrington	17,491	75.1	37.0	49.2	38.1	50.8	15.0	20.0	22.6	30.1	–	–
297	Bideford	19,607	81.0	35.0	43.2	46.0	56.8	13.6	16.8	32.1	39.6	–	–
298	Holsworthy	11,382	76.0	32.1	42.2	43.9	57.8	1.8	2.3	42.1	55.4	–	–
Cornwall													
299	Stratton	8,580	73.7	29.0	39.4	44.6	60.6	–	–	44.6	60.6	–	–
300	Camelford	8,448	76.7	19.7	25.7	57.0	74.3	–	–	57.0	74.3	–	–
301	Launceston	16,773	90.8	30.1	33.2	60.7	66.8	12.3	13.6	46.7	51.4	–	–
302	St. German's	16,545	72.7	37.6	51.8	35.1	48.2	10.4	14.4	24.6	33.9	–	–
303	Liskeard	33,831	58.9	18.4	31.2	40.5	68.8	3.9	6.6	35.7	60.6	0.4	0.7
304	Bodmin	20,493	74.2	24.7	33.2	49.5	66.8	–	–	48.8	65.8	0.5	0.7
305	St. Columb	17,402	77.8	22.1	28.4	55.7	71.6	4.1	5.2	50.6	65.0	1.0	1.3
306	St. Austell	32,073	72.2	10.9	15.2	61.3	84.8	6.7	9.3	53.0	73.5	–	–
307	Truro	42,270	84.0	22.3	26.5	61.7	73.5	5.0	5.9	56.7	67.4	–	–
308	Falmouth	22,052	68.4	20.7	30.2	47.7	69.8	10.7	15.6	34.9	51.0	0.8	1.1
309	Helston	28,402	46.5	15.0	32.2	31.5	67.8	1.7	3.7	29.8	64.1	–	–
310	Redruth	53,628	55.7	9.8	17.7	45.9	82.3	1.5	2.7	44.3	79.6	–	–
311	Penzance	53,517	63.8	17.6	27.7	46.2	72.3	3.0	4.8	42.3	66.3	0.7	1.1
312	Scilly Islands	2,627	106.6	53.8	50.5	52.8	49.5	–	–	52.8	49.5	–	–
Somerset													
313	Williton	19,895	71.5	55.7	77.9	15.8	22.1	5.7	8.0	10.0	14.0	–	–
314	Wellington	22,121	84.1	52.0	61.8	32.1	38.2	20.9	24.8	10.6	12.6	–	–
315	Taunton	35,114	75.8	50.5	66.7	25.3	33.3	16.9	22.2	6.7	8.8	1.6	2.1
316	Bridgwater	33,188	72.6	51.0	70.4	21.6	29.6	9.0	12.4	7.7	10.6	1.7	2.3
317	Langport	18,567	68.2	45.6	66.9	22.6	33.1	13.9	20.4	7.9	11.6	–	–
318	Chard	26,085	75.0	44.9	59.9	30.1	40.1	20.8	27.7	8.0	10.6	–	–
319	Yeovil	28,463	76.7	46.6	60.7	30.1	39.3	15.6	20.3	10.6	13.8	–	–
320	Wincanton	21,311	72.4	45.6	63.0	26.8	37.0	14.4	19.9	12.2	16.8	–	–
321	Frome	25,325	92.4	44.5	48.1	47.9	51.9	26.9	29.1	21.0	22.8	–	–
322	Shepton Mallet	16,957	55.4	28.7	51.8	26.7	48.2	4.2	7.6	21.4	38.7	0.4	0.7
323	Wells	21,342	54.8	35.6	65.0	19.2	35.0	7.9	14.5	10.2	18.6	–	–
324	Axbridge	33,059	63.2	37.9	59.9	25.3	40.1	9.7	15.4	15.5	24.6	–	–
325	Clutton	25,227	68.7	34.0	49.5	34.7	50.5	6.0	8.7	28.3	41.1	0.1	0.2
326	Bath	69,847	75.7	46.0	60.9	29.7	39.1	10.8	14.3	12.2	16.1	2.0	2.6
327	Keynsham	21,615	78.6	28.7	36.5	49.9	63.5	24.5	31.2	24.5	31.1	–	–
328	Bedminster	38,143	47.2	26.5	56.1	20.7	43.9	8.7	18.5	11.3	24.0	–	–

Notes to Table 2
1. See note 7 to the text above on the discrepancies in the printed figures for Hungerford.
2. Plymouth's category of 'Isolated Congregations', too small to be of much significance in most districts, was credited with attendances amounting to an attendance index of 12.9 and a PS of 23.4, the highest such figures in the country. See the Devon section of the text for comment.

Notes

The 'index of attendance' method was pioneered by K.S. Inglis, 'Patterns of Worship in 1851', *Journal of Ecclesiastical History,* XI (1960), pp. 74–86. For further discussion of the Census material see W.S.F. Pickering, *British Journal of Sociology,* 18 (1967), pp. 382–407; D.M. Thompson, 'The 1851 Religious Census: Problems and Possibilities', *Victorian Studies,* XI (1967–8), pp. 87–97; and the latter author's chapter in *The Census and Social Structure,* ed. R. Lawton (1978), pp. 241–86. Parliamentary Papers 1852–3, LXXXIX (1690), Census, 1851: Religious Worship (England and Wales), contains both the Census report and the statistical tables on which this article is based.

[2] The published calendars of MS returns are *Bedfordshire Ecclesiastical Census 1851,* ed. D.W. Bushby, in Bedfordshire Historical Record Society, 54 (1975); *Lincolnshire Returns of the Census of Religious Worship 1851,* ed. R.W. Ambler, Lincoln Record Society, 72 (1979); and *The Religious Census of 1851. A Calendar of the Returns relating to Wales. Vol. 1, South Wales,* ed. I.G. Jones and D. Williams (Cardiff, 1976). No returns have been published for England south of the Thames, but two secondary studies which consider parts of the region through use of Census evidence are A. Everitt, *The Pattern of Rural Dissent: The Nineteenth Century* (Leicester, 1973), which looks at Kent among other counties, and R.M. Goodridge, 'The Religious Condition of the West Country in 1851', *Social Compass,* XIV (1967), pp. 285–96, on the Bristol hinterland.

[3] The MS returns are in the Public Record Office under category Home Office 129, with each registration district numbered as in Table II of this article.

[4] Within the category of Old Dissent are included Presbyterians, Independents, Baptists, Quakers and Unitarians. There are certain objections to this procedure — certainly it is not meant to suggest that all the denominations and, even less, all the congregations were of seventeenth-century origin — but it does provide a crude index of more traditional Dissent in contradistinction to Methodism. As for the latter, all the denominations which the compilers of the Census Report recognized as Methodist in origin and nature (including Calvinistic Methodist) are included.

[5] For the figures for registration counties calculated according to the index method, see B.I. Coleman, *The Church of England in the Mid-Nineteenth Century. A Social Geography* (1980), p. 40. This Historical Association pamphlet also provides some general analysis of patterns of worship for England and Wales, though largely from the standpoint of Anglican fortunes.

[6] In this calculation, as in all others in this article, the figures refer to the non-metropolitan counties of Kent, Middlesex and Surrey, with London being treated as a separate and distinct registration county.

[7] There are inconsistencies in the printed figures for Berkshire. The afternoon attendances given for the various denominations in Hungerford total 7166, but the summary total is given at 6066. Anglican afternoon attendances for the separate districts in the county totalled 29,757 but the county summary showed 26,662 as the figure. Afternoon attendances for all denominations in the county totalled 40,401 but the figure in the county summary is 32,800. Short of going to the MS returns there is no way of correcting these figures. The figures in Tables 1 and 2 of this article are produced by taking the totals as they were summarized and ignoring the inconsistencies. Berkshire seems to be the only county of our ten for which there are such basic errors.

The Diffusion of Tractarianism: Wells Theological College, 1840–49

W. M. JACOB

In this article I propose to consider the inter-related themes of the growth of 'professionalism' amongst the clergy, the development of professional training for the clergy, and the advance of Tractarian ideas outside the universities. Tractarianism was, in general, an avowedly clerical movement, emphasising the authority and independence of the clergy over against the laity and the state. The promotion of professional training for clergy was one of the primary ways which the Tractarian fathers saw as developing 'priestliness' amongst Anglican clergy, and they led the field in establishing seminaries to supplement the general education provided by the universities. Wells has been chosen as the subject of this study because although Chichester was the first college in the field, Wells was more successful in attracting sufficient numbers of men to provide a satisfactory sample for investigation during its first decade, and also because, unlike the colleges of Chichester and Cuddesdon, it was less obviously a strong hold of the Oxford Movement.

The 1830s and 1840s were a fulcrum of far-reaching changes for the established Church of England. Not only were there massive institutional changes brought about by the establishment of the Ecclesiastical Commissioners and the preceding minute examination of the functioning of the Church in all its many and varied aspects, there were a number of parallel changes coming to fruition, the origins of which were much earlier. These changes were largely concerned with the place of the clergy in nineteenth century society.

This change is illustrated by a comment of the editor of the *Quarterly Review,* himself a country clergyman, in 1857: 'Our own generation has witnessed recovery from the dismal apathy which had so long prevailed. True theology has revived, pluralities have been abolished, residence enforced, services multiplied, schools built, while the clergy as a body have displayed a zeal, a diligence and a liberality which will bear comparison with the brightest periods of ecclesiastical history.[1] Victorian clergy developed a myth about the ecclesiastical corruption and worldliness, the pastoral apathy and incompetence of their predecessors in the century or so before 1830. Whilst complaining about political bishops, about pluralism and non-residence, and about the gross inequities in eighteenth century clerical incomes, they reserved their most vigorous condemnation for the alleged secularity, laziness and inefficiency of the parish clergy. Identified, as they believed, in society with the squirearchy, the clergy 'gambled and rode, drank and swore' and frequented 'theatres, horse races, balls and taverns'. Lacking any form of regular theological or pastoral training, most Georgian clergy were accused of being incompetent as well as worldly and lax. Their sermons (when they were original, neither borrowed nor bought) were said to have been 'of unreadable dullness . . . dry, cold and uninviting'. Prayers as well as sermons were dreary, church buildings were uncared for, furniture, vestments and accessories of worship were regarded as sordid and slovenly.

It would seem that in the period between 1830 and 1850 there was a rapid and dramatic change in perception of the clerical role. In pre-industrial England the term 'professional' denoted a person of high social status, closely associated with the governing landowning class, able to live a leisured and cultured life, equipped with a good (but entirely general) education and responsible for a 'problem area' in society. The professional man was not expected to have expert knowledge or skill, nor to accommodate himself to a professional style of life, nor was he thought of primarily as a person who dispensed specific services. This was the pattern of life of the majority of late eighteenth and early nineteenth century clergy.[2]

As a result of socio-economic changes in the eighteenth and early nineteenth centuries occupations became increasingly specialised and the earlier understanding of professionalism changed. The right to be described as 'professional' depended less on social status and much more on skill, and on expert educational qualifications tested by examinations. Changes in medical and scientific knowledge, in land ownership and the expansion of agriculture, commerce and industry, required a mastery of complex technical knowledge.

At the same time the clergy were being subjected to similar pressures. In the later eighteenth century the Evangelicals were steadily raising the ideal expected of a Christian pastor. They encouraged clergy to acquire more theological, pastoral and homiletic skills and a more distinctly clerical style of life. The

Tractarians adopted and reinforced the earnestness of the Evangelicals. The respect for utility that lay behind much of the reform in Church and State in the 1830s put further pressure on the clergy to redefine their role in a society that felt increasingly uncertain about rewarding any but its useful members. Popular anti-clericalism had a similar effect, of pressing the clergy to justify their existence. The strong contemporary emphasis on the virtues of work and duty had much the same effect. Further, during the nineteenth century most of the non-religious functions performed by the clergy, medical, educational, judicial and administrative were detached from the clerical profession. As this occurred the clergy were driven to consider and redefine their necessary functions, the activity which justified their existence, in the new sense, their profession.[3]

Although clergy were always expected to possess many of the qualities and certainly the education of gentlemen and continued to be generalists, filling the gaps in local public services, the emphasis on particular professional skills resulted in pressure for a deliberately professional education for a professional ministry. Criticism of the lack of provision for professional training for clergy began in the 1830s and continued throughout the century. Comment on the inadequacy of training for the ministry focused on three particular deficiencies, the absence of theological knowledge, the want of any real acquaintance with the technical duties of the pastoral office and the neglect of specific moral or spiritual training.

Until the nineteenth century the universities had been the theological nurseries of the established Church.[4] The taking of a degree required profession of membership of the Church of England, heads of houses were normally in orders as were most of the fellows. The purpose of the universities bore a resemblance to a modern theological college. If an ordination candidate was sanctioned and recommended for orders by his college and university he was regarded as sufficiently prepared for ordination. To have demanded a further period of collegiate life after the degree would have seemed absurd. In 1800 50% of the graduates of Oxford and Cambridge entered the ministry.[5]

However, with the growing expectation in the early nineteenth century that there would be a resident incumbent in every parish, it became clear that the universities were unable to supply enough men to serve the remoter districts. The first two specifically 'theological' colleges were founded to meet this need. The first was at St Bees in Cumberland in 1816 where George Law, Bishop of Chester, established a 'Clerical Institution' for the better instruction of those candidates for orders who were unable to obtain a university education. The students, who were boarded out, worshipped in the parish church of which the principal, with the co-operation of the patron, was incumbent, and undertook a two-year course.[6] In 1822 St David's College, Lampeter was founded not merely as a seminary but to provide a general education for non-graduates in remote South West Wales.

In fact, during the 1820s the pressure seems to have been towards the founding of new universities and there was considerable agitation against Oxford and Cambridge.[7] This agitation produced not only Lampeter but also University College, London in 1827 and King's College in 1828, although the theology department was not set up until 1846.

In the discussions between the Bishop of Durham and the Dean and Chapter which led to the establishment of another university, at Durham, to cater for undergraduates from the remote north east, there was considerable disagreement as to whether it should be merely a seminary or a university.[8] Although it was founded as a university, a theology course was introduced at Durham in 1834 and the Report of the University of Durham Commission in 1861 suggested that as it developed it was essentially a university for divinity.

Although the Evangelicals had, many years earlier, seen the value of selecting and training candidates for the ministry[9] and had been involved with the opening of the Church Missionary Society training institution for missionaries in Islington in 1826, the initiative for the establishment of post-graduate seminaries came from amongst high churchmen. In fact, a small number of men seem to have been involved in most of the activities in the 1820s and 1830s. William Otter, who was the first principal of King's College, London, became Bishop of Chichester in 1836 and invited Charles Marriott to undertake the principalship of the diocesan theological college for the preparation of candidates for holy orders which he was anxious to establish in Chichester.[10] Otter was succeeded at King's by Hugh James Rose who had previously been Professor of Divinity at Durham and in whose Deanery at Hadleigh the *Tracts for the Times* had been planned. It had been in Rose's mind that a post-graduate 'Theology School' might be established at Durham for ordination candidates, but ill-health had forced his retirement.[11]

The reasons for the lack of confidence in the ancient universities of the high churchmen in the 1830s seem to have been two-fold. Firstly they had hesitations about the adequacy or security of

Oxford and Cambridge as centres of orthodox theological teaching. The disputes in which some of the more advanced of the Tractarians became involved at Oxford may have caused some more moderate high churchmen to feel alarmed. Secondly, Tractarian writers, whilst claiming that the universities offered a good general education, pointed out that they did not offer any training in the essential background of the priestly life — in theology and the spiritual life. Evangelicals, perhaps because of their tendency to cluster in certain colleges of known Evangelical proclivities and to sit at the feet of their own teachers, such as Simeon, were more sanguine of the universities.

Many conscientious ordinands were accustomed to spend twelve months or so between graduation and ordination in solitary preparation for the bishop's examination. Occasionally small groups of ordinands would go to live with a parish priest well known for his spiritual and pastoral zeal to serve a sort of apprenticeship, rather as in the previous century Bishop Wilson had gathered his Manx ordinands around him.[12] It was this informal pattern that seems to have provided the model for the future theological colleges.

One further factor seems to have contributed to the propitiousness of establishing seminaries in the 1830's. In the radical onslaught of the early 1830s cathedral chapters had been a particular focus for criticism. Even conservative high churchmen felt that the concentration of such considerable funds, as some chapters possessed, in very few hands was inequitable. It was the fear of losing all their endowments that concentrated the minds of the 'golden' canons of Durham on diverting a modest proportion of their endowments towards the foundation of that university. A number of constructive proposals were made for more appropriate uses for chapter funds and one of the most influential was that argued by Pusey in a pamphlet in 1833. He advocated the establishment of institutions, providing a specialised theological education for graduates seeking ordination, attached to cathedral chapters, under the supervision of the bishop. It was not unlike the proposal in Cranmer's *Reformatio Legum Ecclesiasticarum* that 'in every Cathedral there should be provision made for Readers of Divinity, and of Greek and Hebrew, and a great number of students to be exercised in the daily worship of God, and trained up in Study and Devotion; whom the Bishop might transplant out of this Nursery into all parts of his Diocese'.[14]

It was against this background of doubt concerning the adequacy and orthodoxy of the universities, of a realisation that the

endowments of cathedrals were requiring justification by useful-
ness, of a desire for more priestly and professional clergy that the
earliest post-graduate theological college had emerged at Chichester in 1839. The instigators were Bishop Otter, who as well as
being Principal of King's College, London, was the friend and
biographer of Malthus, and Henry Manning, then Archdeacon of
Chichester. Charles Marriott, who became the Principal, was a
fellow of Oriel and a close associate of Keble, Newman and the
Tractarians.[15] However, the foundation was fragile, Marriott
resigned because of ill health in March 1841 and returned to Oriel.
His successor Henry Browne survived until November 1845 when
the college was suspended for six months until Philip Freeman,
author of *The Principles of Divine Service*, was appointed. His
successor in 1854 was Charles Swainson who was non-resident from
his appointment as Norrisian Professor at Cambridge in 1864 until
his resignation of the principalship in 1870. During its first thirty
years the college at Chichester was small in numbers and
precarious in existence.[16]

The second such foundation, which followed at Wells, in the
following year, was a very much more substantial affair. The
ingredients, however, were strikingly similar. The Bishop of Bath
and Wells, George Henry Law, had, like Otter, already been
involved with ministerial training, for he had formerly been Bishop
of Chester and had founded the college at St Bees. Again Manning
was involved. It was at his instigation that W.T.P. Brymer who
was Archdeacon of Bath, put up £1000 to establish a theological
college at Wells. Other financial support was also forthcoming,
F.H. Dickinson, a layman, offered £100 a year for ten years, the
Reverend Lord John Thynne also put up a substantial sum, and
James Law, the bishop's son and Chancellor of Lichfield Cathedral, offered the lease of the Rib, a house at the east end of the
Cathedral, for the use of the proposed college, at a nominal rent.[17]

Although the Bishop's background was as an Evangelical, he
had been an exact contemporary of Simeon and had been a pupil
of Isaac Milner at Queen's College, Cambridge, and a fellow of
Queen's from 1781–4,[18] there is strong circumstantial evidence to
suggest that Wells too was founded under Tractarian influence.
Not only was the idea put up by Manning but Lord John Thynne
was the brother of the Marquis of Bath who was a noted high
churchman and a strong opponent of the Public Worship Regulation Act in 1874,[19] and the patron and friend of W.J.E. Bennett
whose elaborate schemes for the ritualistic 'restoration' of Frome
parish church he financed.[20] Most significant of all, however, was

the man they appointed as Principal, John Pinder, who had been Principal of Codrington College, Barbados. The mathematics instructor at Codrington College, whom Pinder had appointed in 1834, Hurrell Froude, wrote to tell Newman 'I have secured the Principal of Codrington College as an ally and he will be able to prejudice several of the clergy, who have been through his hands'. Froude later definitely denominated Pinder as an 'Apostolical' though one whom he wished he could 'unsawnify'. In 1837 Pinder had published a collection of sermons on the *Book of Common Prayer* in which he drew copiously on Palmer's *Origines Liturgicae* and also possibly on Froude's *Tract on the Liturgy.* Pinder carefully emphasised that the Prayer Book was not 'composed and written for the occasion by our Reformers, but most carefully selected from ancient liturgies'.[21]

The four founders were fortunate indeed in having to hand one of the very few men at the time in England who had particular experience of training men for the ministry. Pinder was capable and energetic. He remained in the job for twenty five years and he clearly had the capacity for gaining the affection of the men whom he trained, for in 1865 on his retirement, former students subscribed £2500 in appreciation of his work to buy four houses in the Vicars' Close, the rents of which were to act as an endowment for the College.

Before the end of 1839 Pinder had sketched out a prospectus for the proposed College for 'graduates at the University desirous of preparing themselves for ordination — the students will attend Morning and Evening prayers of the Church daily. The Course of Study will consist of the Scriptures in the original, Selections from the Early Fathers and other standard Divines, the Evidences of Christianity, Ecclesiastical History in general and that of the Church of England in particular — with reference to Doctrine, Polity, Liturgy, Articles and Canons. The Difference between the Church of England and other Churches and Denominations in these respects — Jewish Antiquities, Practical and Pastoral Theology'. Two hours a day were to be spent in lectures, sermons were to be frequently prepared, enunciation and delivery taught and the sick and aged visited in their homes under the guidance of the parochial clergy, and classes supervised in the Wells Diocesan Training School. Men were to be in residence for not less than twelve months previous to ordination.[22]

This syllabus represents the general emphases of contemporary English theology. The concern is primarily with the Fathers and the doctrinal and the moral as opposed to the critical study of the

Bible and history. What is interesting is the inclusion of practical training. Neither Philip Freeman, who became the third principal of Chichester in 1845, nor Liddon as Vice-Principal of Cuddesdon, later, thought that practical training should be included in the theological college curriculum.[23]

The college at Wells followed the examples of those at Chichester and St Bees in that there was no common life. The men seem to have lived in lodgings in the Vicars' Close and later, in the town. It was only in 1872 when four non-graduates were taken on, because of a crisis in recruitment, that it became customary for students to live as households, which later became the pattern of residence for all students at Wells. The first college to be designed for a common life was Cuddesdon.[24]

The college opened on August 3rd 1840 with four students. They and those who had made the venture possible met at 7 am in the Chapel at the end of the Vicars' Close and after morning prayer and a sermon by the Principal, Bishop Law addressed them. Pinder's sermon suggested that the foundation was open to 'misunderstanding as to its character'. He also suggested that the intention was to make the college if not a diocesan, then a regional college.[25]

By the following term there were ten students and a room over the western cloisters of the cathedral was being used for lectures. In 1841 an unsuccessful attempt was made to establish a hall. By the end of 1842 there were seventeen students in residence and a library had been established and a vice-principal to assist Pinder had been appointed. By 1844 when there were twenty-eight students the Vicars' Close Chapel had become too small for the College to use and the Cathedral Lady Chapel began to be used for College services.[26]

In 1846 under the new bishop of Bath and Wells, Bagot, the position of the College was formalised by a trust deed. Pinder as principal became Precentor of the Cathedral and hence, Wells being a cathedral of the old foundation, the second dignitary of the cathedral after the Dean.[27] The Bishop, the Dean and the Precentor and the Vicar of Wells became trustees of the College and a council, on the model of Chichester, was established. It was set out that there should be four terms each year and that Pinder's curriculum of 1839 should be generally followed and that students were 'to abstain from all games of chance, field sports, balls and other amusements of a boisterous and frivolous nature'. They were also expected to pass an examination at the end of every term.[28]

Wells was clearly sufficiently successful to attract the opposition of the universities. Pinder drew up a memorandum defending the idea of a 'diocesan college'. He quoted Cranmer, suggesting that being under the episcopal eye would be a useful means of moderating party feeling, enabling a bishop to know his younger clergy who, through attendance at a theological college would learn practical hints, be taught to administer the offices of the Church and escape from the temptations of the university to the recollection of the quiet cathedral city.[29] Already it seems, in the first decade of its existence, Wells was attracting the sort of criticism of failing in pastoral training, fomenting party feeling and detracting from the universities, that was levelled at Cuddesdon ten years later.[30]

Such are the bare outlines of the development of the theological college at Wells during its first ten years. The circumstances of the foundation of the college and of the appointment of the principal suggest that, like Chicester, the influence of the Tractarians was present, and Pinder's subsequent defence of the college in his sermon at the inauguration of the college and in his memorandum defending the college suggest that the accusation of fomenting party feeling may not have been entirely unjust. However, any conclusive evidence of this needs to depend on an investigation of the men who were attracted to be trained at Wells and on their subsequent careers.

Such an investigation is possible because the matriculation books for the college suvive[31] and note the university colleges which the men previously attended. It is also possible and instructive from the point of view of seeing how the college coped with the competition from other colleges[32] founded later, to compare the patterns of recruitment during the first ten years of the life of the college with the pattern in its fourth decade. Table 1 suggests that recruitment was good in the first decade but that there was quite a sharp falling away in the 1870's.

Another small but significant difference between the former and the latter periods is that in the former years there were no non-graduates, all the men were occupying the year between taking their degrees and the canonical age for the diaconate, however in the latter period there were a small number of non-graduates.[33] However, the reasons why five out of twenty-two colleges at Oxford and Cambridge produced so many men at Wells must be investigated further.

Unfortunately the matriculation books do not record the home locality of the men admitted, but of the seven colleges, only one, Exeter, has any close regional identity, so this is unlikely to be the

Table 1: Numbers of men matriculated at Wells Theological College 1840–49 and 1870–79

Source: Salisbury and Wells Theological College, Wells MSS *Matriculation Books* 1840–54 and 1854–92

1840	13	1870	13
1841	9	1871	14
1842	16	1872	17
1843	20	1873	14
1844	16	1874	14
1845	14	1875	14
1846	26	1876	9
1847	15	1877	18
1848	25	1878	10
1849	22	1879	13
Total		176	136

A further comparison of the university colleges which the men who matriculated had attended reveals another marked difference between the two decades. As Table II shows, a very considerable proportion of Wells men between 1840 and 1849 attended a fairly small number of colleges, whereas by 1870 this proportion was much smaller.

Table 2: University Colleges from which ten or more men went to Wells 1840–49 and 1870–79

College	1840–49	1870–79
Christ Church, Oxford	21	12
Exeter College, Oxford	21	10
Oriel College, Oxford	13	3
University College, Oxford	14	5
Wadham College, Oxford	11	2
St John's College, Cambridge	12	11
Trinity College, Cambridge	14	12
	106	45

answer. What may be significant is that three of the colleges had senior members who were closely identified with the Tractarian cause. Oriel obviously had very strong Tractarian connections. Keble, Newman, Pusey, Robert Wilberforce and Hurrell Froude either had been or were fellows of Oriel,[34] and it may be significant that 1846, the year after the most distinguished of them, Newman, seceded to Rome, was the only year in the decade that no Oriel man went to Wells. At Christ Church Pusey may have been no small influence and that may account for the seven House men out of twenty-six who matriculated at Wells in 1846 and the five out of twenty-five in 1848.

Trinity College, Cambridge may also have been a centre of Tractarian activity. In the 1820s and early 1830s there had been a small group of high churchmen at Trinity who had become Roman Catholics.[35] The Cambridge Camden Society was founded by the Trinity men, J.M. Neale and Benjamin Webb. W.J. Butler, who founded the Community of St Mary the Virgin at Wantage, was a contemporary at Trinity with some of the men who went to Wells. A number of noted later ritualists were Trinity men, including two of the five priests to be imprisoned for ritualist activities S.F. Green and Arthur Tooth. So were Green's former vicar and fellow curate at St Peter's, Swinton. Other notable Trinity ritualists were Knox-Little, vicar of St Albans, Manchester, F.L. Bagshawe who became master of the Society of the Holy Cross and J.R.A. Chinnery-Haldane, who became Bishop of Argyll and the Isles. A fellow of Trinity, Thomas Thorp, was one of thirteen Tractarians who signed a series of resolutions attacking the Gorham judgement in 1850.[36]

There are no obvious reasons why the other colleges in the list sent so many men to Wells unless they too had strong, though less obvious Tractarians amongst their senior members. Although the evidence is entirely circumstantial there do seem to be grounds for suspecting that Wells, at least during its first ten years, was strongly influenced by Tractarianism. The names of the founders, the sympathies of the Principal and the colleges of its students all suggest this. However, this evidence should not be pushed too far, for one of the other colleges from which a steady stream of students went to Wells was Wadham, which was the leading Evangelical college, and whose warden was Dr B.P. Symons, a leading Evangelical. He had headed the attack on *Tract XC,* was one of the court which tried Pusey's sermon, and had transferred his Sunday chapel to the precise time which prevented the undergraduates from attending Newman's sermons.[37] The conclusions to be drawn are not clear. It may be that some Wadham men reacted against their Warden's autocracy, or it may be that Wells was not as tainted with Tractarianism as might at first appear to be the case.

Further light may be thrown on the development of the College and its relationship with the Church of England if the subsequent careers of the men who were trained there during the first ten years are followed over a thirty to forty year period. This can be done by the use of early editions of *Crockford's Clerical Directory*. Of the 176 men matriculated at Wells between 1840 and 1849, seventy-seven were still alive and beneficed and had entries in the 1881 edition of *Crockford*. Table 3 shows where these men 'served their titles' as curates. This suggests very strongly that the college was very much a regional, if not entirely a diocesan college.

Table 3: Dioceses in which men who trained at Wells between 1840–49, who were still alive in 1881, served their titles

	1840–49	1870–79
Armagh	1	0
Bath and Wells	23	15
Canterbury	2	6
Chichester	1	5
Durham	1	2
Ely	3	4
Exeter	6	3
Gloucester and Bristol	1	6
Hereford	1	6
Lichfield	2	9
Lincoln	3	4
Llandaff	3	0
London	5	5
Norwich	2	6
Oxford	3	9
Peterborough	1	2
Rochester	2	2
Salisbury	12	4
Winchester	1	7
Worcester	3	8
York	1	0

The vast majority of the men served their titles in the southern province and a very large proportion of that majority worked in only two dioceses, Bath and Wells and Salisbury. However, if Wells regarded itself as a regional college, it is odd that while two neighbouring dioceses took the next largest number of men after Bath and Wells, the third neighbouring diocese, Gloucester and Bristol, received only one man in ten years. Again, an answer, but perhaps not the only answer, may be party, for the bishops of the neighbouring dioceses to which Wells men went in any number were old fashioned high churchmen who were at least tolerant towards the Tractarians. Bishop Bagot who was translated from Oxford to Bath and Wells treated Newman and Denison and Bennett with sense and tenderness.[38] Philpotts of Exeter, the persecutor of Gorham, was a determined high churchman who was himself anxious to establish a theological college in Exeter.[39] Bishop Denison of Salisbury was sympathetic and had also, in 1841, spoken of establishing a theological college in Salisbury.[40] Bishop Monk of Gloucester and Bristol, however, had taken a very different line on *Tract XC*, believing that the author wished to reconcile the Church of England with the Church of Rome.[41] This may offer some explanation for the very small number of men from Wells who were ordained in the closest neighbouring diocese. A comparison with the dioceses in which men were ordained between 1870 and 1879 served their titles shows that there is a much broader spread, although by far the largest number in any one diocese are still in Bath and Wells.

If the careers of Wells men who are identifiable in the 1881 edition of *Crockford's Clerical Directory* are examined, a considerable number, as Table 4 shows, were in livings in the diocese and the region, and there was, by then, a more even spread amongst the neighbouring dioceses. There were still only very few (five) who were holding benefices in the northern province.

Table 4: Dioceses containing ten or more men trained at Wells between 1840–1849 in 1881

Bath and Wells	12
Gloucester and Bristol	10
Salisbury	10
Winchester	10

It is difficult to know how to evaluate the careers of the men who were still alive and working in 1881. If evaluation is considered in terms of preferment, then not many achieved 'considerable' preferment in terms of becoming ecclesiastical dignitaries, as table 5 shows, and some of the more solid of these preferments seem more likely to have been due to aristocratic conncections than to personal holiness or pastoral effectiveness. It may or may not be significant that in the first ten years at Wells there were six younger sons of peers and one heir to a baronetcy.

Table 5: Men trained at Wells between 1840 and 1849 who became dignitaries by 1881

Royal Chaplain	1
Archdeacons	1
Canons Residentiary	3
Honorary Canons	4
Rural Deans	6

Again, a consideration of the patrons of the livings of the men surviving from the first decade of the college in 1881 suggests that a number were men of substance, for ten of them had presented themselves to their livings and a further ten had been presented by someone with the same surname as themselves, which suggests presentation to a family living. This would suggest that at least a fifth to a quarter of them had some aristocratic or gentry connection of the rest seventeen had bishops as their patrons but only one of these had been presented to a living in the gift of the Bishop of Bath and Wells. Twelve had peers as patrons, ten had been presented by the Lord Chancellor, two by the Crown, and one by the Prince of Wales. Again, it may or may not be coincidence that two peers, the Duke of Buccleuch and Lord Lovelace each presented two Wells men from the first decade to livings in their gift. Only three of them were presented to livings in the gift of their college, two Christ Church men and one from Magdalen, and an Exeter man received a Wadham living. This small number is a little surprising, especially as two had been Students of Christ Church, two Fellows of Magdalene College Cambridge, and one a Fellow of Merton and another a Fellow of Magdalen College, Oxford. It seems to have been unlikely that attendance at a theological college was in any way significant to a man's subsequent career, but it is worth considering whether there may be further areas of clerical activity which could be investigated and which might offer circumstantial evidence as to the value and influence of a period spent at a theological college. A consideration of the publications, where known, of these men and also of their liturgical practice, where information is available, may reveal further evidence.

Eleven of the men who are listed in the 1881 *Crockford's* list their publications there. Between them they had twenty-seven publications, and the titles suggest that eleven of these publications were concerned with pastoral matters, seven with theological subjects, and one with the religious life. Of the others there were three travel books, three antiquarian or historical studies and one Classical reader. The number of titles concerned with pastoral topics suggests that some at least of the Wells men were affected by the concern for the extension and development of the pastoral ministry, which seems to have been an important feature of the professionalisation of the clerical role during the century. The general range of the topics would also seem to suggest a concentration on theological subjects with a substantial minority devoted to works of general cultural interest.

A few of the publications suggest a very professional and specialist interest in certain pastoral areas. John Cave-Brown, who was one of the first in-take at Wells in 1840, was the author of *Indian Infanticide and its Suppression* and *Plain Words for Soldiers* while he was a chaplain in India from 1851 to 1872. Henry Hawkins, who was at Wells in 1848 and was successively chaplain to Sussex County Lunatic Asylum and to Colney Hatch Lunatic Asylum, published *Work in the Wards, Visiting Day at the Asylum* and *Friendly Words to New Patients* as SPCK Tracts and also contributed to the *Journal of Mental Science.*

Some indication of the liturgical practice of these Wells men who were listed in the 1881 edition of *Crockfords* can be ascertained by reference to the *Tourists' Church Guide.*[42] This was published by the English Church Union and presumably indicates the parish churches at the services of which the members would feel happy. It would therefore seem likely that the liturgy of any church appearing in the *Guide* was acceptable to the ritualist tastes of the members. However, it is important to remember that not all ritualist churches were listed in the *Guide* and that the list of ritualist parishes provided is unlikely to be exhaustive.

Twenty of the 1840–49 Wells men who appear in the 1881 *Crockford's* were incumbents or curates of parishes listed in the *Guide.* All of these had a weekly celebration of the Holy Communion, a frequency that was by no means universal in 1881. Of these twenty, twelve are noted as saying Morning and Evening Prayer daily, publicly in church, a practice in which their principal had trained them many years before. Fifteen of them took the eastward position at the holy table when celebrating the Holy Communion. Eight had two celebrations of the Holy Communion on Sundays, and the second one, later in the morning, would appear to have been choral. Six used only Gregorian chant for their music, seven used only Anglican chant and three used both at different times. Six had candles on the holy table and lighted them at some services, five had candles on the holy table but did not light them. Only four exhibited all the signs of full-blown ritualism, wearing eucharistic vestments as well and of these only two wore coloured vestments, the other two wearing white linen vestments.

This evidence suggests that a significant proportion of men who had been trained at Wells in its first decade were a generation or so later identified by the English Church Union as, in some degree, ritualists. At least two of these had gone a very long way along the path to what might have been regarded as extremism. Henry Whish, who was curate of St Michael's, Brighton, was a member of the extreme ritualist Society of the Holy Cross[43] and Sir James Philipps, Vicar of Warminster, who in 1864 established a training home for women missionaries in his parish. A few members of this wished to follow a religious life, so Philipps then founded a community for sisters dedicated to St Denys the Areopagite in 1879.[44] In 1871 he had also established St Boniface College at Warminster for training priests for the mission field, but the following year the first principal, J.R. Madan, seceded to Rome.[45] In addition a Wells man whose parish was not featured in the *Tourists' Church Guide,* William Edward Smith, who later adopted the surname Sellon, wrote a tract, *Sisterhoods in the Church of England,* in 1849, in defence of the Sisterhood established by his sister at Devonport in 1848.[46]

However, it would be too simple to suggest that Tractarian and high church influence was all-pervasive at Wells. In at least two instances and probably very many more, it was quite clearly not. In 1847 Edward Whateley, son of the Archbishop of Dublin, who could hardly be called sympathetic to Tractarianism, was at the college. Twenty years later his sister wrote an attack on Miss Sellon and her sisterhood in the form of a novel, *Maude, or the Anglican Sister of Mercy.*[47] The danger of reading too much into family connections however, is illustrated by the case of the Hon. William Henry Lyttleton, whose brother Lord Lyttleton was an ardent high churchman who was a member of the committee of influential layman who supported and initiated the Park Village Sisterhood.[48] William Lyttleton, soon after his ordination, for health reasons, went to Germany and there 'imbibed a dose of German philosophy' which, in his own words, made him 'sadly low church'. Controversy followed with his brother, who, supported by Mr Gladstone, frowned on a 'tolerant, ecumenical outlook'. Lord Lyttleton had grave doubts about presenting his brother to the family living of Hagley, for he feared that he might admit into the parish dissenters, whom he considered to be 'to a very large extent in the same category as heathens or infidels or Socinians'.[49] Lyttleton went on to become an extremely active pastor with a special concern for the plight of the poor. He published pamphlets and spoke at Church Congresses, seeking to improve the quality of life of the poor, advocating proper charitable distribution and proper recreational facilities, as well as proper educational facilities, in which 'our aim should be to cultivate human nature as a whole in all its powers — bodily, mental and spiritual'.[50]

It seems likely that only one man trained at Wells in the first decade became a convert to the Roman Church. He was Charles Cox, of Exeter College, Oxford, who was at Wells in 1843, whose name appears in *Rome's Recruits: A List of Protestants who Have Become Roman Catholics Since the Tractarian Movement,*[51] a pamphlet published by the Whitehall Review and sympathetic to the Roman cause.

In general the men produced by the college and the pattern of training offered would seem to have commended themselves to moderate high churchmen like Samuel Wilberforce and moderate Tractarians such as W.K. Hamilton. Wilberforce imported a small number of Wells men as guinea pigs into the Oxford diocese and watched over their subsequent history with paternal curiosity.[52] At the grand opening of Wilberforce's own diocesan college at Cuddesdon in June 1854 Henry Pepys, Bishop of Worcester, in his speech gave evidence that his best young clergy were those from Chichester and Wells.[53] Further, the devotional tone of the early Cuddesdon notices bore a marked similarity to the instructions issued by the first Principal of Wells to his men.[54] In his Charge to the clergy at the visitation of his diocese in 1861, W.K. Hamilton clearly showed that he was influenced by the example of Wells in his establishment of a theological college at Salisbury,[55] and one of his most trusted lieutenants, Francis Lear, had been trained at Wells.

That men like Wilberforce and Hamilton saw the theological college at Wells as an example to follow in the establishment of their own colleges suggests that it stood firmly in the Tractarian tradition and that it may very well have been an important influence in consolidating the influence of Tractarianism outside Oxford. The evidence of the colleges from which most Wells men were recruited during the first decade, as well as the liturgical practices of some of them later, also strongly suggest that the college may have been one of the channels through which the high church revival came to be diffused in parishes.

The Tractarianism of Wells, however, seems to have been more modest, and less obviously partisan than that displayed by later colleges. In spite of Wilberforce, the college he established opposite his palace at Cuddesdon gave manifest evidence of Romish practices with its elaborately furnished Chapel.[56] Hamilton, too, had a definitely partisan objective when he established his college at Salisbury. In 1864 he very carefully drew up a trust deed for his college, borrowing the trust deed from Cuddesdon as a model and insisting that a requirement should be written into it that the Principal and all tutors should make a declaration on appointment that they would conform their teaching to the doctrines of the New Testament and the Catholic and ancient fathers as well as the XXXIX Articles and the *Book of Common Prayer*.[57] It is probably not insignificant for their party positions that during the course of the 1870's four students at Cuddesdon and one student at each of Chichester, Salisbury and Lincoln were members of the Society of the Holy Cross, whilst no student at Wells appears in the list.

Whilst it is very important not to over-emphasise the significance of a single year of training in a long ministry, there do seem to be some common characteristics amongst the men who trained at Wells about whom any information is available and a tendency towards Tractarianism may be one of them, although there were obvious exceptions, as has been noted.

A more general tendency, of which Tractarianism seems to have been a symptom rather than a cause, and of which the education offered at Wells seems to have been a notable example, was towards the professionalisation of the ministry of the Church of England. Although there had been Independent Academies throughout the eighteenth century and the Bristol Baptist College, set up in the 1720s, was followed by new Baptist colleges in Yorkshire, South Wales and London in the early nineteenth century and the Methodists were seeking to establish a theological institution in the 1830s, these institutions offered not so much a professional training for the ministry as a general education for those who were debarred from the universities. This was also the intention of the Anglican foundations at St Bees and Lampeter.

The Anglican theological colleges established in the mid-nineteenth century were rather different institutions, for their aim was to add a professional training to the general education that had already been received at the universities. This is made abundantly clear in Pinder's outline for the College at Wells in 1839. The intention was to provide for graduates a grounding in a knowledge of the Christian tradition, supervision in acquiring professional skills such as preaching and pastoral work, and guidance in the acquisition of an appropriate life-style.

This development of a corporate self-identity amongst the clergy, which was also evidenced at the parochial level, by the growth of clerical meetings and societies with an emphasis on the study of doctrine and of the pastoral task, seems to have been a reaction to the changing nature of nineteenth century society. Other professions were encroaching on the clerical role so it was felt to be important to define it more closely. The growing awareness of the drift of people away from formal religious practice created an impulse for thinking about evangelism. Such factors as these contributed to the desire for a professionally-equipped clergy which, despite strong opposition in the 1850s, largely shaped the ministry of the Anglican clergy by the end of the nineteenth century.

However, because of the disparate nature of the Church of England and its lack of any adequate centralised forum for discussion during the suspension of Convocation between 1717 and 1852, theological colleges were established by groups of individuals as private institutions, it would often seem, to promote a particular theological viewpoint. They served therefore not merely to professionalise the clergy but also perhaps to promote party feeling amongst the clergy in a much more coherent way than between the old 'high church' and 'low church' sympathisers.

The establishment of Wells Theological College and its development during its first decade would seem to provide important evidence both for the professionalisation of the clerical rôle and for the development of Tractarianism at the parochial level. A similar investigation of evidence from other theological colleges over a longer period might shed considerable light on some of the less obvious reasons why the Church of England developed as it did in the second half of the nineteenth century.[58]

Notes

[1]   *Quarterly Review,* Vol CII, p. 468; the editor was the Revd Whitwell Elwin, Vicar of Booton, in Norfolk.

[2]   For an account of the expectations of the writers of eighteenth and early nineteenth century handbooks for clergy see A.J. Russell, *The Clerical Profession* (1980).

[3]   For an account of the very different expectations of mid Victorian writers of handbooks for clergy, see B. Heeney, *A Different Kind of Gentlemen: The Parish Clergy as Professional Men in Early and Mid-Victorian England* (Hamden, Connecticutt, 1976).

[4]   Hooker had described them as 'erected to serve as nurseries unto the Church of Christ', *Ecclesiastical Polity*, Books 7 ch 15, section 4.

[5]   M.A. Crowther, *Church Embattled: Religious Controversy in Mid-Victorian England* (Newton Abbot, 1970), p. 220.

[6]   S.L. Ollard and G. Crosse, *A Dictionary of English Church History* (first edition, 1912), p. 588.

[7]   See A. Heeson, *The Founding of the University of Durham* (Durham 1982), pp. 5–7.

[8]   *Ibid;* pp. 24–6.

[9]   F.W.B. Bullock; *A History of Training for the Ministry of the Church of England in England and Wales from 1800 to 1874* (St Leonards-on-Sea, 1955), p. 24.

[10]   J.W. Burgon, *Lives of Twelve Good Men* (1891), p. 158.

[11]   *Ibid*, p. 97.

[12]   Bullock, *Op. cit.*, p. 11–12.

[13]   See G.F.A. Best, *Temporal Pillars: Queen Anne's Bounty, the Ecclesiastical Commissioners and the Church of England* (Cambridge, 1964), ch VI.

[14]   G. Burnet, *History of the Reformation* (1st edition, 1679), pt.I, Bk III, p. 301.

[15]   Burgon, *Op. cit.*, p. 157.

[16]   R.S.T. Haslehurst, 'A Short History of Chichester Theological College', *The Cicestrian*, Trinity, 1939.

[17]   Salisbury and Wells Theological College Archives (S & WTC) Wells MSS Letter of F.H. Dickinson 28 February 1890.

[18]   Bullock, *Op. cit.*, p. 30.

[19]   J. Bentley, *Ritualism and Politics in Victorian Britain; The Attempt to Legislate for Belief* (Oxford, 1978), *passim*.

[20]   P.F. Anson, *Fashions in Church Furnishings, 1840–1940* (1965), p. 193.

[21]   P. Brendon, *Hurrell Froude and the Oxford Movement* (1974), p. 152–3.

[22]   S & WTC Wells MSS: First Outline of Wells Theological College 1839.

[23]   Heeney, *Op. cit.*, p. 101.

[24]   O. Chadwick, *The founding of Cuddlesdon* (1954), p. 49.

[25]   Quoted in E.L. Elwes, *The History of Wells Theological College* (1923), p. 4.

[26]   *Wells Theological College Calendar, 1853* (Wells 1853), p. 18f.

[27]   K. Edwards, *The English Secular Cathedrals in the Middle Ages* (Manchester, 2nd Edition, 1967), p. 159–166.

[28]   S & WTC Wells MSS Trust Deed 1846.

[29]   S & WTC Wells MSS Pinder MSS.

[30]   Chadwick, *Op. cit.*, p. 70.

[31]   S & WTC Wells MSS.

[32]   St Aidan's Birkenhead 1846, Cuddesdon 1854, Lichfield 1856, Salisbury 1860.

[33]   9 out of 136.

[34]   Burgon *Op. cit.*, p. 206.

[35]   H. Keldamy, 'Cambridge Movement and Christian Unity', *the Times*, 9th January 1982.

36 Bentley, *Op. cit.*, p. 27.
37 O. Chadwick, *The Victorian Church, Part I* (1966), p. 206.
38 *Ibid.*, p. 187.
39 Bullock, *Op. cit.*, pp. 113–114.
40 *Ibid.*, p. 112.
41 Chadwick, *The Victorian Church*, p. 188.
42 *Tourists Church Guide (1879), which contains: The hours of Service in most of the Churches in England, some in Wales, Scotland and Ireland, the Channel Islands and on the Continent, wherein the Holy Communion is celebrated weekly, and shows where Vestments and Altar Lights are used, if Music is Gregorian or Anglican, the Church Free and Open, and the Position of the Celebrant, published by the English Church Union and edited by the Secretary* [J.C. Waram] 9th edition.
43 Society of the Holy Cross, *List of Members 1855–1881*, temporarily deposited in Kent County Record Office.
44 P.F. Anson, *The Call of the Cloister: Religious Communities and Kindred Bodies in the Anglican Communion* (1955), p. 453.
45 Bullock, *Op. cit.*, p. 112.
46 Which was to become the Society of the Most Holy Trinity at Ascot Priory. See T.J. Williams; *Priscilla Lydia Sellon: The Restorer After Three Centuries of the Religious Life in the Church of England* (1965), p. 3, n. 1. The Marchioness of Bath, whose brother-in-law had been involved in the founding of Wells also contributed to Miss Sellon's work in Plymouth: see p. 22.
47 *Ibid.*, pp. 288–289.
48 *Ibid.*, p. 47.
49 B.E. Askwith: *The Tangled Web*, (1960), p. 119ff.
50 Heeney, *Op. cit.*, p. 51.
51 Fourth edition, Corrected and Amplified, 1881.
52 Chadwick, 'The Founding of Cuddesdon', *Op. cit.*, p. 12.
53 *Ibid.*, pp. 20–23.
54 *Ibid.*, p. 49.
55 *Salisbury Theological College Calendar* (Salisbury 1903), p. 17.
56 Chadwick, 'The Founding of Cuddesdon', *Op. cit.*, ch. 3.
57 S & WTC Salisbury MSS Account for the Foundation Deed 1864.
58 I am especially grateful for the help of Mrs Rosemary Pugh, Librarian of Salisbury and Wells Theological College, who made available the records of Wells and Salisbury Theological Colleges for my use.

Henry of Exeter
and the later Tractarians

J. A. THURMER

'Of uncommonly pleasing manners, and elegant mind. He bears a very high character'.[1] So wrote Henry Phillpotts, newly arrived in his diocese of Exeter, of the 'third man' of the forthcoming Oxford Movement, Richard Hurrell Froude.[2] Hurrell was the son of Robert Froude, Rector of Dartington and Archdeacon of Totnes, and Phillpotts met him at Dartington Hall, the seat of the Champernownes.

Phillpotts's approval of Froude was personal rather than theological, but it is matched by his high regard for all the Tractarian leaders. He offered John Keble the living of Paignton[3] and later accepted into the Exeter diocese Keble's curate, Peter Young, whom the Bishop of Winchester refused to ordain priest.[4] Newman wrote in 1835, 'I have been several days in houses with the Bishop of Exeter, who was exceeding gracious, and begged to see me, or rather hoped it, at the Palace'.[5] Phillpotts was in warm and frequent correspondence with Archdeacon Manning, particularly over the Gorham case, until shortly before the future cardinal's change of ecclesiastical allegiance. When in June 1843 Pusey was suspended for two years from preaching within the University of Oxford, Phillpotts went out of his way to make it clear that the suspension did not apply in the diocese of Exeter. Pusey's two sermons at Ilfracombe were printed, and he asked permission to dedicate them to the diocesan. Phillpotts gave this gladly without even reading the sermons, knowing 'that you would not preach anything in the diocese of Exeter which its Bishop would not be glad to hear, or which could give reasonable ground of offence to any sober-minded and faithful Christian'. Shortly before this Phillpotts had confirmed Pusey's invalid son Philip with a degree of kindness and pastoral consideration not always evident to his contemporaries or to posterity.[6] Intimacy between 'that fiend the Bishop of Exeter'[7] and the Restorer of the Church[8] continued until the 'fiend' died in 1869.

Yet, as the historian of nineteenth-century Exeter says, succinctly and accurately, 'Phillpotts was no Tractarian'.[9] He was 52 when

Henry Phillpotts, Bishop of Exeter aged 85 by William S. Hodges 1865.

he became Bishop of Exeter and his mind was fully made up. Tractarianism as a movement or a system was, to him, a mixture of truth and error, the separate strands of which he distinguished with the confidence of an avenging angel. Though he was the warm friend of the Tractarians, and on the same side as them in a number of public contoversies, he and they were of different spirit. To describe and define that difference of spirit is the purpose of this article. This will be done in relation to three matters: the surplice riots and the incident in St John's Torquay, the Gorham case and (more briefly) the revival of Convocation; a question of ritual, a question of doctrine and a question of organisation.

The surplice controversy in the Exeter diocese in 1844 and 1845 is a link with that interest in ecclesiastical ornament and ceremonial which, though largely absent from the early Tractarians (with the exception of Froude) commonly appeared from about 1840 in association with Tractarian theology. What was at issue was not, as in the sixteenth and seventeenth centuries, the surplice as such. Its use for sacraments, occasional offices and by the officiant at Morning and Evening Prayer was well established in law and custom. What varied from place to place and became (briefly) controversial was its use by the *preacher* who in some churches wore a black gown. If the preacher were not also the officiant, he sat in some convenient place, already gowned, before ascending the pulpit. If he were the officiant he changed (probably in the vestry) before mounting the top deck of the pulpit, or wherever the sermon was preached from. The morning sermon followed the Nicene creed. When there was no communion the ante-communion was commonly read from the reading-pew, often the middle level of the three-decker. Afternoon or evening sermons were 'lectures' strictly additional to the prescribed liturgy, and here also the dress of the preacher could be controversial.[10]

The point of the preacher's vesture is illustrated in an undated anecdote about W.F. Hook, who as Vicar of Leeds from 1837 to 1859 played a large part in establishing later Anglican usage, and who disliked the gown as a preaching vestment.

'In a church where he was to preach the consecration sermon, he was requested to wear the black gown in the pulpit. When the Nicene creed was over he did not go into the vestry, but had a black gown brought to him within the altar rails, where he took off his surplice and put on the gown before the congregation with a grave and deliberate formality of manner which to some present who understood the humour of the thing was exceedingly entertaining'.[11]

From 1840 the vesture of the clergy (with other architectural and liturgical matters) became controversial after a quiescence of nearly two centuries. William Palmer, Tractarian Fellow of Phillpotts's own college of Magdalen, performed what may be called the first ritualistic action; after his ordination as deacon on 8 December 1836 he wore the black clerical scarf diagonally over his surplice as though it were a stole.[12] This caused a considerable stir and Pusey advised Palmer to drop the practice lest it should bring the Tractarians into disrepute. Palmer's colleague J.R. Bloxham was Newman's curate at Littlemore from 1837 to 1840 and played so large a part in furnishing Littlemore chapel after the new fashion that Lord Blachford described him as 'Father or Grandfather of all Ritualists'.[13] Exactly contemporary with the surplice riots in Exeter was the first 'ritual' prosecution,[14] the beginning of what was to become a major preoccupation of Victorian churchmen for over half a century.

So to have issued, as Phillpotts did on 19 November 1844, a direction to the clergy to wear the surplice in preaching[15] might look like a partisan action. But Phillpotts, who along with other prominent patrons resigned from the Camden Society over the Round Church affair, was not striking a blow for Tractarianism or ritualism. He was trying to prevent the surplice becoming a party badge, for he hated the spirit of party, and to it he opposed his panacea for all woes, the law.

It was the Tractarian and reforming curate of Helston,[16] Walter Blunt, who started off the Exeter controversy. Preaching in the surplice was one of the things his parishioners complained of, though in this he was only following his predecessor's practice. Phillpotts, in his letter to the clergy, urged them to 'look to the law as sole guide', and, in the question of vesture, to wear the surplice in preaching.

The Bishop's directive occasioned, in the first instance, a characteristic and convoluted controversy with members of the Cathedral Chapter whom, with the Archdeacons, the Bishop had consulted on 14 November.[17] Phillpotts was the last man to give in easily. But having had clear evidence that his order about the surplice had increased, and not diminished controversy — that is, it had had the opposite effect to the one he intended, he withdrew it on 23 December, leaving it to the parochial clergy to continue its use if it was already customary and not offensive.

Such uncharacteristic indecision on the Bishop's part put some of the clergy in a difficulty greater than before; notably the incumbent of St Sidwell's, Exeter, the Rev. Francis Courtenay. He continued to preach in the surplice, a practice of three years' standing in his church, and on Sundays 12 and 19 January 1845 was mobbed in the street after service by large and hostile crowds. The Mayor, fearing that the forces of law and order would be unable to contain the situation, asked Phillpotts to intervene again. Phillpotts rather ungraciously complied. At his suggestion the preacher at St Sidwell's wore the gown and the furore subsided.[18]

At a time when party political feeling ran high and Exeter was 'rough, disorderly and often brutal'[19] Phillpotts, whose abrasive Toryism had already given offence, made the mistake of appearing to countenance popery and ritualism. He was regularly burnt in effigy at the 'gunpowder treason' bonfire in the Cathedral Close, and in this instance popular feeling was 'fanned into anger and action by a local press violently opposed to and consistently abusive of the Bishop — but *more on political* than religious grounds'. (Shapter, p. 17, his italics.) Whatever tactical mistakes the Bishop made, says the same authority, he looked 'solely to the law of the Church as his guide — alike condemning those who exceeded as those who failed in their fulfilment of it'.

Phillpotts, who normally resided not at the Palace adjacent to the Cathedral but at Bishopstow, Torquay, was often present at St John's, Torquay, which was itself involved in the surplice controversy. It was here, on Easter Day 1847, that Phillpotts made it dramatically clear that he was neither Tractarian nor ritualist. The altar had the customary communion plate upon it. But in addition there was, on this occasion, a wooden cross decorated with leaves and flowers, and two small glass vases with flowers. Phillpotts pushed one of these off, not realising that it was attached to the table with string, so flowers and water were spilt on the floor and the offending vase hung in mid-air. Questions of pious decoration and the beauty of holiness were absent from his mind. The issue was simply one of law.[20] Immediately after the service he said to the incumbent, 'Perhaps, Mr Smith, you are not aware that what you have done is illegal'. He appointed a court of enquiry which, after examining the 'ornaments rubric'[21] in its sixteenth-century setting, justified the Bishop in confirming his first reaction. 'As there is no ground on which the act, admitted by Mr Smith, can be deemed lawful, it is my duty to judge that he be admonished, and I do now admonish him not again to offend in the like manner'. With regard to the cross, Phillpotts was prepared to add a devotional consideration to the legal one. 'Instead of exciting the mind to due contemplation of the triumphant issue of our Lord's sufferings, it [the material cross] tends to chain it down to the sufferings themselves'.[22] An adaptation of this argument led some churchmen to prefer the plain cross to the crucifix. But the adjective 'triumphant' should be noticed. To the Tractarians a *theologia crucis* was vital; the church was identified with Christ in his sufferings and should not expect to be popular or successful. But to Phillpotts the church was the society of the glorified Christ and, in principle, perfect. Hence the confidence with which he invoked its law to bring its recalcitrant members to heel. Phillpotts was, to use the language of another time and place, a 'triumphalist'.

None of Phillpotts's controversies caused a greater stir or had more far-reaching effects than that with Gorham. In this he had the strong support of the Tractarians, and his eventual defeat occasioned a movement of secession to Rome so considerable that it bears some parallel to the disruption of the Church of Scotland in 1843.[23] It has been suggested that, in opposing Gorham's move from St Just to Brampford Speke, and so precipitating the crisis, Phillpotts was motivated by partisan hatred of Evangelicals. His biographer accuses him of 'bitter opposition towards the Evangelicals', and calls him 'an open partisan, who consistently and constantly made it his aim to promote men of his own party, and as consistently to persecute or ignore deserving low Churchmen'.[24] But, as a more recent study observes, 'there is some evidence which suggests that this view is in need of modification'.[25] Davies gives only one example to substantiate his charge, apart from appealing to the views of Thomas Latimer, radical Editor of *The Western Times* and himself a scurrilous partisan.

In fact Phillpotts's animus was not directed against Evangelicals in general. With H.F. Lyte, for example, the hymn-writer and Evangelical incumbent of Lower Brixham, Phillpotts had excellent relations.[26] It was directed against *Calvinists*. The point appears in the diary of Phillpotts's first tour of the diocese. On 12 August 1831 he met Mr Sollis, of Wolsery (Woolfardisworthy) who was 'said to be a Calvinist'. But the Bishop found him 'meek, humble, patient, confiding in Providence beyond anyone whom I ever knew . . . I enquired of his preaching, which he professed to be, as I had heard, free from all predestinarian tone — and practically like other good and sober Christian teaching'.[27]

Calvinism declared and preached was the enemy. 'Predestinarian tone' contradicted 'good and sober Christian teaching' because it cut the moral nerve and undermined the Sacraments and discipline of the Church. If there was an invisible church of the elect, the value of human effort was questioned, the Sacraments did not do what they claimed to do and the government and discipline of the bishop was not the unqualified law of God.

So Gorham's contention that regeneration in infant baptism was 'conditional on an act of prevenient grace' challenged Phillpotts's whole theological and ecclesiastical position. That is why, after prolonged *viva voce* examination, he refused him institution to the living of Brampford Speke, and defended his refusal before the Court of the Arches in 1848 (successfully) and before the Judicial Committee of the Privy Council in 1850 (unsuccessfully). When all legal means of excluding Gorham had failed, Phillpotts refused to appoint a rival pastor or to exhort the parishioners to worship elsewhere; he would not be the parent of schism. But he urged the churchwardens to keep watch over the doctrines their Vicar preached, and was prepared, if he received an unfavourable report, to take further legal action, just as he successfully refused licence or institution to other clergymen of similar views.[28] He never ceased to look for a legal authority which might overturn the judgment of the Judicial Committee, and this quest contributed powerfully to his interest in the revival of Convocation which followed close on the Gorham controversy.

On the doctrine of baptism that judgment has remained controversial. As a recent much-used reference work says, 'The secular authorities decided against the Catholic view'.[29] But Privy Councillors (all ordained or lay churchmen)[30] legally advising the Crown on the exercise of its ecclesiastical Supremacy are hardly 'secular authorities', and they did not decide *against* any view of Baptism. They judged that Gorham's view was not clearly contrary to the formularies. They did not require anybody to *hold* it. In this, as in other doctrine cases, the Judicial Committee maintained and extended an existing liberty.

The reason for the decision was that 'devotional exercises cannot be evidence of faith or of doctrine, without reference to the district declarations of doctrine in the Articles, *and to the faith, hope and charity by which the formularies profess to be inspired or accompanied*'.[31] (my italics.) Expressions of confidence in future bliss in the funeral service, for example, did not mean that all departed persons automatically enjoyed that bliss, and expressions about baptismal regeneration might also need to 'be construed in a charitable and qualified sense . . . and those who are strongly impressed with the earnest prayers which are offered for the Divine blessing, and the grace of God, may not unreasonably suppose that the grace is not necessarily tied to the rite; but that it ought to be earnestly and devoutly prayed for, in order that it may be then, or when God pleases, be present to make the rite beneficial'.[32] Liturgical language, in other words, is not the same as legal language; the wording of the services looks to something other than the bare performance of the rite. The idea would naturally not appeal to Phillpotts. But it comes curiously close to the outlook of the Tractarians, who found poetry a guide to the nature of religious truth because it is allusive, sensitive and humble. On the question of Baptism, they were more interested in the preservation of baptismal purity by faith and the right state of heart than in the efficacy of the baptismal act itself. This emerges from Pusey's lengthy Tracts on Baptism.[33] These admit that 'many . . . holy and good men' have not held baptismal regeneration, while some or many of those who do 'use it as a skreen to hide from themselves the necessity of the complete actual change of mind and disposition necessary to them'.[34] It was considerations of this kind that made Pusey 'much more lenient towards the evangelicals on the matter of Baptism than was Phillpotts'.[35] As he said after the judgment, devout and earnest low churchmen feared baptismal regeneration meant an 'actual change in the infant's soul' and they thought it denied 'the need of any further change, by which the grace imparted in Baptism may actually take up all the powers of the man, and being continually enlarged and renewed, may conform the whole soul to the mind of God'.[36] Pusey respected such fears, and was so anxious to defend his own doctrine from lending any colour to them that he proved a great disappointment to some of Phillpotts's more bellicose supporters. William Dodsworth, for example, while paying tribute to Pusey's practice in sacramental matters, criticised his statements of doctrine. 'You seem ready to hide yourself under soft assertions of truths . . . and behind ambiguous statements which can be subscribed in different senses'.[37] Dodsworth was to join Manning and others in the secession. Nor were the complaints all on one side. When Phillpotts's Diocesan Synod at Exeter put out its statement about Baptism in refutation of the Gorham judgment, both Pusey and Keble found the declaration grammatically, if not doctrinally, unsound.[38]

The main impulse to revive Convocation came neither from Phillpotts nor from the Tractarians. But whereas Phillpotts lent strong support to his suppler and more persuasive brother bishop, Samuel Wilberforce of Oxford, the Tractarians held aloof. They did not deny that Convocation was, in theory and principle, the authoritative voice of the Church. But they feared that any revival would be linked with some lay voice and representation. W.E.

Gladstone held that a lay element would be beneficial and would make a revival practically acceptable. Pusey, Keble and Robert Wilberforce could not agree with him. A lay element in Convocation would destroy the last safeguard of Catholic authority.[39]

In any case, a deliberative and legislative body was irrelevant to the main concern of the Tractarians. As Pusey said in the introduction to his University Sermon on Confession, 'We need no *organic* change in the Church, no Convocation, no laws, no enforcement of outward directions, no public discipline. It were to begin at the wrong end. What we need is that men's hearts should be restored'.[40]

Phillpotts was no advocate of lay participation of Convocation either, but he was willing to take the risk. His own Exeter Synod, in June 1851, was a major step in the process of revival. That Prime Minister least favourable to churchly ideals, Lord John Russell, discovered to his surprise that diocesan Synods were not illegal. A month later the House of Lords debated the revival of Convocation. When the formal Convocation of 4 February 1852 sought to petition the Crown for the revival of its powers, the Queen's Advocate, supporting Archbishop Sumner, said that by a statute of Henry VIII[41] business was prohibited without Crown sanction. It was Phillpotts who replied that business meant making canons, not petitioning the Crown, and it was Phillpotts who led a minority of bishops who denied the Primate's power to prorogue on his own authority.

When the revived Convocation was launched in 1855 (in the nick of time, just before the Aberdeen government fell through mismanagement of the Crimean adventure) Phillpotts may well have hoped for a legal authority which would redress old wrongs. He was certainly disappointed. Archaic, unrepresentative, and 'bound hand and foot by disabling legislation'[42] it was no match for Parliament or the Privy Council. Convocation went some way to satisfy ecclesiastical sentiment, which Phillpotts had no interest in. A dignified historical body with echoes of the days of Laud, Warham and Chichele might have appealed to Hurrell Froude, but since it had no independent powers, it was useless in the matter of *law*.

Phillpotts's confident assertion of law as the great weapon of church life left little permanent mark — just as the old warrior's grave at St Marychurch is forgotten, and even the windows which commemorated him in his Cathedral were blown out in the air-raid of 1942. The Tractarians, likewise, would think that the modern church has taken heed of only the footnotes of their teaching, if that. But they, who did not expect success in this world, would be less surprised.

Notes

[1]   H. Phillpotts's Notebook, 24 August 1831, Exeter Cathedral Library 11/85.

[2]   Froude, who died in 1836 at the age of 33, long remained a controversial enigma. The deposition of family papers in the Oratory at Birmingham by the descendants of his younger brother William has enabled a fuller picture to be drawn, notably by P. Brendon, *Hurrell Froude and the Oxford Movement* (1974).

[3]   J.T. Coleridge, *A Memoir of the Rev. John Keble M.A.* (1869), p. 196.

[4]   G. Battiscombe, *John Keble* (1963), p. 315.

[5]   Newman to F. Rogers, 15 October 1835; quoted in G.C.B. Davies, *Henry Phillpotts* (1954), p. 166.

[6]   H.P. Liddon, *The Life of E.B. Pusey* (1983), Vol. II pp. 399–401.

[7]   As Queen Victoria called him; *Journal*, 27 January 1840. Phillpotts and other Tories had thwarted the Government's attempt to define by statute Prince Albert's precedence.

[8]   The subtitle of A.G. Lough's study for the centenary of his death, *Dr Pusey*, published by the author 1981.

[9]   Robert Newton, *Victorian Exeter 1837–1914* (Leicester 1968), p. 55.

[10]   C.J. Blomfield, Bishop of London, in his charge of 1842, recognised the distinction, preferring the surplice when the sermon was a part of the authorised liturgy and the gown when it was not. (Owen Chadwick, *The Victorian Church*, Part I, p. 215.)

[11]   W.R.W. Stephens, *The Life and Letters of Walter Farquhar Hook, D.D., F.R.S., (1885), p. 576.*

[12]   *R.D. Middleton, Magdalen Studies* (1936), pp. 102–104.

[13]   *Ibid.,* p. 31 note 1.

[14]   *Faulkner v. Litchfield*, which disallowed the stone altar in the restored Round Church at Cambridge and provoked a crisis in the Cambridge Camden Society which had sponsored the restoration.

[15]   *A Letter to the Clergy of the Diocese of Exeter.*

[16]   Cornwall was in the diocese of Exeter until 1877.

[17]   A ms account of the whole controversy, written by the prominent Exeter citizen Dr T. Shapter for the Rev. W.H.B. Proby in 1881, is preserved in the Cathedral Library. Davies (op.cit.) gives a full account of events, based on Shapter's narrative (pp.180–191). Chadwick, *The Victorian Church*, Vol.I (pp. 219–220) relies for the Exeter events mainly on Davies.

[18]   A *reprise* in 1848 at St Sidwell's concerned the preacher at the newly instituted evening service. On this occasion the incumbent ceased to allow the church to be used for this novel and controversial exercise.

[19]   Newton, *Op. cit.,* p. 68.

[20]   The same attitude was taken after Phillpotts's death by his son, W.J. Phillpotts, Archdeacon of Cornwall, who in 1874 prosecuted the Dean and Chapter of Exeter Cathedral for erecting an illegal reredos with sculptured figures in Exeter Cathedral; but both the Court of the Arches and the Judicial Committee of the Privy Council upheld the Dean and Chapter — a decision of great moment both for ecclesiastical architecture and for the Bishop's relation to his Cathedral. (*Law Reports*, Admiralty and Ecclesiastical Courts, Vol. IV, pp. 297–379; Cases in the Privy Council, Vol. VI, pp. 435–467.)

[21]   This, printed in the Prayer Book immediately before Morning Prayer, states 'that such ornaments of the church and of the ministers thereof at all times of their ministration, shall be retained and be in use, as were in this Church of England by the authority of Parliament, in the second year of the reign of King Edward VI'. It is substantially a quotation from the Elizabethan Act of Uniformity (1 Eliz. Cap. 2) and was to be the subject of detailed examination in the subsequent ritualist litigation.

[22]   For the whole incident see R.J.E. Boggis, *The History of st John's Torquay,* pp. 71–76.

[23]   See Chadwick, op.cit., p. 250 ff.

[24]   Davies, op. cit., p. 390.

[25]   J.R. Wolffe, in *The Devonshire Association Report and Transactions* Vol. 114 (1982) p. 106, 'Bishop Henry Phillpotts and the Administration of the Diocese of Exeter 1830–1869'.

[26]   B.G. Skinner, *Henry Francis Lyte,* (1974), p. 112.

[27]   Ms notebook, Exeter Cathedral Library 11/85.

[28]   The full story is told in O. Chadwick, *The Victorian Church,* Vol.I p. 250 ff. For the most complete discussion see J.C.S. Nias, *Gorham and the Bishop of Exeter,* (1951).

[29]   F.L. Cross (ed.), *The Oxford Dictionary of the Christian Church* (2nd Edn. 1974), Article 'Baptism'.

[30]   As Chadwick has shown, op. cit., p. 259.

[31]   E.F. Moore, *The Case of the Rev. G.C. Gorham against the Bishop of Exeter* (1852), p. 467.

[32]   Moore, *Op. cit.,* p. 471.

[33]   *Scriptural Views of Holy Baptism,* Tracts for the Times 37, 38 and 39, 1835.

[34]   *Tract 37,* p. 6.

[35]   Nias, *Op. cit.,* p. 10.

[36]   *The Royal Supremacy not an Arbitrary Authority* (1850), quoted by Liddon, op. cit., Vol. III p. 262.

[37]   *A Letter to the Rev. E.B. Pusey* (1850), quoted by Liddon, op. cit., Vol.III p. 263.

[38]   Nias, *Op. cit.,* p. 286.

[39]   Liddon, *Op. cit.,* Vol.III p. 343 ff.

[40]   *Nine Sermons Preached before the University of Oxford* (1859), quoted by O. Chadwick, *The Mind of the Oxford Movement,* (1960), p. 205.

[41]   25 Henry VIII cap. 19 (1534).

[42]   F.W. Cornish, *The English Church in the Nineteenth Century,* Part II (1910), p. 27.

Religion and Voting in an English Borough : Poole in 1859

T. A. McDONALD

'A Tory Dissenter', wrote Thomas Price, Vicar of St. Augustine the Less, Bristol, 'is one of the most anomalous creatures in existence, and is as rare as he is strange and unnatural'.[1] Price's assertion has long been seen as a truism, and the connection between non-conformity, the Liberal Party, and eventually, the Labour Party, has been extensively studied. The aim of this article is to examine this relationship at the level of the individual by establishing the denomination of as much of the electorate of the Dorset borough of Poole as possible, and comparing it with the way they voted.

Why do people vote the way they do? Why should what would appear to be an individual act produce a pattern of uniformity from millions of votes across the country when a general election is held? Today the announcement of the result from the first constituency to declare enables confident predictions to be made for those in the remaining 634, even allowing for regional variations. Modern psephologists (and sociologists) have developed a matrix of factors which they believe help shape the way a person makes his or her choice at election time.

Two standard works on the subject, Blondel, and Butler and Stokes, identify social class, age, occupation, family tradition, and religion as having varying (but interlinked) amounts of influence, although there are variations from region to region and election to election. These factors are particularly significant when it is remembered that many (even perhaps the majority) of voters support the same party throughout their lives.

Today, with the secret ballot, we lack absolute proof of the way individuals vote, relying instead on their statements after an election, or on comparisons between the total votes cast for each candidate and the social character of the constituency. Before 1870, however, with open voting we can see how individuals actually voted and it is therefore possible, using a nineteenth century electorate, to examine two precise parts of the matrix. One is of course voting behaviour and the other is a factor which played a more political role then than it does to today, religion.

Religion and religious problems are woven into the history of England from the mid-sixteenth century, occasionally becoming the dominant strand, often just one of many threads in the fabric of English social, economic and political life. The division of the western Christian church into two main camps was followed in England by the emergence of various groups with their own distinctive ideas of worship and churchmanship and who therefore rejected the established Church of England, a development which eventually had profound consequences for English society. By the early nineteenth century these dissenting groups had become an important section of society and were particularly prominent in trade and commerce. The Acts[2] passed in earlier centuries restricting their activities now appeared to the Whigs to be outmoded and unfair, and in 1828 Dissenters (but not Catholics) were finally allowed to hold public office. Ohter restrictions were removed during the 1830s, such as the insistence that they had to marry in an Anglican church.

The Municipal Corporations Act of 1835 was in many ways the legislation which most assisted Dissenters in their quest for respectability and political power. The abolition of the old, exclusive corporations and their replacement by elected councils meant that they could now attempt to mould society itself into the less formal fashion of their own churches and chapels.

Poole, in the mid-nineteenth century, had a population of just under 10,000 and an electorate of around 500. For centuries it had been one of the south coast's most important ports and its merchants had grown rich from its trade with Newfoundland. After 1815, though, this trade had declined and the town was seeking new forms of industry to compensate for this change in its fortunes. It had returned two members of Parliament since 1341 (intermittantly for the first hundred years) and was one of the boroughs whose Corporation had exclusive voting rights until the 1832 Reform Act.

The town received its first contact with Nonconformity in the seventeenth century, and was visited in 1655 by the Quaker, George Fox. He again visited the town in 1657 and 1658, and his journal records that 'from Ringwood we came to Poole, . . . and we had a meeting there, with sober people, and William Baily, a Baptist teacher, was convinced there at that time'.[3] The Quakers were for a time a flourishing andimportant sect in Poole, and are described in Hutchins' *The History and Antiquities of the County of Dorset* as comprising 'many of the most respectable and wealthy inhabitants . . .'[4] and indeed many of the great merchant families were members. Hutchins, in the third edition adds, though, that the Society in Poole '. . . of late years has well nigh become extinct'.[5] This is confirmed by the 1871 Tabular Statement (The Quakers' annual review of membership) which records only seven Friends at the Poole meeting, and six years later the Quarterly Meeting membership list has just five names.[6]

Another religious minority on Poole were the Roman Catholics. Their numbers in Poole were few until the French Revolution, when several thousand fled to England and one priest settled in Poole.[7] Encouraged by the Weld family of Lulworth, he rented a piece of land in Longfleet, an area to the north east of the town, and established a small chapel which served the area's few Catholics during the first decade of the nineteenth century. Catholicism in Poole received a boost in 1829 when Edward Tichbourne Doughty purchased Upton House, a mansion a few miles from the town and built in 1816 by the great Newfoundland merchant family of Spurrier, and the local priest became chaplain to the new owner.

The Roman Catholic congregation at this time numbered about 120, a surprisingly high figure considering the virtual non-existence of the Catholic Church in East Dorset before the nineteenth century. The figure of 120 is taken from the draft of an article published in the *Poole and East Dorset Herald* in June 1939 to celebrate the centenary of the building of the church, although it was not quoted in the printed article. The surviving Baptismal Register, and the Record of Cofirmations tends to support this figure, and so too does the Religious Census of 1851, when it gives 122 people attending the morning service in Poole's only Catholic church. The records also show that Poole's Catholic community was not of Irish or French origin, for the names of those baptised were typical of the town, such as Dibben, Orchard, Barnes, Nippard, Burden and Stickland.

The first Catholic church in Poole was the result of a vow made by Mr. Doughty when his four year old daughter was gravely ill. She recovered and her father purchased a plot of land in West Quay Road in 1837, and the new church was opened in June 1839, as a realisation of Mr. Doughty's vow.[8] The opening was reported by the *Dorset County Chronicle* as being by the 'Popish sham-bishop of the Western District' and it was irritated by the fact that some of Poole's protestant dissenters had subscribed towards the building. The newspaper was particularly incensed by the presence at the ceremony of the Anglican Rector of Poole, Peter Jolliffe, especially as there was an admission charge of half-a-crown.[9] Mr. Jolliffe ignored the *Chronicle's* attacks, and his attendance was in character, for he showed similar goodwill towards Poole's other non-Anglican churches.

By the 1850s the Catholic church in Poole was well-established with 22 people being confirmed by the Bishop in 1853. In 1856 a new priest, Joseph Parke, came to the town from Birmingham and remained until 1860, appearing as a voter in the 1859 poll-book.

In addition to the Quakers and the Catholics, Poole's other non-Anglicans were the Congregationalists, Baptists, Unitarians, Wesleyan Methodists, and Primitive Methodists,[10] each with their own church or chapel within the town. Of these denominations the Congregationalists were the largest and longest established, having built their first chapel in Hill Street in 1705, some ten years after the first recorded indication of their presence. At that time, though, their numbers were small, totalling only 55 members.[11]

The Congregationalists, as they were in 1859, really date from the year 1759, when divisions within the Hill Street chapel over admitting people who had not been baptised, and between the Trintarian and Unitarian groups, widened into a split. The underlying reason for the division was as much social as doctrinal. One history notes that from the early eighteenth century the Congregational or Independent Church was 'in the fullest sense of the term, . . . a powerful centre of religious life and influence in the town, and it was the spiritual home of a large number of the most influential inhabitants'.[12] In later years 'differences arose between him (The Minister) and some of the more influential members of the congregation, many of whom abstained from being members of the church, that they might qualify for municipal office by occasionally receiving the Lord's Supper in the parish church'.[13] These social divisions tended to crystallize into doctrinal ones, and, almost inevitably, a split occurred. Interestingly, though, in Poole it was the representatives of the 'proper' Congregational Church who were forced to secede, rather than those seeking doctrinal change. In many ways the Congregational Church in Poole illustrates the grey area between English Presbytarianism and the Independents or Congregationalists.[14]

The victory for the Unitarians meant that the Minister and his supporters were forced to find new premises. In 1777 they built a new church in Skinner Street, enlarging it in 1814, 1833, and yet again in 1847. It is an indication of the Congregationalists' importance during the period under consideration in this article that the church Sunday School population numbered over 800, and also that they were expanding, with nine members leaving in 1855 in order to establish a new church in nearby Bournemouth.

Although the Baptists were the first dissenters in Poole, arriving in 1646, they only became firmly established in 1804. Before this year they had worshipped in the Hill Street chapel with the Congregationalists and later in a small chapel in West Butts Street, but their numbers were small. Their re-emergence as a distinct group within the town was assisted by the Congregationalist minister, Thomas Durant, and they became more numerous as the century progressed. New chapels were established in the town's outer areas, and by the 1870s their Poole chapel could hold 500 people.[15]

The Wesleyan Methodists in Poole date from the end of the eighteenth century, with ministers being appointed to the town from 1797. Hutchins noted that 'the Wesleyans have gained ground amongst the Dissenters of Poole, and have considerably enlarged their meeting houses, and provided very complete arrangements for the several details of their religious system'.[16] A few years after Hutchins, in 1879, a new building capable of seating over a thousand people was erected. Short[17] describes this as the 'present chapel' but with its spire and its general appearance would appear to have been a substantial church.

Poole's other Methodists, the Primitive Methodists, are mentioned in Hutchins almost as an afterthought when it states simply that they had a small chapel in North Street. They were first established in the town in 1836 and were granted their own minister two years later. Originally they met in a private house in Cinnamon Lane, but in 1842 were able to build the chapel mentioned in Hutchins. Although they were never a large group, with only three people on the 1859 register of electors being traced as members, they had advanced sufficiently by the eighteen-nineties to build a better chapel.

The final dissenting group to be considered is the Unitarians, the descendants of those who had driven out the Congregationalists a hundred years earlier. They had continued to worship in the Hill Street chapel and although the building could accommodate 400 people, only five members of the congregation are known to be on the electoral register in 1859.

The Religious Census of 1851 provides a guide to the relative strengths of the town's various denominations, and the figures for attendance at public worship on Sunday 30 March of that year are shown below as Table 1.

Table 1: Attendance at Poole's churches and chapels, 30 March 1851

	Morning	Afternoon	Evening
Church of England	2202	2122	1000
Congregationalists	1043	737	1060
Baptists	200	–	150
Quakers	12	8	–
Unitarians	40	–	50
Wesleyan Methodists	463	240	682
Primitive Methodists	178	58	193
Undefined	120	–	166
Roman Catholics	122	–	84
Latter Day Saints	–	12	60
	4380	3177	3445

The town's various dissenting groups therefore made up a sizeable minority[18] of its population, and it would appear that amicable relations existed between them. The assistance of the Congregational minister in re-establishing the Baptists is an indication of this. Similarly good relations existed with the Anglicans, mainly due to the efforts of the Rector, the Rev. Peter Jolliffe, and he warrants a section of his own in Bernard Short's *Early Days of Non-Conformity in Poole* where he is described as doing '. . . everything that lay in his power to help forward the Non-Conformist movement in this town'.[19] Jolliffe's goodwill towards the Roman Catholics has already been mentioned at an earlier point in this article.

Poole's Anglican church was dedicated to St. James, and it was fitting that a fisherman should be the town's patron saint. The church had been founded in 1142 and over the centuries had come to play an important part in the life of the town. This was mainly due to the Rectors, and the Corporation had managed to gain the right to nominate or elect each new holder of the post.

This had caused controversy during the eighteenth century, similar to that over their insistence that only they could elect Members of Parliament, and in 1795, after four years of deliberation, the Court of Chancery upheld the Corporation's rights. In 1791, when the case began in Chancery, the Burgesses chose as the Rector the 25 year old Eton and Cambridge educated member of an eminent Poole family, Peter Jolliffe. He was still Rector when the Poole electorate voted in 1859.

In 1819 the old church was in such a poor state that it had to be completely rebuilt, and the foundation stone was laid at an impressive 'masonic' ceremony at the end of May. Two years later the new church was opened, the first of five[20] new Anglican churches built in the town (or rather, the constituency) within a fifteen year period. During the two years of building services had been held in the Guildhall, to the inconvenience of the Burgesses, and it was perhaps ironic that the Corporation, which had for so long asserted its authority and patronage over the church, found it within its own walls.

Despite the handsome new building, a visitor in 1830 was, according to an article by Bernard Short in 1962, 'shocked . . . to see the church so overcrowded'.[21] The visitor was apparently an 'important member of the Prayer Book and Homily Society' who happened to be visiting Poole and 'told some of the local townsfolk that he knew of a certain lady, . . . who wanted to assist in the execution of an evagelical church at a sea port in the West of England'.[22] The eventual result of this suggestion was a meeting at which Poole's banker George Welch Ledgard was the chief spokesman for those in favour of building a second church, and the Rev. Peter Jolliffe for those against. It was decided to go ahead without financial assistance from the parish. The lady originally being mentioned as willing to finance the project gave £1000 on the condition that she nominated the minister, and Mr Ledgard also gave a considerable sum so that the fund soon reached £4000.[23] Thus the church was built in the High Street and consecrated as St. Paul's in June 1833.

Two more Anglican churches were also opened in 1833, in the outlying areas that were now becoming suburbs of the town. These were in Longfleet and Parkstone and there was a definite political reason for two churches being built. The growth of the outer areas had led to a demand for a church, especially as in Longfleet two disused cottages were being used as a place of worship. The original intention was to build on the boundary of the two parishes and the Hon. W.F.S. Ponsonby, owner of the nearby Canford Manor, offered £1600 towards a new church. Ponsonby's role as a leading Liberal and the belief that he sought control of the town's Parliamentary representation led to the demand for a separate church for Parkstone, most notably by the Parr family. The Parrs had long been active in Poole politics and Freemasonry, and were staunch Tories. When they failed to raise the money to finance a new church they paid for it themselves. The first minister was James Culshaw Parr, previously curate in Poole's third suburb, Hamworthy, and another Parr, John, became vicar in 1858. The rivalry between those building the two churches is well-illustrated by the fact that they were completed simultaneously, but St. Mary's at Longfleet was consecrated the day before St. Peter's at Parkstone.

Poole in 1859 therefore contained a variety of religious groupings and organisations, each with its own place of worship. Anglicanism expanded with the building of new churches during the 1820s and 1830s, and the Dissenters, too, were consolidating themselves in new areas as the suburbs became established and also as neighbouring Bournemouth grew in size and importance. Despite the occasional new chapel being established as early as the eighteen-forties, the main growth in Dissent came nearer the end of the century. The elector in 1859, though, could belong to one of a number of different congregations, and it is this membership which will be examined, and a possible relationship to his voting behaviour sought.

The source for establishing the denomination of members of the electorate were the civil burial registers for the municipal borough which have been kept since 1854. These were not copies of death certificates, but the borough's own record of those interred in its municipal cemetery. In addition to recording the name, age, and occupation or status of the person buried in the cemetery[24] they also state whether he or she was interred in consecrated or unconsecrated ground, and the name of the person performing the burial service.[25] Thus those buried in consecrated ground were Anglican, and those in unconsecrated ground were Dissenters, with the Minister's name revealing the particular church or chapel at which they worshipped. In this way the denomination of 249 of the 1859 electorate (or almost half) were positively identified. Overwhelmingly, though, they came from the old town for most of those living in the outer districts of Longfleet, Parkstone, and Hamworthy, whatever their denomination, were buried in the grounds of their local Anglican church. It was not until 1880 that an Act of Parliament allowed Dissenters to be buried in churchyards by their own Ministers.

Those voters who were not present in the burial registers must be presumed to have left the town, perhaps going no further than Parkstone or Bournemouth. The burial records include a complete index of names, and this was used to check that voters had not been overlooked in the general chronological section.

One of the two poll-books from the 1835 general election, that published by the Conservatives, appeared to be an alternative or confirmatory source for establishing a voter's religion but turned out to be unreliable. Although it is clearly divided into 'Church-men' and 'Dissenters' at least two[26] of those listed were shown by the burial register to be Anglicans and not Dissenters. Several others listed as Anglicans, but who cannot be traced in the registers[27] have a voting pattern which contrasts dramatically with those known to be members of the Church of England.

Another useful source for confirming that an individual was a Congregationalist was the Register of Marriages and Baptisms for Skinner Street Church between 1837 and 1902. This, however produced some anomalies or contradictory information, such as that pertaining to one John Graves. He is listed as an Anglican in the 1835 poll-book and described by the same source as 'Clerk to Longfleet Church'. Both denomination and occupation are con-firmed by the burial register. However, a John Graves is recorded as marrying Martha Goff in 1853 in the Congregational church, and assuming that it is the same man, he would have been 42 years old. This would suggest that he was marrying for the second time and that he was deferring to his new wife's wishes. There were three Goffs on the 1859 electoral register, and two of them (father and son) are known to be Congregationalists, whilst the third was a brother and uncle to the others, and was therefore probably also a Congregationalist.

Another example is that of the stonemason Richard Perkins Collins. He received an Anglican burial by the vicar of St. Paul's church, the Rev. George Morgan, in 1868 and is recorded by the census of 1861 as being 73 years old. (He was 82 when he died according to the burial register.), and living with his 75 year old wife Harriet. The Congregational register has the baptism of a baby girl in 1839 and gives the parents as Richard Perkins Collins and Martha his wife. It would therefore appear that the rather irritating tradition of fathers' perpetuating their name in its entirety has occurred here, and that the baptismal entry is for a son rather than the gentleman in the 1859 poll-book. Because of these puzzles, the burial registers were the only source used for establishing denomination because they were consistent through-out. There are, for instance, no examples of an individual being entered as buried in consecrated ground but with a nonconformist minister conducting the service.

On occasion the wife or children of a member of the 1859 electorate are recorded in the burial register as receiving (say) an Anglican burial, but no entry can be found for the husband. An instance of this is the master-mariner James S. Furber whose wife Harriet died in 1885 and is described as the widow of James.

James Furber could well have been lost at sea, but despite his wife's receiving an Anglican burial, it cannot be assumed that he too was an Anglican, although in virtually all cases where the denomination of both husband and wife is known, they are the same.

One final point is that there are the occasional instances of 'mixed dissent' as for example, Henry Bolton Smith who was a Congregationalist but whose father, Henry Boothby Smith, recived a Baptist burial service, and whose mother, Louisa, was buried by the Primitive Methodist minister. Walter Paull, a hairdresser, is shown by the burial register to be a Baptist but his wife was a Congregationalist, and they were married in the Congregational church. The assistance given by the Congregational minister in re-establishing the Baptist Church in Poole has been referred to at an earlier point in this article and as both denominations shared the same polity, the interaction was not unusual.

The 249 individuals whose religious denomination is known for certain were 134 Anglicans and 115 Dissenters, and this latter category was itself divided into 20 Baptists, 41 Congregationalists, three Primitive Methodists, five Roman Catholics, five Unitarians, 24 Wesleyan Methodists, and seventeen 'others'. These 'others' were definitely Dissenters, but the precise denomination is not known because the minister performing the burial service was not the regular incumbent at a local church or chapel. In some instances he was probably the minister (or assistant) at one of the suburban churches or from Bournemouth, or possibly even farther afield.

An examination of these 249 people by occupation reveals some differences, and these are shown in the table overleaf. The most noticeable difference is the number of Anglicans who are classed as 'capitalists', although in Poole this term is best used to mean 'merchant'. There were 30 Anglican capitalists as against only six Dissenters (four of whom were Wesleyan Methodists) who were capitalists in this sample of half the 1859 electorate. This is perhaps surprising when the importance of the Quakers as leading Poole merchants in the eighteenth century is taken into account, and also when the general historical importance of non-conformists in the early stages of industrialisation is considered. Perhaps the most reliable interpretation of these figures is that they stress the importance of commerce, rather than industry, to a sea-port like Poole.

The other intriguing figure is in the Drink category where, of the fifteen innkeepers or beersellers whose denomination is known,

Table 2: Anglicans and Dissenters by Occupation

	Anglicans	Dissenters
Capitalists	30 (22%)	6 (5%)
Respectables	21 (23%)	31 (27%)
Retailers	29 (22%)	36 (31%)
Craftsmen	24 (18%)	25 (22%)
Farmers	1 (0.7%)	7 (6%)
Drink	14 (10%)	1 (0.8%)
Mariners	3 (2%)	7 (6%)
Miscellaneous	2 (1.5%)	2 (1.7%)

(The categories above are based on the precedents set by J.R. Vincent in his 'The Electoral Sociology of Rochdale'. *Economic History Review*, vol. XVI, no. 1, 1963, and by T.J. Nossiter in his *Influence, Opinion and Political Idioms in Reformed England* (Hassocks 1975).

fourteen were Anglicans.[28] This is perhaps not surprising, given the connection between non-conformity and temperance, but obviously not all non-conformists eschewed drink. Only one Dissenting inn-keeper appears in this analysis, but there were presumably others, for Dissenters were involved in other aspects of the trade. The brewer, Frederick Styring, for example, was a Wesleyan Methodist. Despite this, a ratio of 14 : 1 does seem to indicate a definite connection between occupation and denomination in this instance.

Members of the three categories of Respectables, Retailers, and Craftsmen were drawn from both the Anglican and Dissenting churches, although there was a tendency for there to be a slightly higher proportion of the latter. Thus 31% of the known Dissenters were shopkeepers as against 21% of the known Anglicans, and there was also a slightly larger percentage of Dissenters as Retailers and Craftsmen. The figures for the remaining categories are based on too small a sample to have any real significance, although seven out of eight farmers were Dissenters, as were seven out of ten mariners.

Having used occupation as a criterion for seeking a possible pattern to religious differences, a further step is to use the concept of status, or to be more precise, formally achieved status by virtue of a citizen becoming a Councillor, Alderman, Sheriff, or ultimately, Mayor.[29] Sixty-nine members of the 1859 electorate achieved, or were to achieve by 1885, membership of Poole Municipal Council, and the denomination of 44 of them is known.[30]

It is perhaps worth re-stating at this point that the burial registers, as the most valuable source for establishing denomination, mainly provide information on citizens of the old town. Those people who served as Councillors had to live (or own property) within the town, and were also more committed to remaining there, thus providing a substantial sample for study.

In the event, though, the religious amity was maintained, for of the 44 electors under discussion, 23 were Anglicans and 21 Dissenters. Even the sixteen individuals who held the office of Mayor at least once during their careers managed to produce a split of eight Anglicans and eight Dissenters. It can therefore be assumed from this that Poole's political divisions, bitter though they had been in the past at this level, were not based on religion. An example is given in a detailed account of Poole's local politics, *The Pride of Poole*,[31] when Joseph Knight found himself unable to pay the rent for the franchise of running Poole's market. Two gentlemen undertook to act as guarantors to Knight and both were Reform (eventually 'Liberal') Councillors, John Williamson and William Waterman. Williamson was an Anglican and Waterman a Baptist.

The opening sentence of this article states that 'a Tory dissenter is rare, strange, and unnatural' and it is now necessary to test the truth of this assertion, and also the unstated but corresponding belief that Anglican Liberals were equally rare. In order to do this, individual voting behaviour in the consecutive elections between 1841 and 1865 was studied. Poll-books survive from Poole for eight out of a possible eleven elections, the missing ones being 1831, 1837 and 1868. The only uncontested election in Poole occurred in 1852, but a by-election in 1850 conveniently makes up for this. By studying only the elections between 1841 and 1865, although many of the 1859 electorate voted in both general and by-elections in 1835, the possibility of conclusions being invalidated by the possible discovery of a poll-book for 1837 is alleviated.

The overall findings of voting behaviour based on an individual's religion are shown below as Table 3 :

Table 3: Party Preference of Anglicans and Dissenters

	Conservative	Liberal	Split
Anglican	59.1%	23.6%	17.2%
Dissent	8.7%	80.5%	10.7%

The method used to obtain the percentages quoted in the above table was to total the number of occasions the 249 voters in the sample went to the polls. Thus there were 499 instances of voting by Anglicans between 1841 and 1865, and 401 by Dissenters. Those occasions when voters abstained were omitted from these figures because the 1847 poll-book does not include those who chose this course, and could include people eligible to vote for the first time but who failed to exercise this right.

The figures quoted in Table 3 reinforce the accepted wisdom of a correlation between religion and voting behaviour in the nineteenth century, particularly the nonconformists. The Anglican vote of only 59% is influenced by the fact that on each occasion there there was only one Conservative candidate and there was therefore scope for tactical voting. The elections of 1857 and 1859, in which the same three candidates participated, saw a noticeable amount of this, with consistent Tories suporting a rather radical, independent Liberal against the one backed by the Manor of Canford.[32] Even so, on a quarter of the occasions when Anglicans voted, the choice was solely for Liberal candidates, contrasting strongly with the figure of around 1/12 for Dissenters voting (or to be more precise, plumping) for a Tory.

The Dissenters' preference for Liberal candidates was, as a figure of 80% shows, fairly conclusive and Table 4 gives a more detailed analysis of the way the larger nonconformist church members voted.

Table 4: Baptist, Congregationalist, and Wesleyan Methodist Voting Preference

	Baptists		Congregationalists		WesleyanMethodists	
	Number of occasions voting	%	Number of occasions voting	%	Number of occasions voting	%
Liberal	61	82.4%	127	82.5%	72	82.7%
Conservative	3	4.0%	13	8.4%	6	6.9%
Split	10	13.5%	14	9.0%	9	10.0%

All three groups show a consistent 82% of their members voting only for Liberal candidates, with very little support for the Conservatives, and even split voting was less popular with Dissenters than it was with Anglicans. The other two non-conformist groups, the Unitarians and the Primitive Methodists, had too few members amongst the Poole Electorate for their voting behaviour to be valid, but the figures are shown as Table 5, along with those for the Catholics and the 'others'.

Table 5: Primitive Methodist, Unitarian and Roman Catholic Voting Preference

	Prim. Methodists Number of occasions % voting		Unitarians Number of occasions % voting		Catholics Number of occasions % voting		Others Number of occasions % voting	
Liberal	7	100%	11	68.7%	9	53.0%	43	81.1%
Cons.	–	–	3	18.7%	5	29.4%	5	9.4%
Split	–	–	2	12.5%	3	17.6%	5	9.4%

The 'others' produce figures for the Liberals remarkably similar to the Baptists, Congregationalists, and Wesleyan Methodists, whilst the Catholics, contrary to legend did not all vote the same way as their priest. He plumped for the radical Haly in 1859 but the two ropemaking Cull brothers split for the Tory Franklyn and for Haly, whilst the bone-gatherer, Jeremiah Galpin, plumped for the 'official' Liberal, H.D. Seymour. Only the auctioneer, Adolphus Woolfrey, joined the priest, Joseph Parke, in plumping for Haly. It was, in fact, the Baptists and the Congregationalists who were more likely to vote in the same way as their minister, for both the Rev. John Osborne, and the Rev. Eustace Conder plumped for the Liberal Seymour in 1857 and 1859, as did the majority of their flocks. Table 6 shows the total votes for each of the possible permutations in the elections of 1857 and 1859, the latter being a re-run of the former.

Table 6: Total votes cast in 1857 and 1859 for the various permutations of candidates

	Baptist	Congregationalist	Wesleyan Methodist
Franklyn (Con)	1	6	2
Seymour (Lib)	15	30	20
Haly (Ind. Lib)	6	13	8
Seymour/Haly	7	10	7
Franklyn/Haly	4	2	4
Franklyn/Seymour	0	6	2
Abstained	7	9	3

One final aspect of Poole's religious life was the tendency of a number of leading Anglicans to be members of the Freemasons. The Lodge of Amity had been established in 1765 and despite periods of little activity, was a viable branch in the mid-nineteenth century.[33] Thirty-eight Poole electors were members in 1859, and two others joined in 1860 and 1861. Several of them became Worshipful Master at some point during their membership.

The Freemasons among the electorate were generally from the Merchant[34] and Respectable classes, although there were several who could be categorised as craftsmen and retailers, but recorded by the 1861 Census as being employers on a small scale.

A majority of the Freemasons were Conservative voters, although at least eight were consistent Liberals, and several split, or changed their allegiance on more than one occasion. Martin Kemp Welch, a leading figure socially, who joined in 1854 was always a Liberal voter and was also a Congregationalist, which made him rather an exception among the Freemasons. This was because the characteristic that most of them had in common was their Anglicanism. Of the 38 Masons of 1859, the denomination of 31 of them is known, or can be stated with reasonable confidence,[35] 27 were Anglicans. The others were two Congregationalists and two Wesleyan Methodists.

The American historian R.K. Webb, maintains that religion is 'one of three or four essential keys to an understanding of early-Victorian England'[36] and this would appear to be borne out by this study. Of the various factors which are currently accepted as influencing a person's voting behaviour, age, class, sex, occupation, family and religion, this last example can be clearly seen as having an importance in the nineteenth century that it lacks today.[37] In this study religion ranks with family relationships[38] in producing the most positive results, and the two factors are obviously linked. Nonconformists (of all types) *were* nearly always Liberals, and Anglicans more often than not used only one of their two votes in order to avoid voting for a Liberal. Despite this clear result, the town's divisions were political and not religious. A person's Anglicanism or Non conformity may have helped make him a Tory or a Liberal, but it never seems to have become an issue in itself in Poole's elections.

Notes

[1] Cited in A. Llewellyn, *The Decade of Reform, the 1830s* (Newton Abbot, 1972), p. 205.

[2] E.g. The Corporation Act of 1661, and the first Test Act of 1673.

[3] B.C. Short, *Early Days of Non-conformity in Poole* (Poole, 1927), p. 6.

[4] John Hutchins, *The History and Antiquities of the County of Dorset*, 3rd edition, (1861–1874), vo. 1, p. 60.

[5] Ibid.

[6] From information supplied by Miss Margaret Matthews of Southampton, and

the Religious Society of Friends.

[7]   There were apparently two priests sheltered at Stapehill, near Wimborne, during the eighteenth century according to an article in the *Poole and East Dorset Herald*, 21 June 1939.

[8]   Ibid.

[9]   Ibid.

[10]   The Religious Census of 1851 also has one 'undefined' Protestant Church, and a Church of Latter Day Saints.

[11]   H.V.F. Johnstone, *A Short History of Skinner Street United Reformed Church, Poole, 1777–1977* (Poole, 1977), p. 7.

[12]   W. Densham and J. Ogle (eds.) *The Story of the Congregational Churches in Poole and Parkstone* (Bournemouth, c. 1898), p. 15.

[13]   Ibid., p. 16.

[14]   I am indebted to Dr. Clyde Binfield of the University of Sheffield for his assistance and advice on this topic, and particularly for this last observation.

[15]   This account of the dissenting churches is largely drawn from B.C. Short, *Op. cit.*

[16]   J. Hutchins, *Op. cit.*, vol 1, p. 60.

[17]   B.C. Short, *Op. cit.*, p. 60.

[18]   This, it must be stated, is based on circumstantial evidence. The presence of a majority of Anglicans amongst the electorate, and the size and number of their churches points to the majority being Anglican.

[19]   B.C. Short, *Op. cit.*, p. 46.

[20]   Three other churches are discussed below. The fifth was St. Michael's in Poole's other suburb of Hamworthy.

[21]   *Poole and Dorset Herald*, 5 December 1962.

[22]   Ibid.

[23]   Ibid.

[24]   Opened in 1854 on land donated by the leading merchant family of Garland.

[25]   B.C. Short's *Early Days of Non-conformity in Poole* and various directories list the ministers of the chapels. The dates always match.

[26]   James Cadie and John Osment were both labelled 'Dissent' but were buried in consecrated ground by the vicar of St. James. Osment's wife and son also received Anglican burials.

[27]   Some of them, though, were farmers renting their land from the (very) Liberal Canford Manor.

[28]   There were actually 39 people in the 1859 poll-book who can be classed as inn-keepers, beersellers, etc., but there is no reason to presume that the fifteen discussed in this article are anything but a representative sample.

[29]   As was probably the case in most English boroughs, political and civic leadership was available to those who wanted it, had the necessary social status, and could afford it.

[30]   The religion of some of the remaining 25 can be guessed with a fair amount of confidence, but without conclusive evidence.

[31]   D. Beamish *et. al., The Pride of Poole, 1688–1851* (Poole, 1974), p. 266.

[32]   Canford was now owned by Sir John Josiah Guest, the Welsh iron-master and Liberal M.P. for Merthyr Tydfil.

[33]   H.P. Smith, *History of the Lodge of Amity 1765–1936* (Poole, 1937), p. 475.

[34]   One very important merchant family, the Slades, seem not to have been Masons at this time.

[35]   The Parr family, for example, who built St. Peter's Church in Parkstone.

They do not appear in the Municipal burial registers, presumably being interred in Parkstone, but were obviously Anglicans.

[36] R.K. Webb, *Modern England, from the Eighteenth Century to the Present* (London, 1969), p. 408.

[37] J. Blondel, in his *Voters, Parties and Leaders* (1970), pp. 60–61, discusses the influence of religion on modern elections, reaching the conclusion that 'the precise impact of religion on voting is difficult to determine'. Recent by-elections in Glasgow Garscadden and Crosby, where there are substantial numbers of Catholics, support this view.

[38] It should, at this late stage, be pointed out that this article is drawn from an M. Litt. thesis for the University of Bristol, and it was shown that if people were related, they voted similarly. Even when there was no proven relationship, a shared surname produced the same results.

History, Celticism and propaganda in the formation of the diocese of Truro

P. S. MORRISH

In its section listing cathedral and other capitular establishments *Crockford's Clerical Directory* still prints under the arms of the diocese of Truro the legend, 'see restored to Cornwall 1877'. These words conceal a neglected aspect of the creation of that diocese. The arguments normally adduced in the nineteenth century for dividing over-large Anglican dioceses in England were mostly practical: a diocese might be considered too extensive or too populous, or both, for a bishop adequately to supervise. Rapidly increasing population and a greater depth of pastoral care becoming expected of bishops tended to nullify the gains which were being achieved through railways, penny post and telegraphs.[1] Bishops needed time not only for travelling but also for meeting people, for study, for business at committees and for meditation, and a diocese which was too extensive or too populous might contain so many parishes, clergy and people that its bishop would be unable to devote adequate time to any of his numerous obligations. Furthermore, bishops were unable to retire with pensions before 1869 and in their old age unsuperannuated prelates would have been even less able to discharge their duties. In one case, however, practical arguments were accompanied by two unusual historical and ethnological ones. The separation of Cornwall from the diocese of Exeter was advocated not only on the grounds of population and extent, but also both as a rightful restoration to Cornwall of a status which it had anciently enjoyed, and because the Cornish were alleged to be racially, socially and occupationally different from those living in Devon.

In investigating the sources and significance of these two arguments it is not suggested that they predominated; indeed, some people discounted them. Their role seems to have been both to conciliate lay opinion within Cornwall where the extensive non-conformist community might hardly have been expected to collaborate with a dogmatic Anglican appeal,[2] and to distinguish the Cornish case from a number of other competing claims. The arguments have historiographical interest, demonstrating the persistence and influence of popular history and exemplifying how fragile the distinction between history and propaganda can be. If the one is an academic investigation into past events, the other includes a selective use of such events, possibly torn from their context, to justify or encourage some desired future course. Furthermore, the historical argument itself subsequently underwent a metamorphosis and what had been one justification amongst several became an orthodox description of the whole affair. Finally, the episode also suggests the unwisdom of interpreting the Anglican church in nineteenth-century England exclusively in terms of a reaction to unprecedented urbanisation.

The Royal Commission on the Established Church having only recommended confirming the inclusion of the Scilly Islands in the diocese of Exeter, the subsequent Established Church Act (1836) had done nothing to reduce the size of the diocese. Probably the first public step towards launching the agitation for division was some remarks made by Bishop Phillpotts in his *Charge* in 1842. Together with other suggestions for new dioceses elsewhere, the point was taken up by C.H. Frewen in an unsuccessful private member's bill in 1846.[3] This led to Lord John Russell's rash statement in connection with the controversial implementation of the recommendation by that Commission for a new diocese of Manchester, that plans were also ready for four other new dioceses including a Cornish one.[4] This embarrassed subsequent less enthusiastic administrations and a long agitation ensued until a Cornish diocese was obtained in 1876. This agitation was conducted through the normal channels of Victorian pressure-group politics — public meetings and private lobbying, pamphlets, letters to editors, discussion in such assemblies as Convocation, Church Congress and diocesan conferences, and questions and debates in Parliament. Throughout this long struggle the practical arguments and the historical and ethnological ones were repeatedly deployed but unfortunately the secondary literature has mostly failed to investigate the last two. Indeed, the most satisfactory compendious treatment of all the arguments is in a pamphlet optimistically addressed to Gladstone ten months after he had become Prime Minister by the Rev. W.S. Lach-Szyrma. He summarised the arguments under seven heads: the present diocese was unwieldy, too populous and extensive; next, the reasons for the absorption of the former Cornish diocese into that of Crediton (and, hence, Exeter) in the eleventh century were no longer valid; thirdly, the

Truro Cathedral built 1880–1910

people of Cornwall were for the most part distinct in race and occupation; then, the practical pastoral requirements of Cornwall could only be met adequately by a resident bishop; fifthly, funds were available; sixthly, public opinion was favourable and, lastly, those objections which had been raised were frivolous or unimportant.[5]

Although Truro was not authorised until 1876, the most intensive phase in the agitation was in the 1850s and 1860s. It did not meet with immediate success probably for three basic reasons. There was the apparent novelty of the objective in comparison with the supposed special case and finality of the legislation of 1836. Cautious minds had yet to be reconciled to further development. Next, Phillpotts became increasingly unable to sustain active personal leadership. This tended to reduce the credibility of the argument because a younger man in succession to him might yet be able to cope. Thirdly, there was inadequate political support. Palmerston was unconvinced and during Gladstone's first ministry, as Roundell Palmer observed,[6] the Liberals were divided over additional dioceses. For many years, too, the episcopate was unable to make up its mind. On the other hand, Conservatives under Disraeli were not averse from creating some new dioceses. The politics of the successive administrations of Gladstone and Disraeli after 1868, however, were the background only to the last phase of the agitation and a danger in paying too much attention to the final moves during Disraeli's 1874 ministry is to overlook the preceding decades of pressure and the arguments which characterised them. This is exemplified in P.T. Marsh's *The Victorian church in decline* which gives the impression that the diocese of Truro was largely the invention of Archbishop Tait and R.A. Cross, Disraeli's Home Secretary.[7] They were the midwives, not its parents.

The historical argument was a feature from an early stage. The Rev. John Wallis, vicar of Bodmin and a man of antiquarian interests, published at Bodmin in 1847 a curious local miscellany volume containing items of antiquarian and current interest. In connection with suggestions already made about the division of the diocese, he observed that it would be 'an act of tardy justice' because for 800 years 'we have been deprived of our ancient see'. He noted that Cornwall had been proposed as a diocese by Henry VIII.[8] Wallis's appeal was to equity and local pride, and his originality was not so much in the discovery of ancient precedents which were well documented, but in pointing to their relevance. An offer from Dr. Walker of St. Columb Major in 1854 to help finance division brought the argument out again. In July that year the *Royal Cornwall Gazette* which generally supported the establishment, reported Christopher Wordsworth's reference in Convocation to a see in Cornwall in ancient times, though it was not clear whether he had taken the point from Wallis.[9] Two months later a meeting of Cornish clergy at Bodmin discussed Dr. Walker's offer. The Rev. W. Rogers mentioned Henry VIII's plan in order to suggest that if such a development had seemed reasonable then, it would be more so in the 1850s with a greater population. Wallis suggested that the 'restoration' of a diocese should have been alluded to in the proposed address to Queen Victoria for if the revenues of the ancient see of Cornwall were appropriated to the renovation of the see, they need not go to Dr. Walker or anybody else to finance the project.[10] Wallis had shifted his ground from an almost moralising position where he was safe to one more difficult to defend because there was much uncertainty about the material arrangements for the support of such early bishoprics and because the Ecclesiastical Commissioners were tenaciously endeavouring to implement only that redistribution of assets authorised in 1836. On the other hand, Wallis may have intended that all epsicopal assets in Cornwall whether acquired before or after the eleventh century were morally Cornish and had been misappropriated to support a bishop in Exeter. His point was not added to the address but a petition from inhabitants of Truro at about the same time mentioned that Cornwall had had its own diocese in early times.[11] Though Wallis did not succeed in amending its address, he became honorary secretary of a committee which the Bodmin meeting also resolved upon, and his hand may be seen in the printed 'Minutes of Proceedings' which were subsequently circulated, bearing the sub-title, 'Restoration of a Bishopric to Cornwall'.[12] The Ecclesiastical Commissioners to whom the government referred these petitions, were not empowered to make proposals for new dioceses, but the matter was also brought to the attention of the current Royal Commission on Cathedral Churches which in a special report recommended the division of the diocese though it avoided reference to 'restoration'.[13]

Little was then heard of the historical argument until the Bodmin committee was reconstituted in 1859 and specifically charged to work for the 'restoration' of the bishopric of Cornwall. It sponsored a pamphlet, *A Cornish bishoprick: a statement of facts*, written by the Rev. Arthur Tatham. The aim was to give an account of earlier efforts and to rehearse the factual points about the extent and populousness of the diocese. Its attitude to the historical argument was ambivalent for whilst it pleaded that 'the important question respecting . . . the re-establishment of an episcopal see in Cornwall should be revived', it went on to suggest that 'the diocese of Exeter has a claim, prior, perhaps, to all others, for sub-divison, and that the county of Cornwall ought to be constituted a separate see'.[14] The latter passage seems to imply the creation of something new, not re-establishment. The contradiction was never to be fully resolved. Writing privately to Tatham shortly after its publication, Phillpotts did not comment on the historical argument or the suspect logic, but contented himself with some errors of fact.[15] In a leading article in December based on the *Statement,* the *Royal Cornwall Gazette* not only dealt fully with the practical arguments but also boldly advanced the historical one. 'Exeter is thus unduly large because it was formed by the union in 1050 of two dioceses, Crediton and St. Germans', it explained, the country then having been too thinly populated and devastated to support two, but 'these reasons for the union of the Devon and Cornwall sees, however, available [sic] 800 years ago, certainly exist no longer; and there are urgent motives for restoring the original state'.[16] Such an argument could be double-edged, and early in 1860 the Rev. Reginald Hobhouse observed that antiquity was against them because Cornwall had had no bishop of its own for so many centuries.[17] The committee next prepared a memorandum to Lord Palmerston, the Prime Minister. It referred (inaccurately) to the Cathedral Commissioners having recommended 'restoration' and asked the government to 'divide the present see . . . and erect a bishopric in Cornwall'. This showed the same ambiguity which the *Statement* had manifested. At a meeting in May 1860 Palmerston questioned the committee's deputation. The Earl of Devon explained the extent and populousness of the diocese whilst J.H. Rogers (M.P. for Helston) pointed out that the case of Cornwall stood distinct from other claims in that it would be the restoration of an ancient diocese and not the erection of a new one.[18] The deputation may have thus linked the practical and historical arguments but Palmerston was not impressed and no progress was made. Besides any sense of antiquarian propriety, the historical argument was also a defence against the criticism of novelty: apart from his aversion from high churchmanship, with which some advocates of additional dioceses were identified, Palmerston was unwilling to precipitate a political crisis by introducing a proposal which some of his supporters might condemn as unprecedented. To suggest that legislation to divide the diocese would be tantamount to a return to an earlier *status quo* might have formed the basis of a compromise.

   The government soon came under strong pressure not only from the Cornish lobby but also from another body of churchmen led by Lord Lyttelton who demanded some form of general legislation to permit the Church of England to increase the number of its dioceses at will. The Cornish lobby sought support from that campaign as well as continuing its own.[19] The historical argument, however, tended to be overshadowed by the practical one because the general case for many new dioceses was hardly a suitable context for 'restoration' and because of the doubt cast on its validity by Hobhouse. Neither the debate on Lord Lyttleton's first bill in 1861 nor the discussion in Church Congress that November elicited any substantial reference to 'restoration' and even the petition from the archdeaconry of Cornwall which Bishop Wilberforce presented to the Lords and to Convocation in 1863, avoided the point, as did subsequent debate.[20] That summer Archbishop Longley had visited the diocese to discover local feeling and his subsequent correspondence with Sir George Grey, the Home Secretary, published early in 1864 as a result of a Parliamentary question from Sir Stafford Northcote, elicited no reaction to the argument.[21] Local newspapers which supported the Church of England, were bitterly disappointed but neither the *Royal Cornwall Gazette* nor *Woolmer's Exeter & Plymouth Gazette* alluded to the historical argument in their leaders criticising the government's rejection of the proposal. Later, however, the London-based *Guardian* in dismissing Sir George Grey's arguments as 'flimsy', did point out that Archbishop Cranmer had envisaged a diocese for Cornwall.[22] Bishops Wilbeforce and Browne made another effort in Convocation in February 1865 and although they did not deploy the historical argument, the local press redeemed its previous silence. Shortly after Convocation ended, the *Royal Cornwall Gazette* editorialised with vehemence. There had been Celtic missionary bishops in Cornwall and it condemned Saxon influences and the introduction of an 'Italianate priesthood under Saint Augustine [which] almost extinguished the light of the ancient British church'. It also threw in Henry VIII's plan.[23] The underlying pejorative tone of its reference to Italianate priesthood and the implied approbation of Henry VIII would seem to have been journalistic tricks to seduce all good protestants to the aid of the Cornish party. The *Exeter & Plymouth Gazette* reacted with equal vigour, using the same historical argument.[24] Meanwhile other advocates were mobilised. Robert Scott contributed a letter to *The Times* in which he mentioned the practical difficulties of the diocese and referred to the historical argument as an answer to the charge of novelty.[25] The press and its correspondents puffed in vain and in June Convocation's new petition met with the same evasive and non-committal reply from the Crown through Sir George Grey as before.[26]

A danger in these repeated rebuffs was that the agitation might lose momentum. To some extent this was averted through an abridgement of a learned paper which the Rev. J.J. Carne had contributed to the *Journal* of the Royal Institution of Cornwall in 1867. The original will be discussed further below. The abridgement appeared under his own name in the *Exeter diocesan calendar and clergy list* for that year and was reprinted annually thereafter in the *Calendar* until the diocese was divided. Such repetition could have been the result of editorial inertia but more likely it was a deliberate attempt to keep the historical facts, as they were then understood, and hence the historical argument, before local clergy and anybody else who regularly read the *Calendar*. The abridgement listed bishops of the supposed diocese, with their sees, beginning with Bishop Conan in 936 and ending with the union of the two dioceses of Crediton and Cornwall in the person of Bishop Lyfing in 1042 and the subsequent transfer of the see from Crediton to Exeter in 1050 during Leofric's episcopate. The brief commentary noted that before this Saxon episcopate there had been 'an independent British church . . . in Cornwall . . . refusing obedience to the Roman see'.[27]

The historical argument was used more widely again in the later 1860s. Speaking to a petition from the inhabitants of Cornwall which the Earl of Devon had presented to the Lords, Bishop Browne not only once more rehearsed the practical arguments but also noted that what the petitioners sought was the restoration of the see.[28] Writing on the following day to Tatham, Browne reported the favourable mood of the House, and added, 'Lord Houghton who had opposed me, acknowledged that [my] speech was . . . lucid and had proved that the case of Cornwall was exceptional'.[29] Despite what its spokesman had said to Browne privately, the administration remained unconverted but with Gladstone taking office in 1868 there was some expectation that the change in political climate had come, and the matter was raised publicly by Lach-Szyrma in that pamphlet. On the historical argument he wrote largely as if still defending the project against the charge of novelty:

'The advocates of the Cornish episcopate urge that they are demanding no new privilege, but the restoration of an ancient right, taken from their county for reasons which could not, in the present day, be seriously quoted against their claim . . . This is not only a matter of historical and antiquarian interest, but of ecclesiastical and legal precedent . . . That a see of Cornwall once existed, and flourished for some generations, there cannot now be a shadow of doubt.

The Cornish see was formally abolished on the plea that the frequent incursions of the Danes rendered the open towns of Cornwall insecure. At the period of the Reformation the first attempt was made to restore the ancient see by Archbishop Cranmer in his excellent scheme for suffragan bishops'.[30]

Although Lach-Szyrma believed that history justified the Cornish claim, he did not use the historical argument to demand a share of the endowment of the bishopric of Exeter, as Wallis had, perhaps because that was now seen to be too simplistic.

Meanwhile in parallel to the historical argument, an ethnological one was also being used. Such an argument might seem less plausible and less capable of satisfactory proof, for it would be a matter of opinion rather than of fact whether difference of race, for example, merited a separate diocese. Such a compilation as Wallis's *Cornwall Register* presupposed some chauvinism, and the argument that the Cornish were different and therefore deserved their own diocese was being canvassed by Browne at Bodmin in 1854. He referred to the 'peculiar and very interesting condition of the Cornish people'. According to the *Royal Cornwall Gazette*, he continued:

'The fact of there being a very large proportion of the Cornish people a great mining population, and some of them engaged in our fisheries, renders them an independent, and intelligent, and a self-relying people. And therefore, in some respects they are more difficult to manage; and yet, when managed and rightly led, they are more likely to form a noble and vigorous people'.[31]

The report was a little tortuous but what he probably meant was that miners and fishermen are by the nature of their dangerous employment, a stubborn and close-knit community whose loyalty cannot be won by proxy or at a distance. This may have been as much a criticism of the existing ecclesiastical arrangements as a compliment to the working classes of Cornwall even though as a generalised sociological observation his remarks were probably not inaccurate. However the argument was to move from this apparent truism to a position which implied that any difference of race and occupation justified a separate diocese. Browne's point was incorporated in the subsequent petition from the clergy of the archdeaconry in 1855 which observed that the Cornish were a people 'with their own peculiar needs and feelings'.[32]

The focus was sharpened considerably by Hobhouse in 1860 when he wrote of the Cornish as 'of a different race and of a different tone, habits and disposition, to those of Devonshire'.[33] This introduced the notion of the Celtic-ness of the Cornish in contrast to the supposed Saxon stock east of the Tamar. This more strictly ethnic argument was not immediately espoused by Browne. At Church Congress in 1861 he contented himself with the occupational argument without even referring to any pastoral implications; he merely noted social distinctions between Devon and Cornwall, farming being the preoccupation of the former and mining and Weleyanism of the latter.[34] When he presented the petition from the archdeaconry to the Upper House of Convocation in 1863, Wilberforce similarly noted that Cornish people had a different outlook and needs.[35] By 1865, however, Browne seems to have accepted the ethnic argument as well as the occupational one. Addressing Convocation in February on differences between Devon and Cornwall to justify their separation, he not only reiterated how mining and Wesleyanism characterised Cornwall, and agriculture and the Establishment, Devon, but also added that the one was Celtic and the other Saxon.[36] The point was picked up by the *Guardian* in an editorial which drew attention to the distinctive race and occupation of the Cornish.[37] Browne spoke similarly in the Lords in 1867 in the speech upon which Lord Houghton complimented him, referring to the Celtic and Weleyan propensities of the Cornish.[38] This view that because the Cornish were a different people they deserved a separate diocese, supported statistical arguments in a further petition to the government from the laity and clergy of Cornwall organised in 1869. It stated that besides the historical claim, the 'character and habits of the Cornish people are so far distinctive as to warrant the long expressed wish for a Bishop who should be occupied with the charge of this county alone'.[39] One might suspect that the ethnological argument was being used as a stalking-horse to attack Wesleyanism for Robert Scott had indiscreetly suggested in *The Times* that Wesleyanism had made such progress in Cornwall because of the racial temperament which the Cornish had shared with the Welsh.[40] On the other hand, Celticism was enjoying a revival on its own merits and men like Browne forthrightly mentioned Wesleyanism as another problem.

The flowering of the ethnological argument came in Lach-Szyrma's pamphlet:

> 'no contiguous counties in England contain populations so entirely distinct in race from one another as Devon and Cornwall . . . The Cornish . . . (though of mixed race in the Tamar Valley), are mostly Celts, akin to the other Gaelic populations of these islands and Brittany . . . Till the period of the Reformation, the language of Cornwall was not only unintelligible to Englishmen, but really belonged to a distinct branch of the Indo-European family. It had far more connection indeed with Welsh or Breton than with Anglo-Saxon. The labouring classes of Cornwall, as a rule, are to this day decidedly distinct in character, in habits, even in physical aspect, from their neighbours in Devon; and the differences of occupation (the Cornish being mostly miners or fisherman) widens the result of differences in race . . . A distinct race requires a distinct mode of treatment, and a course of ecclesiastical policy that might be very judicious and desirable for Devon, would be imprudent and objectionable in Cornwall'.[41]

This perhaps owed something to Hegel's notion of the *Bewusstsein* of a people as well as echoing that unsophisticated loyalty which the *Royal Cornwall Gazette* had periodically reinforced with such headlines as 'The Bishopric of Cornwall'[42] and 'A Bishopric for Cornwall'.[43] The same ideas were repeated by Lightfoot in his sermon at Benson's consecration as bishop of Truro.[44]

The final phase of the agitation was less strident. The Cornish lobby availed itself of the momentum of the Conservative victory in 1874 and the decision to create a diocese of St. Albans. A preparatory meeting called at Plymouth early in 1875 by Edmund Carlyon and attended by the Earl of Devon, Lord Eliot, Hobhouse and various other local clergy, resolved to set up a committee 'for promoting the division of the diocese of Exeter'. This title notably avoided the question of 'restoration', the meeting possibly having taken Carlyon's professional advice as a solicitor, that any prospective legislation would not properly concern itself with such speculative matters. The *Exeter & Plymouth Gazette*, however, promptly invoked that shibboleth in welcoming 'the Cornish bishopric which it is proposed to restore'.[45] The *Royal Cornwall Gazette* was more circumspect.[46] The committee was confirmed at the next diocesan conference when what may have been Carlyon's carefully chosen words were potentially confused by the Earl of Devon who moved that 'in order therefore to promote a division of this diocese and the erection of a Bishopric in Cornwall, it is expedient that a Committee be formed, to be called "The Diocesan Committee for promoting the Restoration of a bishopric in Cornwall"'.[47] The title was rather subtle however. It did not claim to be restoring *the* diocese of Cornwall, which may have existed in Saxon times, but *a* diocese to Cornwall. This would still appeal to Cornish particularism but at the same time was not precise enough to incur a critical reaction from those, especially in London, who were studiously avoiding historical entanglements. Unfortunately the subtlty has been sufficient to mislead some subsequent commentators.

The literature which supported the historical argument was considerable and long-established. It may be traced in print to the sixteenth century and a manuscript tradition may be followed to the eleventh at least. That there had been some form of diocese and bishop of or for Cornwall in pre-Conquest times may never have been forgotten. The account in William of Malmesbury was essentially repeated in the sixteenth century by Camden and successive revisions and enlargements of his *Britannia* and its translation into English, culminating in Gough's three-volume edition of 1789, ensured its currency for generations of local antiquaries.[48] Three Cornish writers were especially responsible for the further local transmission of the Malmesbury-Camden story. Richard Carew, who had assisted Camden, and whose *Survey of Cornwall* proved as resilient as *Britannia,* stuck closely to the accepted story — '. . . in ancient times this shire had his [sic] particular Bishops . . .' but Lumigius 'obtained an annexation of Cornwall (lately fallen void) and so made one diocese of that and Devon, as it hath ever since continued'.[49] He was criticised by William Borlase who nevertheless repeated Carew's account though admitting difficulties with the evidence.[50] The story was repeated yet again by Richard Polwhele.[51] For the generation which conducted the 19th-century agitation for the division of the diocese these three writers were the fathers of Cornish history from whom support could be acceptably derived.

Later writers continued the tradition and brought it to the service of the agitators. John Whitaker's *The Ancient cathedral of Cornwall* (1804) was mostly an archaeological account of the parish church at St. Germans, somewhat naive and diffuse. Its first chapter, however, is significant for it exposed the errors, ambiguities and possibilities for alternative interpretation in previous writers from William of Malmesbury down to Borlase over the question of when the Saxon diocese of Cornwall was founded and whether Padstow and Bodmin had any claim ever to have been its see. Picking up a neglected observation in Leland's *Collectanea*, Whitaker showed that the political events of Athelstan's reign made it plausible that the diocese may have been founded then rather than earlier.[52] This was the latest work which Wallis could have consulted. The mid-century saw two more disciplined contributions. Edward Hoblyn Pedler, a solicitor of Liskeard, wrote *The Anglo-Saxon episcopate of Cornwall* (1856). His preface referred generally to recent developments (presumably Dr. Walker's offer) and explained 'whilst the subject was undergoing investigation . . . a proposition was advanced, and seriously entertained, of reviving this ancient Bishoprick, which induced the author to believe that some curiosity would naturally arise to ascertain what is known of the See, as it existed in remote times'.[53] His introduction continued with this train of thought: 'but whether the measure [of union in the eleventh century] was defensible . . . there is an opinion that the exegencies of the present day demand its reversal; and after eight hundred years of acquiescence, Parliament will probably be called upon to reconsider its policy, and to vindicate the wisdom of our Anglo-Saxon forefathers by restoring to Cornwall its separate episcopacy'.[54] The beginning of the agitation had been independent of his own researches but he realised the connection and saw no objection to the lessons of the past, as he may have understood them, being brought to bear upon current problems. Using newly available evidence from Kemble's *Codex*, Pedler was also inclined to date the Saxon episcopate in Cornwall to the reign of Athelstan. Of the merger with Crediton, he moralised: 'the unfortunate Cornish-Celts were left to their own devices, or to such feeble influences as a distant prelate and a few local clergy could exercise'.[55] Ironically in view of the Celtic ethnological argument, it was Anglo-Saxon wisdom which he commended. The topic was re-attacked shortly after Pedler's death by J.J. Carne in the paper already mentioned. Discussing the Saxon period of the bishopric of Cornwall, he referred to the current agitation: 'Cornwall — once the abode of . . . Saint Petrock and many another holy man of God — has for eight hundred years and more been deprived of her ancient see', during which time the population had vastly increased. Hence had arisen the earnest and reiterated petition for 'the restoration of her ancient see of Bodmin, a boon which we feel confident cannot now long be deferred'.[56] The meat of his article, a list of those early bishops, was regularly reprinted in the diocesan calendar and had the approbation of Professor Stubbs.

The Regius Professor of modern history at Oxford indeed

provided notable support. As early as 1851 he had come to realise that a volume tracing the episcopal succession in England was needed even though the task was full of difficulty.[57] He put it in hand and his *Registrum sacrum Anglicanum* appeared in 1858. It traced the succession from Saint Augustine and in an appendix Stubbs rearranged his material to show the succession in each diocese, including the tenth-century successions in the sees of Cornwall and of Crediton. In another appendix he attempted to list the British and Welsh bishops before the 'union' of their sees with the province of Canterbury but although he noted a number of British bishops in Cornwall, he had to admit the unreliability of the evidence, a point which seems not to have troubled the Cornish.[58] His second contribution appeared late in the course of the agitation. Together with Haddan, he devoted just over 30 pages in *Councils and ecclesiastical documents* (Oxford, 1869) to the 'Church of Cornwall' during the Saxon period. Their use of the word 'of' rather than 'in' would seem to be significant for it could be construed to imply that the agitators' view that the church there had been more important at an earlier time was no mere provincialism concocted to bolster their campaign but rather an academically respectable opinion. Very probably Haddan and Stubbs were using the word deliberately for it seems to echo the clause 'dedit episcopatum Cridionensis ecclesiae atque Cornubienses provinciae capellano suo Leofrico . .' to be found in Leofric's missal, with the manuscript of which Stubbs was familiar.[59] That word 'provinciae' would seem to have implied some distinction in the eleventh century between the ordinary diocese of Crediton and the area of Cornwall though whether Leofric, Stubbs and the agitators each ascribed the same meaning to it may be questioned. These two contributions might be dismissed as coincidental, Cornwall being too far removed from Oxford in both distance and thought, had not Stubbs also written, by invitation, a 'History of the Cornish bishopric' for the first issue of the *Truro diocesan kalendar*. This suggests that his work had been acceptable. Probably Benson persuaded him to write the piece because Stubbs's covering note with the text was addressed to him and not to the Rev. H.H. du Boulay, editor of the *Kalendar*. Stubbs was tentative about the commission because the manuscript which he submitted was neither a fair copy nor quite complete, blanks having been left towards the end for details of recent developments. He even suggested to Benson that Carne, 'who has studied the subject very carefully . . . would be better fitted than I am, to teach Cornish men a bit of their history'.[60] Stubbs could not have been aware that Carne had died in 1868. Stubbs's essay, like Carne's, referred to British bishops in Cornwall and to the subsequent establishment of a Saxon diocese there under Bishop Conan early in the tenth century.

Some other historians working outside Cornwall were of less help. The Roman Catholic, John Lingard, for instance, largely ignored any Cornish church in his *History and antiquities of the Anglo-Saxon church*. Adhering strictly to his title, he just noted how the division of the over-large diocese of Wessex had led to the creation of a see at Crediton for Devon to which he appended Cornwall in an end-note.[61]

The historical argument outlived the events which gave birth to it, becoming the orthodox historical account of the affair. This metamorphosis began soon after the diocese had been divided. The first resolution at the first Truro diocesan conference expressed gratitude to God for the restoration 'to the Archdeaconry of Cornwall its ancient organization as a separate diocese'.[62] Contributing an article on Truro to *The Cathedral churches of England* (1884), Edmund Carlyon noted that the 'continuity' of the Cornish see which had existed in the eleventh century and had been broken, was recently restored in 1877.[63] Lach-Szyrma headed a section of his *Church history of Cornwall* (1887) with the sub-title, 'The Restoration of the Cornish bishopric', his account having commenced with the pre-Conquest period.[64] Issued at about the same time, an anonymous pamphlet entitled *The Cornish see and cathedral* (Truro, c.1888) was mainly concerned with progress towards building the cathedral but also looked back over the course of the agitation since 1847 for the 'restoration' of the see. The idea recurs in *The Bishopric of Truro 1877–1902* by Canon A.B. Donaldson. His chronological table and first chapter traced Cornish church history from the fifth century and the second chapter, headed 'Revival', contained an *encomium* of Phillpotts in which he observed that the bishop had lent the aid of his great abilities to the first efforts 'in the direction of the revival of a Cornish see after the lapse of more than eight centuries'.[65] E.G. Sandford devoted a chapter of his *Exeter episcopate of Archbishop Temple* (1907) to 'The Revival of the Cornish see'. Although he cited documents which did not use the word 'revival' (or any synonym), he consistently used it himself and even abused it by referring to the bill of 1876 as one for the revival of the see.[67] He was not alone in this and those responsible for the inscription on the memorial to Carlyon in St. Austell parish church gave the idea lapidary authority, reminding pilgrims of 'Edmund Carlyon . . .

mainly instrumental in the restoration of the ancient bishopric of Cornwall and in the erection of the cathedral church at Truro'. His obituarist in the *Royal Cornwall Gazette* had similarly noted his role in the 'revival of the ancient Cornish see'.[68]

Since the turn of the century, however, the traditional Malmesbury-Camden story upon which the revivalist argument had depended, has been modified by historians. Following the discovery of the so-called Crawford charters and the work of R.R. Darlington in the 1930s and of H.P.R. Finberg and others more recently, the old confidence has gone. A few new facts have been adduced but much is now admitted to be uncertain. It is widely believed that a separate Saxon diocese for Cornwall was not created until 994 and that Bishop Conan and his immediate successors were not diocesan bishops but chorepiscopi subordinate to Crediton. The two dioceses were brought together again early in the eleventh century through the plurality of Bishop Lyfing which was regularised at the expense of the post in Cornwall in 1050.[69] In this light, therefore, it is disappointing that Dr. H. Miles Brown should not have treated the historical argument more fully in his *A Century for Cornwall: the diocese of Truro 1877–1977* (1977).

Though its basis may now be less certain, it would be wrong to dismiss the historical argument as an aberration. There was some strength in it. One characteristic of a diocese is territory and insofar as Cornwall is a peninsula and the Tamar approximately marked the eastern boundary of both what was taken to have been the Saxon diocese, and the diocese of Truro, then in a topographical sense the one was a revival of the other. But topographical identity does not necessarily imply substantial identity. A diocese is also a social organisation and since social organisations are aggregations of people, they predicate a liability to change. The lapse of time between Athelstan and Queen Victoria allowed ample time for change. The context of a nineteenth-century Anglican diocese differed from that of one in the eleventh century even though the Church of England claimed continuity in its episcopacy. Indeed, a distinction may be made between episcopacy itself and the administrative structures and nuances of belief which may depend upon it. On the other hand, as the motion at the diocesan conference had suggested, it could be construed as the restoration not of *the* diocese but of *a* diocese. This alters the logic but few contemporaries rigorously observed the point, least of all Donaldson and Sandford. Next, the eventual failure to maintain a clear continuity in endowment also undermines the historical argument. Up to the middle of the nineteenth century bishops of

Exeter had enjoyed the Cornish manor of Lawhitton which seems to have been held continuously by the see since the tenth century. However the estates of the bishopric were vested in the Ecclesiastical Commissioners in 1869 and though Exeter provided £800 annually after 1876 for the partial endowment of Truro, neither the Truro Act nor the Commissioners' accountancy required or permitted any particular property to contribute to that subsidy. The agitators had hoped for some such ear-marking but eventually had to realise that it was not possible.[70] Thirdly, the title of the see could have been a link with the past but there is no evidence that Saxon bishops in Cornwall had any titular connection with Truro whose site, indeed, may then have been little more than a swampy creek-head.[71]

The essence of the ethnological argument, as it finally developed, was that the racial distinctiveness of the Cornish together with their patterns of employment and society, justified their having their own bishop. The idea of the distinctiveness of the Cornish may also be traced back to William of Malmesbury who implied that the British had become confined to Cornwall.[72] Carew made the same point, noting the similarities between Cornish and Welsh, and the Cornish people's disposition and quality of mind, ancient and present.[73] Some later writers were equally convinced though possibly with less justification. Borlase may not have noted explicitly that they were Celts but in discussing the pre-Conquest period clearly stated that the 'Cornish-Britons' had been hard pressed by the westwards expansion of the Saxon kingdom.[74] Polwhele made similar points, and also linked Cornish and Breton.[75] The view had looked much the same from the other side of the Tamar and Risdon had commenced his account of Devon by referring to how Athelstan had forced the Britons west of that river, making it the boundary which it had remained ever since.[76] These writers were none too precise as to what constituted a Celt or Briton or as to how the Cornish manifested their peculiarities but they encouraged a popular belief that the Celts had been driven westwards into Cornwall and therefore, in uncritical logic, Cornish people of later generations were also Celts and thus to be distinguished from those living to the east.

The question of the distinguishing characteristics of Celts and whether that type predominated in one part of the country rather than another was exercising both the scientific mind and the popular imagination in the mid-nineteenth century. Popular writers had little doubt. Cyrus Redding (1785–1870), a Cornish-born journalist who had pursued his career in Paris and London, was quite certain:

'There is a character of person belonging to the earlier inhabitants of [Cornwall], or arising from some connexion with other than Saxon 'foreigners', which must strike all who scrutinise them with attention. The introduction of the Saxon breed into Cornwall is evident enough; but there are many who exhibit marks of southern extraction, in large black eyes, dark hair, and a swarthy complexion; perhaps the descendants of settlers from the south of Spain at a very remote period . . . The men are strongly made, and more active than those of the midland counties of England'.[77]

Wilkie Collins, whose disinterested but sensitive pen described Cornwall and the Cornish shortly before Brunel bridged the Tamar, observed that it was a county where 'a man speaks of himself as *Cornish* in much the same spirit as a Welshman speaks of himself as Welsh'.[78] Neither of these writers stressed over-much the Celtic element but certainly they pointed to differences. The scientific discussion laboured not only under suspect logic but also from the inconclusiveness of the data which measurements of crania were producing. Nevertheless ethnologists such as David Mackintosh were attempting to define the 'Gaelic' type and found it and its varieties in Cornwall, describing them in much the same way as Redding had; the Saxon type he found in east and south Devon.[79] John Beddoe, using his own index of 'nigrescence' as well as proportions of crania and other indicators, perceived an increase in Celtic types as he travelled south-westwards.[80]

This search for Celtic roots had its critics. Reviewing Collins's book and other publications on Cornwall, the Wesleyan divine and educationalist, J.H. Rigg was sceptical of the alleged differences between Saxon peasant and Cornu-Briton husbandman.[81] The most formidable critic was probably Friedrich Max Müller. He did not endear himself to the Cornish by his refutation of the popular etymology of the place-name Marazion,[82] but his main criticism was launched in lectures at the Royal Institution, London, in 1861, followed by a paper in the *Quarterly Review* in 1867. He postulated the tribal nature of language and saw this rather than blood as the indicator of national identity. The scientific and medical approach had scarcely proceeded beyond the measurement of skulls; a Celt, he declared, 'may become an Englishman, Celtic and English blood may be mixed; and who could tell at the present day the exact proportions of Celtic and Saxon blood in the population of England?'[83] In his subsequent paper he granted that the original inhabitants of Cornwall had been Celts and that its place-names were distinctive but then briskly attacked the idea that the Cornish were therefore still Celts. The Cornish language was full of Norman, Saxon and Latin words; he could give no definition of Celtic blood or skulls and then syllogistically argued that 'Celtic' should be applied to those who spoke a Celtic language, but since the Cornish had ceased to speak it they were no longer Celts but 'true Teutons or Saxons'.[84] Others were content to detach themselves and be cynical or bemused. The querulous Samuel Rundle, incumbent of Stockleigh Pomeroy wrote to Temple in August 1876 that the Cornish people 'are at present too exclusive & clannish. It may be the creation of a new see will foster & increase this feeling'.[85] Having been plunged into the midst of this particularism, Benson soon reported back to Christopher Wordsworth at Lincoln, 'I see what I once believed and which the Cornish are never weary of saying, "Since they are a most peculiar people"; it is quite the truest thing which I have heard them say'.[86]

Taken together, the historical and ethnological arguments were similar to considerations which might be used to test the concept of nationality. Identity of race or descent, community of language and of religion, clear geographical limitations (as a peninsula largely enjoyed) and distinctive political antecedents were even then being identified by J.S. Mill as characteristic of a feeling of nationality.[87] The points raised by Lach-Szyrma could almost be regarded as a commentary on parts of Mill's analysis. It was not a question of seceding from the United Kingdom but only of achieving some ecclesiastical identity, yet the arguments for division brought together elements from which, in other circumstances, secession might spring. Although nationality may be rejected as too strong a term in this context, there is nevertheless county loyalty and identity. Counties were then a lively focus for much social life and any county having to share a bishop with another which had its own social hierarchy, was in some way deficient. Hence the appeal of the slogan produced by Canon Kennaway at the Church Congress in 1864 that where there was a Lord Lieutenant there should also be a bishop.[88] Such an arrangement completed the parallel social structures of diocese and county (or church and state writ small). Cornish identity and Erastianism supported each other.

The ethnological argument also drew support from the church overseas. It did not necessarily follow from an acceptance that the Cornish were Celtic that they therefore deserved their own diocese: the Gospel was for Jew and Gentile alike. Yet there was some encouragement. The *Royal Cornwall Gazette* mentioned the example of the colonial church and Hobhouse referred to it in his pamphlet.[89] The Church of England may have been slow to create additional dioceses at home but new ones had been springing up in

the colonies especially after the launching of the Colonial Bishoprics Fund in 1841, and speaking at its golden jubilee in 1891
Gladstone was to recall how the development of a colonial
episcopate had been an encouragement to the Church at home.[90]
Colonial diocese served natives and British alike though locally, as
in India for example, congregations might be segregated.[91] The
strategy of the Church Missionary Society under Henry Venn the
younger was to develop viable local churches under an indigenous
ministry, and the consecration of Samuel Crowther, a Yoruba, as
bishop of the Niger in 1864 was another straw in the wind.[92] The
idea that a distinguishable racial group deserved its own diocese
may thus have drawn support if only subconsciously and perhaps
misguidedly from the mission field: if African or Indian natives,
however vaguely understood in Cornwall, were to have dioceses
why should not the Cornish? It would be unwise to stress this too
much because it was not a question in Cornwall of an indigenous
ministry or an autocephalous church but merely of a separate
diocese though to the untutored the distinction may not have been
clear.

The final thread in the ethnological argument was quite factual.
Whether Devon was primarily agricultural and Cornwall was
principally engaged in mining and fisheries could be checked from
official statistics. In 1851 farmers (but not landowners), agricultural
labourers, shepherds and farm servants comprised nearly 22% of
the male population of Devon and nearly 17% of that of Cornwall.
Fisherman and seamen comprised 1.8% in Devon and nearly 3%
in Cornwall. Miners in non-ferrous metals comprised less than 1%
in Devon but as many as 17.6% in Cornwall.[93] The argument from
numbers employed was therefore not quite so clear-cut as the
agitators alleged because the respective figures for agriculture
showed less difference than those for mining, and there was
probably some regular exchange of labour between land and
mines. Whether Cornwall was mainly Wesleyan and Devon,
Anglican may be examined in the less certain light of the 1851
religious census which suggested that on census Sunday the various
branches of Wesleyanism in Cornwall together accounted for some
64% of attendances to the Church of England's 28% whereas in
Devon the Wesleyan group was credited with 18.7% to the
Establishment's 59.6%.[94] Curiously, these detailed figures which
were readily accessible, were not referred to so explicitly or
frequently in the agitation as those for the geographical dimensions
of the diocese or the crude total populations of the two counties.
The advocates were not innumerate but their coyness in this

respect seems to beg explanation. They even introduced a note of ambiguity because it is not clear whether the argument based on occupation referred to the people employed or the wealth they produced. From a pastoral angle the number of persons was vital but wealth was not to be overlooked because it would help endow the bishopric. Unfortunately similarly compendious statitstics for comparing the wealth respectively generated by agriculture and mining were not available. Contemporary mining statistics indeed indicated the value of ore raised but agricultural statistics were quantitative.

It is scarcely possible to characterise these two arguments as coming exclusively from any one sector whilst there is no satisfactory way of establishing what the less articulate of the laity were thinking. The background of some of the agitators nevertheless typifies of the variety of people involved. Born in Devonport, the son of a Polish emigré, Lach-Szyrma held preferments in Cornwall until 1890 with the exception of a brief spell in the early 1870s. He deployed all the arguments and the zeal with which he treated the ethnological one was typical of a native by adoption. He was a local official of the 'high-church' party.[95] Browne was born at Aylesbury but married into the Carlyon family and served for many years in the diocese though not exclusively in Cornwall. He also argued on all fronts and continued his support from his chair at Cambridge and throne at Ely. In churchmanship he was opposed to ritualism.[96] Samuel Wilberforce, a notable extra-diocesan supporter of the cause, disliked the extremely high and was disliked by the very low in churchmanship. Though an incumbent in Cornwall from 1832 until his death in 1874, Arthur Tatham was born in Greenwich. On the other hand, Carlyon and Wallis were thoroughly Cornish as were such aristocratic supporters as St. Germans. Successive petitions from clergy and laity in Cornwall touched on most arguments but their signatories were neither wholly Cornish nor all 'foreign'. Amongst lay signatories there may have been a number of Tory-inclined lesser gentry and the local press which supported the cause was indeed normally Tory,[97] yet the project gathered Liberal support as well. The official appeal committee included such Liberals as Earl Fortescue, Earl St. Germans (a former Peelite), Lord Eliot and Sir Thomas Dyke Acland. The grandees of Cornish society were not united however: St. Germans supported it from an early stage but Sir Richard Vyvyan, Lord Falmouth and Lord Mount Edgcumbe, all Tories, each expressed disapproval though their opposition was more on the grounds of different priorities than from a rejection of either of these arguments.[98] Another aspect is perhaps clearer. Not only was there a thematic link between renewed interest in the Cornish language and its literature, and the demand for diocesan independence, both being aspects of Cornish particularism, but also the same people tended to be active in both. Amongst the subscribers to Robert Williams's *Lexicon Cornu-Britannicum* (1865) were St. Germans, Carne and Pedler.[99] Edwin Norris prefaced his *Ancient Cornish drama* (1859) with acknowledgements to Robert Scott and Pedler. Lach-Szyrma became interested in Cornish words and phrases still in occasional use around Newlyn and did field work on them with Henry Jenner.[100]

The use of these two arguments was not unique. The defence of the independence of Sodor and Man, threatened with merger into Carlisle in 1836, had rested not only on practical and constitutional points but also upon the antiquity of that island see and the nature of Manx society.[101] An attenuated historical argument also arose elsewhere, for example in the suggestion that a Northumberland diocese might have its see at Hexham and that Coventry rather than Birmingham might be the see for a new diocese in the Midlands.[102] Both Hexham and Coventry had had some episcopal dignity in earlier times. In these cases, however, the historical argument was not pursued with such vigour as it was in Cornwall; its value was discounted.

These two arguments were not accepted by everybody. The Cathedral Commissioners, it has been seen, eschewed the idea of 'restoration'. Sir Stafford Northcote, later a member of the appeal committee, referred merely to the establishment of a bishopric in Cornwall in a Parliamentary question in 1864.[103] Roundell Palmer speaking to Lord Lyttelton's second Bill in 1867 merely referred to the practical difficulties of the diocese of Exeter.[104] Throughout that decade the government's defence of the *status quo* pointedly ignored both arguments in its assumption that modern communications counterbalanced the practical difficulties. The successful local lobby of Disraeli in 1875, it was subsequently revealed, made only the practical points in its initial submission.[105] Archbishop Tait probably discounted the historical argument because the informal committee including himself which the Home Secretary consulted in April 1876, recommended a *new* bishopric for Cornwall.[106] Parliamentary draftsmen had little truck with pre-Conquest antiquities and a Home Office memorandum to Tait on a number of details referred to the proposed legislation for the 'new bishopric of Cornwall'.[107] The bill itself was 'to provide for the foundation of a new bishopric out of part of the diocese of Exeter'.[108] The nature of the legislation had much to do with this attitude. Dealing with endowment and territory, it had to start from the existing situation, and to be precise and verifiable, which the affairs of Athelstan, Cnut and Edward the Confessor hardly were. There was also at least one effort within the diocese to discount the historical argument.[109]

Both arguments were particular manifestations of broader themes. The use of current historical thought to help mould the future turned history into propaganda. Such an appeal to the past was characteristic of Anglican tradition having been a hall-mark of much apologetic since the Henrican secession, and more recently Newman and his colleagues had sought fresh illumination from that direction.[110] The agitation coincided with the revival of Celtic awareness and they gave each other mutual support.[111] That revival involved a search for precedents and for a folk identity, and was akin to irredentist movements in other parts of Europe, notably Ireland, even though what proved benign in Cornwall was not always so elsewhere. Whether such identity justified a separate diocese may be debated and a criticism of the protagonists could be that they alleged rather than proved this point. On the other hand, the church has frequently made use of secular territorial patterns, and hence the modes of thought attached to them, in making its own administrative arrangements and to this extent there may be justification.

The role of both arguments was to mould public opinion. The ethnological one was particularly directed inwards to neutralise, if not win over, non-Anglicans in Cornwall. It appealed to a sense of community and may be compared with the successful winning over of Joseph Chamberlain to the idea of a diocese for Birmingham.[112] The historical argument similarly had a community appeal. Such an appeal was vital if endowment capital had to be raised principally by public subscription. The historical argument also had an external role, especially in the earlier stages, to counter the criticism of novelty. There was a general role for both arguments, too. Various plans for other dioceses were afoot and since it seemed likely that a wholesale reorganisation such as that done in 1836 would not recur, individual schemes had to take their chance.[113] The basic argument common to all plans was the practical one but although populous, the diocese of Exeter was not the most populous even upon its division.[114] It was indeed extensive and elongated with a see town near its eastern end whilst the tendency of the railway to hug its southern coast posed further difficulties which its bishop confessed and Thomas Hardy utilised, yet other dioceses also had extended lines of communication.[115] Thus if there was little to choose between over-large dioceses in these respects, other factors might be introduced to tilt the balance in the public mind and hasten acceptance of change.

Finally, the Cornish lobbyists had yet one further distinction. Although the accuracy of what they culled from the past may now be questioned, they at least tried to act upon what they thought it indicated and thus went some way towards confounding Hegel's pessimistic dictum about ignorance of historical antecedents.[116] But that peculiar honour probably had little appeal to the man in the pew.

Notes

[1]   Thus Archbishop Longley and Lord Lyttleton respectively in *Chronicle of Canterbury Convocation* [hereafter referred to as *CCC*] (1865), p. 1844 and *Hansard*, 3 clxi (1861), 1944. Sir George Grey for the government held the contrary view (*Hansard*, 3 clxxxviii (1865), 935–6).

In preparing this paper the author has been very much indebted to the Church Commissioners, London, for access to their historical files, and to the Dean of Truro, the Cornwall County Archivist, the Penzance Library, the Royal Institution of Cornwall and the Devon and Exeter Institution for their kindly granting access to manuscripts, newspapers and rare pamphlets. He is also grateful to the University of Leeds for study leave and lest it might seem presumptuous of him to be writing about Cornwall from Yorkshire, he confesses to west-country origins.

[2]   Bishop Benson's initial impression of Cornish Methodists was their eagerness to find fault with the established church: A.C. Benson, *Life of E.W. Benson* (1901), p. 169. Benson may have been somewhat disillusioned because he had been assured by Bishop Temple that the Cornish were ready to receive him with enthusiasm: Truro Dean & Chapter papers [hereafter referred to as TD&C], 1/4 (Temple to Benson, 6th December 1876).

[3]   A detailed account of Frewen's plan appeared in *The Guardian*, 5th August 1846, pp. 231–2. The rather 'high' Anglican newspaper must not be confused with its erstwhile Manchester namesake.

[4]   *Hansard*, 3 xciv (1847), 239. Russell suggested that Bodmin might be the see.

[5]   W.S. Lach-Szyrma, *The Bishopric of Cornwall: a letter to W.E. Gladstone* (London and Truro, 1869).

[6]   Manchester: John Rylands Library. Lyttelton papers (Palmer to Lyttelton, 17th August 1867).

[7]   *op. cit.*, (1969), pp. 201–205.

[8]   J. Wallis, *Cornwall register* (1847), pp. 15–6; cf. J. Strype, *Memorials*, I/ii (1822), 406.

[9]   *Royal Cornwall Gazette* [hereafter referred to as *RCG*], 28th July 1854, p. 6, cols. 4–6.

[10]   *RCG*, 29th September 1854, p. 5, col. 4.

[11]   Church Commissioners, file 1837/i: copy of petition annexed to letter from Palmerston to Ecc. Commissioners, 21st October 1854.

[12]   TD&C, 156/1.

[13]   Cathedral Commissioners, *Second report* (1855), passim.

[14]   TD&C, 156/5. A copy of the *Statement* was forwarded to the Ecclesiastical Commissioners (Ch. Comm., file 1837/i, in-letter 3733/60).

[15]   TD&C 156/7: Phillpotts to Tatham, 24th December 1859.

[16]   *RCG*, 30th December 1859, p. 4, col. 6.

[17]   R. Hobhouse, *The Cornish bishopric* (1860), p. 18.

[18]   *Exeter & Plymouth Gazette* [hereafter referred to as *EPG*], 12th May 1860, p. 3, col. 2; cf. *RCG* 11th May 1860, p. 5, col. 2 and *Guardian*, 23rd May 1860, p. 456, cols. 1–2.

[19]   TD&C 156/17: Wilberforce to Tatham, 15th May 1863; cf. *id.* 156/18 and 156/19 (Lyttelton to Tatham, 7th September 1863 and 29th October 1863). Unfortunately Lyttelton's papers at the John Rylands Library, Manchester, do not contain his end of this particular correpondence.

[20]   Lyttelton's efforts are usefully described in C.E.A. Bedwell, *The Increase of the episcopate* (1906).

[21]   *Parliamentary papers*, (1864) xliv 305.

[22]   *RCG*, 19th February 1864, p. 5, cols. 1–2; *EPG*, 19th February 1864, p. 4, col. 5 and *Guardian*, 7th December 1864, pp. 1177–8.

[23]   *RCG*, 24th February 1865, p. 4, cols. 5–6; for Convocation's debate, see *CCC* (1865), pp. 1837–45, 1875–76 and 1893.

[24]   *EPG, 13th April 1865, p. 5, col. 2.*

[25]   *The Times*, 2nd May 1865, p. 14, cols. 2–3. The letter was published over his initials and he contributed a similar letter to the *Guardian*, 3rd May 1865, p. 435, cols. 2–3. Rector of Duloe and Master of Balliol, Scott as acted as an intemediary for Tatham: cf. TD&C 156/8.

[26]   *CCC* (1865), p. 2355.

[27]   *Exeter diocesan calendar and clergy list for 1867*, pp. ix-xii.

[28]   *Hansard*, 3 clxxxv (1867), 1302.

[29]   TD&C 156/31: Browne to Tatham, 5th March 1867.

[30]   Lach-Szyrma, *op. cit.*, pp. 6–8.

[31]   *RCG*, 29th September 1854, p. 5, col. 3.

[32]   Ch. Comm., file 1837/i.

[33]   Hobhouse, *op. cit.*, p. 15.

[34]   Church Congress, *Report* (1861), p. 72.

[35]   *CCC* (1863), p. 1208.

[36]   *id.* (1865), pp. 1841–2.

[37]   *Guardian*, 12th April 1865, p. 365, col. 3.

[38]   *Hansard*, 3 clxxxv (1867), 1301–2.

[39]   TD&C 152.

[40]   *The Times*, 2nd May 1865, p. 14. cols. 2–3.

[41]   Lach-Szyrma, *op. cit.*, pp. 8–12.

[42]   *RCG*, 6th October 1854, p. 6, col. 1; 20th October 1854, p. 6, col. 1.

[43]   *id.*, 30th December 1859, p. 4, col. 6.

[44]   TD&C 156/66.

[45]   *EPG*, 5th March 1875, p. 3, col. 6 and p. 5, col. 2.

[46]   *RCG*, 27th February 1875, p. 4, col. 3.

[47]   *EPG*, 5th November 1875, p. 8, col. 5. This title for the Committee subsequently appeared on their broadsheet appealing for funds, issued in January 1876 and on a memorandum which it sent to the Ecclesiastical Commissioners on 22nd May that year.

[48]   William of Malmesbury, *De gestis pontificum*, ed. N.E.S.A. Hamilton (Rolls series, 52; 1870), pp. 178, 200 and 204. On the renaissance reception of his work,

see W. Stubbs's introduction to his *De gestis regum* (Rolls series, 90; 1887) vol. I, pp. xci and xcviii, and M. McKisack, *Medieval history in the Tudor age* (1971). For Camden's version, see *Britannia* (1594), p. 126 and the parallel passages in subsequent editions.

[49]   R. Carew, *Survey of Cornwall*, ed. F.E. Halliday (1953), p. 153. This passage is more translation than paraphrase of William of Malmesbury (*De gestis pontificum*, ed. cit., p. 200). Further editions of Carew were published in Devon or Cornwall in 1723, 1769 and 1811.

[50]   W. Borlase, *Observations on the antiquities of Cornwall* (1754), pp. v and 342 ff.

[51]   R. Polwhele, *op. cit.*, (1803–5; repr. 1978), ii 99 ff.

[52]   J. Whitaker, *op. cit.*, i 14–60; cf. J. Leland, *Collectanea*, ed. T. Hearne (2nd ed., 1774), i 75.

[53]   E.H. Pedler, *op. cit.*, (1856), p. iii.

[54]   *ibid.*, p. viii.

[55]   *ibdi.*, p. 105.

[56]   J.J. Carne, 'The Bishopric of Cornwall — Saxon period', *Journal of the Royal Institution of Cornwall*, vii (1867) 212.

[57]   H.P. Liddon offered Stubbs sympathy and encouragement such was the difficulty of the project: *Letters of William Stubbs*, ed. W.H. Hutton (1904), p. 38.

[58]   W. Stubbs, *Registrum sacrum Anglicanum* (1858), pp. 152–3.

[59]   A.W. Haddan and W. Stubbs, *op. cit.*, i 671–704; *Leofric missal*, ed. F.E. Warren (1883), p. 2, cf. Camden, *op. cit.*, (1594), p. 126. Haddan and Stubbs referred to the missal in their *Councils and ecclesiastical documents*, i 691.

[60]   TD&C 74; Stubbs to Benson, 28th October [1877]. Carne's piece was reprinted annually in the *Exeter diocesan calendar* up to and including the issue of 1876; Stubbs's appeared first in *Truro Diocesan church kalendar for 1878*, sect. 2, pp. 1–3. His MS text is preserved in TD&C 76.

[61]   J. Lingard, *op. cit.*, (3rd ed., 1845), i 85–9 and Note F (p. 384).

[62]   Truro CRO: Diocesan conference [proceedings], 25th October 1877.

[63]   *Cathedral churches of England* (1884), p. 236.

[64]   Lach-Szyrma also used the word 'resuscitation' as well as 'restoration' (*op. cit.*, pp. 115 and 118) but does not seem to have intended any elaborate metaphorical distinction by this alternative!

[65]   Donaldson, *op. cit.*, p. 26.

[66]   *ibid.*, pp. 29 and 32.

[67]   Sandford, *op. cit.*, p. 142.

[68]   *RCG*, 3rd August 1911, p. 8, col. 3.

[69]   The literature is extensive, but especially: *The Crawford collection of early charters*, ed. A.S. Napier and W.H. Stevenson (Anecdota Oxon., III; 1895), charter vii; R.R. Darlington, 'Ecclesiastical reform in the late Old English period', *English historical review*, li (1936), 424–426; H.P.R. Finberg, 'Sherborne, Glastonbury and the expansion of Wessex', *Trans. Royal Hist. Soc.*, 5th ser., iii (1953), 101–124, and *Early Charters of Devon and Cornwall* (2nd 1963); P. Chaplais, 'The Authenticity of the royal Anglo-Saxon diplomas of Exeter', *Bull. Institute of Historical Research*, xxxix (1966), 1–34, and F. Barlow, *The English church 1000–1066* (2nd ed., 1979), pp. 211–212.

[70]   On Lawhitton, see *Crawford charters*, p. 107; also the rather unexpected comment in Royal Commission on the Public Records, *Third report* (1919), vol. iii/2, pp. 72–3, and Finberg, 'Sherborne, Glastonbury . . .', p. 121. Archdeacon Phillpotts had had expectations of endowment from some such source (cf.

Guardian, 4th October 1854, p. 752, col. 1) and the Cathedral Commissioners recommended ear-marking episcopal property in Cornwall for this purpose (*Second report*, 1855) but the Ecclesiastical Commissioners promptly minuted that such a proposal was *ultra vires* from their point of view as the law then stood (Ch. Comm., file 1837/i, copy minutes of 26th April 1855). Nevertheless the Cornish claim was repeated in the *Statement of facts* (1859), by the Cornish deputation to Palmerston (*Guardian*, 23rd May 1860, p. 456) and in a petition from the rural deanery of Kerrier in 1869 (Ch. Comm., file 1837/i). Hobhouse was still demanding such a windfall as late as 1875 by when it was a lost cause (*Guardian*, 16th June 1875, p. 771, col. 2).

[71] Cf. Henderson, *Essays in Cornish history* (1935), p. 1. Truro parish church was not consecrated until 1259 and there was a long dispute during the agitation whether Bodmin or Truro should be the see, Sir George Grey using this rivalry as one of several excuses for the government not proceeding with the proposal (cf. *Hansard*, 3 clxxviii (1865), 934).

[72] *De gestis regum*, i 148.

[73] Carew, *op. cit.*, pp. 81 and 129ff. On differences in regional speech in Carew's time, cf. G. Puttenham, *Art of English poesie* (1589), Bk iii, ch. 4.

[74] Borlase, *op. cit.*, p. 44.

[75] Polwhele, *op. cit.*, iii 25 and v 3ff.

[76] T. Risdon, *Chorographical description or survey of Devon* (1811), p. 1. This work was written in 1640 and first published in 1714.

[77] C. Redding, *Illustrated itinerary of the county of Cornwall* (1842), pp. 17–8.

[78] W. Collins, *Rambles beyond the railways* (1851), p. 94; cf. F.W.P. Jago, *The Ancient language and dialect of Cornwall* (1882), p. vii and M.A. Courtney and T.Q. Couch, *Glossary of words in use in Cornwall* (1880), p. xiii.

[79] D. Mackintosh, 'Comparative anthropology of England and Wales', *Anthropological review*, iv (1866), 37–45.

[80] J. Beddoe, 'On the testimony of local phenomena', *Memoirs of the Anthropological Society of London*, ii (1866), 14–16.

[81] *London Quarterly Review*, xix (1862), 16.

[82] Max Müller, 'Are there Jews in Cornwall?', *Macmillan's Magazine*, xv (1867), 484–494.

[83] Max Müller, *Lectures on the science of language* (4th ed., 1864), p. 74. If the distribution of blood groups is significant in this context, then scientific evidence which Müller had sought in vain, suggests there is now no significant distinction between Cornwall and the remainder of the south-west of England, the supposedly more typically 'Celtic' distribution of blood groups being found in parts of Wales, in Scotland and in Ireland though it must be admitted that increased social mobility since the mid-19th century may have had more effect in Cornwall than in those other areas: J.A. Fraser-Roberts, 'The Frequencies of the ABO blood groups in southwestern England', *Annals of Eugenics*, xiv (1947–49), 109–116 and A.E. Mourant and A.C. Kopeć, *The Distribution of human blood groups* (2nd ed., 1976), pp. 65–66. I am indebted to my colleague, Mrs Anne Collins, for these medical references.

[84] Max Müller, 'Cornish antiquities', *Quarterly Review*, cxxiii (1867), 35–66.

[85] TD&C 2/2.

[86] Lambeth Palace MS. 2148, ff. 43–4 (Benson to Wordsworth, 6th August 1877); cf. W.H. Tregallas in *The Nineteenth Century* xxii (1887), 688 and the more recent observations of such writers as A.L. Rowse.

[87] J.S. Mill, *Considerations on representative government* (1861), p. 287.

[88] Church Congress, *Report* (1864), p. 16; cf. Hobhouse, *op. cit.*, p. 18.

[89] *RCG*, 6th October 1854, p. 6, cols. 1–2; Hobhouse, *op. cit.*, p. 16; cf. Hansard, 3 xciv (1847), 377; *CCC* (1858), pp. 25, 52–4 and *Church Quarterly Review*, iii (1876), 188–9.

[90] *Guardian*, 24th June 1891, p. 1051, col. 2.

[91] Cf. F.M. Milman, *Memoir of Robert Milman, bishop of Calcutta* (1879), pp. 46, 81–2 and 106.

[92] E. Stock, *History of the Church Missionary Society*, ii (1899), ch. lv.

[93] *Census 1851: population tables*, part 2/i (1854), pp. 356–9 and 362–5.

[94] *Census 1851: religious worship* (1853), pp. cxcix and ccii.

[95] G.B. Robertson, *History of the English Church Union* (1895), p. 116.

[96] He was 'high' in the pre-Tractarian sense: cf. *Illustrated London News*, 26th December 1891, p. 823.

[97] cf. *RCG*, 14th April 1865, p. 4, col. 6.

[98] Truro CRO: Vyvyan papers, 22M/BO/35/33 (Rogers to Vyvyan, 6th January 1860 and Vyvyan to Rogers (file copy), 7th January 1860); TD&C 3/16 (Falmouth to Temple, 21st February 1876) and 3/19 (Mount Edgcumbe to Temple, 10th March 1876). Mount Edgcumbe later sank his differences and became chairman of the Cathedral Building Committee (*RCG*, 18th January 1878, p. 8, col. 1).

[99] R. Williams, *op. cit.*, pp. v–vi.

[100] E. Norris, *op. cit.*, vol. i, p. x; H. Jenner, 'Traditional relics of the Cornish language in Mounts Bay in 1875', *Trans. Philological Society* (1876), pp. 533–42 and W.S. Lach-Szyrma, 'Le Dernier écho de la langue cornique', *Revue celtique*, iii (1876–78), 239–42. See also M.F. Wakelin, *Language and history in Cornwall* (1875), pp. 24–6 and 211–23.

[101] Royal Commission on the Established Church, *Second report* (1836), p. 2; cf. 6/7 Will. IV, c. 77 (1836), partly repealed by 1/2 Vict., c. 30 (1838), and W.P. Ward, *Isle of Mann and diocese of Sodor and Mann* (1837), p. 157ff. The secondary literature on the incident includes: W. Harrison, *An Account of the diocese of Sodor and Man* (Manx Society, XXIX; 1879); E.C. Wilson, *An Island bishop* (1931), p. 187ff. and, briefly from the political aspect, P.S. Morrish, 'The Manchester clause', *Church Quarterly*, i (1969), pp. 319–326.

[102] On Hexham: Lord Henley, *Plan for a new arrangement of the dioceses* (1834), pp. 21 and 34–6; G.C. Scott, *Additional cathedrals* (1854), pp. 3–4; Cathedral Commissioners, *Third report* (1855), pp. xli–xlii, and W.S.F. Pickering, ed., *A Social history of the diocese of Newcastle* (1981), pp. 24–52. On Coventry: *Church Quarterly Review*, iii (1876), 219–20.

[103] *Hansard*, 3 clxxiii (1864), 680.

[104] *id.*, 3 clxxxviii (1867), 1639–40.

[105] *Appeal for restoration of the bishopric of Cornwall* (1876): copy in Ch. Comm., file 1837/i.

[106] Lambeth Palace: Tait papers, 47/73 (minutes of committee, 6th April 1876).

[107] *id.*, 47/48 (Lushington to Tait, 10th May 1876).

[108] *Parliamentary papers* (1876), I 131.

[109] TD&C 2/2: Samuel Rundle to Temple.

[110] It might be noted that one of the most important mid-century statements by a churchman on the general need for additional dioceses, Christopher Wordsworth, *On a proposed subdivision of dioceses* (1860), was firmly based on common sense and the example of the primitive church.

[111] Wakelin, *op. cit.*, discusses this in detail from the Cornish angle.

[112] P.S. Morrish, 'The Struggle to create an Anglican diocese of Birmingham',

Journal of Ecclesiastical history, xxxi (1980), 79–82.

[113]   R.A. Cross reminded Disraeli on 9th March 1875 that his own and the party's view was that specific legislation for a few new dioceses was preferable to a general enabling act: Disraeli papers, Box 94/B/xx/G.

[114]   *CCC* (1876): Appendix, Report of the Committee on Deficiencies of Spiritual Ministration, p. 31. Thus Exeter diocese had some 960,000 souls whilst York, Durham, Chester, Lichfield, Manchester and Ripon from those which did not share the London area, all had more than one million each.

[115]   *Hansard,* 3 ccxxii (1875), 730–3; cf. T. Hardy, *A Pair of blue eyes* (1873), ch. xi. It was 105 miles by rail from Exeter to Truro and parts of north Cornwall had no railway at all until after division. In other dioceses for example: Carlisle to Barrow, via Carnforth, about 91 miles; Durham to Berwick, 81 miles and Chichester to Rye, 74 miles.

[116]   G.W.F. Hegel, *Werke,* ix (1848), 9.

Reviews

The Archaeology of Hampshire, ed S.J. Shennan and R.T. Schadla-Hall, Hampshire Field Club and Archaeological Society 1981, pp. vii + 121, 34 figs, 2 tables, price £6.50 + 50p postage and packing from the Publications Officer, 2 West Street, Hembledon, Hants.

This volume comprises thirteen papers delivered to a conference on the archaeology of Hampshire which was held in Southampton in 1978. The aim of the conference and now of this book, was to present to the public a synthesis of the great amount of archaeological research work carried out in Hampshire in recent years in the form of a general introduction to the archaeology of Hampshire, while at the same time suggesting to archaeologists the direction in which problem-oriented research might best be concentrated. The contributors had clearly been asked to consider both angles within their own specialist periods. The frequently encountered problem facing editors of the publication of conference proceedings is that of forming a cohesive and well balanced whole from a series of papers which inevitably reflect individual interests and biases. Shennan and Schadla-Hall have done quite well in achieving this balance though inevitably different papers slant in different ways; some, such as that on the Palaeolithic, concentrate on a synthesis and are consequently more useful to the general reader, while others such as that on the Iron Age concentrate on pointing out the gaps in our knowledge and suggesting future research topics, and hence are more useful to the professional archaeologist and are of limited value to the general reader in search of an up to date introduction to the Hampshire Iron Age. The majority of the papers are indeed highly academic in content and the volume is, in the opinion of the reviewer, more valuable to the professional or well-informed amateur. However it is by no means only relevant for these specialists in Hampshire archaeology as many of the papers raise issues and problems which are of country-wide importance.

The first paper, an introduction of Cunliffe to the remarkable background of archaeological work in Hampshire in this century, is followed by eight period-based papers, and a further four on environmental and field archaeological projects. Shackley's characteristically readable account of the Palaeolithic places the Hampshire evidence, as one really has to in that remote era, within its continental or world context and this paper and Jacobi's more detailed and complex paper on the Mesolithic, are mainly works of synthesis. Fasham and Schadla-Hall's paper on the Neolithic and Bronze Age is the first to provide both a description of the archaeology and recommendations for future research. The Champions' paper, however, is almost entirely problem-oriented and deserves serious consideration from archaeologists nots only in Hampshire but elsewhere as many of the points discussed are general for Iron Age studies throughout Britain. Both this paper, and Johnston's highly readable account of the Roman period state that the problem within these periods is not so much lack of material, but lack of material of the right sort to answer the questions now being posed. Hinton tackles the vexed question of the continuity of land divisions from the Roman and pre-Roman periods into the Saxon landscape and discusses the disparate nature of Saxon settlement in Hampshire, while Hughes' paper on the Medieval period is selective and he has chosen to discuss the rise of market towns and the nature of rural settlement within the period. Barton's account of the post-Medieval archaeology of Hampshire traces the changing fortunes of Portsmouth and Southampton to the present day, and this paper with the gazeteer of post-medieval sites is an unusual and welcome addition to the norm.

The next three papers, Barber's on pollen analysis, Coy's on animal bone studies and Renfrew's on plant remains reflect the early stage of development of research in environmental archaeology in Hampshire, although the same is of course true of the rest of Britain. These papers have little in the way of synthesis as so little work has already been done; this is, of course, a mixed blessing, and the benefit is that from the outset well-planned projects can be instituted, aimed at answering specific problems. Indeed, most papers in this volume stress the importance of problem-orientated work rather than the unplanned amassing of further repetitive detail. Shennan's paper, the final paper in the volume, also describes a project, an experiment in intensive planned field-walking over a given area to test on a small scale general hypotheses on the nature of settlement at different periods. This is a most interesting paper and the more detailed publication of the project should be well worth study. The necessity for further field walking rather than excavation is made very clear in many of the papers — the discovery of occupation sites is singled out as the most pressing problem in the Neolithic and Bronze Ages, and even within the relatively well-preserved Iron Age and Roman landscapes, open settlements on non-chalk areas need to be discovered in order that we should understand better the overall nature of settlement in the county. The pleas of most authors for better planned research strategies to pose questions and the organisation of research, field work and excavation to answer them is not new; how to solve this problem within the organisation of archaeology as it exists now is also an old headache. The final four papers, with Shennan's having the most relevance for the general archaeologist and field worker, describe practical techniques which should inspire similar worthwhile projects elsewhere.

Ancient Monuments Inspectorate   SIAN E. REES
Welsh Office, Cardiff

D.E. Johnston, *The Channel Islands: An Archaeological Guide*, Phillimore, Chichester 1981, pp xvi + 144, 40 plates, 71 figs, price £9.50

The archaeology of, the Channel Islands has in the past received a relatively thorough study. After the Lukis family in the 19th century provided a remarkable foundation for study, Kendrick's work on the archaeology of the islands published in the 1930s by him and Jaquetta Hawkes, was a landmark in archaeological survey. Since the 1970s, archaeological work, somewhat neglected after Kendrick's work, has again increased in intensity, resulting in a number of academic studies. Until now, however, a more approachable guide to the field monuments of the islands did not exist, and David Johnston's well written and useful book is therefore especially welcome.

The book is divided into two; firstly there is a general description of the archaeology of the islands and secondly, a catalogue which describes each monument in detail. The first discursive section is divided, conventionally enough, into eight periodic chapters from the geological background to the Migration period, with a final chapter on the history of archaeological study in the Channel Islands. The first chapter, on the geology, sadly too often written in similar works by archaeologists almost as a duty, and consequently either boring or incomprehensible or both, is here treated quite sympathetically with well drawn, clear figures adapted from original sources to be more readily understood by the uninformed layman, and this thoughtful consideration for the general reader is a characteristic of this book. Technical terms are never used without explanation, figures are designed to complement complexities in the text and Johnston seems particularly sympathetic in his anticipation of and response to questions which would be raised by the reader. The chapter on the Neolithic is inevitably the most weighty and vivid because of the extraordinary number of very fine chambered tombs that the islands boast and also because Johnston has himself made a special study of these, but he clearly has carried out detailed fieldwork on monuments of all periods and his utilisation of evidence from continuing or as yet unpublished excavations is particularly useful.

A problem which is perhaps almost inevitable in such a book is how to make the general archaeology of an area comprehensive while telling the story within the confines of the evidence provided by that area. Inevitably some subjects are going to be somewhat thin where evidence is lacking. The chapter on the Neolithic, for example, though entitled 'Farmers and Megaliths' says little of agriculture and agricultural techniques as the archaeology of the islands is poor in such evidence, though this is, of course, vital to our understanding of the Neolithic. On the other hand, in some chapters, Johnston attempts almost too much, and his text jumps between chronologically and subject-based accounts as he tries to place developments within their European contexts, with consequent confusion. This is truer of the chapters on the archaeologically rich and complex periods such as that on the Bronze Age. The chapters on the Roman and

Migration periods are clearer as less archaeological evidence exists for these periods.

The second half of the book is devoted to a catalogue of sites. A large proportion of sites are illustrated in plan, a description of each site is given with clear details of how to find it and whether it is open to the public or on private land. Interesting additional details, such as the folklore attached to sites, and further reading, makes this section of the book an ideal aid to the visitor, and will be a considerable help to the professional archaeologist, especially as Johnston most usefully also often comments on the present condition of a site and whether it is deteriorating. His concern for the well being of the monuments is also reflected by his frequent admonishments of treasure hunters. From the general visitors' point of view, it is a pity, of course that later monuments such as castles are not included, but the Medieval period is beyond the brief of the book. The only slight criticism to be levelled against this section of the book is that there are no references to the plates illustrating individual sites.

The standard of the illustrations is good with the site plans admirably clear, though it is unfortunate that the four Lukis drawings have suffered in reproduction so as to be quite difficult to make out. The number of noted textual errors is small — only the reference on page 38 to an unnamed site on page 00, presumably meaning page 133 is at all important.

Ancient Monuments Inspectorate   SIAN E. REES
Welsh Office, Cardiff

James Dyer, *Hillforts of England and Wales,* Shire Archaeology, Princes Risborough 1981, pp. 64, 18 plates, 20 figs, price £1.95

Here one has a personal contribution to the Shire Archaeology series by the series editor himself: James Dyer, and one immediately feels that this work achieves the commendable aim of the whole series. Into a mere 34 pages of text is compressed a considerable amount of factual information but written so that it is easily assimilated by the layman.

In the introduction the author immediately points out that 'hillfort' is used to refer to a range of field monuments and is often a misnomer but unfortunately, like so many before him, he is unable to think of a better word. He then looks at the principle features of the hillfort in turn, starting with the visually most obvious, the defences. He describes the now generally accepted developmental sequence from palisade, through box rampart to glacis rampart and finally, in the South East, the Fécamp style defence as seen at the Caburn, Sussex. Within this chapter the author includes some interesting statistics for the man hours required to dig the defences of a 22 acre hillfort with a box rampart. He suggests 200 men working an eight hour day could complete the work in 109 days. Unfortunately such calculations are always full of imponderables but it does indicate the magnitude of the task.

The entrances to hillforts are usually the most vulnerable to attack and thus often elaborated upon with inturns, out-turns, staggered entrances, hornworks, gates, guard chambers or a permutation of these. Here the whole range is discussed with the added suggestion that in addition to considerations of defence a 'certain amount of vanity and local pride was responsible for the design'.

More work has been done in recent years on the interiors of hillforts and a chapter is devoted to this, considering the various features that are to be found, including the now widely recognised 'four post structure' generally considered to be a granary. Interestingly the author tentatively suggests that they could be a series of barracks!

In the following two chapters the writer considers the origins of hillforts and how they may well have developed. It is now clear that palisaded hill top settlements were present in the Bronze Age and there are even possible Neolithic precursors. The author then turns to the latter-day hillforts and suggests that some which appear to be of Iron Age design may have been of entirely post-Roman construction and in one case even of Viking date.

Moving from the general to the specific the author examines in detail two hillforts that he has been personally involved in excavating and offers them as typical examples. This gives the reader an idea of what to expect in a medium size and a small hillfort, although the one thing hillforts seem to have in common is that they are all different!

The author concludes with a useful gazetteer of hillforts, with their National Grid references. A glance at this shows the preponderance of such sites in the South and West of Britain. This is one reason why this volume should be of special interest to readers in the South. However hillforts are such dominant monuments of the past that they demand everyone's attention. This book provides the information at a level suitable for the layman or student, but makes no pretension to be opening up any new ground, which is the job of larger and more expensive volumes.

Fishbourne Roman Palace   D. J. RUDKIN

P.J. Casey, *Roman Coinage in Britain,* Shire Archaeology, Princes Risborough 1980, pp. 64, 15 plates, 12 figs, price £1.50

Shire Archaeology books are noted for their striking cover illustrations, but this is the most impressive one yet, bearing a large colour photograph of a coin of the Emperor Claudius. One suspects that this book sells on the strength of the cover alone, because it is not what it might initially seem to be. A superficial glance inside reveals fifteen plates of assorted Roman coins and might suggest that here is a key to the identification of Roman coins found in Britain. It is not, far from it. As the author states in the introduction it is 'an attempt to place the coins in an historical and economic framework which defines the limits of inference within which coins may be used both as dating and as economic evidence'. That will immediately show that this is not light bedtime reading. It is a complex subject dealt with very competently but one feels that it would really only interest the numismatist, the archaeologist or the very determined layman.

The author divides his work into two basic sections. In the former he looks at the Roman Imperial Currency system as a whole. Here he outlines the development of coinage from Augustus up to the 5th century AD with its various reforms and the inevitable debasement of the currency as the central Government became more and more hard pressed. It is an all too familiar story. One has only to look at the new 20p coin.

Many people find difficulty in understanding the relationship of the various denominations, for example how many *sestertii* are there to a *denarius?* This is clearly shown in a set of tables, although it must be stressed that in some cases these are purely speculative.

The second half of the work concentrates on the Roman Coinage in Britain, specifically that found on town and military sites. Villa and temple sites have been excluded as the former produce few coins and the latter produce many, but of an atypical nature.

To analyse the coins from individual sites the author splits the time span involved into a series of periods, either the reigns of individual Emperors or the life span of important coins in lthe currency. This is then used as a basal axis of a histogram against which one coin per thousand notional coins may be plotted. Such histograms give an immediate visual pattern of the coinage found on the sites. The author points out that such patterns reflect 'factors other than the fate or status of individual sites; what we see reflected are largely monetary or political events', which must be rather depressing for the archaeologist.

A final section deals with coin hoards, the motives for hoarding, the likely content of the hoards and what they represent. Often the latter is not what one might expect.

A list of museums housing major collections of Roman coins is included, but it is pointed out that access is usually restricted to those seeking to obtain specific information. One feels that the same thing could be said about this particular book; it is for those seeking specific information rather than for the more general reader, but this is largely because of the nature of the subject.

As the coverage is Roman Coinage in Britain, the content has equal relevance to students in all areas. It should certainly be read by all archaeologists working on Roman sites.

Fishbourne Roman Palace   D. J. RUDKIN

Richard Hodges, *The Hamwih Pottery : The Local and Imported Wares from 30 Years Excavations at Middle Saxon Southampton and their European Context*, Southampton Archaeological Research Committee Report 2 (Council for British Archaeology Research Report 37), London 1981, pp. vii + 108, 60 figs, 12 tables, price £15.00

Despite the renown of Offa and the indications that important things were happening in trade, towns, coinage and the organisation of the state, the Middle Saxon period is in many respects one of the most obscure in English history. With written sources usually brief and laconic, particularly for home affairs, archaeology has much to contribute and Hamwih, Saxon Southampton, is a key site, an international mart that acted as middle man between Carolingian Europe and Saxon England. Hamwih has by now a quite considerable literature and Dr Hodges' new contribution to that literature is of major, indeed European, significance and goes far beyond the concerns of the pottery specialist. Using the analytical techniques, particularly thin-section analysis, that we have come to associate with the Southampton school of archaeology, he divides the Hamwih pottery into thirty-five fabric classes and analyses these with the aid both of mineralogy and of extensive travels in Europe seeking comparative material.

The hand-made Saxon wares are divided according to the tempering used and some of these, particularly chalk (Class 2) and shell (Class 5) suggest low firing temperatures, which agrees well with the experimental evidence (p. 85) that they could have been produced in simple clamp or bonfire kilns, a method which, as the experiments showed, would have left little archaeological trace. It is when Hodges extends his survey from Hampshire to Britain as a whole (Chapter 6. Middle Saxon Pottery : A Review) that the unevenness of our present knowledge of Middle Saxon pottery becomes apparent and for some areas the survey becomes little more than a catalogue of isolated sherds. The core of the book however is the catalogue of the thirty classes of continental import ware. Some, like Tating, Badorf or Beauvais wares are already familiar, though Hodges often has important new things to say about them. His study of Tating ware for example is one of several sections of the book which could have stood alone as an important article in its own right, though his discussion of the role of this literally flashy pottery with its tinfoil decoration as a high-status import seems a little elaborate, for it has been found not only on royal sites but in peasant villages, where one suspects it adorned the mantlepiece inscribed "A Present from Cologne". With Professor Vera Evison's equivalent survey of the Merovingian imports[1] and Charles Thomas's new survey of Early Christian imports in western Britain and Ireland[2] we now only lack a new survey of late Saxon imports of Pingsdorf ware and the like.

[1] I. Evison, *Wheel-Thrown Pottery in Anglo-Saxon Graves* (Royal Archaeological Institute 1979).

[2] C. Thomas, *A Provisional List of Imported Pottery in Post-Roman Western Britain and Ireland* (Institute of Cornish Studies, Redruth 1981).

Hodges has tracked down the sources of many of his imports with greater or lesser precision. They range from the Loire to the Rhine, with a heavy bias towards north-eastern France, Belgium and southern Holland. To anyone familiar with the importance of Ghent and Flanders to Saxon England this will come as no surprise. Some, like his northern French Class 14 Black Wares, emerge as important constituents of the archaeology of the period. Occasionally, Hodges' close familiarity with the mass of detail allows him to forget where those less familiar with it might welcome a little help. Some of the figures show pottery of several different classes with no indication to which class individual vessels belong and the reader is forced to seek this information by complicated cross-checking with the text. Similarly, despite several maps of continental Europe, one misses a single key map showing all the significant sites to help one follow the text. Some places, like Douai or Ghent fail to appear at all. These are minor grumbles however and in general it is not the least of Hodges' achievements that he has forged this mass of detail into a readable and fluent text.

The report is in the twin column offset-litho format which more and more journals are now adopting. This combines economy of space with ease of reading, though a more emphatic division between chapters (which tend to begin almost unannounced half way down a column) would make it easier to find one's way around a complex text. Proof reading and editing are of a high standard. Almost the only misprint noted (p. 43) refers to a Badorf ware pitcher of classis (sic) type. Brought back by King Alfred's fleet no doubt? This book will find an essential place on the bookshelves of all archaeologists working in the early medieval field, whether in Southampton or Stockholm and any serious economic historian of the period will find it required reading.

Ancient Monuments Inspectorate   JEREMY KNIGHT
Welsh Office, Cardiff

Councils and Synods with other Documents relating to the English Church I AD 871–1204, ed. D. Whitelock, M. Brett and C.N.L. Brooke, 2 vols., Oxford University Press, pp. lxxix + 1151, price £65.00

The publication of these volumes, after a gestation period of nearly fifty years, although extremely welcome, is a sad reflection on inflation. When Part II of *Councils and Synods* was published in 1964 it was 275 pages longer, properly printed (not photocopied typescript) and cost £15.00! Otherwise the model of the previous two volumes has been repeated, and there is no doubt that the four volumes together will be remembered long after all their respective editors have passed from this world.

These two volumes covering the period 871–1204 aim to bring together all the *acta* of English ecclesiastical councils or, especially in the earlier period up to 1066, those documents which provide an equivalent insight into ecclesiastical administration and legislation in case where such *acta* do not survive. Although they clearly provide easy access to essential sources for those involved in ecclesiastical history at a national level, they also provide an extremely valuable array of material which should not be overlooked by the regional and local historian, especially in the south of England, where ecclesiastical organisation developed more quickly and with less disruption than in other parts of the country. Thus these two volumes contain, among much other material, the Exeter guild statutes of the early 10th century, documents relating to the new minster at Winchester and concerning a dispute between the sees of Crediton and Cornwall in the late 10th century, and cardinal Imar's report on a manorial dispute between the bishop and monks of Rochester in 1145, all clearly of significance to anybody concerned with the early ecclesiastical history of southern England. The editorial standards are as high as one would expect from those involved in these two volumes, though there is one mistake in the location of manuscripts. The *Textus Roffensis* labelled Rochester Cathedral Library A.3.5., though still the property of the chapter, has been Drc/R1 in the Kent Archives Office at Maidstone for the past decade and more. It is perhaps an interesting commentary on the linguistic ability of even academic historians that the Old English documents have been published with a paralled translation, whereas it is assumed that all readers will be competent Latinists!

Kent Archives Office, Maidstone   NIGEL YATES

Patronage, the Crown and the Provinces in Later Medieval England, ed. R.A. Griffiths, Alan Sutton Publishing, Gloucester 1981, pp. 190, price £7.95

In 1953 K.B. McFarlane attempted to change the long-prevailing emphasis of later-medieval English historical studies on kings and the institutions of central government by devoting his Ford Lectures to the landed aristocracy. For nearly thirty years now some of his pupils and a further generation of scholars trained by them have been seeking to widen his diversification. The publication of these essays by eight contributors in book form is presented as being in this tradition and gives some indication of how far that process has now progressed. They are the products of a symposium held at the University College of Swansea in 1979. Each of these contributions would make an excellent article in any appropriate periodical but it has obviously proved very difficult to find one single common theme to embrace them all. Charles Ross describes the propaganda put out by the usurping dynasties to influence the common people; Anne Crawford writes on the cost to the fifteenth-century kings of maintaining England's queens; Michael Jones on the duke of Somerset's disastrous expedition to France in 1443; J.R. Alban deals with modifications made to England's system of coastal defences in the previous century. The remaining four essays do have the study of patronage in common, which the dust jacket describes as the social and political cement of the kingdom. Here, in fact, it is portrayed rather as the main solvent of national cohesion, the principal.means by which the competing affinities responsible for the persisting evil reputation of the fifteenth century was created. Martin Cherry re-explores the Courtenay-Bonville struggle in Devon and succeeds in shedding some new light on it; Ailsa Herbert describes the parallel disorders created in Herefordshire by the Devereux-Herbert gang. In each case various connexions with the central politics of the kingdom are suggested, but remain problematical. Rosemary Horrox delves into the ceaseless efforts of fifteenth-century towns to secure royal and noble patronage, while Robert Dunning explores the connexions between ecclesiastical appointments and promotions and the nobility and gentry of the south-west of England. All of these essays contain new material, much of it culled from local archive sources. The diversity of their subjects in no way detracts from their individual worth. Only three of the eight contributors are academics. The volume is evidence of the valuable role now played by local archives, their administrators and others outside the academic world in the diversification of later medieval English historical studies.

University of Exeter   B. P. WOLFFE

Keith Wrightson, *English Society 1580–1680*, Hutchinson, London 1982, pp. 264, price £12 (cased), £5.95 (paper).

Dr Wrightson's book — which joins the newly launched Hutchinson Social History of England — is aimed squarely at the student market but should appeal equally to the interested general reader. Extremely well written and constructed, its points are made clearly and convincingly and generalisations are re-inforced with apposite examples. Quotations from the printed autobiographies of the period, for instance, are used to remarkably good effect. The book is a model of its kind and a fine advertisement for the 'new social history'. Dr Wrightson casts his net widely and, in so far as it is possible, offers us a portrait of society in its entirety rather than a close-up of the privileged élite.

At the outset, the author pointedly reminds us that 'society is a process. It is never static. Even its most apparently stable structures are the expression of an equilibrium between dynamic forces' (p. 12). Accordingly, the book is organised into two main sections which deal with elements of continuity and with the forces of change and their expression. Two principal results, Dr Wrightson argues, emerged from the interaction between them. The first was that the localities were penetrated in this period far more deeply than they had ever been before by 'forces of economic, administrative and cultural integration which bound them more closely together into a national society and economy' (p. 13). Alongside this process, however, was an unprecedented extent of 'social polarization'. In the course of his period, Dr Wrightson asserts 'in both town and country a permanent proletariat had emerged, collectively designated "the poor"' (p. 141).

The author's exploration of these two related social phenomena is predominantly local in character, and in the course of it he uncovers significant variations in their chronology and geography. Local and regional historians will be grateful for his careful synthesis of modern research on the early modern English counties but will observe a certain, perhaps inevitable, imbalance. Whereas Essex, for example, the county on which Dr Wrightson's own researches have been concentrated, takes pride of place and merits forty-three listings in the index, counties like Middlesex, Hampshire and Surrey are scarcely mentioned at all. Local communities, however, loom large in Dr Wrightson's considerations and he is entirely convincing in what he has to say about the ties of paternalism and deference, kinship, neighbourliness and moral values which bound them together. 'Community', clearly, was not just a 'thing' or a place. His discussion of law and order, alehouses (on which he has published elsewhere), poverty, and witchcraft, for example, is firmly located in the context of community. 'From the point of view of members of the village community', Wrightson contends, 'the maintenance of order in the sense of restoring good relationships among neighbours might be better served by the avoidance of prosecution than by the stern enforcement of the law' (p. 157). The community framework of riots and disturbances is similarly emphasised, and here Wrightson, like E.P. Thompson, Keith Lindley and others, stresses how orderly, organised and legalistic these events often were. Their 'class conflict' ingredients, he insists, should not be exaggerated. The historian of the problem of order in this period, Wrightson argues, cannot avoid the conclusion that 'much of the drama of the government's statements and the crowds' menaces was indeed theatre' (p. 174).

Wrightson has interesting things to say, too, about family structure, about marriage, about the role of women, and about attitudes to children. Here he takes issue with *The Family, Sex and Marriage in England 1500–1800* (1977), arguing — as others have done — that Stone's interpretation of the emergence of 'affective individualism' virtually ignores the domestic and emotional experience of the great mass of the population.

On this topic, as on others, Wrightson's treatment is not simply descriptive but lively and exploratory. The book's two principal objectives, he announces at the beginning, are to convey something of 'the texture of the social experience of this period', the other to advance 'arguments about the nature and development of English society in the past which will stimulate as much as persuade'. There can be no doubt that the author succeeds impressively on both counts.

King Alfred's College, Winchester   R. C. Richardson

Country towns in pre-industrial England, ed. Peter Clark, Leicester University Press 1981, pp. xiv + 258, price £14.

This volume, one of the series 'Themes in Urban History', is a most welcome addition to the bibliography of urban studies. Comprised of four essays, each based on an original dissertation, to which is added a comprehensive introduction by the editor, it reveals afresh the fascination of the development of English towns and that strange admixture of change and continuity which affects all aspects of local history.

Each essay stands in its own right; each concerns a different community, and those towns themselves reveal their distinctiveness the one from the other. The choice of towns, too, has some special interest for readers of *Southern History* for, excluding Warwick, the other three — Ipswich, Winchester and Bath — belong essentially to the southern part of Britain. The choice, however, is far from arbitrary, for each essay emphasises patterns of life in a slightly different period of time and each stresses some aspect of life peculiar, though not exclusive, to the centre under examination. Thus A.L. Beier in 'The social problems of an Elizabethan country town: Warwick, 1580–90', is particularly anxious to show how the constant problem of poverty was a key element in the decline of the town of his choice. A late medieval economic decline which continued through the sixteenth century and into the seventeenth, despite and partly because of population growth side by side with the economic stagnation. Only after 1660 was there renewed prosperity (a feature not confined to Warwick), as the service trades for county gentry developed. The author also shows how the dominance of the Dudley family was reflected in the lack of economic growth.

In contrast, Michael Reed's, 'Economic structure and change in seventeenth century Ipswich', presents a picture of continuity and remarkable stability. If foreign trade declined, coastal trade largely took its place and while traditional industries were lost, the situation of the town as a stopping place for travellers to East Anglia and as a natural centre for county social life, helped the recovery of Ipswich's fortunes. 'What must have appeared to contemporaries to be decline was instead a change of direction . . .' is the verdict.

Adrienne Rosen's chosen centre is 'Winchester in transition, 1580–1700' and again there is a contrast. Here is a town of great antecedents struggling against political and economic changes of the period. Suffering severely from royalist and parliamentarian alike; partly isolated from the main stream of traffic along the Great West Road through Basingstoke and Andover; yet never succumbing and after the Restoration, like Ipswich in Suffolk, playing an ever increasing part in the social life of Hampshire. Tradition as the county centre held good, but the timely collapse of Southampton's fortunes and the slow growth of Portsmouth as a rival helped Winchester weather political and economic blizzard. Finally there is Sylvia Mcintyre's, 'Bath: the rise of a resort town, 1660–1800'.

Once more there is a story wholly distinct, yet containing the common elements of poverty and declining trade and, perhaps more acutely than the others the problem of suburbs outside the direct control of the city fathers. Bath, however had one special resource — its mineral springs — which, with the ascription of health giving virtues, turned what might have been decline into outstanding success. Beau Nash may symbolize the rejuvenated Bath, but essentially he built upon the resource already available and partially realised before his day.

To each essay is added a full and most valuable bibliography of original and printed material and the book is also completed with a brief but adequate index. Nevertheless four essays, however admirable in themselves, would hardly prove adequate without some indication of the manner in which they relate to the wider study of pre-industrial England and its town life in particular. This is the significance of the splendid introduction by Peter Clark. The four special case studies are placed in their context within the overall knowledge, albeit imperfect, of other comparable towns and our present understanding of urban development in this land.

This is, therefore, an admirable volume. Scholarly, yet eminently readable; setting, as it should, essentially local studies in their wider national context. It is stimulating and one hopes will inspire others to study the towns of their choice, be they large or small, so that a still more comprehensive understanding of their growth or decline, of the impact of demographic and economic change and of the nature of their local politics and structure may emerge. The archives of our towns are often particularly rich and have been too much neglected in the past or used insufficiently in an analytical manner. This book shows what can be done. It should prove a model of its kind.

Bearsted FELIX HULL

Anthony Fletcher, *The Outbreak of the English Civil War,* Edward Arnold, London 1981, pp. xxx + 446, 9 maps, price £24.

Anthony Fletcher's close examination of the events which grew into the civil war will be associated with two 'schools' of historians. It comes at a time of renewed interest in narrative as a historical *genre* and it complements recent work by revisionist historians who have sought the origins of the crisis in the short-term and contingent rather than in the broad sweep of events or in the inevitable conflict of social classes.

Anyone familiar with the staging-posts *en route* to the conflict will recognise the elements which are bound to figure prominently in any account. All are treated intelligently and with fresh insight. Some topics lovingly savoured in university special subject courses are dealt with more briskly; thus the remedial legislation of 1641 'gives a misleading impression of parliament's mood' and the 'paper war', the prelude to armed conflict, is scrutinised in its tactical not in its ideological dimension. Mr Fletcher concludes that 'the civil war came about because of the coincidence of

hopeless misunderstanding and irreconcilable distrust with fierce ideological conflict'.

Parliament emerges here as a body of constantly-changing moods. By
April 1641, and the task of reform still before it, the House of Commons
is losing its way and by the summer there is a palpable 'drift home'. The
progress of mundane legislation — on trade in currants and wool, for
example — is a counterpoint to the dramatic theme, now an indication of
a lack of opposition leadership, now a proof 'that the reforming impulse .
. . was not dead' (though one might query this apparent paradox). Mr
Fletcher's John Pym is a fuller if no less manipulative figure than J.H.
Hexter's, in *The Reign of King Pym*. With Professor Russell he finds it
significant that Pym 'had no county community behind him'.

This book is at its best in exploring the relationship between events at
Wesminster and in the provinces. The two-way correspondence between
Parliament and the country is given all the emphasis it deserves. Chapter
Six considers the petitions from the counties to Parliament, including the
well-known responses to the parliamentary Protestation, and the Kentish
Petition of March 1642.

The Kentish Petition is but one of many specifically 'southern' issues to
appear in these chapters. Naturally London was of key significance. Its
moods exerted untold influence on the conduct of affairs and its leaders
frequently took political initiatives; take the 'Root and Branch' petition,
for example. More generally, as the seat of government London was the
focus for the petitioning movement. The conceptual problem of 'southern
history' emerges here very strongly. Mr Fletcher confirms how in the
south-east the influence of Parliament was powerful and how in the
south-west, another world, a neutral localism prevailed.

The southern historian — and the midland or northern historian — will
find much here to interest him, although no strikingly original view of the
regional or local is developed. Mr Fletcher seems to hover between those
who use 'the county community' as a regular shorthand to describe the
local response and those who deny its universal validity. Such tentative-
ness must be allowed a pioneer, however; in an excellent chapter on 'The
Militia and the Array' Fletcher gets us away from those increasingly
tedious local studies which persist in regarding parliamentary and royalist
war efforts as phenomena to be contrasted, not compared.

This must have been a difficult book to write and it is not an easy one
to read. Those who expect a pure narrative (the blurb invites comparisons
with S.R. Gardiner, which comparisons Fletcher is keen to repudiate) will
be disappointed. The reader may find himself searching for chronological
landmarks which do not always seem to be there. Others will regret that
the analysis stops short in places; some economic and agrarian material of
the kind appearing in recent work by David Underdown would have been
most welcome. But these *caveats* aside, this is an impressive research
achievement which every student of the period ought to read.

Cheltenham   STEPHEN ROBERTS

Hampshire Studies, ed. John Webb, Nigel Yates, and Sarah Peacock, Portsmouth City Record Office, Portsmouth 1981, pp. xxvi + 334, 1 plate, 15 figs., £12.

The collection of eleven essays presented to Dr. Dorothy Dymond to celebrate her ninetieth birthday contains also a list of her publications and a five-handed appreciation which represents her civic activities, the academic world, her pupils, and her colleagues early and late. Dr. Dymond was principal of Portsmouth Training College from 1932 to 1956, and both before and after her retirement was energetic and effective in promoting the study of the history of Portsmouth. The book, well-produced and reasonably priced, is a handsome tribute to her. Of the eleven essays all but two are focussed on Portsmouth, and the title of the book is perhaps a little misleading. In period the essays range from the eleventh to the twentieth century, but only one has a medieval subject and the emphasis is heavily on the seventeenth to twentieth centuries. The writers do not belong to any one school of research, so it is not to be expected that they should show a high degree of consistency either in level of scholarship or in approach to local history. P.D.A. Harvey, on the Portsmouth map of 1545 and the introduction of scale-maps into England, putting the map in its context and showing its exceptional nature, and incidentally providing as much excitement as any of his fellow authors, wears his learning lightly. J.H. Thomas makes heavier weather of the account book of 1666 of the merchant Abraham Jaggard, and J.S. Bromley on the prize office and prize agency at Portsmouth, 1689–1748, is sailing in largely uncharted waters where the reader might expect more navigational aids and find it difficult to see the waves for the breeze. Much less demanding are E.S. Washington's mainly anecdotal study of Roman Catholicism in Hampshire in the 1580s, A.J. Marsh's consideration of the rise of Portsmouth as a naval base under the Commonwealth, and John Webb's account of the brief life of the Portsmouth historian, Lake Allen, and of the early years of his friend, Sir Frederic Madden, whose journal, the principal source, seems to combine Georgian arrogance and Victorian complacency but does not deprive the essay of its charm. Some of the writers use the evidence of Portsmouth history to test and modify accepted views of national history: Patricia Haskell in the longest contribution shows how and why Ship Money was relatively successful in Hampshire; W.N. Yates discusses and tabulates the statistics of attendance at church and chapel in south-east Hampshire in 1851 and in Portsmouth, Portsea, and Gosport in 1881, presenting his conclusions with commendable clarity and a brevity which may stem from his function as one of the book's editors; and R.C. Riley reproves any levity that his offering on the Portsmouth corset industry in the nineteenth century might provoke with a serious-mindedness that can refer to the use of the surplus labour of 'wives to whom the social system allocated inadequate financial support' and conceal a smile in using such a word as 'stochastic'. Others have more limited horizons: Sarah Peacock paints a colourful picture of Portsmouth's

M.P.s and parliamentary elections in the period 1885–1918 without questioning how far the constituency was exceptional or typical; Margaret Hoad on the origins of Portsmouth assumes that her readers have little knowledge of eleventh- and twelfth-century history but much of the geography of Portsmouth. In that essay and some of the others more maps would have helped. A few of the authors might with advantage have made their notes simpler and shorter. Nevertheless, all who are interested in the history of Portsmouth will be grateful for both the publication and the occasion of the book.

University of London   CHRISTOPHER ELRINGTON
Institute of Historical Research

Balleine's History of Jersey, revised and enlarged by Marguerite Syvret and Joan Stevens, Phillimore, Chichester 1981, pp. xiv + 306, 34 plates, 3 maps, 13 line drawings, price £15.00; James Whetter, *History of Falmouth,* Dyllanson Truran, Redruth 1981, pp. 109, 31 illustrations, price £4.95 (hardback), £2.95 (paperback).

These are both curiously old-fashioned publications but nevertheless serious contributions to local studies. G.R. Balleine's *History of Jersey* was originally published in 1950 and this version is a very substantial revision of the original work. Dr. Whetter wrote his history to celebrate the tercentenary of Falmouth in 1961, but the municipality was not prepared to publish it then and it has now been resurrected without any revision at all. It has to be asked in both cases whether the resulting publication is satisfactory and for this reviewer the answer would be in the negative.

Balleine's *History of Jersey* is the standard history of the island but it does not have the status of some late 18th and early 19th century English county histories which, with critical introductions, justify reprinting. What the revisers have done in this case is to use Balleine's model but to enlarge it and, where necessary, modify it, to take account of research undertaken since 1950. It is a pity that the alternative proposal to write a new history was not undertaken instead, although even then this would probably only have been successful if it had taken the form of a series of essays by specialists. The main problem with Balleine's book is that it is substantially an administrative and political history, rather than an economic and social one. The approach also is strictly chronological rather than topical. However, although one regrets that this publication was not conceived totally anew, this revised version of an old-fashioned history will give those who know little about the island a good basic introduction to the main events in its development.

Although Dr. Whetter avoids the chronological approach in his *History of Falmouth,* and divides his work sensibly into a consideration of broad topics, it is an enormous missed opportunity that the text could not, through revision, have benefitted from the considerable amount of work done on various aspects of economic, social and urban history over the past twenty years. As a result many parts of the book are curiously old-fashioned. On p. 84, for instance, he describes the Anglican clergy of the late seventeenth century as showing a 'lack of spirituality and a excessive concern for their material wants'. Religious developments in the nineteenth century are dismissed in less than one page. There is no analysis nor indeed use made of the religious census of 1851 and, particularly disappointing, no reference to the fact, well highlighted in the local newspapers, that Falmouth was a centre of Tractarian controversy at an exceptionally early date.

One good point about both these books is that they do seem to have made some use of archive sources, even though there is no record office as such in Jersey, and not simply relied on printed ones. It could, however, be argued that much better use of such material could have been made in both cases.

Kent Archives Office, Maidstone   NIGEL YATES

Jane Hayter-Hames, *History of Chagford,* Phillimore, Chichester 1981 pp. xiv + 143, 33 plates, 7 figs, price £7.95.

Miss Hayter-Hames' family has a long association with this small mid-Devon town and her book reveals her own affection for her birthplace. It is therefore sad that her book can only be described as an unfortunate example of the outdated, untrained, antiquarian approach to local history. It is full of uncritical generalisation and speculation, unleavened by any serious attempt at historical analysis and interpretation. The development of Chagford's economy and social structure, and the changes in its population, appearance and administration are not in any way adequately treated. Nor does the author show any knowledge of landscape history or vernacular architecture.

It is evident from the text that she has consulted a number of original sources, but without making the best use of them — the Protestation Returns and the Tithe Apportionment are reproduced simply as lists of names. She places much emphasis on the churchwardens' accounts, a potentially valuable source dating from the late fifteenth century. However, the inaccuracy of the transcript of these upon which she relies has been pointed out by a reviewer in last year's *Southern History* (p. 254).

Her work is further marred by the absence of adequate references for her sources — it is hardly sufficient to cite as a reference 'a pamphlet, 1618, in the Bodleian Library, Oxford' (p. 46). Her bibliography, which indiscriminately includes both printed and original sources together, frequently omits author's initials and even some of the titles of their works. There is no general description of the physical features and geography of the parish, and the only map is a small-scale geological representation of the whole county. Miss Hayter-Hames' approach is sometimes whimsical — she acknowledges the assistance of her ancestors, retells local ghost stories, and believes in the existence of ley-lines (one of which links St. Michael's, Chagford, in a line of similarly dedicated churches running down the country).

The excellent printing of the text and the attractive black and white illustrations and old photographs are not equalled in quality by Miss Hayter-Hames' text. Her style is uninspired and reads in places like a schoolgirl essay. The phrases 'no doubt' and 'we can well imagine' occur in almost every paragraph.

The early chapters on the pre-history and early medieval history of Chagford are composed largely of naively applied generalisations from secondary sources. This produces such absurd and meaningless statements as 'In 1017 Cnut became the first Danish King of England; and Chagford, like all England, was required to pay its danegeld for the upkeep of the king', (p. 11) and 'feudalism dwindled gently away' (p. 49).

Her attempt to interpret Chagford's Domesday entries is not happy. She is obviously unaware of W.G. Hoskins' excellent article 'The Highland Zone in Domesday Book' which no attempt at Domesday reconstruction in Devonshire should ignore.

In the latter part of the book she deals with the main families of Chagford separately from the rest of its history, a method which makes the content of these chapters somewhat repetitive. An undue emphasis overall is placed upon the larger landowning families, especially her own, and there are four pages of genealogies of the lords of the manor.

The author herself confesses in her introduction: 'I have serious doubts about my abilities as a local historian; my Latin is negligible, and my knowledge of English history incomplete'. The number of unfortunate mistakes in her text bears this out. For instance — the uncouth neologism in Judge Whyddon's Latin motto 'nigrog;' ('nigroque' when correctly expanded) p. 58; the erroneous identification of Gelliwig (recte Kelliwic) with Callington (see N.J. Pounds in *Devon and Cornwall Notes and Queries* Jan 1958. xxvii p. 39); and the assumption that since Chagford's medieval rectors had the cleric's courtesy title 'sir', they must have been knights participating in the Hundred Year's War (p. 31)!

It is a pity that this obviously attractive and interesting town, a market centre for the agricultural settlements fringing Dartmoor and of importance in the medieval tin trade, should be so poorly served by its local historian.

Kent Archives Office,   SUSAN GARLAND
Maidstone

Edward Bradby, Seend: A Wiltshire Village Past and Present, Alan Sutton, Gloucester 1981, pp. xii + 243, 46 plates, 5 maps and plans, price ¡6.95 (cased), £3.95 (paper).

To those readers brought up in the Hoskins tradition which regards local history as primarily the study of the rise, progress and eventual decline of the local community this very thorough parish history will come as a disappointment. The varied aspects of the history of the village are treated topically; themes such as the different types of communications, public utilities, the land, cloth trade, local crafts and trades, church and chapels, schooling, public houses and clubs, homes, law and order provide the structure of the book, and there is no sense of the chronological development of life in the parish from the Middle Ages to the present day.

Nevertheless the book is a mine of information about the history of Seend. The author has used not only the obvious printed authorities but has made full use of manuscript material in the Wiltshire Record Office. The original open fields and the enclosure between about 1650 and 1700 are touched on as far as the rather limied evidence permits, the development of a local iron industry in the later nineteenth century is fully recounted, the account of the inns begins in the seventeenth century, and there is a long chapter on schooling in the nineteenth and twentieth centuries. The book is excellently illustrated both with numerous plates and some useful maps and plans. Despite the weaknesses of its approach the book is scholarly and substantial, and a useful contribution to Wiltshire history.

University of Reading   C. W. Chalkin

Wiltshire Coroners' Bills, 1752–1796, ed. R.F. Hunnisett, Wiltshire Record Society, vol. 35 (1980) pp. liv + 239, price £10.00 + postage, from M.J. Lansdown, 53 Clarendon Road, Trowbridge.

This volume is dedicated to the Society's president, Professor R.B. Pugh of the *V.C.H.,* one of the great names of English local history. It contains an appreciation of his work and a very full bibliography of his writings.

This reviewer has been left with the feeling that nothing could tell us more about the lives of Wiltshire's eighteenth-century inhabitants than this record of sudden deaths among them. The fascination both with individual cases and with the exciting possibilities of aggregating is endless. Coroners' bills may be only a few short lines reporting inquests to Quarter Sessions for the simple purpose of claiming payment, but what a window they open on to conditions and attitudes. The dangers of earning a living are revealed as people fell into things, had things fall on them, fell off things, over things or had things run over them. Perhaps no one in eighteenth-century Wiltshire could swim, for if there was any form of water around they drowned in it: often intentionally. At a very serious level there is important information here on such matters as suicide, violence within the family or between neighbours, child-minding when unsupervised children fall victims to all manner of accidents, and especially interesting data on infanticide, a subject recently taken up by a number of social historians. Even when the inquest found a case to answer it is clear that the, usually unwed, mothers were rarely convicted. Industrial hostility appears with three workers shot while part of a mob attacking the house of a clothier, while six months later, in 1791 an unfortunate clothworker was mangled in one of the very machines whose introduction was most probably causing the hostility between workers and employers.

Recreation had dangers as well as work. Drunken brawls produced death at revels, skaters fell through thin ice, and an unfortunate bell ringer was carried up fifteen feet before falling to his death.

The real interest lies in the bills presented by the coroner for the North Wiltshire district from 1752 to 1796. Those presented by the South Wiltshire district are much briefer, conveying only: 'accidentally drowned' or 'burnt to death'. Such is the role of chance in historical research. Some regional historians have a goldmine in a source which elsewhere offers only the possibility of a perfunctory counting or listing. Only professionals, and especially visiting trans-Atlantic ones, choose their patch of England because of its archives.

The editor is a specialist in the area in which this volume falls, and the editing, prefacing and indexing are excellent.

University of Southampton   JOHN RULE

Somerset Maps: Day and Masters 1782, Greenwood 1822, with introduction by J.B. Harley and R.W. Dunning, Somerset Record Society, Taunton 1981, pp 37 + 15 map sheets, price £9.10 (in slip case), £7.60 (in plastic bag) from Local History Library, The Castle, Taunton, TA1 4AD

These two maps are among the earliest to cover the county of Somerset at the scale of approximately one inch to a mile. A third is the Old Series Ordnance Survey of 1809–17, which is being reprinted by Harry Margary, Lympne Castle, Kent. Neither of the maps being considered here has been reprinted before, and original copies are now scarce and expensive. A very real service is therefore provided to students of Somerset history. The Day and Masters' map is divided into nine sheets, and Greenwood's into six sheets, all presented folded to fit onto a bookshelf in either a maroon slip-case or a clear plastic wrapper.

The value is greatly enhanced by a splendidly-detailed introductory booklet, which sets out the background to the changing cartography of the county. The two maps concerned here span either side of the introduction of the Ordnance Survey sheets, and the Greenwood maps benefit from the new trigonometrical surveys and design features of the official maps. There is also a contrast presented in the biographies of the cartographers. Knowledge of William Day remains fragmentary, while his collaborator, Charles Harcourt Masters, is perhaps better remembered as an architect concerned with the planning and rebuilding of Georgian Bath. In contrast, much more is known about Christopher Greenwood, because of his national standing as a cartographer. Greenwood, in partnership with his brother John in offices in Regent St., London, saw opportunities to publish new county maps to replace the outdated eighteenth-century versions, and pushed ahead at great speed to cover large areas of the country faster than the Ordnance Survey could match.

For the student of regional cartography, there is also an excellent description of the technical production of the two maps. They are examined in the context of the geodetic survey and triangulations for the map, the topographical surveys, and the drafting and engraving involved. This section illustrates the great advances made in cartography between the two maps, and also the differences between the cartographers in the depth and breadth of their associations with the wider world of map production. Greenwood's was the more sophisticated, Day and Masters' the more original.

Perhaps the greatest value of the booklet is to be found in the section dealing with landscape history in the maps of Day and Greenwood. The local historian and historical geographer in particular will find the regional treatment of landscape change between 1782 and 1822 very informative. As such it will make an admirable companion to the recent Somerset volume in the *Making of the English landscape* series by Michael Havinden. The changing landscapes of the Somerset Coalfield, the Levels, the Parrett, South Somerset, and Exmoor are variously outlined at this crucial stage in the transformation from rural to industrial England. An appendix finally sets out bibliographical notes on the maps and a facsimile reproduction of the 'prospectus for and subscribers to C. & J. Greenwood's maps'.

For its combination of scholarly care and attractiveness to a wider public, the Somerset Record Society are to be congratulated on the production of this fine example of map reproduction and interpretation.

University of Sussex   BRIAN SHORT

John Webb, *Portsmouth Free Mart Fair: The Last Phase 1800–1847*, Portsmouth Papers no. 35 (1982), pp. 22 (illus), price 75p.

John Webb is an experienced historian, a professional who knows the national context into which a local study should fit. Apart from its value to those interested in a part of the past of a famous city, this pamphlet is a useful contribution to the· history of recreation and provides a local example of the conflicts over popular leisure activities between the 'respectables' and the 'roughs'. By the beginning of the nineteenth century Portsmouth fair like other famous urban fairs, St Giles' at Oxford for example, or the great Metropolitan fairs, had ceased to be a primarily trading occasion, (although John Webb demonstrates that this function never became negligible), and become a leisure provider for the lower orders. Lasting for two weeks to the 'respectable' trading interest of the city it was not only disruptive of business but also afflicted the city with a floating scum of pickpockets, tricksters and prostitutes. The last at least one would presume were not lacking in a seaport at any time of the year. The streets were filled with noise and drunken brawling. 'Respectability' finally closed the fair in 1847.

In detailing the range of amusements associated with the fair, not only on the ground itself, but also in private premises hastily transformed into dancing and beer gardens, the author usefully supports the thesis recently advanced by Dr Cunningham that there was no vacuum between the decline of traditional sports and the rise of mass organised sport in the second half of the nineteenth century. Rather there was a remarkable upsurge of a lively popular culture depending on a professionally supplied entertainment. By understanding the rude and vigorous nature of this new use of leisure time by the lower orders, we can see why the 'respectable' classes were so concerned to control it.

This is a most useful study of processes of change which were taking place at the same time in many English cities and towns.

University of Southampton   JOHN RULE

Records of Cornish Schools, Cornwall Record Office, Truro 1981, pp. 27 + 12 illus, price £1.20.

This is a welcome, useful and comprehensive summary guide to the records of Cornish Schools available in the County Record Office whose staff, judging from the articles they have contributed to the *Journal of the Royal Institution of Cornwall,* have an evident interest and expertise in this particular field.

A clear, informative and factual introduction tracing the development of education nationally and with special reference to Cornwall is followed by four different lists. The records of educational charities and endowments are dealt with separately from those of elementary schools both listed in alphabetical order according to place. More detail is given of the records relating to charity schools including the names of the charity or founder or type of school, the archival reference of the document, a brief description of it and its date (mainly eighteenth and nineteenth century material). Of additional assistance to the user are the references given to the reports of the charity commissioners and the Board of Education, including such reports for schools without other sources in the Cornwall Record Office.

The list of records of Cornish elementary schools makes extensive use of abbreviations, to which a key is first set out, and a shortage of space has prevented the inclusion of details about the schools themselves or records other than the nine most common categories. However, further information about elementary school records should be relatively easy to discover from the Record Office Catalogue, whereas the more miscellaneous material relating to the 'charity schools' would be more difficult to track down. Here the compilers of the handlist have performed a valuable service, drawing together the relevant records from all categories-borough, parish, diocesan, private, official and the office's collections of facsimiles.

An additional bonus is the two lists of school boards and the grouped managers which succeeded them with their dates of foundation and the names of the schools they covered. A final list is given of 'Additional Sources' such as Acts of Parliament and reports together with two short but useful bibliographies. The twelve black and white illustrations showing several different examples of the material available provide the student with an idea of the structure and content of the records, although being photocopies they cannot convey the original appearance of the document as well as photographs. But photographs would have increased the cost of this very modestly priced booklet which is securely bound and fairly well produced. Perhaps more use of darker type and underlining would have enhanced the clarity of the lists. An inset on accessions in 1981 brings the handlist up to date and a note at the front on office opening hours and appointments is sensibly included.

Well-produced subject-based handlists are invaluable aids to the searcher, particularly in the case of the records of education, attractive and popular sources much exploited now in their own right, and as part of larger local history projects, but which are usually scattered among half a dozen different record categories according to provenance, i.e. county council, parish private and public (DES) records. The investigation of charity schools especially could entail lengthy searches through family papers, from which, by the publication of this handlist, the Cornish student has now been saved.

One may hope that it may eventually be feasible for the staff of the Cornwall Record Office to pursue their good work further by surveying (and hopefully acquiring) the records of the 56 schools included in the list but for which no records have yet been deposited.

Kent Archives Office   Susan Garland
Maidstone

David Large, *Radicalism in Bristol in the Nineteenth Century* Bristol Record Society, University of Bristol 1981, pp. 20, price £1.00.

This paper emerged from a lecture and so has the brevity and sweep dictated by the latter's format. In it, Mr. Large reviews the main events in a long history of organised protest in his city, but with the greatest emphasis on the first half of the nineteenth century. As a review, it is stylish and lively. For a city most people link with the fires and violence of 1830/1 Bristol appears to have been rather a quiet place — its real Radicalism, whether working or middle class, seems to have been the prerogative of a rather restrained minority. Its middle class was too solid for a general dislike of the aristocracy to take hold but apparently not nasty enough to engender any very considerable working class antagonism. The last decades of the century are rather rushed over — one hopes a second pamphlet will follow on this. As an outsider I would have liked to see rather more on the social/geographical components of protest as the city grew. But, all in all, this is a valuable addition to local studies of radical movements and should certainly be on every university library's shelves and course lists.

University of Sussex   JOHN LOWERSON

Ports and Resorts in the Regions ed. E.M. Sigsworth, Hull College of Higher Education 1981, pp. 206, price £2.50.

One important, and often militant, contribution to the professional development of local and regional studies in recent years has been CORAL (the Conference of Regional and Local Historians); loosely structured, often strident in its voice, it provides workshops and seminars on a number of themes, aiming to shake complacency, open avenues for comparisons and offer new perspectives, largely for those in higher education. Some of its proceedings have been published and this is the latest to appear, eight papers on ports and seven on resorts. This circulation of tidied-up conference offerings is to be welcomed, given the problems of modern publishing, but the results are uneven. With three exceptions, those by Marshall, Beckett and Walton, the authors focus in so sharply on their chosen place and its slot in time that virtually no reference is made to other areas, nor to their work's place within wider regional debates and conceptual problems in the discipline itself. It could have been overcome, to an extent, by a critical introduction and a review of each section. This reviewer has a particular interest to declare here — he chaired one of the sessions and tried hard to draw out some of the themes common to the different contributors. To appreciate the significance of this volume it is really necessary to acquire the relevant issue of CORAL's newsletter/journal where the debates are recorded and that is a pity, although a good reason for joining CORAL! What one gets in this volume is a rich mine of local information, systematically worked over and, on the whole, rigorously presented. Liverpool, Hull, Cleethorpes, Margate, Lynton, Brighton and so on are laid out for inspection (alas without enough maps on the whole). But the reader then has to draw the threads out and it needs more than this to fill the hopes of CORAL.

University of Sussex   JOHN LOWERSON

University of Sussex Centre for Continuing Education: *Hastings Voices*, Brighton 1982, pp. 74 (illus.), price £1.60; *Scarpfoot Parish: Plumpton 1830–1880*, ed. Brian Short, Brighton 1981, pp. 57 (illus.), price £2.00; Sue Farrant, Kevin Fossey and Adrian Peasgood, *The Growth of Brighton and Hove*, Brighton 1981, pp. 66 (illus.), price £1.80.

The three titles reviewed here follow closely on the four discussed in the last volume of *Southern History*. The Brighton and Plumpton pamphlets can be considered together, since both result from the work of evening classes run by the Centre. *The Growth of Brighton and Hove*, dealing with the period 1840–1939, is the sequel to Dr. Farrant's *Georgian Brighton* reviewed last year, and adds much detail to the general picture outlined in Gilbert's *Brighton, Old Ocean's Bauble*. The beginning of the period is marked by the arrival of the railway, which had such a great effect on Brighton. In the succeeding years the town had to respond to changing patterns of holiday-making, partly caused by that, but was able to diversify into other activities, gradually becoming the regional centre that it remains today through population growth which took it from 47,000 in 1841 to 147,000 by 1931. Much of Brighton's growth was westwards, spilling into Hove parish, where population grew phenomenally from 2,500 in 1841 to 55,000 in 1931. Though the two towns remained separate for local government purposes, Dr. Farrant rightly points out that they should be seen as one conurbation during the period.

The pamphlet fascinatingly describes the physical growth of the two towns, showing by means of 'dot maps', using evidence from directories, how the fashionable residential area moved westwards. A special study is made of the Stanford estate in Hove, which was developed for building after 1870. The Stanfords were former tenant farmers who owned land in the right place, and urban rents in Hove, as in the Eastbourne and Edgbaston recently described by David Cannadine, provided the foundation for an opulent life-style that included, besides Preston Manor in Brighton, a house in London, a fishing cottage in Norway, a house in Madeira and a yacht. The last two chapters are credited individually to two members of the class; one well discusses the effect of transport on urban development, while the other comprises a preliminary survey of the terrible slums of the later 19th century which were the complement to the fashionable streets and squares. A concluding section suggests ideas and methods for further research.

Scarpfoot Parish: Plumpton 1830–1880, unusually for publications of the Centre, deals with a rural subject. Like many Sussex parishes, Plumpton lies in a long strip across varied geological strata from chalk in the south to Wealden clays and sandstones in the north, giving a scattered settlement pattern and varied land use. It too was greatly affected by the railway, which caused a concentration of settlement in the centre of the parish, where a new church and the village school were built. Like Dr. Short's study of Hailsham reviewed last year, *Scarpfoot Parish* includes sections on occupations, social structure, and social life, using the Census returns, parish registers, and local newspapers. The tithe map provides material for sections on agriculture and landownership. Since both the chief landlords were absentees Plumpton was far from being a 'closed' community, and the size and shape of the parish seem to have been one reason why the only resident gentry, the rectors, wielded relatively little power. Unfortunately, the available source material for the history of ordinary people's leisure activities is much less than that found at Hailsham, and it is only those of the gentry of which we know much.

Both pamphlets have striking black and white Astralux covers. But it is a pity that the text pages in each are rather unattractive to look at, with a tiny size of type that causes problems in the A4 format: *Scarpfoot Parish* has unbroken lines 20 to 25 words long which are tiring to read, while the unjustified margins of the Brighton pamphlet's double columns have a ragged effect. The scale of maps and diagrams often contrasts disconcertingly with that of the text. In *Scarpfoot Parish* pagination is the opposite of normal.

Both pamphlets also inevitably suffer to some extent from being compromises between the independent work of class members and the editorial control of the tutor. The standard of editing and proof-reading is not perfect in either, and *Scarpfoot Parish* contains some indigestible writing as well as scrappy paragraphing. Secondly, both publications, like earlier ones of the Centre, emphasise that they contain only interim findings. Evening classes, like research for theses, do not always result in neat and compact conclusions, but the reader may sometimes feel that he is being given less than the titles of such works seem to imply.

Hastings Voices represents a new venture for the Centre, since it comprises edited transcripts of interviews concerning life in Hastings and St. Leonard's c. 1900–40 undertaken by the Hastings Modern History Workshop, which is run by the Centre. The occupations of those interviewed include servant, maid, shop assistant, and netmaker. The chief themes dealt with are work and subsistence, social life and politics, and general 'welfare' (health, schooling etc.). As well as the national depression of the 1930s, Hastings also suffered, throughout the period, from its own individual decline, expressed in the 'down-market' trend of its resort facilities. It is notable, nevertheless, how many of those interviewed refer to eating meat regularly, though fish was naturally also an important article of diet. Social classes were more sharply defined than they are today, though interviewees differ about how much snobbery resulted. Of interest to the folklorist is the survival in a 20th-century urban environment of the 'wise woman', whose advice was always asked by neighbours on questions of illness.

The transcripts are described as 'edited', but it is unclear how far. Hesitation is only rarely apparent, and there is much less 'rambling' than one would expect from oral testimony. The questions put can be surmised from the recurrence of some themes, but it would have been fairer to the reader to list them in an appendix. What people remember spontaneously has a different validity from what they remember when asked; frequent references to trade union matters or to the incidence of Fascism in the town suggest a high degree of political awareness which the inhabitants of Hastings are unlikely to have felt. A third, though minor, reservation is about the restricted social origin of those interviewed, most of whom would probably be called working class or lower middle class. It would be interesting to have more oral history evidence (as distinct from memoirs) from the upper reaches of society as well; we know little, for instance, about domestic service as seen from the employers' point of view (e.g. how, where, and on what terms servants were hired).

The pamphlet has a useful centre-spread map and many well chosen photographs. Readers who know Robert Tressall's *The Ragged-Trousered Philanthropits* (1914) and its portrait of Hastings as Mugsborough will recognize the town described here as the same place — a tribute, surety, to the essential truth both of that novel and of this publication.

Victoria County History of Sussex   T. P. HUDSON

Angela John, *By the Sweat of Their Brow: Women Workers at Victorian Coal Mines*, Croom Helm, London 1980, pp. 245, price £11.95; Joan Burstyn, *Victorian Education and the Ideal of Womanhood*, Croom Helm, London 1980, pp. 185, 8 plates, price £11.95.

It is not inappropriate that these two books should be considered together. The pit brow woman, the subject of Miss John's study, was the very antithesis of the Victorian ideal of womanhood so sedulously cultivated by the middle classes and examined here by Mrs Burstyn within the context of Victorian education.

Miss John's book concentrates on the efforts made to restrict women's work in the mines in the 1880s. It is organised into three sections. The first is devoted to the exclusion of women from work below ground before 1880. The second part examines the life and work of the pit brow women. The third and major part of the book concentrates on the significance of the attempts to exclude women from the pit brow.

Miss John contends that the pit brow debate was part of the larger debate on women's employment generally. An unlikely combination of coal owner and suffragist was allied against the miners' union and others. Coal owners did not wish to see their profits eroded by the need to replace women with male labour or machinery. The suffragists opposed exclusion of women from the pit head because it conflicted with women's right to work and their, the suffragists', hopes for future legal and political equality. For the miners, the women represented cheap labour. There were also the coal owners who supported exclusion because, coming from areas where women were not employed at the pit head, they did not see why their competitors should benefit from this source of cheap labour if they could not do so as well. In short, each side used the issue of the pit brow women for their own, larger purposes.

Broader issues similarly motivated the parties opposed to higher education and defenders of the ideal of womanhood. They genuinely feared for the economic stability of the country: the growing loss of male labour and secure professional status which would be the logical consequences, in their opinion, of the higher education of women. Mrs Burstyn concentrates on this opposition to higher education for women. She examines in detail opponents' arguments in order to show how serious a threat the movement for higher education was to the ideal of womanhood: the woman who never worked, married young, ran her house and servants and cared for and was an inspiration to her family.

The opposition marshalled their arguments forcefully and succinctly. Not only did they oppose the higher education of women on economic grounds but members of the medical profession argued — and professed to be able to demonstrate scientifically — that women's brains were inferior to men's because women's inferiority in both mental and physical pursuits was obvious. They argued that physiologically the sexes were suited to different occupations. More dramatically, they argued that no woman could follow a course of higher education without becoming sterile. In short, women were unfit to compete with men in the professional and business world: the ideal of womanhood was entirely consistent with medical facts.

The clergy were ardent defenders of the ideal of womanhood. They helped define it and gave it a spiritual dimension. Women were the moral guardians of society. Using the bible as evidence, they argued that intellectual competition would destroy the modesty of Christian women and that careers would take them away from the duties of motherhood. To sum up, opponents of higher education tried to prove that the Victorian ideal of womanhood was based on sound principles and that to go against these would destroy the whole fabric of society.

Finally, Mrs Burstyn argues that higher education for women was accepted by the end of the century, not because the opposition had been defeated but because the ideal was impractical, was unrealistic economically — and intolerable to the women themselves. It is a lively, well-written book, as is Miss John's. Between them, they make useful contributions to the history of the women's movement and Croom Helm are to be congratulated for being prepared to publish these theses.

Portsmouth City Records Office   SARAH PEACOCK

Roger Penn, *Portrait of the River Medway*, Robert Hale, London 1981, pp. 192, 37 plates, 1 map, price £7.95.

By the end of the third chapter of *Portrait of the River Medway*, after a mere 25 pages, the reader could be excused if he enquires of himself what it is that he is reading. Already Mr Penn has touched on palaeontology and geology (his description of the High Weald), on Neolithic, Celtic and

Roman technologies, on the origins of place and river names, on botany (the life of the nettle), on Tudor politics (Admiral Lord Seymour) and on the proposed extension of the privately-owned Bluebell Railway. Unfortunately the author persists with this style of writing and, personally, I found this a difficult book to read.

There can be no doubt that this is a well researched volume and one can almost believe the publishers' blurb which says that 'the Author . . . walked the entire length of the river including the headwaters and many of the tributaries' — but one wonders how many extra miles were added due either to enthusiasm or to finance. Tonbridge is a legitimate subject since the Medway flows through the town but to devote 3½ pages to Tunbridge Wells which is neither on the river nor owes its origin to that particular water suggests a need to produce a set number of words to fulfil a contract. Some of these words, too, are old e.g. '. . . this rare sunny day in July . . .' (p. 59) '. . . those fifth-century barbarians . . .' (p. 85) and '. . . a third second-century Roman ship . . .' (p. 141 — no mention of two other ships).

Portrait of the River Medway is a book for the modern tourist wanting to know what should be seen and not too concerned with the accuracy of the information because, unfortunately, there are silly mistakes which appear to indicate either careless or hurried preparation of the text. In the chapter on Maidstone, for example, it is said that '[the Palace] was restored to Cardinal Pole by Mary and finally disposed of by Edward VI' and the builder of Maidstone prison and Mote House is given as David instead of Daniel Alexander. There is, however, much in the book that would attract visitors to the area and it must be seen as a popular guide rather than a serious study.

Kent Archives Office,　　　　　　　　　　　　　　B. G. THOMAS
Maidstone

Directory of British Oral History Collections Vol. 1, ed. Anne McNulty and Hilary Troop, Oral History Society, Bristol 1981, pp. 60, price £1.95. James Nye, *A small account of my travels through the wilderness,* ed. Vic Gammon, Queenspark book 11, Brighton, 1981, pp. 56 (illus.), price 90p. Jack Cummins, *The Landlord Cometh,* Queenspark book 10, Brighton 1981, pp. 48 (illus.), price 60p.

Oral history, which has found great favour with many local and amateur historians, still lurks on the edges of academic respectability, if only because, in the words of the entry made by Shepherds Bush Library in the first of these volumes, 'the information acquired was found to be largely inaccurate, for the most part inconsequential, and in any case (where substantial) already available in written sources'. Fortunately this is a by no means universal experience. The Oral History Society's first *Directory* is to be welcomed, offering as it does a place/region as well as subject index. It lists 231 collections, public and private, with holdings ranging from songs and work to early flying and the experiences of Methodist ministers, though not necessarily both together. Anyone using this valuable resource frequently would be well advised to purchase a new binder for it — the staples fall out after a couple of openings. Every library should have it, so should every local historian.

By comparison, the latest products of Queenspark have a material sophistication which reveals how far cheap publishing has travelled recently, and their contents are much stronger stuff, although their origins in a concern with 'people's history' are the same. This reviewer, who commented on one of the texts at an early stage in its preparation, was pleased to find himself listed as one of the 'work team' within — perhaps there is a lesson here for all those of us who list their every helper in prefaces; make them feel part of it. Vic Gammon's edition of Nye's diary (oral history in print) has a much greater than local interest. Nye (1822–1892) was a poet, musician, gardener at Ashcombe House by Lewes (in a more recent incarnation the official residence of Sussex's vice-chancellor) and a Calvinist and sermon-taster, born again, who saw God's hand in everything. There are times when the spirits of the seventeenth century and Baxter run through these pages. For anyone interested in religion at the lower levels, this is a must.

The other work, by Cummins, is one more familiar in style and message to most modern readers, perhaps too much so. From interviews and text we see a Catholic turned secularist, a worker-poet and first world war rifleman — into the trenches yet again. Sadly, Jack Cummins died the day the book went to press — oral history's rescue role sharply illustrated. Both booklets are well-produced and illustrated and bargains at the price. The Nye diary is outstanding.

University of Sussex   JOHN LOWERSON

T.X.H. Panchaff, *Alderney: Fortress Island,* Phillimore, Chichester 1981, pp. viii + 86, 7 figs, 35 plates, price £1.95.

There have been other books and at least one television series about the German occupation of the Channel Islands but this small volume concentrates on Alderney and tells of the horros perpetuated by the officers and men of the *Wehrmacht* whilst occupying a small part of Britain.

Alderney: Fortress Island is a strictly factual book and as such contains passages that could be upsetting. Unfortunately these descriptions of, for example, the treatment of Poles are essential in a true report on life on the island between July 1940 and May 1945. The author, in 1945 an officer in Military Intelligence who questioned the German garrison, has attempted to end the rumours that have circulated concerning the enemy occupation of the island. There is no attempt to draw conclusions or to make excuses for the régime that administered the Channel Islands; this is a book that puts the record straight and is a necessary addition to the written history of World War II.

Kent Archives Office   B. G. THOMAS
Maidstone

The Fight for Bristol, ed. G. Priest and P. Cobb, Bristol Civic Society 1980, pp. 128 (illus.), price £2.95.

Published to mark the seventy-fifth anniversary of the founding of the Bristol Civic Society, this book records the change in attitudes to planning and architecture in Bristol since 1945, and the resultant changes in the face of the city. The ten contributors to the book are activists in the amenity movement in Bristol, and so the book concentrates on the changing relationship between the planners and amenity societies with an emphasis on the impact of public or community opinion on planning issues. The book is divided into three parts. The first section gives the background to the problems facing the city planners in 1945, how the problems were tackled, the rise of public concern and protest, together with the formation of new amenity societies. The second section consists of case studies: the Outer Circuit Road, the Avon Gorge and the Grand Spa Hotel, Kingsdown and the Hospital Board, and the City Docks. The third section details the changes in the 1970's as the amenity societies grew stronger and more forceful in their advocacy of particular ideas: new uses for old buildings, urban renewal, conservation programmes, and open spaces, trees and woodlands.

Bristol provides so much material for a study of the implementation of planning policies, and the authors provide a good account of planning iniatives and changing attitudes, particularly in the 1960s and 1970s. New concepts, such as the Broadmead shopping centre and grandiose road schemes designed to appease the dominant motor car, are described as arethe advances of the developers in the private sector, in the form of insensitive office development, and the public sector with the destruction of so much property to provide space for the hospital and the university. The destruction of communities and districts, together with familiar and reassuring townscapes, are shown as the contrast. Examples of the more recent conservation counterattack, including conservation of old buildings and the creation of a new park, allow the book to end on a note of hope.

Interesting as the book is to read, one is left with an impression of blandness as one puts the book down. This reviewer would have welcomed a frank assessment of the real impact of amenity societies on Bristol, an analysis of successes and failures, together with the lessons to be learned from them and a view on whether amenity societies lead or follow public opinion. Fashions in planning form the theme of the book — are the authors confident that conservation will not prove another fashion?

Perhaps some of the answers will be given in a centenary publication of the Bristol Civic Society!

Maidstone   PAUL OLDHAM

Sussex Bibliography 1980, ed. E.A. Hollingdale, East Sussex County Library, Lewes 1982, pp. 64, price £1.00 + 20 pence postage and packing.

Since 1974 the East Sussex County Library has produced annual (on one occasion biennial) lists of new books and articles on Sussex, historical and otherwise, aided by the West Sussex County Library, and in the present case by the West Sussex Record Office. The term 'bibliography' probably suggests to the user a more coherent compilation than the pamphlet here reviewed actually is: it is seriously deficient in both arrangement and scope.

The arrangement of entries is first A to Z by subjects, and then A to Z by places. The system seems to have been to enter items if possible under place, if not then under subject, but not under both. The place names used are not logically chosen; sometimes they are parish names, sometimes not. A user looking up Treyford would not find Hooksway in Treyford parish, which is under 'H'; Chilgrove in West Dean is similarly under 'C'. There are separate entries for Beeding and Upper Beeding, referring to the same place. Places are not always correctly located; e.g. Little Thakeham is in Thakeham parish, not Storrington. The subjects seem to have been chosen at random and are often misleading. There is an entry for agriculture but another for enclosure, one for canals and another for Royal Military Canal, one for walking and another for the South Downs Way. The headings on page 17, taken almost at random, include geology, ghosts, golf, gypsies, health, hearth tax, heraldry and history (the last has six oddly assorted titles). The largest group of entries — nearly 5 pages — is for biography and autobiography; many of the people named are unidentified or unidentifiable. The lack of cross references means that the user looking up archaeology would not realize that many entries in the 'places' list refer to particular excavations. The only way to use the pamphlet, in fact, is to read it right through, which surely negates the idea of a bibliography.

The scope of what is included, too, is uncritical. Alongside serious and scholarly articles and books is much that is secondary or of ephemeral interest, but there is no indication which is which. Anyone interested in the history of, say, Shoreham, would not discover that the recent *V.C.H.* volume (entered under 'history') contained one of the most detailed accounts of the town ever written, but instead would find only references to two newspaper artciles and one leaflet. Such an approach may satisfy the general enquirer, but to the serious local historian, especially the inexperienced, it is unhelpful. On the credit side, the bibliography includes many unusual references which the user is unlikely to have come across by himself. It is a pity that the arrangement and scope of the pamphlet tend to obscure them.

Victoria County History of Sussex ⸱T. P. HUDSON

Christopher Hibbert, *The Court at Windsor,* Penguin Books, London 1982, pp. 240 (illus.), price £4.95.

First published in 1964, revised in 1977 and now published by Penguin Books in 1982, Christopher Hibbert's *The Court at Windsor* is no learned treatise on political or constitutional developments. It is not a book about architecture nor is it a disquisition on the development of court etiquette. It is quite simply a domestic history in the sense that it relates to a home — Windsor — and the people who lived there, the kings and queens of England. Mr Hibbert looks at their personalities, their preoccupations, their pleasures and the routine of their lives at Windsor. It is an amusing and light-hearted book. The later chapters are made up of the sort of copy which is the very stuff of the better sort of gossip column. The illustrations are numerous and well-chosen. There are lush coloured photographs of pictures of the castle and surrounding countryside from the Royal Collections. It is a nice book.

Portsmouth City Records Office SARAH PEACOCK

ANNUAL REVIEW OF PERIODICAL LITERATURE

The articles listed below were mostly published in 1981. Archaeological, geographical or sociological articles have generally been excluded. The review aims to cover both national and local journals but any significant omissions should be brought to the attention of the review editor who will arrange for their inclusion in a subsequent review.

Abbreviations

AC	*Archaeologia Cantiana*
AHR	*Agricultural History Review*
DCNQ	*Devon and Cornwall Notes and Queries*
DH	*Devon Historian*
Econ HR	*Economic History Review*
FLTR	*Friends of Lydiard Tregoze Reports*
HR	*Hatcher Review*
HT	*History Today*
JEH	*Journal of Ecclesiastical History*
JHMS	*Journal of Historical Metallurgy Society*
JRIC	*Journal of Royal Institution of Cornwall*
Man	*Manuscripta*
MA	*Medieval Archaeology*
PDNHAS	*Proceedings of Dorset Natural History and Archaeological Society*
PLDLHS	*Proceedings of Leatherhead and District Local History Society*
SANH	*Somerset Archaeology and Natural History*
SDNQ	*Somerset and Dorset Notes and Queries*
SH	*Sussex History*
Sur AC	*Surrey Archaeological Collections*
Sus AC	*Sussex Archaeological Collections*
TBGAS	*Transactions of Bristol and Gloucestershire Archaeological Society*
TDA	*Transactions of Devonshire Association*
TMBS	*Transactions of Monumental Brass Society*
WAM	*Wiltshire Archaeological Magazine*
WANHSAB	*Wiltshire Archaeological and Natural History Society Annual Bulletin*
WF	*Wiltshire Folklife*
WI	*Wealden Iron*

(1) General Articles

R.W. Bushaway discusses the oak-apple day custom of carrying branches from Grovely Wood to Salisbury Cathedral, in *HT* xxxi 37–43.

Brian Carne contributes a third article on the triptych in Lydiard Tregoze church, in *FLTR* xiv 23–46.

Jean Morrison chronicles the history of the Great Barn, Avebury, which now houses the museum of the Wiltshire Folk-Life Society, in *WF* ii (2) 25–8.

P.H. Robinson describes and illustrates the Devizes Museum Collection of Wiltshire banknotes and related items, in *WANHSAB* xxvii 7–12.

P.A.S. Pool provides a valuable exposition of the tithings of Cornwall, their origins, functions and decline, with tables and maps, in *JRIC* viii 275–337.

Richard Coates lists *addenda* and *corrigenda* to the English Place-Name Society's volume on Sussex, in *Sus AC* cxviii 309–29.

(2) Before 1500

A.G. Pugsley discusses Devon's 'leahs', a feature of Saxon settlement, in *DCNQ* xxxiv 313–19.

Heinrich Härke re-examines an Anglo-Saxon shield from Petersfinger, near Salisbury, and is able to show that the accepted view that such shields were laminated is a myth, in *MA* xxv 141–4.

Katherine Barker uses the topography of Sherborne, Beaminster and Wimborne to examine some problems of early ecclesiastical settlement in Dorset, in *PDNHAS* cii 107–11.

Michael Cowan tries to identify the site and course of the battle of Searoburh, AD 552, in the vicinity of Old Sarum and Salisbury, in *HR* ii (11) 3–11.

E.W. Holden and T.P. Hudson describe Saxon and medieval salt-making in the Adur valley, using all the available archaeological and documentary evidence, in *Sus AC* cxix 117–48.

R.B. Pugh takes issue with Malmesbury's claim that its first borough charter was granted in AD 880, and shows that no town may claim to be the oldest borough in England, no pre-conquest kings granted charters to boroughs, however defined, and no event in Malmesbury's history is known to have occurred in AD 880, in *WAM* lxxxiv-lxxxv 133–6.

J.H. Harvey identifies the scattered Templar properties in east Somerset, in *SDNQ* xxxi 135–41.

J.H.P. Gibbs reconstructs the medieval buildings of Dunster Castle, in *SANH* cxxv 1–15.

Mary Whitfield surveys the documentary sources for the medieval field systems of south-east Somerset, in *SANH* cxxv 17–29.

E.C. Norton discusses the medieval floor tiles of Christchurch Priory, their designs and the evidence they provide for the medieval tile industry in Dorset and Hampshire, in *PDNHAS* cii 49–64.

W.J. Blair continues his valuable series of calendars of medieval deeds of properties in Leatherhead, and with J.H. Harvey examines the architectural and documentary evidence for the building known variously as the Chapel House and Old Rising Sun, Fetcham, in *PLDLHS* iv 86–96, 118–33.

J. Edwards describes a medieval wall-painting at Hales, in *TBGAS* xcix 167–9.

Daphne Stroud discusses the relationship between the Salisbury *Magna Carta* and the three other surviving exemplars, and suggests that Salisbury's may be a copy made for Elias de Dereham shortly after the charter was granted, in *HR* ii (12) 51–8.

Clive Orton considers the development of the Surrey White Ware tradition and the supply of pottery to the London market from the mid 13th to the late 15th centuries, in *Sur AC* lxxiii 49–92.

W.M.M. Picken provides a painstaking edition of Oto of Bodrugan's charter of 1320 to East Looe, which quotes in full Lucy Russel's charter of c.1220, in *JRIC* viii 350–7.

Hugh Kitching offers an account of the Augustinian priory of Maiden Bradley, near Warminster, founded as a leper asylum in 1152, to its dissolution in 1536, in *HR* ii (12) 70–7, and discusses the three Wiltshire enclaves, Swallowfield, Wokingham and Hurst, transferred to Berkshire in 1844, in *WANHSAB* xxvii 2–3.

H.F. Owen Evans discusses a reputed monumental brass of Ela, Countess of Salisbury, at Lacock Abbey, in *TMBS* xiii 35–40.

Nicholas Orme, in an important study of education and learning at Exeter Cathedral between 1380 and 1548, argues that its clergy were highly literate and maintained the educational interests fostered by cathedrals before the establishment of universities, in *JEH* xxxii 265–84; he also discusses the medieval chantries of the cathedral, in *DCNQ* xxxiv 319–26, and its vicars and annuellars, in *TDA* cxiii 79–102.

B.G. Awty analyses the continental origins of Wealden ironworkers between 1451 and 1544, in *Econ HR* xxxiv 524–39.

C.J. Dudley dates, describes and illustrates the small portrait carvings of the pulpitum in Canterbury Cathedral, in *AC* xcvii 185–94.

William Smith offers a detailed analysis and description of a 15th century manuscript book of hours in the parochial library at Steeple Ashton, in *Man* xxv 151–63.

J.N. Hare suggests a new interpretation of the demesne lessees of 15th century Wiltshire, in *AHR* xxix 1–15, and describes the fortunes of a well documented chalkland village, Durrington on Salisbury plain, in the late medieval period, in *WAM* lxxiv-lxxv 137–47.

H.J.M. Stratton and B.F.J. Pardoe provide a history of Chertsey bridge, first constructed from timber by royal licence in 1410, and its replacement by the present handsome stone bridge in 1780, in *Sur AC* lxxiii 115–26.

(3).1500–1750

S.R.C. Poulter surveys the Court connections and varying fortunes of the Stydolf family, who held Norbury manor in Mickleham, and other estates in London and Surrey, between 1475 and 1662, in *PLDLHS* iv 99–101.

Sir John Winnifrith reveals the remarkable continuity and stability of land ownership in Appledore between 1500 and 1900, in *AC* xcvii 1–6.

M.L. Zell examines the Crown estate in Kent and what happened to it between the mid-1530's and the accession of Elizabeth I, in *AC* xcvii 53–70.

A.H.A. Hogg re-examines the history and provides a description of an Elizabethan redoubt on West Wickham Common, in *AC* xcvii 71–8.

Jeremy Goring provides a 'multiple biography' of members of the Elizabethan borough jury of Lewes, which exercised a semi-autonomous role in the government of the town, in *Sus AC* cxix 157–72.

A.R. Morris considers the effect of the Reformation legislation on Sussex schooling, and endorses recent views that it was not as catastrophic as was once thought, in *Sus AC* cxix 149–56.

James Barber uncovers Sir Francis Drake's investment in Plymouth property, in *TDA* cxiii 103–8.

K.D. Henderson transcribes and annotates the will of John Bayley, mayor of Salisbury, who died in 1600, in *HR* ii (12) 86–91.

D.E. Williams describes some post-medieval pottery in the second part of a report on excavations at Chatham, in *AC* xcvii 261–73.

Victor Chinnery notes some members of the Salisbury Joiner's Company and their products in the early 17th century, in *HR* ii (11) 32–5.

Suzanne Eward describes the wayward career of Stephen Jefferies, a 17th century Salisbury chorister appointed cathedral organist at Gloucester, in *HR* ii (11) 26–31.

B. Frith provides biographical details of Abel Wantner, a 17th century unpublished Gloucestershire historian, in *TBGAS* xcix 170–2.

L.M. Costello discusses the Bradford Poole case, a 17th century conflict in Devon between the common law and the stannaries, in *TDA* cxiii 59–77.

J.H. Bettey discusses sheep farming in 17th century Dorset, in *PDNHAS* cii 1–5, and drovers and the movement of livestock in the 17th century, in *SDNQ* xxxi 158–61.

Selby Whittingham contributes a brief biography of the Salisbury painter John Greenhill (1642–76), with a list of his paintings, in *HR* ii (12) 58–69.

R.K.G. Temple reports on the significant discovery of 'what may be the only surviving manuscript eye-witness account of the battle of Maidstone in 1648', in *AC* xcvii 209–20.

K.D.M. Snell considers, with a lavish use of graphs and statistical data, agricultural seasonal employment, the standard of living and women's work in the southern and eastern counties of England between 1690 and 1860, in *Econ HR* xxxiv 407–37.

Gertrude Morey examines the founding of the free school in South Molton by Hugh Squier (1625–1710), in *DH* xxiii 7–11.

R.A. Lever provides a note giving details of conditions and rents from seven Ashtead farm leases for the period 1692–1727, in *TLDLHS* iv 141–4.

(4) After 1750

G.J. Davies describes Dorset's trade in tobacco, in *SDNQ* xxxi 216–18, and gives a graphic account of wreck and plunder in 18th century Portland in *PDNHAS* ciii 1–4.

Sue and John Farrant show how the decline of the once prosperous fishing town of Brighton from the late 17th century was reversed by its transformation from the 1740s into a major resort, which by 1820 was growing fast, in *Sus AC* cxviii 331–50, and the former illuminates downland estate management practice in *c*.1800 with the help of the surviving memorandum book of William Roe of Withdean, near Brighton, in *Sus AC* cxix 173–80.

Colin Edwards edits the itinerary of William Wynne's first visit to his Cornish estates in 1755, in *JRIC* viii 338–49.

M. Richards describes two 18th century Gloucester gardens, in *TBGAS* xcix 122–6.

Eileen Hornby examines the importance of the musical festivals held annually in 18th century Salisbury under the patronage of James Harris, in *HR* ii (12) 78–85.

D.A. Crowley discusses the business that was conducted in the 18th century manorial courts of Downton, and shows that the records created were sophisticated, business-like and of great local importance, in *WAM* lxxxiv-lxxxv 148–60.

David Butler describes some connections between iron-making in Sussex and in Scotland in the 1760s and 1770s, in *WI* 2nd series i 24–31.

H.B. Jameson analyses some new evidence concerning indentured servants who left Bristol for North America between 1763 and 1768, in *TBGAS* xcix 127–40.

Ena Cumming shows the wave-like fluctuations in illegitimacy and bridal pregnancy in Ottery St. Mary between 1602 and 1837, in *DH* xxiii 25–9.

J. Boyle provides an interim report on some significant discoveries about Edward Hasted and his History of Kent, in *AC* xcvii 235–59.

C. Staal uses some recently discovered correspondence to chronicle William Cookworthy's early struggles to turn Cornish china clay into satisfactory porcelain, in *JRIC* viii 267–74.

J.P. Dodd provides a detailed account of Dorset agriculture between 1800 and 1854, in *PDNHAS* cii 7–14.

Rodney Cruse describes the activities of a family of dew-pond makers living at Imber on Salisbury Plain in the 19th century, including details of the method of construction, in *WF* iii (2) 18–24.

Desmond Hawkins uses letters addressed to Sir Thomas Grove, M.P., to examine Victorian politics in south Wiltshire, in *HR* ii (11) 12–18

Tiffany Hunt describes the activities of a group of 19th century ceramic collectors in Salisbury, including James Nightingale and Raphael Read, in *HR* ii (11) 19–25.

Mark Baker describes aspects of the life of the Wiltshire agricultural labourer of *c*.1850, in *WAM* lxxxiv-lxxxv 161–9.

U.W.R. Casebourne considers the industrial archaeology of the Great Western Railway secondary main lines, in *WAM* lxxxiv-lxxxv 170–9.

K.H. Rogers selects some of the word portraits by Canon J.E. Jackson, the Wiltshire antiquary and scholar, of his parishioners at Leigh Delamere in *c*.1850, in *WANHSAB* xxvii 4–6.

Bruce Coleman discusses Exeter in the 1851 census of religious worship, in *DH* xxiii 2–6.

Helen Harris looks at 19th century granite working at two sites in western Dartmoor, in *TDA* cxiii 29–51.

M. Waters analyses the work force of Chatham dockyard in *c*.1860, in *AC* xcvii 79–94.

C. Miller details the history of the Gloucestershire Steam Plough Company in 1860–2, in *TBGAS* xcix 128–56.

Roy Day provides a comprehensive account of the Wiltshire iron industry, centred on iron works at Westbury and Seend, between 1855 and 1949, in *JHMS* xv 18–38.

E.B. Short describes the important Bridport textile industry, in *SDNQ* xxxi 205–9.

J.B. Walker provides an interesting statistical analysis of child mortality and public health in Lyme Regis between 1856 and 1979, in *PDNHAS* ciii 5–12.

Roger Homan discusses the Society of Dependents, a 'peculiar' sect in

West Sussex, from 1850, using oral evidence and manuscripts belonging to its members, in *Sus AC* cxix 195–204.

D. Stephenson follows up an earlier article on Kentish door-knockers and boot-scrapers, in *AC* xcvii 137–57.

J.R. Goddard continues his acccount of the Mormons in the Steeple Ashton district of Wiltshire, in *WF* iii (2) 15–18.

Joan McNeile describes the career of Mrs. Arthur Newell (1852–1923), who founded a cottage industry in embroidery at Fisherton de la Mere, near Wylye, in *WF* iii (2) 25–6.

Peter Brandon uses letters and diaries to describe the Sussex connections of Philip Webb, William Morris and their circle, in *SH* ii 8–14.

Salome Pelly, daughter of John Wordsworth, bishop of Salisbury (1885–1911), describes her childhood at the bishop's palace, in *HR* ii (11) 40–4.

Elizabeth Mullins recounts memories of childhood days at Shaw, near Swindon, during the first world war, in *FLTR* xiv 1–2.

Frances Haveron describes the Pisé (compressed soil) technique of building developed by J. St. Loe Strachey at Newlands Corner in *c.*1915–20, in *Sur AC* lxxiii 141–5.

Arthur Wakeling recounts further details of the life and anecdotes of Arthur Whitlock, a Pitton farm labourer who died in 1943, in *WF* iii (2) 3–14.

The Local Historian

Journal of the British Association for Local History

Editor: Dr Kate Tiller, Extra-Mural Tutor, Department of External Studies, University of Oxford

Reviews Editor: Robin Chaplin, Staff Tutor for Midland History, University of Birmingham

Each 64-pate issue contains
- articles by specialist writers covering areas of interest to both the amateur and the professional historian
- extensive book reviews section
- listings of recent publications from local societies
- readers' letters
- news notes on related activities

Subjects dealt with in recent issues include
Census returns from Victorian villages
Historical evidence from photographs
Land-tax returns and urban development
Roads in the eighteenth century
The heritage of landscape
Charitable bequests and their recipients
How to write a town trail
Whither local history?

Readers and contributors are drawn from tutors, research students, librarians, archivists, adult education groups, and local historians at all levels

'. . . invaluable reading both for amateur and professional historians. Indeed, I welcome the imaginative and constructive effort to bring them together which the journal presents.' — **Professor Asa Briggs**

Four issues a year   Annual postal subscription: UK £5   Overseas £5.50

Sample copy and advertising rates available on request from the publishers. Pleas quote **Southern History** when writing.

Published for BALH by the
National Council for Voluntary Organisations
26 Bedford Square, London WC1B 3HU

MIDLAND HISTORY

Vol. VIII   1983

Editor: Christopher Dyer, University of Birmingham

Published annually at £5.00 for individuals, £6.00 for institutions

Orders to the Business Manager,
              School of History,
              University of Birmingham,
              P.O. Box 363,
              Birmingham,
              B15 2TT.

NORTHERN HISTORY

Vol. XIX   1983

Editor: G.C.F. Forster, University of Leeds

Published annually at £6.50

Orders to the Secretary,
              Northern History,
              The School of History,
              The University,
              LEEDS LS2 9JT

Vol. XVI, No 69   APRIL 1983

ARCHIVES
Journal of the British Records Association

The Wellington Papers 1790–1978: by R. J. Olney

Record-Keeping in the Medieval Borough: Proof of Wills: by David Postles

The Methodist Archives: by William Leary

The Records of the Worshipful Company of Stationers and Newspaper Makers (1554–1912): by Robin Myers

A Medieval Archive from Trinity Hospital, Salisbury: by William Smith

Cosmopolitan Correspondence: A Calendar of the Letters of Georges Cuvier (1769–1832): by Dorinda Outram

Archives and Records of the Institution of Electrical Engineers: by Lenore Symons

The Records of Engineering Firms and their Treatment in the Scottish Record Office: by J.H. Sime

British Records Association Annual Conference 1981

Report and Comment   **Reviews**   **Works Received**

Published twice yearly   Honorary Editor: A.S. Cook

Articles, publications for review or notice, and enquiries from intending contributors should be sent to the Editor, *Archives,* at India Office Library and Records, 197 Blackfriars Road, London SE1 8NG. Enquiries about subscriptions and requests for single copies should be sent to British Records Association, The Charterhouse, Charterhouse Square, London EC1M 6AU.

Annual subscription: £8.00 (£10.00 for subscriptions through agents or book-sellers); free to subscribing members of the Association (details sent on request).

Parliamentary History

Parliamentary History is being launched in response to a resurgence of interest in parliamentary history in Britain and America.

The Yearbook is being planned to cover the whole spectrum of British parliamentary history from the middle ages to the present century, including the Scottish and Irish parliaments. It will include articles and communications on parliamentary and electoral history, book reviews, conference reports and a bibliography.

The Management of the Elizabethan House of Commons: **Edwin Jaggard**
The Council's 'Men-of-Business'
M.A.R. Graves
Wardship in the Parliament of 1604
Pauline Croft
The House of Lords and the Appellate Jurisdiction in Equity 1640–1643
James S. Hart
The Electioneering of Sarah, Duchess of Marlborough
Frances Harris
Charles Lucas and the Dublin Election of 1748–1749
Sean Murphy
The Parliamentary Reform Movement in Cornwall 1805–1826

The Organization of the Conservative Party 1832–1846: Part II: The Electoral Organization
Norman Gash
Gladstone, Land and Social Reconstruction in Ireland 1881–1887
Allen Warren
The Last of the Lancastrians
A.J. Pollard
The Politics of the Excluded: Tories, Jacobites and Whig Patriots, 1715–1760
J.C.D. Clark

Book Reviews

ISBN 0-86299-065-3   £12.50   ISBN 0-86299-066-1 (paper) £7.50

Published Annually in November

Alan Sutton Publishing Limited 17a Brunswick Road Gloucester GL1 1HG

Vol. LV No. 132   November 1982   Price: £4.00

BULLETIN OF THE
INSTITUTE OF HISTORICAL RESEARCH

Edited by F. M. L. Thompson

UNIVERSITY OF LONDON: INSTITUTE OF HISTORICAL RESEARCH
SENATE HOUSE, LONDON, WC1E 7HU

THE ENGLISH
HISTORICAL REVIEW

Editors: A.D.Macintyre M.A.,D.Phil.
         P.H.Williams M.A.,D.Phil.

The English Historical Review is the oldest quarterly journal of historical
scholarship in the English speaking world. It carries articles, shorter notes
and documents (all the products of original research) on all aspects of
medieval, early modern and modern history. Although there is a natural
bias towards British history, the journal regularly contains important
contributions on the history of other countries, particularly of Europe.
Extensive book reviews.

1983 annual subscription £27.00 (student rate £13.50)

*Send cheques (made payable to Longman Group Ltd) and requests for
further information to: Wendy Crowdy, Dept S.H., Longman Group Ltd,
Westgate House, Harlow, Essex CM20 1NE. Tel. (0279) 442601.*

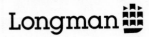
Longman